op
3-

BETWEEN TWO WORLDS

'Wandering between two worlds, one dead,
The other powerless to be born . . .'

MATTHEW ARNOLD

J. M. M., photographed by Burt Martinson, 1935

The Autobiography of

JOHN

MIDDLETON

MURRY

Between Two Worlds

JULIAN MESSNER, INC.

New York

'Ce qu'on dit de soi est toujours poésie. S'imaginer que les menus détails sur sa propre vie valent la peine d'être fixés c'est donner la preuve d'une bien mesquine vanité. On écrit de telles choses pour transmettre aux autres la théorie de l'univers qu'on porte en soi. La forme de "Souvenirs" m'a paru commode pour exprimer certaines nuances de pensée que mes autres écrits ne rendaient pas.'

RENAN

CONTENTS

5

ILLUSTRATIONS

6

To Betty

CLOUDS OF GLORY

I WAS born in Ethnards Road, Peckham, on August 6th, 1889. I was, I am told, a very big baby, weighing something between eleven and twelve pounds. Since my mother has always been slight and slim, and was only nineteen years of age when I was born, I must have been a heavy burden for her to carry. She needed a beautiful baby to recompense her; and, if one may trust the photograph of myself at about a year old, poised apprehensively on a photographer's swing – forgotten property! – I was a beautiful baby. To judge by the same photograph, and to compare it with one of my mother taken at about the same time, I was very much my mother's son. She was a beautiful woman, or rather a beautiful girl; and to me, she is so still. When I look at her – on the rare occasions when we meet – I see clearly in her the woman whom, as a little boy, I thought so beautiful.

As a little boy, I dumbly resented the fact that she could not always be beautiful. Poor women cannot afford to be beautiful; and we were poor. We had lodgers in the upstairs part of our small house – kind, but to me quite shadowy people called Mr. and Mrs. Somersby. I did not mind that. What I did mind was the squalor in which my mother was involved. My resentment is summed up in a single picture. Probably it is the first of my distinct memories, for the event must have happened when I was about two years old, and nearer two than three.

We had a penny oil lamp. It was like a small bottle of coarse greenish glass, with a little tin cap on top through which came a wick like a piece of thick string. It gave a shabby, smoky, yellow flame, by no means as bright as that of a single lucifer match (as my grandmother always called them). It had no chimney, nor was it possible to fix one; though at one time it had carried a tin

9

reflector. About that lamp there was to me something indescribably mean and sordid. Compared to it, a candle was a splendid thing, splendid in brightness, splendid in extravagance.

This little lamp was peculiarly mine. With it I went to bed, and through staring at its pitiful yellow flame, which trailed dully off into a wavering tail of smoke, I grew to resent it. There was nothing comely or good about it. The wick had to be poked, up or down, with a hairpin – and I did not like to see my mother take a hairpin from her hair to prod the flame about. Moreover, it was an evil little lamp: if it was overturned, the oil poured promptly out of the bottle, and was ablaze. And, because it was dangerous, it was put well out of my reach. It smoked away on the remote bare mantelshelf – a gloomy mockery of light.

On the occasion I remember this little lamp was alight in the day time. Probably it was a foggy day in winter. And it was washing day. So I was alone with the little lamp in a room with a bare floor, which may have been my bedroom; and no doubt I was playing. How it happened, I do not know; perhaps I clambered on a chair to the mantelshelf. Somehow the little lamp was overturned. The oil ran out on to the bare boards and blazed, and I cried out. Perhaps I called out what had happened, for I was a precocious little boy. Anyhow, my mother came running in with a fibre doormat in her hand, and beat out the flames with it. I thought it very brave of her, as it was. But printed on my memory ever since is the figure of my mother with bare arms, with an old cloth cap pinned on her hair, beating the flames with a dirty doormat. The bare boards, the stink of oil, the evil little lamp lying empty on the floor – and my mother. It may be that I afterwards invested this memory with a total sordidness which I, at the moment, did not wholly feel. But of one thing I am certain. The cloth cap pinned to my mother's hair was ugly to me then; and I resented it that my mother was involved in this ugliness.

I had learned to read at two; and at two years and a half I was taken to the infants' class of the Rolles Road Board School, somewhere near the Old Kent Road, by the kind little daughter of a neighbour. I remember almost nothing of the school itself; but I have a distinct memory of being taken there for the first time. There were many gloomy arches, and I was frightened. The arches seemed so big and dark; they loomed over me. There was a teacher, grey-haired and forbidding, with a pince-nez and a flannelette blouse, who was surprised that I could pipe my multiplication-table up to twelve times without a mistake. I remember plaiting vari-coloured strips of paper into chequered squares. Little baskets like birds' nests also come back to me, but whether I wove one of them I do not know. Nor have I any idea of my own how long I was at Rolles Road Board School.

Assuredly, I cannot have been an 'infant' for long; for it is graven in my memory that at the age of seven I was in the Ex-Seventh (Ex= Extra) standard of a quite different Board School, at Bellenden Road. That was in a different part of Peckham, and a far less gloomy one. I myself was rather proud of this strange achievement, by which at the age of seven I was at the top of a superior sort of board school – a Higher Grade School was its technical name – with a handful of boys much older than myself. If I had not been proud of it, why should the refrain, 'Seven in the Ex-Seventh', have lingered in my memory, with a note of triumph? Perhaps it is as well that I should have shared my father's feeling of pride. To-day, I have a small boy of my own, who is now seven. I should be truly appalled if he knew what I knew at his age – the problems at the end of Pendlebury, algebra up to quadratics, a good deal of chemistry and geology, history that included a delving into the developments of the Curia Regis, and I know not what besides. My father used to preserve an essay of mine on Gothic Architecture, of all things, written impromptu at this same ripe age of seven, which received fifty out of fifty marks.

It is a grim process to reflect upon – this early education of mine: grim in itself, for it involved the complete obliteration of a child's childhood; for which, when I later came to know of what

I had been deprived, I used to blame my father: grimmer still, when later I realized that in my father's eyes, and perhaps also in fact, there had been for me but one way of escape from a life of squalor and futility, and I ceased to blame him, and acknowledged with gratitude that he had done all he could for me.

It must have been hardly more than a blind and feverish urge in him that drove him to educate me when I was a tiny boy, and get me educated. Education, he must have felt, was the secret; but what education itself might be he did not know. It was something which he himself had not. So, instead of teaching me to write his own firm and beautiful hand, he put me at the oddest fences. There was, for instance, at the end of the *Victoria Spelling Book* (so called to commemorate the 1887 Jubilee) from which he taught me to read, a list of Latin phrases: *Noli me tangere; Nemo me impune lacessit; Finis coronat opus*, and the like. This to my father was Latin – part of that education which he had not, of the knowledge which he did not know. So I must learn it. The idea of buying me a simple Latin grammar never occurred to him. He did not realize, any more than I did, that Latin had a grammar. All he could tell me to do, and all I did, was to learn by heart four or five pages of those hieroglyph phrases and their English equivalents.

History, for the same reason, was dates; and I became a prodigy at dates. But here fortunately the barrenness was mitigated, because my grandmother possessed some volumes of an illustrated *History of England* which had been published by Cassell's in penny weekly parts. This book I loved. It had a picture of Egbert being rowed by seven 'tributary princes' down the Dee, which satisfied my imagination of how a king should behave. The big rowing boat was homely; but there was a kingly difference between it and any rowing boat I could imagine. And the Dee itself, which the artist had indicated summarily, seemed vast and simple as an ocean. Others of the pictures were more mysterious. I knew them and their titles; but I did not know what they meant. I did not love them the less for that. One such picture represented,

in a highly dramatic fashion, 'Non-Jurors surprised . . .' by whom,
I have forgotten. They had their swords out and were burning
papers in the flames of magnificent candles, in huge candlesticks,
with wax dropping generously about. The room had mighty
curtains, and the Non-Jurors, grasping their swords, had their
heads turned backward in alarm. I could not discover who the
Non-Jurors were; but I thought them very fine men.

Better even than the pictures were the long chapters at the end
of each volume headed 'Social Life', which told of rich and
lovely dresses, of long pointed shoes, and butts of wine, such as
that in which false Clarence was drowned – there was a picture of
him, in trunk hose, being thrust in upside down. But my most
distinct memory of these particular chapters is a description of
Doctor Johnson with two verses ascribed to him:

> If a man who turnips cries,
>   Cries not when his father dies,
> 'Tis a sign that he had rather
>   Have a turnip than his father.

That seemed to me very funny indeed, and I had a vague idea
that it had been written specially for me. It seemed to have no
connection at all with History. Turnips were funny vegetables.
Their function was to interrupt the placid course of History. For
another fact which I seized upon early was that in 1714 Lord
Townshend introduced the Turnip. To introduce a turnip was
funny in itself. And funnier still was that this introduction was
called the Rotation of Crops. That meant to me a turnip spinning
wildly round at the end of a string.

The second verse which Dr. Johnson had composed for me
was this:

> I put my hat upon my head
>   And went into the Strand;
> And there I met another man
>   With his hat in his hand.

13

This was distinctly mysterious. In the first place, it was hard to pronounce. It was a long while before it occurred to me that I must not say: 'With his hát in his hand', but 'With hís hat ín his hand'. And in the long while before that discovery I had time to meditate on the meaning of the quiet and innocuous phrase 'With his hat in his hand'. It was funny. I had no doubt about that. But I couldn't see the joke. That condition of mind is strange to me now; but it was very real in those days. Things were funny, though you could not see the joke. You *knew* they were funny; and you laughed, just as though you had seen the joke. In later years, this mysterious condition was recalled to me by Edmund Gosse's *Father and Son*. There he describes how *The Pickwick Papers* affected him, as a small boy. He began to laugh before he had opened the book. He read a perfectly serious statement: 'It was a fine, sunny day', and it struck him as so irresistibly funny that he had to put the book down, convulsed with laughter and tears. *The Pickwick Papers* affected me in precisely the same way; and so did this verse of Dr. Johnson. It *was* funny. That I should understand how or why it was funny was irrelevant.

I owe very much to those bound volumes of *Cassell's Penny History*, for most of the few shafts of light which pierce the darkness of my early childhood seem to terminate on one of its pages. They, and a volume of *The Pickwick Papers* with the first nineteen pages missing, were my chief delights. Hard after them came a little dark green volume which had been given to my mother on her marriage by her Sunday school teacher, called *Health in the Home*. It had woodcuts of the nervous system, the brain, and the heart: of a healthy foot and a Chinese woman's foot; it told how some little children who were carried as cherubs in a great Papal procession in Rome, were gilded all over, and they died. That was to show how necessary it was to keep the pores of the skin open. I felt sad about those little children. More fearful, and more exciting, was the account of a Canadian, called Alexander something or other, who was shot in the stomach. The wound did not close up, but left a permanent hole through which the doctors could look inside. When he drank nothing but water, the walls of his stomach were lovely to behold – pink and healthy; but when he drank a glass of whisky, they turned purple and angry. There was to me an awful fascination in peeping through that hole. One of those shafts of light, of which I have spoken, pierces the years and shines straight through that hole upon the iridescent wall of Mr. Alexander's stomach.

There were very few books in the house – ten or a dozen at most – and I tried to read them all. I ploughed through a novel by Bulwer Lytton called *Paul Clifford, Highwayman*, but I could make nothing of it. I grappled also with an isolated volume of Macaulay's *Essays*, containing a review of 'Malthus on Population'; but my chief reward was something 'funny' at the end, where some of Macaulay's lighter verses were printed. There I came across his account of a coach journey from London to Cambridge; the song of the Roundhead: Sergeant Obadiah Bind-their-Kings-in-chains-and-their-Nobles-in-Links-of-Iron (which was funny); and the story of the news of the Armada, with its thrilling ending:

> . . . Till the red glare on Skiddaw roused the burghers of Carlisle.

That was a rich haul, from such a book. But one book there was which, to my subsequent regret, I could not bring myself to read. It was *The Pilgrim's Progress*. Had it not been for its terrifying pictures I should have read it as eagerly as I read *The Pickwick Papers*. But it was filled with crude oleograph pictures of Giant Despair. There was even one such on the outside of the red cover, but that was gilt, and comparatively harmless. The highly-coloured ogre outside, however, was too much for me. I could not run the risk of coming again upon him unawares, as I once had done. So I left *The Pilgrim's Progress* severely alone.

I was, in fact, a timid little boy, who, even though he was 'seven in the Extra-Seventh', could not sleep without a knotted towel for company. I was ashamed of this; but it made no difference. I must have my knotted towel, to save me from night-terrors. I suppose that these came chiefly from my reading, for my own children, whose reading is of the most casual, are not greatly afflicted with them. Once, I remember distinctly, a fearful nightmare followed immediately upon reading a Christmas number of *The Graphic* lent me by a neighbour, which contained a comic picture of a pack of little devils with tails and toasting forks dancing round a curmudgeonly old man. Rather fearfully, I had laughed at them; but when they surrounded me at night, I howled with terror, until I was taken into the big bed beside my mother.

For that haven I would make straightway whenever I waked in the night. Or rather I would try to make for it. But the dangers of the journey out of my bedroom, across the landing, into my mother's room were so terrible that I would wait, quaking and frozen, in bed, with my throat parched, unable to utter a cry. At last I would gather my courage together and make the awful plunge. But worst of all, for the paralysis and speechlessness it imposed upon me, was a curious abstract night-terror which recurred again and again. Even when I could speak, I could never explain it. Nor can I now. Great circles of light would bear down upon me, with sickening swiftness, narrowing as they came. I was the centre upon which they converged. Just before they touched me, they would speed back again, widening and widening: till everything was one terrible pattern of circles, coming and going, with absolute regularity and a fearful speed, with the point that was me for their centre. When long afterwards I came to read of 'the velocity of light' as an absolute maximum of speed, I felt that I had already a ghastly familiarity with it. It had been exercised upon me many times.

I must have been about three or four years old when we moved from Ethnards Road, which is a turning off the Old Kent Road, to the part of Peckham near East Dulwich; and much of what I have been describing belongs to the age between four and seven. The new house, in Copleston Road, was the scene of my night-terrors and my agonizing journeys across the landing. But there is one vivid memory which may belong to Ethnards Road. It is of a bearded doctor (whose name was Dr. Davies) coming to see me. I sat up in bed, trembling, while he put his thermometer under my arm. I was terrified of it, and him. It was only measles. But the doctor's black beard and my mother's frightened face were alarming. And I sensed in a childish way my mother's desperate anxiety. It was not altogether for me. She was afraid of what my father would say when he knew that she had called in the doctor.

This absolute impossibility of calling in the doctor haunted my childhood. And once, when I dislocated my thumb rather badly, it led to my being tortured by the local chemist for ten minutes, quite in vain. I had eventually to be taken to Guy's Hospital. That was when I was seven. By that time I was able to realize how brave my mother had been in calling in Dr. Davies, without telling my father. My mother, you must remember, was a girl of twenty-two, inexperienced and anxious. My father was away at work from eight in the morning until after midnight. Seeing that I was really ill, my mother, to whom my father's will was law, disobeyed him. It must have been a fearful struggle for her: and her two terrors, terror for me, terror of what my father would say, were plain upon her face.

My father was ten years older than my mother. She looked up to him; and there were good reasons why she should. Not only was he a handsome man, but he was a man of integrity. He was obstinate, short in his temper and short in his views; but he was a man. And my mother knew it. Although she suffered under his domestic rule, and the time came when she would confide something of what she suffered to her small son, she would always insist, as she dried her tears, that 'your father is a good man'. He was. But he was obsessed with the fear of insecurity. He had seen the ugliness of the world from close quarters when he was a little boy. When he was a little boy – the only son in a family of girls – his had been the sole burden of responsibility for an irresponsible family. He had had to keep things straight, and he had known how easy it was for them to go crooked. No one, in his family, had

given a damn what he did, or what became of him. I believe that
he even paid for his own schooling, such as it was, at one of the
old National schools. Certainly, it was entirely on his own
initiative that he had worked for and obtained a post as boy-
messenger in Somerset House, which eventually became a temporary clerkship, then, after another struggle, a clerkship on
the permanent establishment. In the Higher Division clerks in
Somerset House – superior beings, educated at the University,
with private rooms where they lunched on a half-bottle of
claret – my father saw embodied a higher way of life: the way of
life of the gentleman. He saw that it was good. He did not aspire
to it himself. For himself it was sufficient that he should lift himself out of the lower class, and save himself from being sucked under
in the welter of fecklessness which threatened him. But his son
must achieve the miracle: his son must become a gentleman. I
believe that if, one day, I had become a Higher Division clerk in
Somerset House, and had rung the bell for my father, his bliss,
as he appeared before me, would have been as entire as Othello's:

> If it were now to die,
> 'Twere now to be most happy; for, I fear,
> My soul hath her content so absolute
> That not another comfort like to this
> Succeeds in unknown fate.

And, sometimes, such is the weakness of the flesh, I grieve a little
that I should have denied him this satisfaction or its analogue,
which it was once in my power to give.

Since this was his ambition, it may seem strange that he
should have looked so sternly on the summoning of a doctor when
I was ill. After all, it was necessary, in order that his ambition
should be fulfilled, that I should be alive to fulfil it. The explanation, I think, is simple. He did not admit it as a possibility that I
should die. My destiny was to fulfil his ambition; it was inconceivable that it should be interrupted. In like manner, he never
conceived it as a possibility that I might suffer from the system of

intensive cultivation he applied to me. My goal was simple and evident. My manifest purpose in life was to be what he wanted me to be. The idea that a small human being might have needs of its own would have been confusing to his simple soul: therefore it gained no lodgment in it.

Since, then, it was impossible that I should be really ill, to call in a doctor was sheer waste of money. That it might even be worth five shillings (for that was what it cost) that the fears of his girl-wife should be allayed never occurred to him, as it never occurred to him that it was a little hard for a girl so naturally gay and loving as my mother, to be alone in the house from eight in the morning till after midnight. If he, in order to earn a little extra money, made no bones about going straight on from his work at Somerset House to work at a sweated wage as ledger-clerk to a Penny Savings Bank, why should she complain? She did not complain, but she suffered. Her instincts were overridden. Instinctively, she felt that the cheeseparing went too far; instinctively, she felt that it was a crime that her small son should be worked so hard; and, just as instinctively, she felt that it would be not only futile but unfair to complain. All that my father did – as he not infrequently said – was done for us. It was for her sake that he took charge of a pitiful little legacy of £30 which was the only money of her own she had ever had. That wonderful £30! Fairy gold, changed dully into an entry of figures in my father's little account book. My mother cried over it. God knows what she would have done with it if she had ever had it in her purse. Something rash and regal, I hope. Or, perhaps, she would have been afraid to spend it – it was not long before she became afraid to do most things she wanted – and, perhaps, that would have been the best. She could have put it under her pillow and had golden dreams. For my mother had her dreams. Once, in a desperate burst of confidence, she told me that she wanted to be a gipsy and live in a caravan. That was a deadly secret between us. What my father would have said, in those days, if he had known that that was his wife's dream, I cannot imagine. Of all fantastic, impossible things – to be a gipsy and live in a caravan! It was the sheer antipodes of all he stood for.

But behind my father's determination and my mother's dreams was the fact that we were poor: that, in order to pay our way and scrape together something against the rainy day, it was necessary for my father to work fifteen hours a day and to come home fagged to death in the small hours of the morning. I saw him only on Sunday; he saw me, except on Sunday, only asleep. But he left me my task to do out of school-hours every day, and on Sundays the joy of our meeting was mitigated by the fact that I had to spend all the morning in doing prodigious sums – 'long tots', they were called. I don't know that I resented it; and I do know that I hated to get them wrong, because that upset my father: and to 'upset' my father was the one thing to be avoided in our house. But most of all I was conscious of a fearful boredom with these monotonous sums; and even to-day I cannot bring myself to add up a row of figures without an inward groan, that echoes from those bleak Sunday mornings at the wobbly round table in the sitting-room.

Our move from Ethnards Road to Copleston Road was a step up in the world. We no longer had lodgers, and the new house itself was bigger – the rent was 8s. a week – and altogether more exciting than the old one. It had a garden-plot behind, which my father had no time to tend, but in which I planted nasturtium seeds with the help of a clothes-peg. All round the garden-plot was a black fence. At the bottom lived a widow called Rivers, who had an only son called Charlie. He had reddish-gold hair and was altogether superior. Although, at one time, he had attended the same Board School as I, he had been translated by means of a scholarship to a secondary school. I climbed up to peer at him, sometimes, through the trellis work on top of the black fence. There he lay, with his red-gold hair bright against his black coat – his mother was emphatic on her widowhood – shooting with an air-gun at a tin chimney-pot, set up for a target at the end of his garden. That seemed to me an entirely appropriate activity for one so superior as he. Thus would the Olympians spend their days.

I crept down from my peep-hole awe-struck, and smitten with a wild and impossible desire to get a scholarship and have an air-gun. One day I got a scholarship: but an air-gun I never had.

This aristocrat of fifteen dwelt at the end of the garden. On the left-hand side was a turbulent jovial family of boys. They were sternly ruled by their mother, a rotund little woman encased in a tight bugled bodice, above whom her big sons towered. But she laid about among them with a cane, as with a flail; till the biggest of them was howling. Their father was a kindly harassed-looking man who was something in the Post Office, and a sedulous photographer. Probably he also was under his wife's dominion. To me, from my post of observation through the fence, the life of the boys consisted of glorious games, punctuated by thrashings: extremes alike unknown to me. They built enormous ships, real two-deckers, with cannons made of drain-pipes, and a crew of four or five, whereas I rowed solitary with a broom on a pair of household-steps with the loop of the safety-rope for my rowlocks. Eventually, the boys took compassion on me and invited me across. I was disappointed. Their games were more glorious to watch than to take part in. It was not merely that they were boisterous; they had an odd trick of sexuality, which may have been animal and harmless enough, but when exhibited as it sometimes was before a boy of six or seven, frightened and repelled him. By this time I was perfectly used to the innocent tricks of the boys at school, and was at least an interested spectator of their strenuous efforts to piss higher than one another against the slate slabs of the urinal; but the habits of my neighbours belonged to a different order.

Anyhow the scenes of which I was the reluctant and astonished witness put a barrier between my neighbours and me. So I turned to my neighbour on the other side. She was a little girl – the only child of a rather happy-go-lucky, generous pair called Mr. and Mrs. Pinnington. Mrs. Pinnington even smoked cigarettes – an unheard-of thing in our neighbourhood in the mid-nineties. But she adored her little girl; and Edith Pinnington was adorable. She was a year or two younger than I. She was exquisite. Her face was delicate, and her voice clear and sweet. She loved to walk about her garden holding a little parasol, while I admired her with that complete and ineffable devotion which little boys can give to little girls. But she acknowledged it. It was understood between us that we were sweethearts, though we never spoke the word. Nor do I remember that we were much in one another's house. Chiefly we played our separate games in the two gardens; yet each paid attention to the other's game, and was somehow included in it. She was certainly a tenant of the house I used to build between the dustbin and the fence, though she never entered it; and I was the chosen partner of her promenades, though I never walked with her. Sometimes I went to her house to tea, and sometimes she came to mine; but then we played decorously indoors.

She had a brown squirrel in a revolving cage, which was marvellous. On my side I had a mongrel brown terrier dog, called Gyp, of whom I was very fond. He was inclined, as dogs are, to bite things, which did not endear him to my father, who held that dogs should behave rationally. Particularly Gyp enjoyed crunching the cheap wooden draughtsmen with which my father and I used to play on Sunday evenings. He had many a beating for that. But the draughtsmen were irresistible to him; and every time we put them out to play on Sunday evening one or two more would bear the tell-tale indentations. During the terrible winter – 1895, I think it was – when the drops from the pails of water we carried from the standards in the street froze hard and black like halfpennies where they fell, Gyp disappeared. Day after day I hunted for him, before I went to school and after I returned, and for some reason I can see myself plainly on these miserable expeditions, in a reefer coat with brass buttons, and carrying a long stick in my hand.

At last I found Gyp, shivering and cowering at the top of some steps leading to the front door of a house in our road. Instantly, I felt that something was wrong. Why was he there, and not in front of our house that he knew so well? Why was he only half-pleased to see me, as though he remembered that he had loved me once and could do so no longer? Why was he wounded and bleeding? Why was he half-afraid of me? Even now, forty years after, I do not know the answers to these questions that vaguely tormented me. I know that my heart was heavy as I carried him home. If anyone had told me, five minutes before, that I should not be happy at finding Gyp, it would have been incredible to me. Yet here he was, and I was miserable.

The episode of Gyp remains a mystery. I wanted to take care of him, and make him well again; and I believed I could do it. But suddenly he disappeared again while I was away from home – at school, perhaps: I do not remember – and I was told that he had been taken away and destroyed. That was anguish. And to the anguish was added a misgiving. I do not know why, but I felt that I was not being told the truth about him. Perhaps, in this, I was utterly mistaken. But the doubt has lain perdu in my heart for forty years. Nor have I ever had the courage to resolve it by a plain straightforward question to those who should know. I have never been able to take the risk of getting the answer I shrink from getting. But I have never had another dog since Gyp, and never shall.

The wounds in a small boy's soul are strange and past finding out; and a grown-up cannot be blamed for inflicting some of them. Our children must forgive us, for we know not what we do. It was nothing to one small boy that he was overworked, or that he was lonely; it was little to him even that he dreaded his father's disappointment at his failures at school or in examinations. These things hurt for a day, for a week, for a month, may be, but they healed and were forgotten. Somewhere, somehow, he could understand them all. Why they happened was plain and palpable. Death itself was no great terror. Edith Pinnington died, whom he loved; his grandmother whom he loved died also. He was sad, but the sadness left no scar. But the mystery of the death of his brown dog is a wound that rankles yet.

CHAPTER II

GOD AND THE POLICEMAN

AT the end of Copleston Road was a railway cutting, behind a high brick wall. Alongside this wall ran a narrow passage up the hill to the road next above. This passage was called – at any rate among the children – by the sinister name of Cut-throat Alley; and it was as much as your life was worth to go through it in the dark. In the daytime its terrors vanished; but it still had its thrills, of which the chief was to run down it at full tilt, with the noise of one's feet ringing metallic against the walls, and to pull oneself up sharp before running into railings of the house that faced it in Copleston Road. This great pleasure took a keener edge in winter, in the hoop-season, when you dashed headlong after your spinning iron hoop down the alley, and to the task of checking yourself was added the ticklish business of grabbing your hoop before it escaped you.

One day when I was alone I failed in this. My iron hoop bounded in front of me, beyond my reach. It sped across the road, soared over the low iron railing of the opposite house, and crashed into the basement window. For a split second I stood aghast and frozen; and then I ran, pursued by furies. I never looked back, till I was plunged and hidden in the area of our house. Nor, so far as I remember, did I say a word to anybody of what had happened. The thing was too awful. Policemen, prison – all the dread things that my imagination could conjure – were involved in this, if the secret were ever known. I kept it to myself. How I explained away the loss of my hoop, I cannot remember. Day after day I lived in terror of a policeman knocking at the door and asking for me. As the days became weeks, the load slowly lifted, until at last I began to feel guiltily free. But it was months before I dared go through Cut-throat Alley again.

There was another such incident, when I was about the same age. I had some cousins who lived at New Cross. They were the sons of a publican who had married my father's sister; they were a little older than I and altogether more astute and knowledgeable in the ways of the world. One day they came to fetch me to their home. I had a halfpenny to spend. We crossed Peckham Rye safely, and were walking along the Brayards Road when we came to an Italian ice-cream man – a 'Jack', they called him. I had had, and had always obeyed, strict instructions never to buy ice-cream from a 'Jack'. They kept their ice-cream under their beds, and heaven alone knew what it was made of. In consequence ice-cream was far more of a luxury to me than to other little boys; for I could never afford to buy any, except from the 'Jacks'. They sold water-ices by the farthing's-worth, in dark blue glasses, shaped like tiny tumblers, whereas in a shop a halfpenny was the lowest price. On the rare occasions when I had a halfpenny, I could not bear to plunge it all in a brief ice-cream.

So, when my cousins stopped by the gaudy barrow, I was already a divided man; therefore, a lost one. Conscience said that I must speak up, and say that it was forbidden me to buy a farthing ice. But a kind of eagerness to please which has since been one of the trials of my life was already at work in me. To my cousins farthing ices from the Italians were a matter of every day – and of two or three times every day, for they had much more pocket-money than I. I could not appear 'superior' before them. Nor could I have them regard me as a prig. And, I suppose, in some part of me there was a desire for the ice-cream; but that was a faint motive in comparison.

I paid my farthing, received my farthing change, and with it my deep blue glass of water-ice. Perhaps I enjoyed it. I hope so. But, to judge from my later character, it is doubtful. Probably I was far too nervous; and probably it was my nervousness that made me do the fatal thing. I dropped the glass to the ground. It broke in pieces.

'Jack' said straightway that I must pay for it – a penny. No doubt my cousins had a penny between them; but they were not going to pay it for me. The help they gave me consisted in maintaining stoutly and brazenly that the glass was not worth a penny. Such help was merely an added burden to me. It infuriated 'Jack', as well it might, for even in those incredibly cheap days the glasses probably cost him a penny each. He had been quite reasonable, and if they had not tormented him, he would doubtless have let me go on my promising to bring him the penny as soon as I could. But my cousins' braves exasperated him, and he turned his exasperation upon me. Although he took my second farthing, he spurned it and declared that he would put the police after me. My cousins laughed at this; but I felt that their laughter was hollow. As we moved off, they did their best to encourage me; but I felt that their encouragement would have been no good to them had they been in my place. For me, at any rate, the sunshine day was darkened for good. Once more I was haunted by visions of a policeman knocking at the door and asking for me.

These two happenings are among the most vivid memories of my childhood, and it seems to me significant that this should be so. For there is something mysterious about the terror they caused in me. I am puzzled to understand why I felt completely unable to tell my mother about it, but suffered the terror to prey upon me in secret for weeks. For my offences were ridiculously innocent: in the case of the hoop, pure accident; in the case of the glass, a mere peccadillo. Of a guilty conscience, in the ordinary meaning of the phrase, there can have been no trace in me. I must have known that I was not to blame. But that made no difference. An inscrutable and unspeakable Power had gained a hold of me. I incline to believe that the fear was primitive, like the fear of the savage who breaks a taboo. As I understand it, no savage ever deliberately breaks a real taboo. That is inconceivable; for if he could deliberately break a taboo, it would follow inexorably that it was not a real taboo. Thus there can be no question of personal responsibility in the breaking of a taboo. It is not something which a man does, but something which happens

26

to him; the arbitrary Powers, who lie in wait, seize hold of him
The child knows this dread fear: the horror of the thing which
must not be done, which no soul willingly or wittingly could do,
but yet is done. It is prior to all morality. It scorns intention,
and considers only act.

Compared to this, the experience of sin was nothing. That
may be because I had not much experience of sin as a little
boy. But there is nothing peculiar in that. Small children *are*
innocent. The grown-ups who find them guilty of depravity,
as they still sometimes do, are themselves depraved. I can remember only one instance of 'depravity' in myself. I had a girl cousin,
sister of my braves of the ice-cream glass, of about my age. One
day in summer, when I was eight, she stayed a few days in our
house, and we slept in the same bed. Under her instruction I
knelt on the bed before her with my night-shirt tucked under my
armpits while she lay on the bed before me with her night-gown
tucked under hers. In this wicked and delectable contemplation
we were nearly surprised. Perhaps we were surprised. If so, my
mother, who was entering the room, had the good sense not to
show it. We guilty ones, who had flopped down on the bed at
the noise of the door-handle and were pretending to be asleep,
were at any rate convinced that we had not been caught.

In this matter I had no doubt at all that I was engaged
in something 'wicked'. But the wickedness was wholly external.
It consisted, as it always did, in my deliberately doing things that
I was supposed not to do. But as for my *being* wicked, such a
notion was completely alien to me. Occasionally, I felt in myself
that what I was supposed not to do was wrong; in which case
I simply did not do it. But the discrepancy between my small
private morality and the elaborate public morality round about
me was great and ominous. Roughly, this private morality of
mine was limited to 'Do as you would be done by'. I would
never have dreamed of stealing a penny from another boy, or
of taking one from my mother's purse; but when, at Christmas,
there was a store of good things in the cupboard of the *chiffonnier* –

an indispensable article in such a home as mine, pronounced *shiffaneer* – I had no scruple whatever in pilfering continually. My sole concern was that my pilfering should not be detected. Therefore it was very gradual – at the rate of two or three almonds, a dozen raisins, one rich mixed biscuit, and a couple of caramels or so a day.

It will be observed that my principle 'Do as you would be done by' not merely did not forbid my naked enjoyment with my cousin, but rather encouraged it. That was delectable to us both, and only the more thrilling because we knew it was wicked. But even if it had not been wicked, it would have been thrilling enough to me. I had never seen a girl naked before; and it was many years before I did so again.

As I was a non-moral, so was I a non-religious little boy. That is not to say that I did not believe in some sort of God. I believed in at least three. Most potent and most dreadful was the mysterious, unnamed, unformulated Power who was out 'to get you', who sent disaster upon you if you failed to cross your thumbs when you went under a ladder, or if you missed a target which you rashly set yourself to hit with stones. His mode of operation was peculiar. Suddenly, in the midst of an idle trial of skill, such as stepping only on the cracks between paving stones, or guessing the number of paces from one lamp-post to another, he would impart to you the shattering knowledge that if you failed to step on the cracks, or if the paces turned out to be more than a certain number, he would 'get you'. You were thus the recipient of a kind of malign inspiration. The Power who sent it had no good luck to offer – it would have been contrary to his nature if he had – the utmost that he yielded, and that grudgingly, was a momentary dispensation from disaster. His only redeeming feature was that he suffered himself to be cheated. Thus, when the paces to the lamp-post began to look dangerously like being more than the number, you could stretch your paces till they were giant-strides, huge leaps of thrice the normal length. It was not that he had a streak of kindliness in him which made him wink

teaching a Sunday School class was simple and excellent. He read us story-books – Ballantyne and W. H. G. Kingston. The whole school sang a hymn together at the beginning, and one at the end of the proceedings: but for Mr. Gittins' class, at least, the hour between was one of secular enchantment. Even at that age I thought Mr. Gittins very kind, but I look back upon him now with affection and astonishment, and wonder what spirit of humanity possessed that little man to walk a long distance every Sunday afternoon simply to make small boys happy. If Unitarianism had done no more than to give some scope to the Mr. Gittinses of this world, it would be abundantly justified.

Moreover, the Unitarian School was held in a Church Hall which was also fitted as a gymnasium. If we arrived early we could try to do tricks on the parallel-bars, or swing on the climbing-ropes. One evening every week we went there to be taught gymnastics, by other kindly young men, who saw to our instruction for an hour before they commenced the serious business of their own exercise. So that the Avondale Hall was the scene of my happiest hours as a little boy, except on one painful occasion when I was cast to be Little Boy Blue in a Waxworks Show at a Church Concert. I had to wear strap shoes of shiny patent leather, which hurt me abominably; I had to be carried on like a motionless figure, and with a stiff mechanical movement apply a tin-trumpet to my lips, and blow. The whole performance was torment.

By this time we had left Copleston Road. My father had saved up enough to buy the lease of a house in Worlingham Road, a turning off Goose Green. It cost £214, I remember, because I was called upon to assist in the calculations, and this prodigious sum of money made a durable impression on me. It was a smaller house than that in Copleston Road, but it had a real garden. There my father's career as a gardener began. This was possible because he had been able to give up some of his night-work at the Penny Bank. He had been taken on to the establishment in Somerset House, and was no longer in the precarious position of a temporary clerk. I went with him one night to a mysterious junk shop in the neighbourhood where, after some bargaining, he bought for 6s. 6d. a second-hand lawn-mower – a Green's 'Multum in Parvo': for the first time my 'Latin' came in handy. Soon after came a brand new garden-roller, then a garden-hose with an attractive winder. He was now fully launched, and, with *The Amateur Gardener* to guide him, he began to grow noble tomatoes in huge green boxes in his greenhouse. He re-sowed the lawn (which was about the size of a billiard-table) and stretched elaborate entanglements of white cotton to protect his seed. This admirable occupation of my father had the effect of making the garden a precarious playground for me. In fact, it was definitely safer not to play in it at all.

I was eight years old when we went to Worlingham Road. In spite of the garden, it was not a change for the better. Near to Copleston Road were the still lovely parts of Camberwell – Grove Hill Road, Grove Lane and the rest – running down on the south side through Dog Kennel Hill, unspoiled by trams, to East Dulwich. It was a beautiful neighbourhood then, and I absorbed something from it that I needed badly. For the country was an unknown thing to me. I was taken to the seaside for a holiday every year; but the seaside, though the sea itself was exciting enough, meant poky lodgings in a dim suburban street like that I came from. When my cousins spoke of the village of Tuddenham in Suffolk, whence their father the publican had come and whither they returned annually; or my friends, the Thompsons, told me of their holidays at Addlestone in Surrey, the Country they spoke of was infinitely more remote from me than the places where my holidays were spent – Yarmouth, Hastings, Margate and Brighton. But I had one brief and glorious glimpse when I was seven years old, and my father, seized by an unaccustomed spirit of adventure, declared that we should have our holidays in Jersey. That was a magnificent dream, from the voyage in the *Lydia* down Southampton Water to our arrival in the late evening on the quay at St. Helier. My father carried me ashore. Someone asked him for a fill of tobacco, and my father gave him a halfpenny. Afterwards, he explained to me that in Jersey there was no tax on tobacco, and a halfpenny would buy a whole ounce.

So the strangeness of Jersey began. I was enchanted by the fact that the halfpennies and pennies were strange. At the little half-French boarding house where we stayed, we had dessert: all kinds of fruit served with separate plates and different knives and forks. That was marvellous. And in the streets and on the sands I heard more French than English: that was thrilling. Everything was different, rich and strange. The names – Plemont, La Corbière, Mont Orgueil – were resonant as no English names were resonant. The cider apples were red, the sands were yellow, the sea was green – all absolutely, as in a dream. And things happened accordingly. My father found a gold bracelet on one of our expeditions; on another we walked across the causeway to the lighthouse at La Corbière, and it seemed to me like walking a tightrope with the dark unfathomed caves of ocean sheer on either side. It was a *pays de Cocagne*. And when, a week or two after we had returned, the *Stella*, the sister-ship of the *Lydia*, went down on the Casquets, and more than two hundred lives were lost, I felt as one might feel who had braved the dangers and tasted the wonders of the Hesperides, and returned to tell the tale.

Sometimes I went on more commonplace holidays with my grandmother, who was my mother's mother. Then we went to Hastings, and stayed in a not very salubrious street, in a little house, tenanted by a corporation dustman called Hipgrave. It was only rarely that I got as far as the beach, or the romantic heights of Hastings Castle. Judged as a seaside holiday, the whole thing was a farce. But a holiday it surely was, and one of the best. I adored my grandmother, and she adored me. Her one idea was that I should have a good time, and she considered that I myself knew best how to get it. So I played all day long with the dustman's children who, as denizens of Hastings, took no account of the sea. I was allowed to be as grubby as was necessary; I was given a copious supply of pennies, and sent to buy all that *I* wanted for my birthday party, which I gave to the little Hipgraves. Probably, I should have been completely spoiled if my grandmother had had the care of me for very long; but as things were, the freedom she gave me was purely beneficent. And, when I come to remember what a wise and sweet old woman she was, I think that she knew well what she was about. She had an instinct for life. She had known what hard times were; she had been through a kind of poverty which even my father's family had never known: yet she was completely unsoured. She had brought up her two daughters – my mother and my aunt – to be gentle and generous. They had learned from her to be tender. Experience has taught me that this quality of tenderness in woman, which my grandmother possessed so abundantly and which flowed on through her two daughters, is rarer than I imagined. After all, these were the only women I knew: and this quality was the same in them all. They were all gentle and generous. Though they could not have expressed their feeling in words, they felt that to reckon every penny, to scrape and save, to pinch and squeeze, was an offence against human dignity. My father's code, they felt, was all wrong.

True, they were women, and he was a man. But neither my grandmother nor my aunt had led sheltered lives. For many years my grandmother had been the bread-winner of the family; and all her life long my aunt has had to battle with the world by herself, at times in circumstances of great misery. She has been successful in business by her own efforts, and fallen into poverty after comparative affluence, purely because of her own trustfulness and generosity. She has had a single child who died in infancy. Yet, to know her, one would think she had led a life of unbroken happiness.

CHAPTER III

METAMORPHOSIS

I HAD a blind hunger for the country. Once when I went on holiday to Margate, by the Thames steamboat, my father took me for a walk which led us by the edge of a ripe wheatfield. The golden corn, the chalk-white field, the red poppies in the corn — all were brilliant in the midsummer sunshine; and they shone in my memory for years. Indeed, they still shine there. But to see the country, as I did, in glimpses on a seaside holiday was not enough. Thus seen the country was at once vivid and unreal, vanishing like a magic-lantern view. I wanted something more, and something different. And yet, had I been asked if I would like to live in the country, I should probably not have known what to reply. That anyone should *live* in the country was almost outside the range of my real imagination.

But the hunger worked blindly in me. With one or two companions I used, on Saturdays during the summertime, to undertake an immense walk to Bromley in Kent. Probably, Bromley is completely suburban by now; but in the middle 'nineties it was open enough to be the real country for me. There were trees we could climb, streams we could dam and fish and paddle in, acorns we could gather in September, and even blackberries. It was our favourite expedition; its charm was bitter-sweet, for no sooner had we arrived (it seemed) than we had to be thinking about returning home. We talked of making a little tent, and a trolley on pram-wheels, so that we could camp there for the night, but that was a dream, golden and impossible.

My hunger for the country was, in fact, inextricably mixed with a longing to light fires, to cook food, to sleep in a tent in the open with two or three companions of my own age. I had read in a book of a pleasant old tramp who used, when he caught a hedge-

35

hog, to cook it in a delectable fashion. He would cover it with a paste of clay like a dumpling, and put it in the glowing ashes of his fire. When the time was come, he broke open his clay dumpling, and lo! the prickles and the skin came away with the clay, leaving pure, succulent and smoking hedgehog. This seemed to me so marvellous, that for many months to live on hedgehogs cooked in this fashion was the absolute of felicity to me. But it was many, many years before I even saw a hedgehog; and when, four years ago, one actually came into my garden in Hampshire, I was as astonished as my children, and it never entered my head to kill it and cook it in a clay ball.

Nowadays, I suppose, the small boy in a city is enabled, through the Boy Scouts, to satisfy this deep desire to pitch camp, to be on his own and to fend for himself. If it is not so, it should be so: for the desire is as healthy as it is profound. In one form or another, it haunted me throughout my boyhood. I longed to be a member of a small tribe of boys – not more than six in all, nor less than three – who lived in complete independence alike of grown-ups and of girls. Not that I disliked girls; on the contrary I liked them, and I very much wanted to have a sister of my own. But this business of camping, of independence, of the tribe, was one for males only. Girls had their honoured place, but it was not there.

The loftiest height to which this constant dream attained was reached some years later, when I had won a scholarship, and become by a miraculous transformation a public schoolboy. Then, at about fourteen, with one or two cronies, I would spend hours talking of a marvellous boat that we were to build. What tiny fragment of substance this dream of ours possessed was derived from the *Boy's Own Paper*, which had a series of articles telling you 'How to build a sailing sharpie'. These we studied with utter self-abandon; in our imaginations we built that sharpie plank by plank. When it was finished, it occurred to the eldest of us – a boy called Harvey – that, after all, a sharpie was only suitable for inland cruising. What we needed was a sea-going

J. M. M., age 10 in Christ's Hospital uniform

boat. Straightway, we became scornful of the sharpie we had built, and set about designing – well, a sea-going boat. Week after week we made designs and elaborate scale-drawings. On Sunday afternoons we would steal off with a billy-can, some cocoa and condensed milk, light a fire in a sequestered coppice, and while the billy boiled argue heatedly with one another on the best arrangement of the cabin. Evening after evening we would snatch the chance of a ten-minute walk together, listening to Harvey while he dreamily piped us to quarters on our vessel. It was always night when we were voyaging. Harvey was usually at the helm, I was doing something important on the bowsprit, and Porky Allen was cooking down below. Then the helm was made fast, and we sat down to a meal of fried bacon and coffee. 'It's your watch, to-night,' Harvey would say to Allen or me. 'We ought to make Le Havre by four in the morning.' And so the boat, and we, with our eyes focussed on the light of the binnacle, dreamed on.

How many nights, at school, I went to bed as one of the crew of that phantom-ship going below, I cannot say. They must have been hundreds; for in that dream I lived more or less continuously until Harvey left the school. Then Allen and I were left alone; and somehow, without Harvey, we had not the heart to continue. Perhaps also, Harvey's imagination was more buoyant than ours. Without his splendid assurance to uplift us, we lapsed back into sordid and despairing consideration of ways and means. We had not the wherewithal to begin to build a twelve-foot dinghy, or even a model yacht, if we had suffered our minds to descend so low. At that time there was not even a rudimentary workshop at the school, where we might have slaked our passion to build something. For us, it was dreams or nothing.

In this I have outrun chronology. The footsore expeditions to Bromley belonged to the time when I was eight or nine, and living beside Goose Green in East Dulwich. At the end of our garden, immediately after we settled there, a big ginger-beer factory was built, of which my father complained bitterly, with good reason: for, in the summer at least, the men began to work at dawn, clattering the crates of ginger-beer bottles on to the heavy drays. At one time, my father tried to promote a petition among the residents of the street against the nuisance; but they were apathetic, and my father's protest was confined to the boycott. Never a bottle of Batey's ginger-beer was brought into the house; the name of Batey was never mentioned. It was a religious taboo, and it wrought so upon my mind that I came to believe that Batey's ginger-beer was almost a kind of slow poison, pervaded by black-beetles and other foreign bodies. The firm has flourished since; but to this day I have never dared to taste its brew.

But the ginger-beer factory was not an unmixed evil. A stream of drays, each with two stout horses, issued from its gates in the morning; and much of the success of our longer expeditions depended on our being able to steal a lift behind, where there was a convenient footplate. With luck, we might be carried far over Peckham Rye towards Catford – a good two or three miles of our journey. And in the morning the drivers were not so quick to flick their long whips to cart-tail, nor were other little boys so alert to cry maliciously 'Whip behind!' as they were later in the day. Then they never failed to betray one. The appetite for *Schadenfreude* was highly developed in the little boys of my generation; they were very, very far from being 'class-conscious'.

My parents would have frowned heavily upon this gutter-urchin behaviour of mine, if they had known it. I was intended to be highly respectable; and I myself was reasonably anxious to be respectable. We boys of the Bellenden Road Higher Grade Board School, though we had no notion what Higher Grade meant, were conscious of a definite social superiority over the boys of the neighbouring Board School in Choumert Road. They were to us 'the Choumert blags' (short for 'blackguards'), but we were afraid of them. It was their habit, when there was a fall of snow, to invade our playground and bombard us out of it. We averred that they put stones in their snowballs, which may have been true; but that was no reason why we should all retire precipitately into our building – all save one, by name Wally Bampton, a boy of thirteen or so, who invariably rushed into the midst of the Choumert host, like a Shakespeare hero, and clove an unavailing lane in their midst. They were as frightened of him, as we of them.

Meantime, I was working hard for a scholarship, under an able but disappointed schoolmaster called Wylie. He was, like others of his kind, impatient with stupid boys, and easily exasperated. He put vigour into his canings of the unruly ones; and I can see him now, a spot of high colour in his cheeks, and a fierce light in his eye, raising himself on tip-toe in his eagerness to put all his force into the blow. He was a tallish man, with a waxed moustache and a very high collar. His handwriting was clear and firm; and his notebooks (made at the Training College) which he some- times lent me were beautifully neat and methodical. Moreover, he had an accomplishment very unusual among board-school masters of that day: he could speak French fairly well. He had spent several holidays in France; and he lodged with a French family which had settled in the neighbourhood. Yet, for some reason, he never gave me a French book to read. I had to be content with the melancholy passages at the end of *Bué's First French Book* – about Leonidas and the Spartans and the rest. If only I had been given *Les Trois Mousquetaires*, I would have found some way of making it out. It was not until ten years later, at the end of my time at Christ's Hospital, when a young master fresh from Cambridge gave us some of Ludovic Halévy's stories to read, that I for the first time became interested in what a Frenchman was saying, and French became more than a boring matter of grammar and genders to me.

Still, I made progress under Wylie. Ours, unlike some other of the London Board Schools of that day, was one with no parti- cular interest in scholarships, and no highly developed technique of cramming for the examination. Nor had anyone any clear

39

idea of the relative value of the scholarships for which I was entitled to compete. By a stroke of good fortune, at this moment my father, who had at one time been a temporary clerk in the War Office, happened to meet his old chief. To him he spoke of my being prepared for a scholarship, and of his difficulty in deciding for which school to try, and Christ's Hospital was mentioned. Then Mr. Simpson told my father that he himself was a Christ's Hospital boy – an old Blue, as we call it – and he urged my father to do all he could to get me there. That decided it. I was to try to get one of the six scholarships which Christ's Hospital had been lately compelled to throw open to elementary schoolboys; and I succeeded. My trepidation, when I was summoned to a viva voce examination at the London School Board offices on the Victoria Embankment, was fearful. Though nothing was said, as some thirty of us were ranged in our places in the Board Room before the examiner, I knew that we were placed in order of examination. There was no mistaking the intelligence in the dark eyes of the small boy whose impressive name – Percival Hermann Charles Allen – was called first, or the comparative obtuseness of those at the other end. And I was sixth.

I pulled myself together. I had the feeling, when I summed up the five in front of me, that I ought to be higher than sixth. About Allen I was doubtful; but I thought I was more than a match for any of the other four, if only I could get a fair trial; and somehow I must lift myself out of my precarious position into one of safety. At this juncture my very lack of specialized scholarship instruction served me well. I had accumulated a store of general knowledge – precocious, unhealthy, in a sense unreal – but still the fruits of my own reading and discovery. Suddenly, we were called upon to read aloud – a passage about Uncle Toby. The pages of print, without chapter-heading or title, went round. I waited for the question which I knew must come. It came. 'Could anybody say who was the author of that passage?' For the first, and only time, I had the advantage even of Allen. But in my eagerness I was confused and gulped out that the author was Tristram Shandy. At which the examiner laughed, and I recovered. 'I mean Laurence Sterne'. The examiner was visibly surprised. 'Do you know anything more about him?' I said I knew that he was a clergyman, that he lived in the middle of the eighteenth century, and that he had written another book besides *Tristram Shandy*. 'How do you know that?' 'Because I've read it.' He seemed to be incredulous. 'What is it called?' '*A Sentimental Journey*.' 'Do you remember anything about it?' 'Not very much,' I said truthfully, 'because it's hard to remember. There are so many dashes. But I remember about the dead donkey.' Then he asked me: 'Did I know of any other novelists who lived at the same time?' Yes, I did – I knew of Fielding and Smollett. Could I name any books they had written? I could. '*Humphrey Clinker, Roderick Random, Peregrine Pickle*.' 'But you've not read any of those?' No, I hadn't. 'Then how do you remember the names?' 'Because they are funny.'

Again, it was good luck. The names of Smollett's novels had stuck in my head ever since I had read them in the social chapter of my grandmother's *Cassell's Penny History*; and by some fluke a little threepenny copy of *The Sentimental Journey* had been in my hands. I hadn't enjoyed it; but I had read it. I liked strange reading. I liked to accumulate new words; and I even liked to use them in a pedantic way. Occasionally, but definitely, I was moved by their vague poetic suggestions. Once one of the masters at school had written on the blackboard:

> Yet once more, O ye laurels, and once more
> Ye myrtles brown, with ivy never sere
> I come to pluck your berries harsh and crude
> And with forc'd fingers rude
> Shatter your leaves before the mellowing year.

By this I had been secretly enchanted. 'Harsh and crude', in particular, had delighted me, I know not why: for I had never seen, much less tasted, a myrtle-berry. And 'shatter your leaves' gave me an exquisite pleasure. 'Scatter', I could have understood; but 'shatter' – because I did not understand it – gave me a physical thrill. There were lines of *Hamlet*, too – part of which we had once read – that I rolled delectably on the tongue of my imagination:

> 'Tis not alone my inky cloak, good mother,
> Nor customary suits of solemn black,
> Nor windy suspiration of forced breath . . .

The master who made us read these was a black-avised, beetle-browed man, named Grubb, who himself wore solemn black. It befitted him, for he was that portentous thing, a Freethinker, an Atheist. And perhaps in consequence, he was the only master in the school who had a real taste for good literature. But I was with him only for a month or two, before I was shot, like a rocket, from the second to the fifth standard.

To all these masters I now said good-bye. My viva voce had been successful. I was raised to second on the final list, and my parents were given notice that I must be presented for medical examination at Christ's Hospital. Now that the strain and excitement of scholarship examination was over, I was dismayed at the thought of leaving home. I said farewell reluctantly to two masters in particular at Bellenden Road – to Mr. Wylie and Mr. Hazlitt. To Wylie I was grateful for his coaching; towards Hazlitt I felt an odd kind of admiration. I do not remember what he taught me, or even that he taught me at all. But there was a grave and kindly austerity about him which made a deep impression upon me. He was stern, yet not severe; and he was never exasperated. If I had been asked why I admired Hazlitt, I should probably have said that he had a nice face. But that face, which I believe I never saw again, has remained vivid to me ever since. It is before my eyes for me to study now; and now I can recognize what it was to which I dumbly responded. There was a moral beauty in Hazlitt's face. He, I should now conjecture, had an ideal of education, a desire to

42

make boys into men, which barely entered the mind of the board-school masters of those days. He made some simple, yet subtle, appeal to the rudiments of manly pride in us little boys, so that when we marched past him we would pull ourselves together and be amply rewarded by the flicker of a friendly smile. For I was not alone in my admiration of him. Dozens of us felt the same about him; and not one of us could have expressed what he felt. And now it seems to me simple enough; we felt that the others were just schoolmasters: but Hazlitt was a man.

To him I said good-bye: good-bye to the dark stone stairs and the shiny green and yellow rooms of Bellenden Road, to the conkers and jews'-harps and peg-tops and marbles of the little board-school boy, to the slow meandering home on dusky winter evenings up Oglander, along Musgrave, and down the Undine roads, to the baked-potato man at the bottom of Lordship Lane, to my companions at the school and the Sunday School, to Bill Adams who walked from far the other side of Peckham Rye to bring me three shining new pennies of 1901 for a keepsake. I felt sad; I felt that I should never see these things, these faces again. And the feeling was true, though not the fact. I saw many of these things and these faces again. My parents did not move house again for some three or four years after I entered Christ's Hospital. I was among the familiar things and the familiar faces in my holidays; but henceforward there was a subtle and ever-growing veil interposed between me and them. It was not my fault; I was caught up in a process: I was being lifted out of my own social class into another. Where I had moved freely in my neighbourhood – an equal among equals – now I was constrained. I began, secretly, to be ashamed even of my home and my own parents. I had glimpses, at Christ's Hospital, of a dignity of life that was altogether new to me. I acquired an utterly new standard by which to judge things which I had previously not dreamed of judging at all.

43

CHAPTER IV

DITTIES OF NO TONE

IT was in January, 901, that I entered Christ's Hospital, which was still in Newgate Street. The boys who lived in London were allowed to go home on 'passes' on Saturday afternoons, though they had to be back by seven o'clock; and, for some time, I still felt that my home in East Dulwich was my home. Christ's Hospital was a kind of bewildering dream, with brief intervals of lucid wakefulness.

But the dream was vivid enough. I was awe-struck before the august figure of Richard Lee, the Headmaster, in gown and bands, when we were called into his room on the second or third day to receive his homily. 'Keep innocency, do the thing which is right, and that shall bring a man peace at the last.' The words were graven, automatically, upon my memory as though an oracle had spoken; but the words had no conceivable relation to myself. They and I moved, as it were, in different dimensions. And so it was in the class-room. We board-school boys, who had no Latin, were placed in a special form – Little Erasmus Special – where we were taught Latin at extra speed in order that we might cease to be unmanageable oddities. But to me *mensa* was un-utterably strange, I could not come to grips with it at all. What little I learned, I learned parrot-fashion; and I was a very bad hand at learning parrot-fashion. What I really needed was Cornelius Nepos and a crib. Instead, I stumbled painfully through Kennedy.

I was, as I have said, a rather pedantic little boy, with the trick of using big words out of my store. The school w.c.'s – 'bogs', we called them – were inadequate in number, and there was always a crowd waiting to go in after breakfast. As I was lurking timidly on the edge, a boy of about my size turned to me and said: 'Have you got any bodge?' I had not the faintest notion what he meant. (Actually, he was asking for toilet paper.) But I was all politeness.

'I'm very sorry,' I said, 'but I'm a new boy, and I don't yet understand the vocabulary.'

I uttered the word 'vocabulary' very precisely, in what I imagined to be the tone of perfect courtesy. There was a moment's dead silence, while he stared at me, dumbfounded. Then he slapped my face, well and truly. 'That's a fotch,' he said. After a pause, he added, 'And bodge is paper. Have you got any?'

'No,' I said.

'Well, why didn't you say so?'

Then he plunged back into the crowd, while I – I grieve to say – slunk away into a dark corner of a cloister and cried.

For a little while, the six of us who entered the school by the same way at the same time used to foregather together to compare experiences, and comfort one another; but gradually we were absorbed into our Wards. Our being 'scrub' members of 3's, or 16's, or 5's, as the case might be, became more important to us than the bond of our common entry.

Of this process of absorption into the tradition and ethos of a great and unique school, it is in the nature of things impossible to speak. It happened in the main unconsciously. But the process was attended by discomforts which might be magnified into moral struggles. For example, my parents and, in particular, my aunt, in their endeavour to make things easy for me, had cultivated one of the school beadles, who had the immediate control of our goings-out and our comings-in. They tipped him heavily. That did not matter. What did matter was that they treated him as something more than their equal. At first, I was too bewildered, too little adjusted to the school, to be aware of this. But in a month or two I was sufficiently sensitized to notice that this beadle treated me in an uncomfortably familiar way. If I ran into him, he would stop me, and say, in a loud and oily voice: 'And how is master Jack Murry getting on?' No one in the

school called me Jack; no one in the school knew that I was
called Jack – we did not use one another's Christian names: still
worse, the beadle never addressed any other boy in that fashion.
It was all because my relatives would speak familiarly of me to him
as Jack.

I grew to hate the sight of that beadle. I longed to tell my
aunt that she must not be more than decently civil to him; but I
was fond of my aunt, and shrank from hurting her. And even
when she would say to me – for it was she who came generally
to take me home on Saturday – how kind the beadle was, I held
my peace. I knew that he was not kind; on the contrary, he was
'slimy' as we used to say. My boy's instinct was sound in this
case; and I never found reason to withdraw my inarticulate
judgment that he took a subtle pleasure in compromising me.
My feeling of shame eventually grew so intense that I even shrank
from going out on Saturday. To see in the distance my aunt, who
was waiting for me by the lodge, conversing affably with that
beadle and then to run the gauntlet of his pretended amiabilities,
as he stood with his hand on my head, was a torture to escape
which I would have forgone the pleasures of a half-holiday.

I was becoming a little snob; but, looking back, I cannot see
what else could have happened. I was engaged in shedding a
skin, and the process of growing a new one took many years. In
comparison with the way of life of which I now had glimpses, that
of my home seemed sordid and devoid of dignity. When my
classical master invited me, as a reward for my neat Greek handwriting, to tea at his house in Little Britain, it was an education
in the possibilities of intimate living. His shining silver and smooth
napery I savoured like a little gourmand: the starched print dress
of his housekeeper was clean and cool to my eye, like a plunge in
the sea. I could no more help comparing these manners with
those of my own home, than I could help observing and delighting
in them. They were, indeed, refinements; luxuries compared to
the monastic austerity of the school itself. But that monastic
austerity of the school implied the same judgment on the life

to which I was accustomed. It was dignity against vulgarity. The blue bowls from which we drank our tea, the long oak tables at which we sat, the plain plank beds on which we slept, all passed a silent verdict on the shoddiness of the furniture at home – a home furnished at the end of the 'eighties when the taste of the English lower middle class reached a nadir.

I was very fond of my parents; but I became silently critical of them. In a vague way I wanted them to be different. I did not want them to be richer; I wanted them to live differently. And one holiday it struck me suddenly, with an awful despair and a guilty consciousness of treachery, that there was not a single object in the whole house which I should have been glad to have for its own sake. This was, in its own small way, a tragic realization, though its full significance was concealed from me; but it was serious enough to make me miserable for days.

This happened some three or four years after I had entered Christ's Hospital and was the culmination of a slow ferment of unconscious estrangement. I was at odds with myself. And I had other reasons for being miserable, though there was none which gnawed at me so painfully as this. But one was serious enough. For some cause or other I had, almost immediately after entering the school, become lethargic. I was not lazy; perhaps I was not really stupid: but I could take no interest in my work, outside the one favourite subject of history, which was an unimportant subject on the Classical Side. My vanity received many blows from the day when my form-master, for some atrocious false concord, told me that I was 'a little owl, and should put my head in six bags'. It was a new and devastating experience for me to be called a fool, and to know that I deserved it; and it was the more galling because Allen, who had headed the scholarship list, was in the same ward as I, and had become my bosom-friend. He seemed to take to Latin and Greek as a duck to water. While I was floundering about at the muddy verge, he was swimming gaily in the middle of the pond. And he was eight months younger than myself. But galling or no, there was nothing to be

47

done. He shot ahead of me at the first examination. He went up two forms; I scraped one.

But we were good friends, and I accepted it with a fair grace, and made up my mind that he was abler than I. My real trouble was with my father. He had naturally come to the firm conclusion that I was abler than Allen, and that it was merely due to special coaching that Allen was in front of me on the scholarship list. Now that the field was fair and no favour it would be proved that I was the better man. My one duty, in my father's view, was to beat Allen. Accordingly, every week when I reached home, I was cross-examined on this matter. Was I ahead of Allen? I parried or evaded the question as long as I could by declaring, quite untruly, that there was no order in the form, whereas in fact we changed places every day. For my own part, I was now quite accustomed to being beaten by Allen: I took it, indeed, as a matter of course. But to have told my father the truth would have plunged him in the sulks, and my mother in consequential misery, for weeks. Anything was better than that. So I began to lie valiantly, and to give my father to understand that we were always neck and neck.

> Each changing place with that which went before
> In sequent toil all forwards do contend.

I was not in the least worried about the lie. My one concern was to prevent the real situation from becoming known to my father. In this I succeeded, until the school was moved from Newgate Street to Horsham. Then, unfortunately for me, the authorities introduced the nefarious practice of sending out a detailed school list in the holidays after the midsummer examinations. The true situation was revealed: Allen was a whole form above me. There was an explosion; and thereafter, my summer holidays every year were made miserable, not merely for me but for my mother also, by the expectation of the arrival of that devilish school list.

But for this constant poison, my school-days would have been happy enough. It seemed, and still seems monstrously unjust

48

that my father should have estimated my diligence, and even my character, solely by my capacity (or rather my incapacity) to overtake Allen. I knew that I had done what I could; I felt that my father's attitude was quite unreasonable, and that he had deserved the lies with which I fed him. And when, eventually, the lethargy of mind with which I had struggled so long began to dissipate, and I did (to my own astonishment) overtake Allen on the Classical Side, I had not the faintest joy in telling my father the good news. The sympathy between us had broken down completely.

So it came about that, after the summer of 1902, when Christ's Hospital was moved into the country, I was happier at school than at home. Though I was no particular good, either in class or at games, I enjoyed myself. I positively loved the summer-term and the cricket, though it was not till it was far too late that it was discovered by my house-master that I was abominably short-sighted and could not see the ball. Nevertheless, I once had the ecstatic pleasure of making fifty – no more, no less – when it was badly wanted in a house-match. And house-cricket, as we played it in Maine A, had many charms. We possessed no good cricketers; but we made up for it by playing as a team. There was a pleasant feeling of comradeship in the house, which made this possible; and we had the satisfaction of winning the House cricket cup in our own unstrained, unorthodox fashion.

Christ's Hospital, as was said by the Charity Commissioners (to whose reforms was due my own admission), is *sui generis*. We were familiar with the phrase, before we knew what it meant, because it was often quoted by dignitaries at Speech Day. It is true: Christ's Hospital is unique. It is a public school into which money cannot buy entrance. Wealth is automatically excluded from it. It follows that unless a boy has ability enough to win an open scholarship at the University, the working of the school demands that he should be superannuated at a point at which he can secure a situation in which he can maintain himself. The old and intimate connection between the school and the com-

49

mercial life of the City of London was just beginning to break down in my day, simply because the commercial life of the City was passing out of the hands of the individual merchant houses, into which old Blues for generations before had been steadily recruited. During my own eight years at the school, two of the Lord Mayors of London were old Blues. But that, I imagine, was rather the glorious finale of an old era, than the triumphant beginning of a new one. The removal of the school from Newgate Street to Horsham did really presage the gradual weakening of a centuries-old bond.

The time had been when Christ's Hospital, more than any other school, supplied the staffs of the great merchant houses of the City. A hundred years ago, there was the tiny handful of boys – the Grecians – for whom the school could supply exhibition (in the good Shakespearian sense) to the University. These were one or two, at the most three, every year: and their obvious destination was the Church. Beneath them were the Deputy Grecians, unfitted, whether by ability or other causes, to proceed as Grecians to the University. The relation between the Grecian and the Deputy Grecian is enshrined, to the edification of historians and the perennial glory of the school, in the relation between Coleridge and Charles Lamb. There was always a tinge of condescension in Coleridge's attitude to Lamb, a trace of deference in Lamb's attitude to Coleridge, which only the old Blue, and perhaps only the old Blue who remembers the glory of the Grecian in Newgate Street, can intimately understand. For the Grecians in those old days were visibly the lords of the school. When the masters were not actually teaching they disappeared from the school precincts. The domestic authority in the Hall was the Warden, in the wards the Matron – a being far inferior to the august Grecian, who listened to her conversation and her complaints with a *distrait* and preoccupied air. With his velvet cuffs, his multitudinous buttons (which all small boys firmly believed to be stamped out of pure silver), with his coat of superfine cloth and his gracefully drooping girdle, he sat on the

polished granite stones, plumb in the middle of the Grecians'
cloister, itself plumb in the centre of the school. He was, indeed,
the cynosure of every eye, the observed of all observers: he was
more, he was the navel and centre of the life of the school.

Charles Lamb, disqualified from Grecianship by the stammer
which would have made it impossible for him to take orders,
went, as befitted a Deputy Grecian, into the relative dignity
of the old East India House. If he had been superannuated in
Erasmus, he would doubtless have entered an ordinary mercantile
house. In the world's eyes, Lamb was in a far better and securer
position than Coleridge ever attained; but never in his own.
Coleridge had known the glory of Grecianhood, from which
Lamb had been excluded.

With the removal of the school and the introduction of the
system of two house-masters, senior and junior, resident in each
ward (which now became a 'House'), it was inevitable that something of the glory of the Grecian should depart. But for some little
time there was a silent and tenacious resistance against the consequences of change, of which the tradition vaguely persisted
even when I became a Grecian of the third parting, in 1905.
Since my new house-master – a kindly and humane but rather
indolent cynic named Sainte-Croix – had known me as a scrubby
little boy of twelve, it was not possible for me to stand on my new
dignity; so far as my relations wi h him were concerned, I definitely belonged to the new and inferior race of Grecians. But
with the new Headmaster it was different. We had good reasons
for believing that he was not a classical scholar of the exact type
to which we were accustomed. Indeed, we tried him out, and
discovered that he would let pass a shoddy rendering of a kind at
which F. H. Merk, the real classical master of the Grecians, would
have winced, visibly and audibly. We came to regard it as
something of an insult that the Headmaster should affect to teach
us at all; and our sense of insult passed occasionally into downright
indignation.

One occasion was memorable. The Classical Grecians

possessed a fair-copy book, in which from time to time a rendering into Greek or Latin which was judged exceptionally good by Merk was copied by the fortunate author. It was a real distinction, coveted and respected as such; and it was so seldom conferred that a single fair-copy book went back some forty years. Men whom we knew by repute as distinguished and middle-aged old Blues were represented in it; and we could tell by the jet-black ink and the blotted loops of the old copies that they belonged to the quill-pen age. Merk himself, who had been a Grecian and a Balliol scholar, used a quill. He was thus in all respects qualified to be what he was in fact, the jealous upholder of the traditions of the fair-copy book.

To our dismay, the Headmaster announced his intention of taking the senior Grecians for Latin prose. Merk announced this to us with a detached and frigid voice; and we knew that he disapproved as thoroughly as we did ourselves. We wrote our proses with a half-heart and a bad grace, convinced that we were wasting our time. During one of these perfunctory performances, we noticed, with real apprehension, that the Headmaster was turning over the pages of the fair-copy book. We feared the worst. It promptly happened. During the next week, no less than three of us were commanded to immortalize our renderings in the book. We were in a quandary. Our first impulse was to explain the situation to Merk; but that on consideration we rejected. It would have put him in an impossible position, and involved him in a sort of conspiracy with the Grecians against the Headmaster. So we decided simply to ignore the Headmaster's command, and to hope that he would forget all about it. It was not to be. Very probably he had sensed our reluctance to obey; and he was peremptory with us when he found that no additions had been made to the book. There was no escape: we copied our versions in, feeling guiltier at heart than any downright offence could have made us. Then we waited for the next hour with Merk. When we settled down to whatever we were doing, we watched him furtively. He went over to the book, which (as he well knew) had been missing from its place for a day or two, turned over the pages with pursed lips, read, came to the end, sniffed faintly, then with his face to the window and his back to us, squared his shoulders – a Herculean gesture characteristic of the little man – and stared silently outside. We were the tongue-tied witnesses of a minor tragedy.

It was told me, when I was at Oxford, by one who should have known, that Merk was one of the finest sixth-form masters of his day. I can well believe it. Although I was not the type out of which his aptest pupils were made, I received very much from him. The first authentic thrills of the experience of poetry came to me from him. With the dryness and reserve that marked him, he never said an explicit word concerning the quality of the Catullus, the Theocritus, the Plato which we translated to him; but he subtly enforced upon me an attitude of reverence for the text. He made me feel that they were precious; until the moment came when I knew they *were* precious – that here were clear voices – Μῶσα λίγεια – sounding directly to me out of the past. The muffling mists of dictionary and commentary were rolled away; and the bright clear landscape, which is classical antiquity, stood suddenly revealed. Phrases, like phrases of music, began to grave themselves upon my mind: scalding phrases –

> Nunc in quadriviis et angiportis
> Glubit magnanimos Remi nepotes –

silvery phrases –

> ἁδύ τι τὸ ψιθύρισμα καὶ ἁ πίτυς, αἰπόλε, τήνα

sad-sweet phrases –

> οὐ μ’ ἔτι παρθενικαὶ μελιγάρυες ἱμερόφωνοι,
> γυῖα φέρειν δύναται· βάλε δὴ, βάλε κηρύλος εἴην
> ὅς τ’ ἐπὶ κύματος ἄνθος, ἅμ’ ἀλκυόνεσσι ποτῆται,
> νηλεγὲς ἦτορ ἔχων, ἁλιπόρφυρος εἴαρος ὄρνις·

53

all, as I gathered them to myself, making harmony together – or rather one never-ending, ever-varying melody, played on that distant pipe which Keats so clearly heard, piping to the spirit ditties of no tone.

To Merk alone I owe it that my ear could catch fragments of that melody, of which neither he nor we ever spoke. There was in his scholarship an austerity, which made no pretence of capturing the ineffable, yet shrank fastidiously from flamboyant paraphrase. It insisted on precise and definite terms. With him translation was translation: nothing more, but nothing less. We rendered baldly, but so accurately that the imagination remained sensitive to the original phrase entire. We were not suffered to deceive ourselves with the fantasy that the quality, or the quiddity, of the text was transfused into our English. The Greek or the Latin stood clean apart, its magic essence uncontaminated by our clumsy symbols. They were mere motions of the voice to signify that we understood all that could be understood. We had done the works: the descent of the grace was not Merk's affair, nor any man's. If neither he nor we presumed to conjure it down, then we might, perhaps, be found worthy to be sometimes visited. In his heart was the religious humility of the priest before the sacrament.

One discovers these things, years afterwards: fragments of the past, treasured unconsciously, one knows not why, yield up their secret to contemplation. And it may be that I have hit upon the answer to a question that has always puzzled me. Why was it, I have wondered, that I had no religion at school? Never for one moment can I recall feeling the need or desire for religion. As befitted a Religious, Royal and Ancient Foundation, there were services galore, though there had not been many at Newgate Street, where we had no school chapel. Christ Church in Newgate Street served us on Sunday mornings (when my own main office was the peculiar one of tickling the feet of a bigger boy) and the School Hall on Sunday evenings. But at Horsham there was morning chapel every day, and an evening chapel for the saints' days. This was one of the innovations which we felt it our duty to resent; but there was not much substance to our resentment, or at any rate to mine. In my own fashion I enjoyed the services: partly for themselves – to the mind of a boy accustomed to Unitarianism, the Prayer Book services are like sherris-sack after years of thin potations – partly because they bore a necessary part in the process of my transmutation. Since religion, in any deeper sense, was unknown to me, I made no bones about desiring to be confirmed into the Church of England like the majority of the boys: for which purpose I had to be baptized by the Headmaster. Beyond my appreciation of the fact that I had the School Chapel to myself, this meant nothing to me. It was a queer ritual which must be decorously undergone. I underwent it decorously. I was distinctly curious to discover whether anything would happen when the Bishop laid his hands upon me; but nothing did happen, and I was not disappointed.

CHAPTER V

PERSONA-HUNTING

MANIFESTLY, I was a boy from whose composition the nerve of religious susceptibility had been omitted. When I came to read Lucretius, I was satisfied with his account of the nature of things: more than satisfied, because his mighty phrases called forth an echo from some cavern of my soul hitherto unknown to me. The dim beginnings were awakened of an imaginative awe before the immensity of the universe, and the facts of birth and death. His tremendous simplicity in facing ultimates shook my schoolboy indifference, indeed, but it did not send me to religion for consolation: on the contrary, the wound Lucretius made was its own medicine.

> Quare etiam atque etiam tales fateare necesse est
> Esse alios alibi congressus materiai
> Qualis hic est avido complexu quem tenet aether.

To that impassioned insistence which makes of bald prose majestic poetry; that all-conquering, all-devastating hunger for the truth, as for a power which works its own salvation and forbids, as unworthy, any recourse to consolations more personal, I did dimly respond. It was the grander background, as the firmament is the background of the warm and palpable night, of the wistful acknowledgment of my wayward and beloved Catullus:

> Nobis, cum semel occidit brevis lux,
> Nox est perpetua una dormienda.

But these responses were embryo within me. In so far as I had a creed, I found it in the classics, and above all in Lucretius. That was more intimate to me than anything in my own nominal religion, which then seemed to revolve about a matter with which

I never had, and never have had, any real concern – my personal survival. I loved the Apostles' Creed; I enjoyed saying: 'From thence he shall come to judge the quick and the dead': but it had no meaning, except as a piece of mythology. Death was no problem. Not that it was wholly unreal. In fact, I had come to unusually close quarters with death while I was at school. One afternoon, when I was about fifteen, I was bowling at the cricket-nets to a boy of my own age called Connor, when suddenly there was a clap of thunder, which struck like the blow of a mallet on my head. I fell to the ground. I scrambled to my feet, and made a wild dash for the little wooden hut at the edge of the field. The rain poured down. Some two or three of us were gathered there, half-stunned. When we peeped out, we saw Connor lying still, in the nets near the wicket. We ran out to pick him up. I grabbed his ankles, and dropped them again. There was a queer sensation in my fingers, as though the flesh they had touched had suddenly become inelastic. 'He's dead!' I whispered. And when we looked in his face we knew it was so. His eyes were dead. A thin line of mucus was between his lips, and an odd bead of solder on the hinge of his spectacles.

Had Connor been a friend of mine, perhaps I should have felt differently; but he was not. What impressed me most was that death was a very simple business. What Connor had felt was what I had felt – a great bang on the head – only his was harder. You were alive: then you were dead. It was all over. The notion that I should meet him again in some hereafter was grotesque.

οἴη περ φυλλῶν γενεή, τοίη δὲ καὶ ἀνδρῶν

I had not got to Homer when Connor was killed; but when I did, that line of Homer satisfied the demand of my experience. Connor had been knocked off the tree in April by a big stick, as I might swipe off a thistlehead. Others fell naturally, brown and sere, in November droves.

But if I could not be depressed by the fact of death, I found a good deal of imaginative pleasure in the sadness of the idea of death. I liked to hear, and to read aloud, the twelfth chapter of Ecclesiastes.

'Remember now thy Creator in the days of thy youth, while the evil days come not, nor the years draw nigh, when thou shalt say, I have no pleasure in them . . .
'Also when they shall be afraid of that which is high, and fears shall be in the way, and the almond tree shall flourish, and the grasshopper shall be a burden, and desire shall fail: because man goeth to his long home, and the mourners go about the streets.
'Or ever the silver cord be loosed or the golden bowl be broken, or the pitcher be broken at the fountain, or the wheel broken at the cistern.
'Then shall the dust return to the earth as it was: and the spirit shall return unto God who gave it.'

But the effect of that was not at all to make me remember my Creator in the days of my youth; it was to induce a rich and languorous melancholy, akin to that which visits one in later life, at re-hearing a strain of romantic music, which one first heard many years ago, sitting outside a café at evening with parted or departed friends. Then the precariousness of life, the fact that youth grows old, that love can bear it out to the edge of doom, but not beyond, that what was once an ecstasy is now a vague and melting wisp of memory – all these sad thoughts are sweet in such a moment; and we touch the hem of the garment of the goddess who

> dwells with Beauty – Beauty that must die;
> And Joy, whose hand is ever at his lips
> Bidding adieu.

Of her I must have been an unconscious schoolboy votary. She was the goddess whose footprints I saw in my musings in the school chapel, when I let the service roll about my ears and dreamed. Her voice sounded alike in the words of the *Nunc dimittis* and the love-songs of Catullus. Everything was turned to her praise, tuned to her sorrow. If Homer's heroes were brave and berserker, the sweet war-men were dead and rotten; if the gulfs of the sea had not washed down Ulysses, time had swallowed his body, and his spirit lived only to remind us that it happened far away and long ago. If I walked with my friends on a summer evening after chapel, and built castles in the air and ships on the sea, the dreams were suffused with the drowsy ache of wondering where we four should be; how distant, how forgotten, five or ten years hence. If I had really known, my sadness would have been bitter indeed.

But as it was, it was my luxury, my one contact with something beyond the everyday, terrestrial world. My soul, or what I imagined to be my soul, seemed half-inclined to ascend and leave my body blissfully at peace. It was my opium dream, with this difference that it left me feeling good. In such a moment, not merely did I feel good in myself; I felt that it was good to be alive, to be at school, to have my friends for friends. In such a moment I dreamed myself into prodigies of magnanimity towards my enemies as well. In imagination, I said magnificent, simple, soul-shattering things to them, so that they changed and regarded me with affection tempered with awe. Even old J.B. – James Barnard, the senior mathematical master, whose sarcasms over my pitiful failure with analytical geometry made me go pale – would come up to me and say: 'I'm sorry, Murry: I have misunderstood you', and I would smile bravely and forgive him. That indeed was no minor miracle that I allowed myself. The old fellow, who had more than his pound of flesh from me before I escaped him by becoming a classical Grecian, ran true to form to' the last. First, when he knew that I had been made a classical Grecian, he stopped me and said: 'They must be running very short of material over yonder', nodding his head towards the Classical school: and last, when I had secured a tolerable classical scholarship at Oxford, he stopped me again – my short cut to

59

school ran perilously near his house – and grunted: '£100 a year. H'm. Well, who *could* have believed it – of *you*?'

To tell the truth, I could never believe it of myself. I had come, in the process of my struggle through the school, to have a profound mistrust of my own capacities. At one time I had resigned myself, with a despondent stoicism, to being superannuated as a Deputy Grecian. Week after week, term after term, my Greek prose was returned to me, by S. E. Winbolt, who was the Deps' form-master, as almost incorrigibly bad, and I grew more and more depressed. It was, I am ashamed to say, at moments very hard to keep myself from weeping: for Winbolt was a debonair and generous soul, who was himself rather distressed by my shocking performances, and seemed to find their badness almost as unintelligible as I did. The more I struggled, the deeper I got into the mire. By the time the midsummer examinations came on, I was beaten beforehand. The far-off days when I had entered into examinations with confidence seemed as remote as a star. For me everything depended on the result; I must either be somewhere near the top or be superannuated. I could expect no mercy – no charity mark such as is sometimes, very justly, given to boys when they are examined by their own masters, who know that they possess capacities that cannot out under pressure of examination. For on this occasion, I learned with a sinking heart, a well-known Oxford classical tutor, J. U. Powell of John's, was examining us. The conclusion, so far as I was concerned, was foregone.

To this day I cannot understand what happened in that nightmare examination. All I distinctly remember is Winbolt reading out the result of the Greek Prose, with a raised eyebrow. I was top. 'That is remarkable,' he said, ' – and gratifying,' and he smiled. I was completely bewildered, not knowing whether to laugh or to cry. The thing was fantastic and incredible. I was still completely bewildered when, a week or so later, J. U. Powell himself arrived, and we were called in to him one by one to hear his general observations on our papers. I opened the door and saw my *deus ex machina*: a dark-haired, rather untidy man, with his red master's hood all awry. He was encouraging towards my timidity. 'I liked your papers – very much, on the whole.' Then he paused. 'But I don't think you are really a classical scholar. But you will do well in Greats.' That, in my condition, was oracular in its authority and its darkness. I had long since ceased to believe that I should ever go to the University; and as for speculating what I should do when I got there – that was wholly outside my range. But Powell's sentence remained with me, and I extracted, incredulously, its astonishing implication. It took for granted that I would get a classical scholarship of some sort to Oxford.

I could never bring myself to take that for granted. The distrust of my own capacities which had accumulated during my previous five years at the school could not easily be removed. I could not regard myself as responsible for the surprising reversal of fortune which had overtaken me: it was not a thing that I had achieved, it had simply happened to me. Just as I had formerly a foreboding that I was doomed to do worse than I was, now I began to have a foreboding that I was doomed to do better than I was. But it was still in the nature of a foreboding – uncomfortable and ominous.

This was borne in upon me, pretty clearly, a few months later. In consequence of my fantastic performance, I was now a classical Grecian of the third parting. In the winter the classical Grecians competed for the Charles Lamb medal for an English Essay. One of these medals was in the school museum; and I had long admired it. Indeed, it is a beautiful thing – one of Wyon's completely satisfying designs. It was a simple silver medal, unaccompanied by any wad of calf-bound volumes. And that appealed to me. It was as near as one could get to the straightforward Greek wreath of bays which was appropriately part of the design of the medal itself. But most of all I desired it because it was struck in honour of Charles Lamb, whom I had now begun to read and admire and to consider the noblest and most human of all old Blues.

The method of competition was that, on the appointed morning, the subject was given out. We had three hours to ponder and to write, and then sent up our essays anonymously with a distinguishing motto. That first term of mine as a Grecian the subject was 'Literature and Journalism'. The theme pleased me; and I remember opening with the episode of Dr. Johnson knocking down a bookseller-publisher for whom he had been hacking. It struck me as somehow symbolic of the inward relation between literature and journalism; and I tried to extract its significance. With a half-conscious salute to Charles Lamb's convivial shade, I signed myself '*Nunc est bibendum*', and thought no more about it for a day or two. But then, in a ruminative way, I began to reconstruct my essay; and discovered, to my surprise, that it seemed to me good – so good that I could not believe that I had really written it as I imagined. But after a painful effort to recapture as many as I could of the actual sentences, I convinced myself. Straightway, the sense of foreboding came upon me; and I 'knew' that I had won the medal.

Indeed, I had. If anyone had the wit to unmask me, I should, I felt, be revealed as an impostor; but since nobody offered to expose me, and I was quite incapable of doing it myself, I was burdened, henceforth, with the reputation of being a budding man of letters. I say, burdened, for amongst the Grecians I was definitely one of the least literary. I read Kipling, like any other boy, and considered *Stalky and Co.* a sheer masterpiece. After him Anthony Hope, Rider Haggard, Seton Merriman and Conan Doyle were my men. In a rather different order, I liked and re-read Lamb's *Essays* and Boswell's *Johnson*, and in an incalculable fit I had bought myself a copy of Arnold's *Essays in Criticism* which had lately come out in the new 'Everyman Library'. With English poetry I had no truck at all. While other boys read Shelley and Browning, I found them incomprehensible. Since I had occasionally to learn some English poetry by heart – for 'repetition' under Merk – I chose Tennyson as the least puzzling. But even from him I chose the classical pieces – the translation from the Iliad and *Ulysses*: and only once can I remember launching out into *The Idylls of the King*.

Then spake King Arthur to Sir Bedivere:
'This sequel of to-day unsolders all
The goodliest fellowship of ancient Knights
Whereof the world holds record. Such a sleep
They sleep, the men I love. I think that we
Shall nevermore at any future time
Delight our souls with talk of knightly deeds
Walking about the gardens and the halls
Of Camelot, as in the days that were.'

It seems to me pretty thin stuff to-day, as I begin to unwind it
from the bobbin – I could go unwinding, apparently, for ever –
but I rather enjoyed it at sixteen; and it certainly marked the
acme of my taste in English poetry then. But even Tennyson I
should never have dreamed of reading for my own pleasure;
and I generally escaped the compulsion of finding a piece of
English poetry by bringing up to Merk something of Catullus, or
Theocritus, or Homer, or Lucretius. They had a charm for me
that no English poetry possessed.

How impervious to English poetry I was I can recapture from
the memory that a long passage from *Endymion* was set us, at about
this time, for Latin Hexameters for the Richards medal.

And now as deep into the wood as we
Might mark a lynx's eye, there glimmered light
Fair faces and a rush of garments white,
Plainer and plainer showing, till at last
Into the widest valley they all past
Making directly for the woodland alter.
O kindly muse! let not my weak tongue falter
In telling of this goodly company,
Of their old piety, and of their glee,
But let a portion of ethereal dew
Fall on my head and presently unmew
My soul; that I may dare, in wayfaring,
To stammer where old Chaucer used to sing.

63

There follows the lovely description of the procession before Endymion in his chariot. It was almost gibberish to me; nor was I even curious enough about it to read it in its context. I copied it down blindly, as it was dictated; but never dreamed of borrowing a Keats to see if I could make it mean anything real to me. Yet the effect of the passage stuck in my memory, enhanced by the very obscurity in which I found and left it. That glimmer of fair faces, that rush of garments white in the darkness of the woodland ride became a strange sensation. The shade of the forest, the obscurity of the unknown context, blended into one; the glimmer and the rush of white were indistinguishable from the gleam and movement of the passage before my mind's eye. That sensation was thenceforward Keats for me: real, indeed almost physical; and it remained unchanged for years.

Assuredly, I was the last sheep to have the wolf-skin of a literary reputation thrown over him; and it was embarrassing. One of my fellow-Grecians approached me with the proposal that we should take in *The Spectator* together. Since it was obviously my duty to accept, I accepted, with a secret resentment at the waste of threepence a week. It was wasted, for my conscientious struggles to read *The Spectator* were soon abandoned; and I was content with the prestige that accrued to me from having a pile of back numbers on my study window-ledge. It was a trivial, but a typical example of the false position in which I found myself for some years to come, and of a deep-seated weakness of my own character, of which about this time I came to be uneasily conscious. People would take it for granted that I had certain interests and a certain knowledge which I did not possess. I, still essentially a stranger to this new world of culture, would conclude that I ought to have those interests and possess that knowledge. Ashamed to acknowledge my poverty, I would allow it to be understood that the interests and the knowledge were really mine. I assumed the virtue though I had it not.

Maybe I judge myself altogether too leniently; and I should simply write myself down at this time, in intellectual and other things, a humbug. But that is not quite how I see it. I can see it only as part of the half-conscious struggle of a *déraciné* to take root in a new environment. In respect of culture, my home-life had been meagre in the extreme; I was a scion of the most completely disinherited section of modern society: the urban lower middle-class, whose sole conscious aim in life appeared to be to distinguish itself from the proletariat. The manual worker had his tradition: his pride in his craft, his sense of solidarity with his fellow-workers. He was at once an individual and a member of a whole. But the black-coated proletarian of thirty and forty years ago was starved alike of creative satisfaction and of social contact. His one hope of salvation was to develop an interest, or a hobby. None were developed in my home. We lived in a jealous and sterile seclusion. From this I had emerged in virtue of a board-school education as sterile as the life from which it rescued me. It had been entirely superficial: at no point had it touched my dormant imagination, nor awakened in me any sense of wonder or of awe.

With my entry into Christ's Hospital all this was subtly changed. From disinherited, I became an inheritor. I was received into a tradition, and knew the meaning of solidarity: suddenly, I, the spiritual waif of modern industrial society, was endowed with ancestors – and noble ones, named and nameless. When I stared at the simple tablet in the cloister: 'Here lyes a Benefactor: let no one move Hys Bones', there was an inarticulate upheaval in my soul. It thrust out a root into the remote and silent past; it was stirred by a new significance and a new nobility. But my responsiveness to the gift of the richness of which my life had been devoid was so complete that I was overwhelmed. There was no 'I' any more. And the process of growing a new self was tardy and invisible. I could not wait for that. How could I, when it was only after many years that I knew that it had happened? In the meantime, I had to build some sort of habitation for myself. I gathered the materials wherever I could find them, followed eagerly any chance indication of the pattern to be followed. Pertinaciously and silently I groped my way into a *persona*.

CHAPTER VI

COMPENSATIONS

PERHAPS it was very fortunate for me that there had been the long lapse from the precocious cleverness with which I entered Christ's Hospital. Had it lasted, I might have accepted it as my destiny to achieve the goal of my father's ambition, the Higher Civil Service. The road would have been smooth and straight, and there would have been nothing for me to do but follow it. But my long lethargy of hibernation, or metamorphosis, gave me the chance to develop a blind but stubborn recalcitrance to a career.

At first, I accepted my father's destination quite placidly. It was so remote; its attainment depended upon so many improbable preliminary achievements, that I would have accepted the office of Prime Minister or Astronomer Royal with as good an outward grace, and as deep an inward scepticism. I indulged my father's vicarious ambition, with a small boy's cynicism; though I was not unaware that there was some appearance of reason on his side. By this time he had, by dint of hard work, raised himself from the position of supernumerary clerk at Somerset House, first to a post on the establishment, then to the rank of Second Division Clerk, and finally, to that of a minor Staff-officer. If he had done all that, from his beginnings, it stood to reason that I should do far more, from mine. It was a matter of simple arithmetic.

But now I knew better, just as I knew that it would be foolish to attempt to convey my better knowledge to him. It was now the time when my situation in the school was most precarious, and I was in imminent danger of being superannuated as a Deputy Grecian. In the course of one of my father's soul-shattering inquisitions at home, concerning my graceless position in the School List, I had desperately asserted that what I needed was more books. Why I should have pleaded this improbable excuse for my failure passes my comprehension now, unless it were a

66

combination of the need for some excuse for my failure, and my genuine desire to possess certain books which I had read, for my own – Mackail's little book on *Latin Literature* I particularly coveted. However, it was a lucky stroke on my part. Instead of pleading a lethargy, which he could not understand, or a defect of capacity, which he could not admit, I had put forward something concrete and tangible, which he could grasp. Books, was it? Why, then, of course I must have them. And, to do the generous heart of my father justice, I am convinced that, had the demand been for £50 worth of books, he would have supplied it somehow. It was in accordance with the plan.

However, my difficulty was now to provide him with a convincing list of books that I required. It was agreed that I should consult my form-masters, when I returned to school, and send my father the list. This arrangement suited me. I had in mind to tell Merk and Winbolt, in a casual way, that my father was making me a present of £5 to buy books, and ask them for the names of any books they would recommend me to read. I had only been back a week or so, when my father upset my diplomatic design, by writing direct to my house-master to say that I had told him that I needed certain books for my work, that he was anxious to supply them, but he did not know what to order. Naturally, I was called in to my house-master's study to explain this unprecedented letter, for it was well known that the school supplied all the books we needed. The situation was awkward; and no doubt my attempts to extricate myself were clumsy. To have explained the whole position was beyond my powers. But I did convey to my house-master that my father was unreasonably ambitious for me, and expected impossibilities. To this at least my house-master was sympathetic, and he ended by saying that he would ask my father to come down to have a talk.

That filled me with dismay. I knew, only too well, the attitude of humility towards 'a gentleman' that my father would take towards my house-master in the discussion; and I was ashamed. I went hot and cold within whenever I thought of the meeting –

and I thought about little else during the intervening fortnight. My sense of coming humiliation entirely overwhelmed my sense of relief at the prospect of my father's burdensome expectations of myself being abated by the judgment of authority. I took no thought at all of my father's coming disappointment. That, I felt grimly, he had deserved. The humiliation he would inflict upon me in my house-master's eyes was my sole concern.

Perhaps in the main, as the sequel will show, it was the prospect of social humiliation which tortured me; but it was inextricably mingled with other feelings which I could not disentangle then. Beneath my miserable unease was a conflict of 'values': my new 'values' were threatened by an eruption of the old ones. I had long since given up the attempt (if I ever seriously thought of making it) to explain to my father that education at a board-school and education at Christ's Hospital were totally different things. There was no connection between them: only a great hiatus. In the former, education was wholly external – a matter of doing and knowing things; in the latter, it was internal – a matter of being something. To talk, therefore, as I knew my father would talk, as though Christ's Hospital were merely a part of the notorious 'educational ladder' – a mechanical contrivance for getting one further off the ground, for enabling one to achieve 'a better position', twenty rungs off the ground instead of six – was an outrage, the more deadly because it was unconscious. What did, what could it matter to Christ's Hospital, whether I climbed by its means into the Higher Civil Service?

I do not know what actually happened at the interview between my father and my house-master, which lasted perhaps a quarter of an hour before I was called in. The meeting of the three of us was an anti-climax to my strained nerves, and I remember little indeed of it, save that I felt immensely sorry for my father when I saw him sitting engulfed in Sainte-Croix's big arm-chair. It suddenly seemed intolerably sad that we should be so far apart; and a great wave of physical tenderness for him surged over me, such that, had we been alone, I should have hugged him and kissed him. As things were, my eyes swam, and he almost dissolved out of my sight. Then Sainte-Croix relieved the tension. 'I've been telling your father,' he said, 'that your interests have become too generalized to make you the ideal examinee – any longer; and that I think the only thing to do with you now is – to give you your head.' My father nodded sagely. But I doubt whether he understood what Sainte-Croix meant: translated into his terms, at any rate, it meant that Sainte-Croix would not give a button for my chances of the Higher Civil Service, and that the best thing for my father to do was not to worry about it, and to let me alone: and I doubt whether he meant any more – except that, in some indefinable way, he was on my side. 'As for the books' – by this time I had forgotten that it was a matter of books at all – 'I think it an excellent idea; and I am going to get a list from Mr. Winbolt.'

The affair was over. It seems like a storm in a teacup, but for me it had been a convulsion: the final tearing-up of the roots that united me with my father. I did not realize it then; all that I realized was the agony of mind I had endured. That had been as real as a toothache. But, as I have hinted, it had a curious sequel: the more curious, perhaps, in that it never occurred to me until to-day to connect the happenings. I remembered merely that one followed the other – at how long a distance, I forget.

The incident I am about to relate has been an unlaid ghost in my memory for years. There has always been a tinge of mystery about it, as though it occurred in the uncertain land between sleep and waking. Some little time after my father's visit I began to feel rather ill – not genuinely ill, but below normal in ways schoolboys do not take into the reckoning. I began to sleep badly and to have vivid, nightmarish dreams: and once or twice I waked up in the night to find myself talking. I was now a house-monitor: and therefore absolved from the medical super-intendence of the matron. So I jogged along, feeling tired but nothing worse, until one day she caught sight of me and insisted that I was looking unhealthily pale. I must be sickening for the 'flu. So off I went to the school infirmary, gladly enough (for it was a pleasant place). I confessed that, so far as I knew, there was nothing wrong with me. The doctor, Aldersmith, who was an ideal doctor for schoolboys, took a specimen and muttered something about 'a trace of albuminuria', and kept me there for ten days. It was agreed that there was nothing wrong; but still a rest, and a glass of port twice a day – a wise and favourite remedy with Aldersmith – would do me good.

No doubt it did. But when I returned, I still slept badly, and still found myself talking in my sleep. This interested the senior monitor in the dormitory – a big and sanguine-looking boy, G——, for whom I had an aversion. He dabbled in hypnotism, in concert with the Grecian of the house: which for some reason offended me. As a would-be hypnotist, he fastened eagerly on my sleep-talking, and took to sitting by my bed and scientifically stroking my forehead. I endured this resentfully until one night it came into my head to give him a run for his money. Pretending sleep, I began to ramble to some purpose, and commenced a vague and hazy story of a palace in Northern Italy. He, wishing to indulge his expertize in such phenomena, and persuaded that I was in a trance, plied me with leading questions, as I knew he would. Night after night I developed a truly wonderful story, of which the upshot was that I was the illegitimate son of the Duke of Aosta. The story was most circumstantial, though I forget the circumstance; but I felt at the time that it was a very creditable effort in invention, and I experienced the glimmerings of a true artistic satisfaction in the manner in which I allowed the dreamy narrative to be dragged from me. Yet at the same time, it was not wholly an invention; for the story, once it had been begun, unrolled itself before me in a kind of vision. I did no conscious thinking about it; and, indeed, during the daytime it would have vanished completely from my memory, if it had not been for the conspiratorial benevolence with which G—— sometimes glanced at me.

His spare time was largely occupied in compiling an enormous *procès-verbal* of my lucubrations, which was, of course, sedulously concealed from me. G——'s mind was made up from before the beginning: the waking Murry knew nothing of the sleeping Murry's activities, nor was he to be informed about them. And I took a wicked delight in observing G——'s elephantine pretences of a normal attitude towards me. He was the last person on earth to play any part convincingly, except to himself. But one day, to my consternation, I discovered that he was reporting the whole affair to Sainte-Croix. I have said consternation; it should be rather trepidation: for I now believe that it had dimly been my aim that it should get to Sainte-Croix's ears. And one night soon after, I heard the softly padding feet of the house-master, coming to take up a position by my bed. I then felt something of the mingled fear and delight of the artist who confronts the connoisseur. Sainte-Croix was no fool; and I gave him of my best, in substance and in manner – so good it was that I was more than half-convinced myself. Then I waited for a summons to his room. It came. Evidently he had studied the story: for his questions were wholly directed to finding out what I actually knew concerning the personages whom I had involved in it. I knew very little; but I did know enough to be fairly sure that the external structure would stand. But to Sainte-Croix, I maintained a sturdy ignorance. I knew I talked in my sleep, but nothing more.

I am afraid that I really enjoyed that battle of wits. And my house-master, if he had his suspicions, concealed them well. I left his room with the feeling that I had been successful. Successful in what? First perhaps, I think, in planting in his mind a tiny seed of romantic doubt concerning myself; but really more important, of which the former was only the crude symbol, in convincing him that I was in myself an interesting person. And in this, I believe, I did succeed. At all events, he began to take an interest in me, and to give me the run of his books, by which I profited. He was a pretty good historian; and through him I came to read Stubbs and de Tocqueville.

It is a queer story. But the mystery is gone from it now. It was my dream-vindication of myself from my previous humiliation. The connection is plain: the long mental torment, the slackening of the strain, the physical debility, the sleep-talking, and, finally, the instinctive exploitation, in the interest of my consuming and unconscious purpose, of my new disability. The exploitation was instinctive; for, indeed, it was much less deliberate than this narrative makes it appear. There was very little calculation in my queer conduct – so little that, for thirty years it has seemed to me a mysterious aberration, which only now I am able to explain to my satisfaction.

But I must, at this time, have been a fairly accomplished actor: for another incident returns to me (because in it again G—— and my house-master were involved) which is almost incredible. As I have said, I had a violent aversion to G——. I disliked him altogether: there was something damnably furtive about him. An equally pronounced trait in my character, to which I have referred, was an unconquerable reluctance to confess that I was ignorant of any matter of which knowledge was imputed to me. I would look wise, and trust to not being found out before I had acquired the knowledge with which I was falsely credited. On this occasion my refusal to confess to ignorance landed me in a fantastic position.

It is in the nature of the case that I am unable to say exactly how I was led into this position. But evidently, G—— had been hinting, in his ponderously roundabout way, at the existence of immorality in the house. Since I, at this time, was supremely innocent in matters sexual, I could only look wise and pretend to knowledge. Which, doubtless, I did. The next thing my conscious memory records is that – this time to my genuine consternation – I was solemnly led by G—— into the house-master's room to confirm his story of immorality in the house. The conversation was almost wholly between G—— and the house-master, and conducted entirely in dark and inscrutable hints, from which I could gather nothing. I had not the faintest notion of what the boys, whose names were mentioned, *could* have done. There was, indeed, absolutely nothing on which my mind could seize. But there I was, assumed by them both to be silently corroborating a story of which I understood nothing at all. Certainly, I had been in the changing-room with G—— when apparently he saw certain things happen; most certainly been with him when he cross-questioned a certain small boy. Obviously, I ought to have seen what he saw, and to have learned what he learned from the cross-examination. I was a monitor; and evidently I was supposed to know these things. I looked wise and kept silence.

Now, if I had been a different and a nobler sort of boy, at this point I should have spoken out, and confessed that I was completely ignorant of the whole affair: that I had seen and heard nothing, and did not even know the nature of the offence of which the boys were being accused. But how on earth, if I had chosen the nobler part, could I ever have explained how I had become so deeply involved? G—— would have been dumbfounded. Had he not been speaking to me for days about it? And had I not taken an intelligent part in the conversation? I was trapped; and, to be honest, my one concern was to escape from the house-master's room without being detected for an impostor. To be fair to myself, there was no question in my mind of innocent boys being condemned on the evidence of my silence. If they were innocent – of I knew not what – then their innocence would be obvious, for (as it happened) one of them was something of a friend of mine – not an intimate, indeed, like Harvey and Allen – but more than a mere acquaintance: for we had long been in the same form together. I liked K——. He was a boy of furious temper, who invented bodyline bowling by instinct; but at bottom he was a generous soul. If he was innocent, I should know. But, unfortunately, I felt that he was not innocent. He and the younger boy had one of those queer friendships that I could never understand, and I was inwardly certain that, when they were taxed with their unknown offence, they would not be able to deny it.

73

And so it was. Neither of them was expelled, as they might have been; but K—— was birched instead – a humiliation which he never forgave. The house received a solemn pi-jaw from the Headmaster; and not long after G—— left the school, in the odour of sanctity. The upshot of the episode is as queer as the episode itself. K—— became a distinctly closer friend of mine. Probably I felt very guilty towards him, and did what I could to make amends for my cowardly behaviour. At any rate he bore me no grudge for what had happened, though he conceived a vindictive hatred against G——, with which I sympathized. Indeed, in my own mind there was no doubt, either then or now, that K—— was morally a much finer type than G——.

The impulse that leads to schoolboy homosexuality is, I confess, beyond the range of my experience. But I have since learned, from a friend of mine who is a psychiatrist of genius, something of the causes of it. To him both those cases – of K—— and his 'tart' – would have been perfectly simple. Both those boys (I now remember) came from homes where there had been a domestic disaster. K——'s father had lived apart from his wife for many years: L——'s mother had died almost at the moment he entered the senior school. I can see the broad black band round his father's bowler hat (which brings back the period) when he came to see L——. L——, indeed, I knew but slightly; but if ever there were a boy starved of a mother's tenderness, hungering for it, cherishing a vindictive hatred against the world because he had been cheated of it, it was K——. But, instead of being understood, the boy was broken: he left the school, hating it and hating everybody; and to this day I can see the snap of his white lips together, and the murderous flash of his eye, when he was the victim of some slight injustice such as would slide like water from a duck's back from other boys. But instead of killing somebody, he was killed.

But what am I to make of myself, whose ignominious and characteristic part in this affair I have faithfully recorded? Assuredly, I have no judgment to pass: I am concerned merely with the pattern which unrolls itself when I look back into my school-days. It seems nothing short of amazing that K——, of all people, should have borne me no grudge for what I had done. Yet I gave him no explanation; indeed, I was quite incapable of explaining my conduct to anybody. No doubt I tried to be friendly towards him afterwards; but he was the very boy to have spurned any such friendliness with contempt. The only solution I can offer (and I feel it is the true one) is that K—— felt that I really *was* friendly towards him, as indeed I was, and he responded to it.

The story is not yet ended: and the finale is typical. The whole affair had left me gasping and bewildered, but with one clear feeling: that I had been elevated on to a moral perch, where I had no right to be; where, if I had had the right to be, I did not want to be: and still less did I wish to share it with G——. I must get down without delay. My method of getting down was singular. I cultivated my new friendship with K——, and arranged with him that we should break bounds and the school rules by having tea together in a cottage on the Horsham Road every Sunday. There accordingly we met, together with a third crony, an able and excellent fellow; and there we talked smut together. Perfectly harmless, indeed innocent smut, as I was to realize later at Oxford, where I encountered a kind of smutty talk which gave me physical nausea as well as a sense of proportion about the Sunday-afternoon conversations of K——, H—— and myself. We thought ourselves pretty desperate fellows, as we smoked our occasional cigarettes, and talked our amateurish bawdy: but we never forgot to enjoy our tea.

That, so far from giving me a guilty conscience, put me to rights with myself. I was free from the imputation of being a moral prig; and, in my usual fashion, I acquired a good deal of new knowledge without revealing my previous ignorance; but, since the conversation never turned on homosexuality, I remained pretty well in the dark concerning the nature of K——'s offence. Nor can I really remember what we talked about. I know it was quite unlike the stuff with which I was sometimes staggered at

freshmen's breakfasts at Oxford: stuff best described, by implication, in the comment made by one of the senior men – himself no
chicken – who remarked drily at the end of a nauseating story:
'After that, Bum' – so the second-year teller was familiarly called –
'you had better pull the plug!' But the more clearly I remember
what our conversation was *not*, the more difficult it is to establish
what it was. My one definite recollection is that H—— recited:

> King David and King Solomon
>   Led very pleasant lives
> And amused themselves exceedingly
>   With various kinds of wives.
>
> But when old age came on them
>   They both had serious qualms;
> So King Solomon wrote the Proverbs
> And King David wrote the Psalms.

Which struck me mightily then, and amuses me now. Beyond
that, I suppose we had a few bawdy limericks between us, though
I must have been hard put to it to make a contribution in that
kind; and a good deal of discussion of the dirty words we hunted
up in our Latin and Greek dictionaries – or rather the big Liddell
and Scott, and Lewis and Short, which we borrowed from the
Grecian of the house.

In this way, indeed, I accumulated a good deal of knowledge;
but it was rather classical than sexual. The exciting gloss: *sens.
obsc.* after a Greek or Latin word seldom gave me any hint of what
the obscene meaning really was. It passed me decorously on to
another Greek or Latin word with the same intriguing label. The
only satisfying method was to look up the references, and read
them in their contexts. It was, no doubt, an altogether unworthy
way of learning Greek and Latin, but it certainly was very good
for me. And when I acquired, one holidays, in the Farringdon
Road, an Aristophanes, a Catullus, and an Ovid, all unexpur-
gated, and all with copious Latin notes, for a penny a volume, I

had plenty to occupy me. Then it was that I appreciated the withering invective of

Glubit magnanimos Remi nepotes

and the malicious and bawdy humour of

Languidior tenera cui pendens sicula beta.

But the English analogue of this direct and blazing obscenity of Catullus and Aristophanes I could never discover; I have since come to believe that it does not exist, and that the advent of Christianity made it impossible. When sex became infected with sin, then pure obscenity – 'pure' in the moral as well as the scientific sense – became extinct. A faculty of the human consciousness, a province of human experience, simply disappeared. In every human advance there is loss as well as gain. The slow and painful struggle towards the conception of man-woman love involved the degradation of obscenity from the sunlight into the darkness: from a pure into a festering thing. Nor have pure love and pure obscenity ever lived together – yet. The nearest they ever came to living in amity was in Shakespeare. When Mercutio and Romeo were bosom-friends, for a lightning moment in Shakespeare's imagination, then there was a glimpse of a harmony yet to be won. O brave and debonair and manly Mercutio! When you called to Romeo over the orchard-wall, obscenity and love for once laughed with one another.

MER. I conjure thee by Rosaline's bright eyes,
By her high forehead and her quivering lip,
By her fine foot, straight leg and quivering thigh
And the demesnes that there adjacent lie,
That in thy likeness thou appear to us!
BEN. An if he hear thee, thou wilt anger him.
MER. This cannot anger him: 'twould anger him
To raise a spirit in his mistress' circle
Of some strange nature, letting it there stand
Till she had laid it and conjured it down.

That were some spite: my invocation
Is fair and honest, and in his mistress' name
I conjure only but to raise up *him*.

That is not the obscenity of the classics; it could not be. It is
different, and gentler: but it is an achievement.

The obscenity of the classics startled and amazed me.
Granted I was only an adolescent schoolboy in search of dirty
words, I got far better than I deserved from Aristophanes and
Catullus – the salutary shock of a world of sex, that might have
been dark and furtive, as it were scorched into purity by a glaring
sun. The sheer absence of all English equivalent, save some
shocking and sordid periphrasis, for the stark and simple words –
ἔστυκα γὰρ – brought me to a boyish realization of their primal
innocence. I knew, though I could not have expressed it, the
difference between obscenity and dirtiness; and as I recognized it
in my mind, so I recognized it by its effects. Aristophanes created
no prurient itch within me: rather he stunned me first, and then
bleached me, till I was capable of shaking with a sort of savage,
golden laughter, over the mysteries which he worshipped by pro-
faning.

I knew the difference well: for by this time I had learned
masturbation. I had no doubt at all that masturbation was a
deadly sin. There was no need, to convince me on this point, of
the vague and alarming rumours of its terrible physical effects –
rumours which, I have since been told, are seriously exaggerated.
If the President of the Royal College of Physicians himself had
come to assure me, as I understand the modern 'sexologist'
assures his patient, that the practice is, in moderation, harmless,
it would have made no difference to my feeling. For the first
time in my life, I was self-convicted of sin. This act of mine was
wrong: my mind, my body knew it. Had I been a little savage,
brought up alone upon a desert island, still I should have known
it, in just the same primitive way.

And so I struggled against the enemy. I kept a secret diary, wherein I marked the days when I succumbed with an ominous red-ink cross, and I concentrated all my effort upon having no more than one red cross in a week. Gradually I got to the point where there were only three red crosses in a month, then two – then Heaven be praised – only one: and, by the time I left school, I had reduced it to a rare and mysterious aberration, which I could almost regard as a case of daemonic possession. Nor did I ever breathe a word to anybody about the trouble; nor did I ever regard it as, in any sense, a religious affair. I resented, more deeply than before, pi-jaws, whether from the Headmaster at school, or from the dear, good Bishop of London in St. Mary's at Oxford, about purity and chastity; I loathed the whole atmosphere of corporate pre-occupation with sex.

But never, for one moment, did I regard the obscenity of the classics as giving me licence for my sin. Their obscenity and my depravity belonged to different orders, as different as light and darkness. I did not reason about it; I knew it. The struggle in myself was the most elemental thing I had known. I might as well have tried to restore an amputated leg to my body by argument, as to reason myself out of the immediate, incontrovertible conviction that self-abuse – a truer word – was a festering sore in my own integrity. In some dim way, I wanted to be myself; and it was for the victory of my self that I was fighting. And the same self that was weakened and undermined by my depravity, was strengthened and purified by my contact with classical obscenity.

Within a year or so the victory was virtually won; and my last year at school was very happy If I had gained no confidence in my own abilities, I had some trust that things would not turn out so badly. Nor did they. I won the gold medal for classics a year before my time; and there was a momentary flicker of hope that I might be of the Balliol scholarship class, after all. But Merk, and I, knew better. 'Whatever I was', he assured me with the suppressed half-smile I loved to see on his lips, I was not 'a scholar', and I knew it was true.

'Whatever I was' . . . What was I? I had not the faintest idea.

Part snob, part coward, part sentimentalist – all these elements were in me: an amorphous being, with an uncomfortable premonition that I was not going to fit, and therefore with the feeling that I was safer at school, where I had now shaped out for myself some kind of fourme, in which I could lie *perdu*, than I should ever be at the University or in the great world: neither popular, nor unpopular: resigned to a certain ineffectiveness: willing to accept any concrete goal proposed to me, provided it was sufficiently remote to enable my inchoate mental reservations to take shape in the interim: inclined to regard any definite decision, any irrevocable commitment of myself, as 'the acting of a dreadful thing' in the sense of Brutus' experience.

> Between the acting of a dreadful thing
> And the first motion, all the interim is
> Like a phantasma or a hideous dream:
> The genius and the mortal instruments
> Are then in council; and the state of man,
> Like to a little kingdom, suffers then
> The nature of an insurrection.

An unattractive personality: and it is difficult for me to disentangle any good point, unless it were a capacity of some sort for warm affection. The masters and boys that I did like, I liked very much indeed; and, ever since, at the age of thirteen, I had ceased to be an only child and had been blessed with a small brother, I had discovered in myself a great tenderness for little children. Much of my holidays was spent in taking this little brother of mine on all kinds of expeditions; and a good deal of my school time, as soon as he learned to read, in writing an elaborate story for him, in weekly instalments, concerning the adventures of a rabbit which we saw in Bushy Park. I borrowed a primitive typewriter in order to print this story so that he could read it himself. But, since he was a very lovable small brother, I can hardly reckon this a virtue to myself. When I was at home, working in a tiny room I called my study, he would sit in the armchair beside me patiently for hours, without making a sound, waiting for the moment to come when the books would be shut and we should go out together. Once, for some reason, I was impatient with him, and spoke angrily. He was amazed; then his lip quivered, and the tears came, and he sobbed: 'You go back to your school: that's all the bes'.' Since he always looked forward eagerly to my coming home, this was a truly terrible thing for him to have dragged out of himself: it betokened the complete collapse of an ideal for him. I knew what it was to have my heart wrung.

But for the most part, my brother and I were happy indeed together. Soon after he was born my parents had moved from East Dulwich, first to Ewell, then to Kingston-on-Thames, and finally to Hampton Wick. In none of these places did I possess, or make, any friends. It was not to be expected. By this time I had become the public-school boy, able neither to mix with the neighbouring children, who were not of my class, nor with other public-school boys (if I had wanted to) whose parents were in a different class from mine. My parents and I lived in complete aloofness. But now that I had my small brother for a companion, I was well content with this isolation. At Ewell, we would go off blackberrying for the day together, I pushing him in a little folding chair, begirt with baskets. When we had found a little lawn sur-rounded by brambles, he would be deposited in the middle, and I began picking. As soon as I worked my way out of his sight, he would call to me, and I would answer. He could not see me, but I could see him; and my eyes would delight, and my heart be thrilled, in his loveliness. I was happy then. And even now it seems to me that most of the simple, immediate, unalloyed happiness I have known has come to me when I have been alone with a small child.

However that may be, it is certain that my holiday companionship with my small brother influenced me in ways beyond my knowing. It encouraged me in a tendency to which I was already prone – to live my real life in a kind of dream-world, withdrawn from contact with the world of reality. But this dream-world had little to do with the day-dreaming of which I was often guilty. It was a real condition of human living, wherein I could completely forget myself. With my brother, I was not concerned to justify or defend myself; there was no need to play a part, or to pretend anything at all. He was he, and I was I, as Montaigne said of La Boéthie. He trusted me implicitly, and that was all I wanted. We were in contact with one another, immediate, close, and unoppressive; and the burdens of the outer life (which even then were heavy enough on me) dissolved away. This, it seemed to me, was the life which was mine; this the world to which I belonged. The other was like a play upon a great stage. I learned my part, and now at last I had learned it so well at school that it was almost second nature. At the university I should have to learn a new one; perhaps I should learn that also well. After the university would come yet another, and another. But the real I would live, unless he died, somewhere off-stage, in the brambles and the sunlight of a September afternoon talking to a small brother — self-forgetful, at peace, and unafraid.

CHAPTER VII

OXFORD

WHEN the time came for me to sit for a scholarship at Oxford I had
confidence enough in my 'star', though not in myself, to be pretty
sure I should 'get something' if the Fates were moderately kind.
But it looked as though the Fates would be unkind. When I
entered the great hall of Christ Church I was possessed by such a
sense of inferiority that I was panic-stricken. My clothes were all
wrong: that was the first horror. Then I was completely overwhelmed by the carefree confidence of my fellow-competitors,
and when I reckoned up that at most one in ten would 'get something', I felt that my claim to take precedence of a hundred or two
of these easy gentlemen was ridiculous.

Anyhow, I spent the night in my rather dingy lodgings in
Museum Street lying wide awake. I could not sleep at all; and I
spent the time taking bitter note of the incomparable variety of
chiming clocks in Oxford. If I did not sleep, I moaned to myself,
I should be a bundle of nerves with an empty and aching head on
the morrow: and naturally my impatience made sleep the more
impossible. I shut my eyes, and the darkness seethed and spangled.
Spread over three nights, it was a miserable experience.

I returned home, with the bitter knowledge that I had done
about as badly as it was possible for me to do. But it turned out
to be not so bad as all that. I had failed in my first choice, which
was University College; but I had succeeded in my second, which
was the extra £20 of a Junior Hulme Scholarship at Brasenose.
The reason why I had not put it first – for the difference between
£100 and £80 a year was very important to me – was that the
reputation of Brasenose was distinctly forbidding to such a timid
one as I.

I do not know whether this central, aching *fear* of mine is common to many men. This very morning, opening my letters at the breakfast table, I was surprised into awareness of an emotion so characteristic of myself, so knit into the accepted texture of my life, that it passes by unnoticed. I had asked an acquaintance of mine to do me a trivial favour – the kind of ordinary thing I do for others twenty times a week as a matter of course – and there lay his letter in reply. Almost unconsciously I had put it aside unopened. Now, having read the others, I realized that I was avoiding it. Yet still, I could not bring myself to open it. I was *afraid* of it. What was I afraid of? Not of the refusal it might possibly, but very improbably, contain. Intrinsically, the granting of this favour was of about as much consequence to me as the loan of a box of matches. There was only one thing I could have been afraid of – namely, the human hurt that a refusal would cause me. I had exposed myself to this possibility of being hurt, and I wished to God that I had not. Far better, I thought, never to have asked for it and lived on in the persuasion that one had only to ask, for it to be given. What was a favour worth, even a great one instead of this trivial thing, in comparison with the acuteness of the pain of apprehending a rebuff? All these thoughts passed through my mind while I stared at the unopened letter; and then came a weary realization of how little the essential substance of myself had changed. In this respect, I was at forty-five what I had been at fifteen. And that gave me comfort and a sort of Dutch courage. 'Past cure, past care.' I opened the letter. Naturally, the favour was granted.

That sudden reminder of the depth of my essential timidity serves as a key to open the chambers of forgotten misery into which I entered as time drew near for me to go to Oxford. Various people had spoken to me ominously of Brasenose. It was a college full of 'bloods', with a reputation for making the life of its fresh-men a little hell on earth. These warnings, which had dissolved away in the pleasant haze of my last summer term at school, now took formidable shape and substance and filled me with dread. I had no clear conception of what a university 'blood' might be.

They were familiar enough to boys from other schools, where they were hatched; but the structure of Christ's Hospital allowed no room for the species to develop. To my imagination they were fearsome animals, whose principal habit, according to my information, was to burst into a freshman's rooms at all hours of the night, demand unlimited beer and whisky, make havoc of his furniture, and, as like as not, dump him stark naked into the middle of the college quadrangle. In face of the prospect of meeting these creatures, the ordering of my first dress-suit, instead of being a cheerful occasion became a gloomy and funereal affair – the decking out of a victim for sacrifice.

By the time I got out of the train at Oxford, my face was set and my heart was thumping. I grossly over-tipped the licensed pirate who clapped me into his miserable hansom, scornful as I knew of my extremely undistinguished and unbloodlike luggage; and I was vicariously revenged when the lodge-porter treated him *de haut en bas*. That commenced a friendly feeling in me towards the lodge-porter which endured till the end of my days at Oxford. At such an age, one has no sense of perspective; and I was compelled to ascribe his courtesy, which made no distinction between the shy scholar and the noisy 'blood', to some innate refinement: which, indeed, the porter may well have possessed. But it was not till years after, when I had occasion to return to Oxford not dishonourably, that it struck me that it might equally have been due to the wisdom of experience. He had seen many generations come and go – emphatic 'bloods' and timid scholars – and he had learned that it was the timid scholars who remained to become his real masters – the fellows of the college. But whether his wisdom was innate or acquired, it came to the same thing. The courtesy was there, and it comforted me.

He led me to my attic rooms overlooking the Radcliffe Camera. I was enchanted with them. The enormous lump of coal that blazed upon the fire, and roared wastefully up the chimney, welcomed me into a kingdom of more generous living than I had known; yet withal I was remote, and, I thought, as far from the

85

possibility of casual disturbance as it was possible to be. When the scout clashed my curtains together and asked me whether I wanted anything more, I should have answered, if I had had the courage, that I wanted only to be left alone.

But that was futile. Plunge after shivering plunge had to be taken. I returned, a little breathless, after dinner in hall to find someone already in my rooms – a dark-haired man, with a scholar's gown all awry, and his hands in his pockets, looking quizzically at my meagre array of books. 'My name's Goodyear,' he said abruptly. 'I thought I had better get in first. I want you to join the Pater Society. It's the only literary society we have.' He gave an odd snorting laugh. 'I founded it.' Somehow it seemed to mean that that was the oddest reason he could think of for my joining it. Certainly, it was good enough for me: for I liked him at sight. He switched abruptly on to a new subject. 'This isn't a bad place,' he said. 'Not half as bad as they make out. In fact, it's really better than those intellectual forcing-houses.' That comforted me greatly; and though there was time for my heart to sink into my stomach again after he had left, while I waited for the visitation of the second-year men about which I had been warned, Goodyear had given me something to hold on to, when they poured into my room. I was not utterly annihilated while they drank my beer and cross-examined me and criticized my cigarettes, which I had brought with me from London and I knew were none too bad. They decided, fairly quickly, that I was no particular use for their purposes, though one, having asked my weight, which was some eight pounds over nine stone, decided that I might as well be 'tubbed', in a peremptory but quite friendly way. Another – the same who afterwards told 'Bum' to pull the plug – while the rest were cascading out of the doorway, turned with a smile and said a loud and kindly 'Good night!' The others took the cue from him; and a series of perfunctory 'Good nights!' sounded above the clatter of descending feet.

Nothing worse than that? I could hardly believe it. But there was nothing worse. Indeed it was all far better than my

most rosy dream. Not only were my fellow classical scholars –
two from Wellington, one from Charterhouse – delightful people
in themselves; but two at least of them were excellent athletes.
Since I took to them, and they to me, I was enabled to make my
athletic contribution to the college, so to speak, vicariously. I
genuinely admired their prowess. I should have liked to be a good
cricketer and a good footballer myself: for, oddly enough, I have
always enjoyed playing games. Even rowing I enjoyed, and it was
a real grief to me not to be able to put on the extra stone in weight
that would have made it worth while to give me a real trial as
bow in the college torpid. Since I had not then, and never have
acquired, anything of the intellectual's conventional contempt for
sport, my new friends and I could live amicably together. That
aptitude I owed to Christ's Hospital. I had not suffered under the
tyranny of athletes; therefore I never conceived the vindictive
hatred of athletics which consumes the mind and heart of so
many intelligent and sensitive boys while they are at school, and
manifests itself afterwards at the university in a smouldering and
ill-concealed contempt for the athlete. If I had had to endure
beatings at the hands of boys who were my intellectual inferiors
and certainly not morally my superiors, whose authority came to
them simply because they were in the XI or the XV – as many
boys like me at other public schools had had to endure them –
then, without doubt, I should have felt as vindictive and contemptuous as they. But I had no such bitter experience of the
brainless, oafish athlete in authority; and my new friends certainly
did not belong to the type. Instead, they stood between me and
any untoward contact with it.

Indeed, they satisfied very completely what has always been
one of the main terms of my definition of a friend. A friend is a
person with whom one feels safe: and I felt safe with these men.
If I had asked myself what sense of safety I brought to them in
return for the sense of safety they bestowed on me, I should have
been hard put to it to reply. It seems to have been a one-sided
arrangement, unless – as it may possibly have been, though I have

forgotten – I fortified them a little on the intellectual side. True, my need of security was far greater than theirs. For them life in college was a natural extension of the life to which they had been accustomed, at school and at home: for me it had, once more, something of a *salto mortale* that left me naked in a new world. Since I did not show it, and never spoke of it, it is unlikely that they ever guessed it.

Anyhow, thanks mainly to them, my first year at Brasenose was completely unlike what I had feared. It was in the main a very happy time indeed. My classical tutor, H. F. Fox, was a man in a thousand. Generous, sympathetic, happy-go-lucky, a fine scholar, a fine cricketer – he let in upon me the breath of a larger air. I admired him without reserve; and when he had broken down my timidity I found that I could speak to him more freely than I had ever spoken to an older man. He was a liberal and free-thinker of what is now, alas, the old school. Liberalism was a positive faith in him; it meant for him not a meagre *laisser-faire*, but a large, warm-hearted, impulsive generosity. Matthew Arnold and Clough and Browning he liked, Ruskin he revered; but *Sartor Resartus* was his Bible. He pressed it upon me; and was a little disappointed that my response was less than ecstatic. But I found it very difficult. I had no experience of my own to give me the clue to it. Keats would have understood my trouble. 'We read fine things, but do not understand them until we have gone the same steps as the author.' That, certainly, was the case with me and *Sartor Resartus* at that time.

But Fox's great influence upon me was not intellectual at all. It was not his accomplishments I admired, but him. Quixotic, wayward, he was always completely human. The warm breath of impulse was in all his saying and doing. He was described to me, more than once, with a touch of disdain, as a great school-boy; and I resented it. Such a misconception, I knew, could arise only from blindness, or envy. Fox was wholly alive; and he was determined to remain alive, even if it cost him the reputation of irresponsibility. He would not suffer the fine point of his soul to be blunted by conformity: and his soul had a very fine point indeed. It was not a separate thing to be tended and cared for. There was not a touch of preciousness in him. But always there was the flicker of life, delicate and strong, in his eyes, his speech and his movement. Careless he was, but never clumsy; and if there was, as there surely was, something boyish in his love for his fragile and beautiful wife, that – I was wise enough to know even then – was because there is, and always must be, something boyish in true love. He told me one day of a little speech made by someone he admired which ended with the words: 'Those the gods love die young – they never grow old.' Evidently he loved that thought, and because he loved it, I treasured it. It was true of him.

I owe H. F. Fox something far better than this halting tribute; but even so much it is some relief to pay. For the time came when he disapproved of my conduct. Perhaps, if I had had the courage to tell him everything, he would have supported me even beyond the utmost limits of his liberal tolerance; but one of the major curses of my life has been my complete inability to confide my inmost heart, even to my truest and most proven friends. It is easier to me to make the world my confidant than to drag the words out of myself in speech to a friend. It is a strange incapacity, for which I have suffered deeply enough, at times indeed almost intolerably. For, by an equally strange capacity, I seem to attract confidences. And friend after friend, in a long and grim succession, has come to feel that because I attract confidences and do not return them, I am a sinister and inhuman figure. Maybe I am, but if it is so, it is not for the reason they suppose. I do not deliberately invite confidences, neither do I deliberately withhold them; and I imagine (as a matter of simple psychology) that a man who deliberately invited confidences would be the last to receive them. As for my deliberately withholding them, nothing is less deliberate: *c'est plus fort que moi*. And, beneath even that, is the curious sense that I have nothing to tell – nothing, at least, that can be told. What (in course of time) I had to tell Fox was that

I had fallen in love with a married woman, and that I was leaving Oxford to live with her. But what had those words to do with the reality of what I felt, or was doing? If I could not make him feel what I felt, as I knew I could not, it was far better not to speak at all. So I kept silence; and I left him to discover the worst. Since I knew it must happen so, I felt a grim, self-torturing delight in doing nothing to mitigate the shock of his disillusion with me. Since he must believe bad of me, let it be the worst.

But my heart was oppressed, many times, with the thought of the hurt my seeming ingratitude must have caused him; the impulse would come to me to try to explain, and my mind would embark upon one of those prodigious letters with which Coleridge sought, in vain, to set himself right with his friends. But if I wrote them, certainly none was ever posted. It seemed, in the end, more decent and more dignified to keep silence. But one day, years after, at the very end of the war, I met Fox unexpectedly in a restaurant at Golders Green. There was no escape. He beckoned me to sit down beside him; and I knew the war had made him old, as it had made me also old. Now it seemed fantastically irrelevant even to begin to say that I was sorry for what had happened – in that other life. I told him simply that my wife was very ill with consumption, and that I was there, in Golders Green, searching for a house for her. He looked at me from under his grey eyebrows, and said 'I'm sorry'; and because I knew he *was* sorry, a lump came into my throat. Then he pushed back his chair, saying he must go, and went off to pay his bill. I sat, staring at the toast he had left untasted – he never could abide thick toast – and thinking back. Suddenly, I was conscious of his arm round my neck and his hand patting my coat-lapel. 'Now, my dear boy' – he paused. 'Don't *you* go and get consumption.' And he was gone, for ever.

I don't suppose that the memory of Fox is dearer to me than to hundreds of other Brasenose men; and it may be that, unknown to me, a worthier hand than mine has drawn a truer picture of him. If it be so, then I am glad. But when I think back to find the secret of his singular and enduring appeal to me, so that he became, in some sort, a part of my own finer consciousness, it lay, I think, in the fact that he had kept unimpaired, nay, cherished and encouraged, his man's tenderness. The tenderness of a woman is a lovely thing; but the tenderness of a man is a miracle.

Fox, in some inexplicable way, was Oxford to me. I felt grateful to Brasenose itself, even, primarily because it gave scope and freedom to Fox, to do in his own way his incomparable work of education. While I had Fox for my tutor, I worked: even drudgery – of which he himself imposed none upon me – became a kind of delight, from the exceeding desire I had not to let him down in the Schools. For this cause alone I wrestled with the dreary *apparatus criticus* of Robinson Ellis's big edition of Catullus until I had mastered it, though it was ashes in my mouth. And I did not let him down. But, so soon as Moderations was over, and I passed out of Fox's hands, there was no such personal motive to operate upon me. I relapsed into the egoist. What I did not like, I avoided. The idea of success in the Schools for its own sake had never appealed to me; for the sake of a possible career, it positively alarmed me, for by this time I was out of humour with the idea of any career at all, and in the mood of feeling that, unless I were wary, I should be entrapped and become a don through sheer lack of courage.

Indeed, it was hard enough to keep myself running straight till Mods were safely over. New influences were disturbing me; slowly and imperceptibly there was taking place a great upheaval in my being. I think that I can understand it well enough now; but at the time it was mysterious.

It began, as I trace its onset now, with my first and my only reading-party. Towards the end of my first long vacation Fox invited my three friends and me to read for a month with him at Snape in Suffolk. For economy's sake, I rode my bicycle all the way from Hampton Wick, where I lived, to Snape in a single day. Since I was ashamed to let it be known that I could only thus afford the luxury of going on a reading-party I pretended that this was simply an eccentricity of mine, and that I enjoyed riding 120 miles a day on a bicycle. On this occasion I did enjoy it. I enjoyed riding clean through the most famous streets of the City of London at five o'clock in the morning – I had started out at 4 a.m. Besides me and the men flushing down the streets with a great hose, there was nobody stirring, and as the tyres of my bicycle made a swift crisp noise on the wet roadway I sang for the very pleasure of being thus alive.

As it had begun, so it went on. The whole of that reading-holiday was delightful to me. I did very little reading; but I persuaded myself that it was far more important that I should be enjoying myself. Here – in this gay, free, careless life – was something of which I had been cheated by circumstance, and I meant to drink my fill. Someone had lent us an old sailing dinghy in which we careered down the Alde and battled our way back again up to Snape bridge. It was a part-fulfilment of my schoolboy dream. What was probably at best good fun to my companions was a wild delight to me. When they went off to play golf, I would take out the boat alone, and generally succeed in running myself aground. Then I waited, blissfully, for them to return and extricate me. The estuary of the Alde was then a marvellous piece of country – soaked in sunshine – and for the first time in my life I entered into a care-free, country existence which I felt to be my rightful heritage.

From this time forward it seemed to me quite impossible to endure spending my vacations at home in a small villa in a row of small villas. As soon as my month was over, and I had returned to my London suburb, my mind was filled with a single purpose – to find some place in the country where I could live in vacations. It was not an easy problem to solve. The income from my scholarship and my school exhibitions was all I had, and it left only a narrow margin. But I reckoned that if I could find lodging in a farmhouse for £1 a week, I could manage. So I explored a column in *T.P.'s Weekly* which was called (I think) 'Friends in Council' – or, at any rate, by some name which signified that it was not concerned with the ordinary type of profit-seeking advertisement. There I found the offer of being received into a farmhouse in Gloucestershire, in terms and on terms that struck me as friendly indeed. Accordingly, I wrote and explained myself, and received an encouraging reply.

I sent off my belongings to Oxford by train, on the day for going-up, and started off on my bicycle before dawn one October day for Stow-on-the-Wold. The road from Stow to Waterloo (with which I was to become familiar) enchanted me that autumn morning. It was my first experience of Cotswold country, and I loved it at sight. When at last I rode through the stackyard and had my first glimpse of Waterloo Farm lying remote in a still hollow, I felt that the Fates were being kind to me.

To this day I am not sure why the Thornhills – for that was the name of the farmer and his wife – took in such a lodger as myself. Assuredly, it was not for profit: for they certainly made none out of me. I never asked them the reason; but I suppose it was for the sake of company. Waterloo was a remote and lonely place – the last lost end of the postman's daily tramp from the town in the valley, so that he had a little hut in the copse beside the farmhouse, where he could stay until the time for his return tramp to begin. Twenty good miles and more, sometimes with a heavy load of parcels, every day except Sunday, with a climb, I suppose, of nearly 700 feet. For Waterloo stood well above the 900 ft. mark, with Cutsdean Hill, more than 1000 ft., a little to the north-west. At Waterloo I felt that I was on the windy roof of England, and I loved the place.

As it happened, I was to love the people more. But on that day my shyness was such that I barely glanced at the sitting-room and the bedroom which were to be mine, as Mrs. Thornhill showed them to me. She was a small bird-like woman with a charming smile; and she was astonished when, having settled to come for the whole of the Christmas vacation, I refused her invitation to tea, on the plea that I did not like riding in the dark, but in fact through mere shyness. As I rode away up the slope in front of the farmhouse, I knew that she was still standing at the doorway to watch me. So I stopped and waved my hand. That seems, in retrospect, to be a characteristic gesture of mine, as though friendliness were easier to me at a distance.

During that term, I thought more about the coming adventure at Waterloo than I did about my work. To me it was one more plunge into the unknown; but it had, as I well knew, another meaning also. I was slipping my moorings at home. I was glad and sad to do it; glad, because I had come by now veritably to loathe lower middle-class life in a poorish suburb. I could not bear to be exhibited to the few local acquaintances of my family any more as 'my son, who had won a scholarship to Oxford'. I had no friends of any kind of my own age; I knew no older men who shared my interests; indeed, I knew no educated men in the neighbourhood at all: I was by now completely *déclassé*. Away from home, as I had discovered at Snape, I had a place in society; I was naturally received amongst people whose manners I enjoyed. I talked to attractive girls at tennis-parties, shyly indeed, but not without the feeling that the pleasure was mutual. At home, I was completely cut off from every kind of social inter-course; and had it not been for the presence and the company of my small brother – now between six and seven – my loneliness would have been desperate indeed. And he, I sadly realized, though he still scampered out of school to meet me where I waited for him, had begun to prefer the company of children of his own age to mine.

More than anything else it was the thought of not seeing him in the vacation that saddened me. The break with my home I knew, or believed, to be inevitable; and it was fortunate that I could make it with the half-true excuse that I could work better away. I represented my forthcoming stay in Gloucestershire as a sort of prolongation of my summer reading-party, to the satisfaction of my father. For my mother I was indeed much more con-cerned. I had been, since I was a little boy, her cavalier; and in a boyish way I was still proud of her. I knew, moreover, that I was

94

her chief, if not her only escape from a straitened kind of existence against which she was still rebellious, and that, without me at home, the year would be dull indeed for her. But that, I thought, was no fault of mine. It could not hold me back.

A terrible to-do about a very simple thing, it may be thought. But the severance from one's family is not a simple thing: and I knew well enough that this severance was, somehow, final. Henceforward, I was at home as a visitor merely; it ceased to be home to me.

CHAPTER VIII

ET EGO IN ARCADIA

WHEN one December afternoon I got out of the train at Stow-on-the-Wold, with an aching head after a riotous end-of-term party, I might, for my sense of homelessness, have been disembarked on a jetty in the Antipodes. I was forlorn, indeed. Mr. Thornhill – John Thornhill, as I learned to call him, and as he lives in my memory – was there with the dogcart. He wore a battered deerstalker hat of brown tweed, covert cloth gaiters and stout driving gloves; and his face was red-brown with exposure on the hills. He was, though I did not know it, as shy of me as I was of him; while we slowly pulled up the hill from the station into the town, we said barely a word. He talked only to the stout Irish mare, whose quarters gleamed in the lamplight. When we reached the town, he disappeared into the Swan to collect his parcels, and also – as he told me weeks afterwards – a stiff whisky to keep his courage up under my companionship during the sixteen miles to Waterloo.

It was a silent ride; but the Irish mare went gallantly. When she flagged a little, John Thornhill had merely to whisper to her, caressingly: 'Come now – Bess!' and the lovely beast flung herself forward as though wakened suddenly out of a dream. Thornhill leant forward with one hand on his thigh, sucking at his old briar, and I was amazed at the bond between him and his mare – something completely simple, the like of which I had never known, in the presence of which I felt myself to be the rootless, unstable thing I was. And once again, when he bade me tuck the rug tighter round myself, I felt in his voice that man's tenderness towards a man, which is so strange, so precious, and so rare.

At Waterloo, I settled myself in my room. For two or three days I saw practically nothing of the family. I turned over my classics, I suppose, but the only book I can remember reading there was Maeterlinck's *Serres Chaudes*, the sight of which is fixed in my memory as something supremely incongruous. In the afternoons, I walked and bicycled, and listened, enchanted, to the sound of the hunting-horn coming from far across that Cotswold country. Mary Thornhill, the daughter, of about my own age, brought me in my meals. I stood by the fire watching her lay the table in the lamplight; but never a sensible word could I find to say. It was 'Yes, thank you' and 'No, thank you'; until I began to hug to myself the queer solitude that was creeping round me. So that I was startled out of myself when, one breakfast-time, Mary Thornhill brought me the invitation from her father: 'Would I like to drive to market with him?' 'No, thank you,' came by sheer automatism, so shrinking-shy was I.

Then, as I learned afterwards, the Thornhills despaired about me, and nearly gave me up as a bad job. Mrs. Thornhill was convinced that the life I led was thoroughly unhealthy; but how to drag me out of it, she had no idea. And Thornhill, now that his overture had been refused, was reluctant to try me again. But, urged by his wife, he did; and I, who had had a full week in which to ponder on the curse of a timidity which must have looked like churlishness, was only too eager to respond when, once more through Mary, there came the question. 'Father wants to know whether you would like to go for a ride?'

'I should like to, very much; but I don't know how to ride.'

'That doesn't matter. He'll teach you.'

To learn to ride a horse was another dream of mine; but now that the chance had come, I was a bundle of nerves. Not that I cared at that moment a single rap whether I broke my neck, but the thought of making an utter fool of myself in front of John Thornhill was grim indeed. For by now, although I had not spoken a hundred words to him, I admired him completely. His rich, gruff voice, calling 'Mother!' through the house; above all the sight of him sitting easily on his great mare as he rode off to do his round on the thousand-acre farm, with his crop thrust between his thigh and his saddle, while he lit his old briar – these satisfied me wholly. I wanted to be like him. The thought of making myself ridiculous in his eyes was a torment.

No doubt, I looked as white-faced as I felt when I went out into the yard to mount Gipsy – a lighter and younger Irish mare. I obeyed instructions faithfully about mounting, got a good grip of her mane in my left hand, and went up. Anyhow, at the first shot I was in the saddle, but without an atom of confidence that I could stay there. There seemed no earthly reason why I should stay there. The connection between Gipsy and me seemed quite fortuitous. I was like a billiard ball on the tip of a conjuror's nose. So long as Gipsy decided to keep me balanced on top of her, so long I should stay. For a while she seemed content to do so, while we followed Thornhill out of the yard. He opened the gate. As it swung back, it gave Gipsy a shove on the haunches and away she began to trot. The fortuitous connection between us was over. 'Grip with your knees!' called Thornhill. I gripped with my knees; and, miraculously, there I still was, but being bundled igno-miniously up and down like a sack of potatoes. It was, I knew, an insult to Gipsy to be ridden thus. 'Rise in your stirrups!' called Thornhill; and I rose in my stirrups. But my idea of the moment to rise, and Gipsy's were different; instead of bumping up and down, I now bobbed. '*Feel* her!' said Thornhill. But *how* to feel her?

Then, for a miraculous second or two, I had a glimpse; for a second or two, there was a sort of rhythmic peace between Gipsy and me. But no sooner I had touched it, than I was jerked out of it again. Then she started a sort of motionless trotting that drove me to despair. I bobbed and bobbed and bobbed. 'You want a pair of real breeches,' said Thornhill. 'You can't ride in trousers.' Willing to be excused though I was, I could not let that go. 'It's not my trousers,' I panted. 'It's me. If I could ride, my trousers would.' And he laughed. Then, slowly, as I toiled through the afternoon, the moments of rhythmic peace grew longer, and I was secure enough in my perch to look about me. We entered a great pasture field, which I had not seen before – it takes time to explore a thousand-acre farm – and I was gazing about me, when suddenly Thornhill thundered off on his mare, at a full gallop, his head turned to watch what would happen to me. Gipsy put down her head and flew after. For a moment, I was lost, like a man who cannot swim plunged into deep water. Then I emerged. I was still on Gipsy's back, and the air was rushing about my ears. Suddenly I felt absolutely safe, and my one desire was to go faster, faster – to catch up with the great haunches of Thornhill's mare and the hooves that spurted bits of turf. Nay, this was wonderful. Nothing in life that I had known could compare with this. This exhilaration was absolute.

And I owed it all to Thornhill. When I pulled up beside him, he was smiling. 'How's that?' he said. I could not answer; but my eyes were shining. 'Will you ride with me to-morrow?' he said. And again I did not answer. I only laughed. 'You've done well – very well,' he said, and I felt it might be true.

When we reached home, it seemed impossible that I should retire to my solitary room; and it was. It was taken for granted that I should have tea in the farm kitchen with the family. Nor, from that moment, did I ever have a meal by myself again at Waterloo. Then there began one of the few completely happy times of my life. I was, simply and truly, made one of that family. Every day I rode the round of the farm with Thornhill, or I drove with him to market at Stow or Andoversford; every day I learned something that seemed to me worth learning. I leaped fences and walls on Gipsy, I stood with Alan Thornhill – an apple-cheeked boy of twelve – under the tall trees waiting for a shot at the wood-pigeon, I began, very modestly, to ride to hounds with Thornhill, following his lead obediently, and trying to fathom the mystery of how he knew beforehand the line the fox would take when it broke cover; until, in a little while, it was the Thornhills who had to remind me that I had come there to work at my books. Where-upon I would make a good resolution, and chain myself impatiently for two hours to Cicero, chafing till the moment came when I could be up and away on Gipsy with Thornhill again.

As I bring back to memory those Cotswold days, I am repossessed with the old desire to have a horse of my own. It has lain, perforce, dormant for many years, and probably it never will be satisfied; but there, I recognize with a sort of smiling consternation, it is, smouldering hidden yet unabated. In those Cotswold days, it almost burned me up. It came within an ace of changing my whole life. My thoughts were busy all day long on the single problem: How could I so contrive my life that a horse should always be part of it? I even conceived the fantastic notion of offering myself as a stable-lad to Sir Charles Nugent at his training establishment near by. True, I was sane enough to put that out of my head, but not before it had turmoiled me for a week. Finally I decided, as the only practical solution, that I would enter the Indian Civil Service, for which to ride a horse was necessary.

So that was settled. There was, at least, nothing chimerical about that plan; and I was completely serious about it. Now, indeed, I had something more than an excuse for my new passion. Leaping over practice fences all day long was now part of my work; to ride discreetly to hounds essential to my education. Nor had I any real compunction any more in asking my father, for the first and only time in my life, for some money. At the instigation of Fox, who considered that I was run down, the College had generously increased my scholarship by £25 a year, on condition the money was used to spend part at least of my vacations in the country. With this, and some heroic economies, I could meet half-way John Thornhill's suggestion that he should keep a horse for me. He would keep it at the bare cost of its feed; I would keep myself at Oxford for the bare cost of mine. He reckoned he could buy me a horse which would do me credit for £30, if he went the right way about it. So I made up my mind to ask my father for £30, destination unknown; and I went home for Christmas to get it.

All through my life, it has been a peculiar agony to me to ask anyone for money; and I have so contrived things that it has only been necessary on two occasions. This was one of them. My father, whose anxiety about money was morbid, managed to saturate the situation with the maximum of misery: I had the sense that I was engaged in filching the ruddy drops that visited his sad heart. And my own moral position was precarious. However much I had succeeded in convincing myself that I would enter the Indian Civil Service – and in that respect my conviction was now entire – I was conscious of a certain casuistry in my self-persuasion that it was necessary for me to keep a horse in order to prepare myself for my career. The horse-riding test was no part of the I.C.S. examination; it followed a year afterwards. However, that would have been near enough to satisfy my elastic conscience: but I knew that my father was utterly opposed to my choosing the Indian Service. Nothing but a desk in an office in Whitehall would satisfy him.

Those two or three days at home at Christmas were a nightmare. My father's glumness, my mother's suffering, and my own unease turned my distaste for home almost to loathing. Out of my happiness at Waterloo I was plunged into this – all for the sake of a wretched thirty pounds, which my father could easily afford. Since I was a tiny boy, I ruminated cynically, my education had cost him not a penny. He was, I knew, no longer poor. He had made his modest way in the Civil Service, and with the meagreness which he enforced upon my mother, he saved a generous proportion of his income; and now, for the sake of thirty pounds, I must eat dirt. At that moment I hated my father. I thought of the meanness to which his life had slowly been reduced, until all his native freedom and generosity had been slowly extinguished, and I loathed all that he stood for with a nausea almost physical. Extravagance, or no extravagance; conscience or no conscience, I would have no truck with that. No matter what I did, if only it was a repudiation of that deadly thing, it was justified. I thought of the portraits of my father and mother in the family album: once, they also were young and debonair – and now?

Those few days at home were crucial. The contrast between my home and Waterloo was terrifying. There were moments when the morbid fancy seized me that the cavernous space of the dark winter night was some strange neutral stuff in which different kinds of reality were hidden, like metals in a rock: you journeyed through the darkness from one world to another. Then my uneasy terror changed into a sort of cynicism, as I remembered the fate of my mother's poor little legacy. This thirty pounds was my mother's; since she would never get it, I took it in her stead. And I was quite content to let my father believe that I had 'run into debt' – an enormity which in his mind took rank with Roman Catholicism and a protective Tariff. It spared me the necessity of a more elaborate invention. And, to fill my cup of iniquity to overflowing, I intended to declare roundly that I would not enter myself for the Home Civil Service, but the Indian. Since it was only under the influence of Waterloo that I had come to think seriously of the Civil Service at all, my decision was at least an outward sign of grace. Whatever the motive, I had turned my mind to the necessity of a career. If I had brought myself to put on harness for the sake of a horse – it was appropriate, and at least as good as putting it on for the K.C.B. with which my father's ambitious dreams sometimes decorated me. Had my father known all the facts, I thought riotously, perhaps he would have given me the thirty pounds as a reward for virtue. But I knew my father; I knew he was incapable of listening to the facts, and I knew I was incapable of trying to tell them to him. For him, the Indian Civil Service – I knew not from what association, perhaps Jos Sedley, for there was a paper-back copy of *Vanity Fair* in the house, which he had read, or maybe from some connection between the I.C.S. and Kipling, whom (without having read) he abominated – was a kind of oriental Saturnalia. The road to Mandalay was the road to ruin, lined, I suppose, by Nautch girls, and along which the ne'er-do-well company of Indian Civil Servants rode furiously on horseback.

I believe that if my father had known that his thirty pounds (my mother's thirty pounds) was to be spent on a horse, he would have had a paralytic stroke. A horse! Wine, women, cards and horses: and the most terrible of these, by far, was horses. To him they were merely things to bet on; and gambling was his sin of sins. There was some reason for his horror. When he was a youngish man, he had moved for a while in a rather fast set. I have a dim baby recollection of being taken one evening to a magnificent set of rooms in the Old Apothecaries' Hall, and being put to sleep while my father and mother played cards. Those august rooms were, I afterwards learned, the rooms of a Secretary of the Society of Apothecaries, a man of altogether higher social standing than my father, and a very convivial fellow – who ultimately pushed conviviality to the point of suicide. How the connection between him and my father arose is a mystery; but the vague story was that one night my father, having dined too well, played a disastrous game of cards, at the end of which he had lost seven pounds – six weeks' wages. He had paid his debt, by a great effort, and had taken a vow never to drink to excess, and never to play cards for money. I don't believe he ever put money on horses; but the Apothecary certainly did, and the Apothecary killed himself.

Gambling – horses – the Indian Civil Service: they were all one, I think, to my father's mind. I am mildly astonished that he did not turn a rabid teetotaller as well. But the queer thing about my father was that, with all his extreme obstinacy, his morbid anxiety about money, his fanatical Gladstone worship, mysteriously combined with an equally fanatical detestation of the Irish, he was no Puritan. There was no principle at all that I could find underlying his various asceticisms. He was, if soberly considered (which is probaby beyond my power to do) an astonishing combination of contradictory obstinacies. He believed that the Irish could only and should only be ruled by a rod of iron; yet he believed himself to be an ultra-democrat. He hated soldiers – except for the purpose of suppressing the Irish. All foreigners, without exception, were rogues. Yet again he was a violent anti-Imperialist, who had been willing to run risks in protesting against the Boer War, and whose one major doubt of the moral magnificence of the branch of the Home Civil Service to which he belonged was due to the fact that Sir Alfred Milner had at one time been Chairman of the Board of Inland Revenue. That was as though a Mahommedan had crept into the Papal Chair.

No, it is impossible to make anything of that fantastic congeries of prejudices which served my father for opinions. Indeed, I have never until this moment realized quite how strange they were. I took them for granted too many years ago. They were facts of nature, as inscrutable and indubitable as earthquakes: and earthquakes were precipitated by any challenge of them. Since my mother and I preferred to live as peaceably as we could, they never were challenged. Indeed, some of them were never even defined. We knew, by instinct, the point at which a danger zone began. There had never been a specific ruling, or a specific earthquake, on the subject of horses; but I knew perfectly well that for my father horses were one of the symbols of perdition. And heaven alone knows how he would have reacted to the thought of an Irish mare! It would have seemed to him an apparition straight from Hell, like the black dog of medieval witchcraft.

There was another odd thing about my father. He was secretly convinced that I should come to a bad end. There was, so to speak, one strait and narrow path to virtue for me. It was simple enough; it led straight from the board-school to the public school, from the public school to the University, from the University to the Board of Inland Revenue. In my father's peculiar vision of things this path appeared to stretch dizzily, like a tight-rope, over a moral abyss. So far I had swayed perilously along it; but my father never believed I should really get to the end. The Devil would have me. I should fall headlong, like Satan, on to the burning marl of some disreputable profession and a pauper funeral. When, finally, I took his thirty pounds, and almost in the same breath declared that I did not even intend to try for the home Civil Service, he had at least the satisfaction of knowing that his profound mistrust of me as a moral being was completely justified.

And yet I loved him; and yet I admired him. In spite of the intolerable cleavage between us, it seemed to me that it needed only the touch of a fairy's wand to make him manifest as the splendid thing he was. His strange, fantastic prejudices were a kind of veil between him and the outward world. They would disappear in the twinkling of an eye, if only the magic word could be uttered. But I knew well that I should never have the power to utter it.

When I left home, I was so jangled and on edge that I half-doubted whether I should really find John Thornhill waiting for me at the station at Stow. When I saw him there, and the glimmer of the lamps on Bess's haunches, I was overwrought nearly to tears. In a bare three weeks this man of forty odd had become the most solid thing in my life; and, for some inscrutable reason, it seemed that I was almost as dear to him as he was to me. This was, indeed, a mystery, and we were enveloped in its warmth as we drove along.

'If only you knew *how* glad I am to be back!' I said.

How could he know? He knew nothing of my home; and, even if I had tried to tell him, it would have been incomprehensible. I did not try. From the beginning it had been understood between us that I was a homeless fellow. Else why should I be at Waterloo? I had a mother only, who lived abroad on a small pension, and sometimes came to England. Her I had been to see in London, and she had given me the money to buy the horse. Such a simple fantasy, into which I escaped naturally, was by this time more real to me than the fact. I had to believe in someone who would have given me the money willingly; and in my mother I had such a person. What more natural than that I should endow her with the material capacity she did not possess?

But, no doubt, behind this was a very real snobbishness. I wanted to blot out my origins. It is always said, and most of my life I believed, that snobbishness is an ignoble attitude. But now that I have long since overcome all sense of shame at my own origins, I have a tenderer judgment of it. That is what always happens. While I was in fact ashamed, so long I knew that my snobbishness was in fact ignoble. Its source was ignoble. While I was afraid lest my weakness should be uncovered, my very fear was itself the ignobility. But when I ceased to feel shame or fear, when I knew, incontrovertibly, that I was simply I, then at last I was free to see that my snobbishness had not been wholly ignoble, and that, mixed with it, hitherto indistinguishably, had been an aching desire that my parents should be something that I could love and admire without reserve. A boy feels a terrible hunger to admire the thing he loves. Where it is not possible, it sets up a profound conflict within him. He is forced, long before he is spiritually strong enough to endure it, to judge where he loves. And he evades the necessity he has not the strength to meet. He blots out the reality he cannot face.

My fantasy had changed since my school-days. I had no longer any desire to invest myself with a halo of inherited glory; I was more or less content to be what I was. But even to be what I was demanded fantasy. My new legend, of my mother living on a small pension, was truer to reality than the facts themselves would have been. I acknowledged the bond with my mother; I repudiated the bond with my father. That was the truth of my feeling then.

But it was not all the truth. Though I was willing enough to obliterate my origins, I was not at all willing to forego the adventitious prestige that had accrued to me. I was ready to forget that I had been a board-school urchin; I was not so ready to forget that I was an Oxford man. Certainly, it would have been difficult enough to do; and I do not know how I should have set about it in those days. But I suppose that I was as near as I ever could be to my real self in the kitchen at Waterloo. There I had no need, and therefore no desire, to defend a precarious position. If I had dropped from the clouds, I should have been the same to them, and they to me. Or so it seemed. And if I was, perchance, for them the 'gentleman', I was only so by the same right and in the same sense as the other lodger who afterwards came to live with them – a French *enseigne de vaisseau*, who employed a long leave in learning English.

But that was later; and since that chance contact with a young French naval officer had a great influence on the course of my life, it must wait a little. Now I was simply back at Waterloo, enjoying life with John Thornhill as I had never enjoyed it before, and was never to enjoy it again. Day after day I was with him, at market, round the farm, to hounds. I met his farmer friends so often that they began to take it for granted that I was a farm-pupil, and I found myself involved in discussions concerning theaves and tegs which were bewildering. Because John Thornhill had taught me how to tell what meat there was on a shaggy sheep, I prodded and pulled them in the pens to see whether I could guess how high the bidding would go: and I was sometimes taken for a knowledgeable young man. Sometimes I had to imbibe so much whisky and water that when the market was over, I could barely stand, and Thornhill himself would be inclined to nod. But Bess would fling up her heels, and dart like an arrow from a bow in the ostler's hands, and away we careered the eighteen miles over the frozen hills and iron roads from Andoversford. The cold air sobered me well, so that I arrived with nothing more terrible than a ravenous hunger.

But best of all were the long days riding together. I had a smart pair of breeches now, a pair of black riding boots, and a hard hat fixed to my collar. At last the horse had come, on trial – a light brown mare – and though she had an alarming habit of jumping a wall in two instalments, one on to the top and one down again, I was thrown only once. But Thornhill was dissatisfied with her; he thought her too nervous altogether. So back she went: but not before I had one or two glorious days with her. One remains in my memory.

When I have listened, as I often have had to do, to all the humanitarian arguments against fox-hunting, this memory comes back to me, and I am silent, set in opposition to others' easy dismissal of an experience which they have never known. The day which I remember had begun wet and miserable; the scent was poor, and nothing much had happened all through the morning, except that we got wetter and wetter. By the afternoon the field had melted away, till there were only a handful mainly of farmers left. But the day had cleared, and the Master was pertinacious. Somewhere about three o'clock he began to draw a great hill-side cover. No sooner were the hounds thrown in than even I knew that this time they meant business. Suddenly Thornhill thundered up the hill away from the cover, and I followed. Towards the top he paused, and I looked at him inquiringly. 'I know the way she'll go: she's bound to.' Hardly had he spoken than I could see the hounds streaking away diagonally across the slope of the hill we had climbed. Over the top we went, and waited. Suddenly: 'There she is!' cried Thornhill. I could not see her; but there were the hounds streaming along just below me, and no pink-jacket within half a mile of them. Then began a noble hour for me. Thornhill's knowledge of that country was marvellous. By a hundred indirect crooked ways we kept up with the hounds. Thornhill's Bess, who had to carry thirteen stone, was tired; but on she went. I was thrown; but I managed to keep hold of the reins, and scrambled on again. By minor miracle after minor miracle we were there all the time.

Then came a check. By now, to me, everything was a dream. In a dream the Master arrived, with his great horse in a lather. And there were, for one supreme moment, the three of us alone, just looking at one another. Then came the whippers-in. Six in all, and all in pink and velvet but ourselves. By now I had forgotten all about the fox. The hounds were feebly threading in and out the wood beside us in the dusk. Nobody seemed to care. Everybody seemed slightly drunk, inclined to smile at nothing, and loth to depart. But the mist was thickening. 'Good-night, gentlemen!' said the Master.

And he and his hounds moved westward up the hill; and Thornhill and I moved eastward, up the hill also, for the wood lay in a valley. When we reached the top we turned. They had

reached the top also   A great bar of dark cloud went clean across
the sky, and below it was a bright space of washed and faded
green. Against it were the horsemen; the Master was plain to see.
Suddenly he blew his horn. It sounded forlorn and magical in the
half-light, like Roland's horn at Roncesvaux. Then we saw him
take off his cap to us, and ride on over the hill. That western sky,
that note of the horn, that gesture, have lived in my mind ever
since; and that is why, when well-meaning people overwhelm me
with arguments to prove that fox hunting is unworthy and
degrading, I remember and am silent and I shake my head.

Nay more, fox-hunting was a passion with John Thornhill;
and a nobler, more generous, warmer-hearted Englishman never
trod the earth than he. Maybe he has no fame; in that, he is like
thousands of Englishmen of his kind. Maybe he understood little
beyond his job – but is there a manlier job in all the world than
farming, a job that gives a man a juster pride or implants in him
a truer humility? At least, I never talked with John Thornhill on
anything, but I found myself talking more truly, more 'in the
middle of the note' than I should otherwise have done. He came
of yeoman stock. He slept in a great oak bed, with his own name
carved upon it; but it was the name of a John Thornhill dead and
gone three hundred years ago. 1609 was the date of that bed:
about the time that Shakespeare was writing *Antony and Cleopatra*,
and perhaps beginning to wonder what disposition he should
make of his own bed. Shakespeare and John Thornhill – these
are England to me – 'the heart of generosity'.

Technically speaking, John Thornhill was no longer a yeoman
when I knew him. He was a tenant-farmer of lands which had
been acquired by a rich solicitor, who lived, I think, in Gloucester.
The son had inherited them and retained the shooting rights. He
was a decent fellow, about five years older than myself, and kind
enough always to ask me to shoot with him when I was there.
That was embarrassing, partly because shooting did not interest
me, but more because I did not want to be in the camp of the
'gentlemen', over against John Thornhill. It seemed to me

preposterous, against nature, that Thornhill should be the tenant and Stoddart the landlord. Rather than be the witness and the accomplice of this unnatural relation, I preferred to make excuses and disappear on horseback for the day. And probably to that cause is due the fact that now, when I live in a country where not a few opportunities of good shooting come to me, I have no impulse to take them, whereas I know – only too well – that the old passion to be on a horse again smoulders unabated within me. My values, in this matter, are John Thornhill's values still.

He was – such was his nature – far more concerned than I when the time for my examination in Classical Moderations drew near. Before I left Waterloo to return to Oxford in mid-January, he had begun to reproach himself with tempting me away from my books. I stoutly assured him that I should do all the better for having forgotten them completely. And Mrs. Thornhill, who knew better than I how deep his concern really was, would point out the obvious fact that I had come pale and peezy-weezy to Waterloo, and was leaving it tanned and with a man's appetite – all in two months. Whereat John Thornhill would ruminate, and say, 'There's something in that, Mother', and brighten up. But I had to promise to write to him to tell him whether I had grown rusty.

For a little while after I returned to Oxford I worked hard, with something of a guilty conscience. Perhaps I worked too hard, or the Oxford climate after the Cotswold air got me down. Within a fortnight I was feeling nohowish, as Keats called it. So Fox wafted me away, in his new Vauxhall car, to his new house on Boars Hill, and into another period of happiness. So that I began to wonder which was the more beatific beginning of a day – breakfast in the kitchen at Waterloo, or breakfast alone with Fox in his bare whitewashed room. He made his wafer-toast at the fire, and boiled his coffee in a special saucepan; and I was made an equal sharer in the feast. Then with a glance between his rugged grey eyebrows and the top of his crooked spectacles, he would thrust one of his letters across to me. 'What d'you make of

that?' Sometimes, there seemed no earthly reason to suppose that
I should make anything of it: so completely were the matters outside my experience – letters, I remember, from a friend of his who
was gold-mining in the Yukon, on thorny questions of finance.
'What would *you* do?' Fox asked half-fierce, half-laughing. 'He
seems a very nice fellow', I would say feebly. And that was
enough for Fox. 'Will he ruin me, or make my fortune? I
wonder.' And then he would break into praise of his friend. They
had once, I fancy, been schoolmasters together, and T——,
making Fox his only confidant, had suddenly thrown it up and
gone West after gold, and Fox had become a sleeping partner in
the enterprise, through which he lived vicariously on the Yukon.
Since T—— was a hero of Fox's, he must needs be one of mine.

Then Fox would swoop down to Oxford in his Vauxhall,
and I would work. It was easy to work up there: so that, when the
moment came for me to descend into the Schools, Fox said to me:
'You've nothing to worry about. It's not a question of you getting
a first, but only of what kind of first you will get.' And that made
the examination easy. I felt I could sail through anything with
Fox to egg me on, just as I would ride anywhere with Thornhill
to show the way. As it turned out, my first was a good one – one
of the best, second only (I was told) to that of a member of a
family which, in these things, has always borne the palm.

'How was it?' said Thornhill to me at the station, the moment
he met me. I said I *thought* it was all right. 'You arranged about
a telegram?' I said I had. Then we settled down to enjoy ourselves again; or perhaps the truth were better told if I said that
Thornhill settled down to make me enjoy myself again. While I
had been away, I had bought him a new hunting-crop with his
name and mine engraved upon it, to take the place of the old ash
stick he had cut for himself. He said I shouldn't have done it;
but I knew that he was pleased. It would have seemed odd that
such a little thing should please him so, if I had not guessed that
he knew how much of true affection went with it. I tried to
heave my heart into my mouth. 'Big John', I said – we were Big

John and Little John to each other – 'it's all I could afford. But if ever I grow rich, I'll buy you *such* a farm, and I'll build myself a little house on the edge of it, and I'll keep three hunters, and you shall have three – and we'll hunt five days every week, and go to market on the sixth'.

Alas, I never have grown rich; I never even managed to take the modest path to security of the Indian Civil Service, although it was then as fixed and solid before me as the hard high road itself, along which Bess was thundering us to Waterloo. But, luckily for my happiness, in those days I did not doubt. Everything was certain; every line met in a point of purpose. My riding, my examination – all made one. There was room now even to think about falling in love. And I did.

My memory tells me that I did it in the village church. But that report is strange; for I cannot believe that I went to church of my own motion. Perhaps it was that Mrs. Thornhill went to church and I went with her for company; or, may be, I saw my sweetheart out walking, and learned that she lived at the Vicarage: therefore church was the likeliest place to find her. But that my first *vision* of her was in church, there is no doubt. A couple of rows in front of me, next to an overwhelming parson's wife, sat a lovely girl, with a complexion so transparent that, while it delighted, it frightened me. Her blood, as Shakespeare used to say, peeped through her skin. Her hair was fair, but not blonde; and her nose was wonderful. It was small, with a trace of arch to it, and the curve of the nostrils was absolutely sensitive: probably what Keats meant when he described Fanny Brawne's nostrils as 'painful'. I could not take my eyes from her profile. It was to me the outward and visible sign of an inward and spiritual grace.

I found out that she was not the daughter, but the niece of the vicar, and the country-side report – which proved to be quite unjust – was she was treated as little better than a servant by her aunt. My youthful chivalry was fired, I was the appointed rescuer, I would marry her and carry her to India. So I sent her a note, by some devious means, asking if I might speak to her. Shortly after, came a note from her aunt requesting me to call. In fear and trembling – for I knew I was in for it – I appeared at the Vicarage and submitted humbly to a lecture on my breach of decorum ; but I could feel, as I bowed my head, that the aunt was not really very angry with me, and I was not altogether surprised when I was invited to stay to tea. But my beloved brought it in, and I was hard put to it then to keep my head. I felt that I had been horribly clumsy to have put her in a position so embarrassing; and my heart thumped as I saw the colour come and go in her face.

We hardly spoke to one another, so shy we were. I felt that she was, at least, not wholly displeased with me. But I knew there was trouble ahead. For the aunt, though she was by no means the tyrant I had imagined, but rather of the generous self-indulgent sort, was sensitive to class distinctions. Her condescending references to the Thornhills and her repeated suggestions of intimacy with the family of the local landowner made me regret my precipitate invitation to her to have tea with me at Waterloo. To have made myself the instrument of a snub to the Thornhills was intolerable.

But Mrs. Thornhill did not see it in that light. She liked the girl for her own sake; and still more she disliked the vicar's wife. She regarded herself as involved with me in a campaign, or a conspiracy, to rescue a princess from a prison; and all her woman's instincts for match-making were kindled. She would gladly have submitted to a hundred snubs if she thereby furthered the cause. So there was a series of constrained and unsatisfactory visits. I went to the Vicarage and played bridge; and my sweetheart and her aunt came to see me at the farm. But what I really wanted was that she should ride with me. It seemed unnatural that she should not share my passion; and since I was become, for a brief period, a sober-minded young man with a sense of future responsibilities, I reasoned gravely with myself that, as my wife in India, she would need to ride no less than I. Not that

I spoke to her of this: I hardly spoke to her of anything, but I did convince myself that delight and duty went hand in hand. And I persuaded her to persuade her aunt to let her go riding with me.

One afternoon I went to fetch her. I took down with me a saddle and bridle for the little grey mare, whose usual duty was to pull the tub-cart at the Vicarage. She mounted safely, though I could see that she was nervous. But now it was my turn to instruct and reassure, till we arrived at the farm. After Mrs. Thornhill had admired us – for this was no small victory in the campaign – we set off again for the serious business of the day. For an hour or more it went well. The little grey mare trotted sedately, and though my sweetheart was too tense to talk, I felt that she was enjoying it in a desperate sort of way. Her pale transparent cheeks began to take on a rosy flush; and a wisp of her fair hair fluttered free. She looked lovely, and I was happy. But my mare was feeling impatient. She was not used to being kept at these quiet paces for so long, and was eager to fling up her heels. She began to be troublesome at the gates. At last, when I had opened one into a big pasture field, with a few scattered and stunted trees, and let the grey mare through, my mare began prancing about. It was one of our daily gallops; but I dared not let her go. I remembered the galvanic effect of Bess's gallop upon Gipsy. The more I held her in, the more she played the fool.

Then, what I feared would happen, happened. The grey mare pelted off down the field, and went straight for one of the trees to brush her rider off. My mare was much faster, and I managed to overhaul the grey mare quickly enough to turn her aside. But the girl's eyes were shut: she had given up. I grabbed her rein; but it was all I could do to slow up my own mare, and for a horrible moment I was tugged between the two of them. So I grabbed at the girl instead. But, though I caught her, I could not hold her. Fortunately, her feet cleared the stirrups, and the grey mare was clean away, before the girl dropped, fairly softly had she but known it, on to the ground. But she had fainted already.

Looking back, I suppose that was a perfect romantic situation; but I did not like it at all. Though I was pretty sure she was not really hurt, I was not certain; and I covered up my anxiety by feeling cross. That would, very likely, be the end of our riding together, I thought as I held her. A real romantic hero would have tenderly kissed her. I was far more concerned that she should come round quickly; and I felt she *ought* not to have fainted. Just like a girl! sums up my crude reaction. But when she did open her blue eyes and smiled at me, I was happy enough; and when she told me that she had been very stupid, I denied it vehemently. No doubt, I was in love.

As it happened, I never did ride with her again – a few days afterwards I went back to Oxford – and, I believe, I only saw her once again. That was during the summer term, when she was going to London, and I met her train at Oxford station. I was in love with her still; but shortly afterwards she and Waterloo and the Thornhills and all my purposes, in which all these were blent together, faded out of my life, in a manner which I will try to tell. I reproached myself, and I was miserable about it; but I could not prevent it happening. 'A greater power than we denies all this.' I had designed my life to a pattern to fit Waterloo; my love for my sweetheart, though not itself part of that pattern, needed that pattern to support it. To marry her, I needed to become a young man with prospects. I knew it from the beginning; and it was because I had become (in my own mind) a young man with prospects at Waterloo that I allowed myself to fall in love with her: and had it been in my power to remain the young man with prospects I believed myself to be, I should have remained in love with her.

But the pattern broke all to pieces. Were I a more important sort of man, I should say boldly that I had a 'daimon' – an impersonal power that drove me on. For truly, while the pattern was breaking, I was miserable indeed. I should not have suffered one half so much, had I been able to feel that *I* was responsible for breaking it. Instead, I felt, helplessly, that something was happening to me, completely beyond my power of control – something which I did not desire. I desired the pattern. I wanted the Thornhills, wanted my sweetheart, wanted the career which made them possible, and wanted it, not merely for their sake, but for its own. I wanted all the certainty, of which these people and these things were part, and wanted it more desperately than most young men. My whole life had been one of uncertainty and insecurity, and my soul was sick of it all. If ever a young man hungered and thirsted after security, it was I. Yet I put it away.

Had it been I that put it away, I should have reckoned myself a hero. But it was not I. I had no desire which conflicted with the desire for the security which was now within my grasp: no desire, or dream, to see a goodlier girl than my sweetheart, to meet finer friends than the Thornhills, to do anything but credit to my college, to have another or a better life than that of an Indian Civil Servant.

Why then did the pattern collapse? I suppose that this narrative of mine, if it is truly written, is the answer to that question. If it is truly written it will contain the answer to the question which soon began to torture me, and tormented me for many years afterwards. Why did I simply let myself drop out of the lives of the Thornhills and my sweetheart, and let them drop out of my life? Why did I leave them without a word – of thanks, of gratitude, of memory, of regret? I felt the thanks and the gratitude: the memory was always precious; the regret was bitter indeed. Yet I said not a word.

CHAPTER IX

FAREWELL TO WATERLOO

THE pattern I had woven for myself at Waterloo had been complete. What I was going to do was settled among us all. Even Alan Thornhill insisted on being part of it. He was to go to India as my factotum, to see that my horses were cared for properly. In vain I pointed out that the work was done by native servants: he was sure that there was a way. And now that I had fallen in love with the girl with whom Mrs. Thornhill 'had always believed' I ought to fall in love, the arrangement had received its final perfection. There were no loose ends, no uncertainties – unless the passing of the examination itself were one. I could not honestly believe it was.

But the Thornhills could. The examination of which I was still awaiting the result was in their eyes the first part of the examination for India. That was how I also saw it now. But since I myself felt fairly certain of the result, I was not prepared to notice that John Thornhill was worrying over it. But he was. His appetite began to fail; he had no stomach for his breakfast. Since his habit was to rise at five in the morning, drink a quart of thin Somerset cider, and spend three hours about the farm, before he returned to breakfast, this was an untoward thing. But it was not till afterwards that Mrs. Thornhill let me into the secret, and I knew the cause.

When the telegram came, it was towards evening, and we were all in the kitchen together. The spark of triumph in John Thornhill's eyes was wonderful to behold. It was as though the dream were his not mine, of which the foundation stone in reality had now been well and truly laid; and for some odd reason I suddenly felt sad. At supper I was only half the man I should have been, in the midst of the laughing and the gaiety. I put it down to the fact that I must have been worrying unconsciously, and I said so. 'We'll put that to rights before we go to bed', said Thornhill. He went down to the cellar for a bottle of sloe-gin; and, with that between us, we played cards, as our habit was, till bed-time: half-past nine. Then Mrs. Thornhill and Mary said 'Good night'. We're coming later,' said Thornhill. Mrs. Thornhill smiled, as she shut the door. After a little while Thornhill descended into the cellar again, and returned with another bottle of sloe-gin. 'We're going to get outside that before we go to bed', said he.

We did. What we talked about that night I do not remember at all. My face slowly fixed in a broad smile. At last the moment came when Thornhill said distinctly: 'We'd-better-go-bed'. I solemnly agreed. But the problem was how to get there. I tried to rise, but sank back helpless in my chair. He tried to rise and he sank back helpless in his chair. We looked at one another for a long time. 'We-must-put-out-the-lamp', he said. Again, I solemnly agreed. Luckily the table was solid, for we both leaned heavily upon it. I had sense enough to hold the base of the lamp while John Thornhill blew. His breath seemed to go anywhere but down the chimney. Then one gust found its mark, and, quite unexpectedly, we were in the dark. We had not bargained for that.

In the faint red glow from the dying fire we groped our way to the door. Thornhill stood in the doorway and I clung to him. We peered into the hall, as into an unknown place. A dim lamp was burning. 'Stairs!' said Thornhill, as though he had not expected them to be there, and I wonderingly echoed 'Stairs?' Then an inspiration seized him. He went down on his hands and knees, and began to crawl towards them. I went down on my hands and knees, and crawled after him. After that there is nothing in my memory but a vision, distinct and unfading, of John Thornhill's broad backside, tight in the good grey breeches that the Moreton tailor made, on the stairs immediately above me –

the Pole Star by which I steered my own uncertain course to bed.

Since, to judge by several recently published books of reminiscences, I stand a fair chance of going down to literary history chiefly as a drunken man, or at least a protagonist in drunken scenes, this is the scene I should like to be judged by. It is, at any rate, one of my most vivid visions and my dearest memories. When I think of all the implications of that preposterous pilgrimage – all that is symbolized for me in the picture of that broad backside – I feel that I should be more than content to be remembered as the young man with whom, and for whom, John Thornhill on that night got drunk.

There are those, I know, who regard it as an abomination that a man should be exalted by wine. They would, of course, say 'degraded'. It depends, no doubt, upon one's personal experience. But I have never known my friends, or myself, degraded by wine. To me, personally, who am by nature a silent and tongue-tied person, wine has always been a liberation – an occasional and beneficent ecstasy, in the true sense – a breaking-down of the barriers of the self. Under the influence of wine, I have never done anything of which I was ashamed, and I have done and said many things which I am glad to have done and said: things which, but for that influence, would have remained unsaid or undone. And so, it may be there is a good reason why people who have known me should be inclined to remember me as I was under the influence of wine; just as I myself remember very vividly incidents of such moments. Almost always they have in my memory a praeternatural clarity, and sometimes a praeternatural significance, as though the hidden meaning of a whole life-situation had been made plain. *In vino veritas* is a truth, in my experience.

But to prevent my witness to the beneficence of wine being perverted, I should add that I am, either by nature or economic necessity, an abstemious person, who passes sometimes months on end without tasting strong drink of any kind. In this respect, and I hope in some others, I am of Shakespeare's mind:

Therefore are feasts so solemn and so rare
Since, seldom coming, in the long year set,
Like stones of price they thinly spaced are,
Or captive jewels in the carcanet.

I am not one of those who, by constant use of stimulants, do
verily 'blunt the fine point of seldom pleasure'. *That*, I feel,
is almost to degrade a god into a boon-companion or even a
household drudge.

Although I did not know it at this time, that vision of John
Thornhill was to be final. That memory ends a whole brief and
most precious chapter of my life; and the unconscious agent of
the undoing of the pattern of which John Thornhill and I had
thus celebrated the triumphant inception, I had met at Waterloo.
Maurice Larrouy – *enseigne de vaisseau 1ère classe* – had been to
Waterloo before ever I came, and he had returned for a fortnight's holiday at the beginning of this Easter vacation. He was
strangely unlike my romantic idea of a French naval officer; but
that made him only the more remarkable to me. He carried a
very large head on a very small body: in his big pale face were set
vivacious dark eyes, which rolled and twinkled and gathered into
their dancing orbit all the nascent gaiety of the household. Everybody laughed, at him or with him – somehow it was all the same.
He smoked an incredible number of Russian cigarettes: smoked a
half-dozen while he was in the bath in the morning so that it was
always advisable to get there before him. There was no difficulty
in that on most days, for he did not come down to breakfast.
Only suddenly, without warning, he would be up betimes. But
generally it was about ten o'clock before we saw the smoke
filtering out of the bath-room window.

Larrouy was also a man of immense physical strength and
endurance. He could bend the stout iron of a croquet-hoop in
his hands; it seemed not to matter to him whether he had any
meals at all; he appeared to feed on cigarette smoke. And one
day he told me a story – he was a submarine-commander – of a

voyage in an early type of French submarine from Toulon to Bizerta in a Mediterranean storm. Everybody was sick almost to death: vomit was everywhere. The crew slipped on it, rolled into it, and slept where they rolled. The stench was inhuman. Larrouy himself had barely strength to navigate the ship. His cigarettes, and his own inability to sleep, enabled him to endure. When they got to Bizerta, more than half the ship's company had to be carried ashore straight to hospital. 'I slept – two whole nights and days,' said Larrouy.

But beside all that, he was a writer. He had already published two novels over his pen-name, René Milan, which was afterwards to become famous, even in England, during the war as that of the author of the amazing narrative: *L'Odysée d'un Transport Torpillé*. But the novels he was writing now were queer and powerful imaginative stories of the world of pre-history, of great Asian movements and migrations. He gave me one to read, and I was deeply impressed by it. He looked through the dozen French books I had brought with me – French 'symbolists', Rimbaud and Mallarmé amongst them, with whom I was trying to grapple, chiefly because men whom I knew at Oxford appeared to think highly of them – and he asked me the point-blank question concerning Mallarmé: 'How much did I understand?' I had to confess that it was very little indeed. 'How could you? Even a Frenchman, even a very intelligent one, doesn't understand much of Mallarmé.'

Then he pressed home the attack. If he, a naval officer on active service, whose impulse was to use his scanty spare-time in writing. nevertheless spent all his brief leave in England in order to learn the language, why did not I, who was not yet caught in the toils of a profession, spend my holidays in France? It was, he plainly but politely suggested, mere dilettantism for me to pretend to read the ultra-modern French poets, when I could not sustain a conversation with a French railway-porter. 'I am strange to you, am I not? A queer fish?' I nodded. 'But think how strange you are to me – how strange is all this!' And

he waved a hand to include me, and Waterloo, and the countryside. 'Have you never thought how strange may be, to someone,
all these things you take for granted? Believe me, *everything* is
strange. One must know it. Why do I like to imagine things' –
he put his hand on his own book – 'so remote and far away?'
I shook my head. 'Because, when I live in that world, I can feel
the strangeness of this one – all of it – not England merely, or Indo-
China – but my own country, my own profession, my own self.'

That was how Larrouy would talk to me. Sometimes my
fancy would shape him to me as a queer creature from another
world, like one of Wells' Selenites or Martians. His great head, his
omnivorous intellectual curiosity, and the impression he made of
being an explorer long since inured to the absence of the warm
atmosphere of affection which was the breath of life to me,
produced in me an eerie feeling, almost of personal hostility,
towards him. Yet I liked him: I could not resist his gaiety. But I
wanted to resist his arguments. I wanted, still more, to resist
him. He was trying to uproot me altogether. Yet that was unfair
to him. He had no deliberate design of doing so. He was simply
Maurice Larrouy, speaking his mind to a convenient Englishman. That I felt his attitude alarming and himself a menace was
due to my own limitations, and I suppose also to some vague and
unconscious desire to overcome them.

When he departed I kept up a correspondence with him, in
which he for his part continually urged me to make a long stay in
France. Like a good Frenchman, he held that Paris was indeed
the centre of the civilized world; and he offered me the services
of a shipmate of his, who now had a shore job in the Ministry of
Marine, to find me a cheap and decent room and generally show
me the ropes. There seemed to be no escape. Reluctantly I
wrote, gratefully accepting his offer for the Christmas vacation.
Reluctantly, because it meant for me yet another plunge into the
unknown. Never, I believe, was there a man less avid of new
experiences than I. I have now, as I had then, a truly formidable
inertia, which tells me that my one desire is to be left undisturbed.

It is only by a process of cheating myself, that I can, of my own free will, uproot myself even momentarily – by making arrangements so long before that the future dislocation is unreal, and then gradually being drawn into a position such that the pain of breaking the engagement is greater than the pain of keeping it. It was not at all that I did not want to go to Paris: I did. More exactly, what I wanted was the experience of having gone to Paris: what I did not want was to pay the price of the experience. In such a connection, it is ridiculous, I know, to talk of the price of the experience. But that very ridiculousness is an index of my idiosyncrasy. I knew I should have to pay a very real price for the experience.

Once I had agreed to go, and settled the date, my whole existence was tense with the new decision. The coming event cast a shadow before. Hardly a day passed but it struck me with a kind of terror that I was a whole day nearer to my doom. More subtly, my centre of gravity semed to shift; my whole polarization to change. With a speed almost sickening, I lost all grip on my work at Oxford. If I worked at all, it was now in a kind of dream. At the touch of this new influence the pattern and the certainty which had filled my life at Waterloo dislimned and dissolved.

But there had been an intervening time – the summer of that year – when the new poison was working obscurely, and I was merely neutral. Not that I knew it. When I met my sweetheart at Oxford station towards the end of the summer term, I was unconscious that anything had changed. The intoxication had gone, but not the certainty. And it was for the purpose of making money enough to buy myself a really good hunter, that I applied to the Appointments Board for a tutorship for part of the summer. Since my qualifications were now, theoretically, of the best, I got a good tutorship without difficulty. My temporary duty was to help Lord Charles Hope get through Responsions, at a salary which was more than generous.

Unwittingly, I secured the post on false pretences. For I was asked by the Appointments Board whether I played golf; and, since I had dabbled with a nondescript collection of golf clubs at school and at Aldborough, I cheerfully replied that I did. Had I foreknown that I should be required to instruct in Latin prose one who was to be among the most famous of Oxford golfers, I would have bitten out my tongue rather than make a claim so fantastic. All that could be said for me was that I was so ignorant about golf that I did not even know that I knew nothing about it. Twenty years later I tried to play golf seriously, and by dint of inhuman concentration – possible to me only because I was using golf as another man might use whisky, to stop myself from thinking – I succeeded at the end of a year in reducing my handicap from infinity to 12. Then, for the first time, I really knew what I had done, twenty years before, when I offered myself as a golf-playing classical tutor to the future amateur champion of France.

However, if Lord Charles Hope was disappointed in me, he concealed it perfectly. And, indeed, even had I been a golfer, he would have no need of me at North Berwick, where I first went to tutor him. But such was my ignorance that I only vaguely perceived the sanctity of that famous links and only dimly appreciated the excellence of the play I witnessed. True I was impressed by the extraordinary contortions of Ben Sayers while he was willing, by some compulsive ritual of his own, a long putt into the hole; and I was impressed in a quite different way by walking a round in the company of A. J. Balfour. He had just given, or was just about to give, the Romanes Lecture at Oxford, on some question of aesthetics; to which I listened, less in intelligent appreciation of his speech, than in childish wonder at the fact that he was speaking, so far as I could tell, quite extempore. In those days, this struck me as a prodigious achievement, well-nigh superhuman; and I was distinctly surprised to find him human and affable on the golf-links. Though he played with intense concentration, he asked me some questions about what I was doing at Oxford, and what I proposed to do afterwards. To this last question I found myself saying that I did not know.

But more important in my history than these chance contacts with celebrities was my voyage of discovery in a rank of society quite new to me. For the first time in my life, I was living in a great house – and Hopetoun House with its view across the Forth is, in my memory, a very great house indeed; and I was overwhelmed by the sheer opulence of it all. That there should be so many rooms, each perfectly appointed, was a standing wonder to me. But I kept my end up with a brave assumption of insouciance. Indeed, I was surprised and gratified by the ease with which I adapted myself to my new environment. I positively enjoyed being valeted, and my only concern was that the valet should think my clothes worthy of his attention. Still more did I enjoy a life in which every meal had its own particular pleasure for me; where eating was not a mere necessity, but a delight enhanced by its own satisfying ritual. It was natural, instead of being a nuisance, to dress for dinner; it would have been crude and clumsy, somehow ungrateful and boorish, to do otherwise.

The ease with which I entered into this way of life, the pleasure I took in it, set me idly wondering sometimes in bed at night. Since it was so easily taken for granted by others that I was used to it, what, I speculated, would have been the effect had I really been brought up in it, had I never known anything different? The only conclusion I could come to was that I should have become a very convincing member of the aristocracy. Accordingly, I came to that conclusion: nor did I ever change it. And it comforted me greatly. It put an end, once and for all, to the sense of a possibility of intrinsic social inferiority which had haunted me for many years. Next after this, came a genuine acknowledgment of the comeliness of this way of life. These manners were good manners, not in a conventional, but in an absolute sense, and though, no doubt, it seemed to those who were born to them that they were only possible on a basis of wealth, it was not so in fact. I could imagine these manners 'in widest commonalty spread'.

But most of all what I gained was the secure conviction that I could move quite freely and naturally in any walk of society. That I was very reserved was part of my elemental structure: I was equally reserved, equally unforthcoming, whatever my surroundings. Only a happy accident could break down the barriers behind which my essential self was hidden, or imprisoned; and, as Waterloo had shown (though I did not clearly realize it then), when the barriers did go down, there was no essential self to emerge. What I really was, was something infinitely plastic and suggestible, with no 'determined character'. Either I was on the defensive, and took the outward colour of my surroundings by the kind of wary accommodation which I had practised for so many years that it was second nature; or, in the rare moments, when my defences were down, I assumed a more intimate colouring, a deeper dye: but neither in it was there anything of my own. To the influence of a H. F. Fox, or a John Thornhill, I was completely receptive: at most I wanted to be what they seemed to want me to be. Without excessive effort, I became that thing; and for a time I was happy in being poured in what I truly believed to be my natural mould. Nor did I ever escape from it of my own free will. All that happened was that this passive self of mine became entangled in another process.

Thus it was with me in the winter of 1910. I was entangled in the process of going to Paris. Maurice Larrouy's friend had engaged a quiet room for me in the Rue Gay-Lussac, overlooking the Luxembourg gardens. The money from my tutorship had dwindled sadly in the effort to pay some debts. Instead of the £50 I had planned to take with me, I had perhaps half; and I was determined that it should last me the full seven weeks of my vacation. Therefore I would live like a hermit, and read Bergson in his native city. What precisely was the point of my going to Paris if I lived like a hermit, I did not ask myself. It was so natural and comfortable to me to lapse back into the hermit state that any such untoward question would have been promptly suppressed.

I arrived at the Gare St. Lazare in the very early morning. It was barely dawn when I and my luggage in a clop-clopping *fiacre* trickled past the Arc de Triomphe, and were shot out into the arms of a blinking and dishevelled red-headed garçon at the hôtel. At one stroke my store of French had dwindled to a conditioned reflex of 'Merci, non', or 'Non, merci'. I felt horribly exposed; and my one desire was to scuttle, like a hermit crab, into another shell. It was 'Non, merci' to the garçon's offer of breakfast, though I was famished; and to the very end of my seven weeks in Paris I never once had breakfast in the hotel. Later, indeed, it was for economy's sake; but for the first two weeks it was for pure terror. Yet, so paradoxical was my condition that I looked forward with dread to the arrival in Paris of an Oxford friend who knew Paris pretty well and had promised to spend the last two weeks with me. I wanted to be alone; yet I hated to be alone. Such was I.

After some hours of Bergson, I ventured out of the fastness of my little room with its desk and its bookcase. The first major event was getting a meal. Restaurants at 1 franc 25 were plentiful in those days, and after wandering up and down the Boulevard St. Michel I chose the nearest one. Once in it, I congratulated myself, for instead of the carafe of *vin rouge*, they offered a *demi* of milk. This appealed to me as being the better investment. Economy was a mania with me at the moment. I forthwith conceived the idea that one substantial meal a day was sufficient. In the evening only, I would dine at the restaurant, for what I needed besides I would go to a Café Biard where a black coffee cost 10 centimes and a white one 15.

Further, since I observed that ten per cent discount was given if you bought dinner tickets in a solid block, I invested in a block, and congratulated myself that I was sure of the one meal a day to the end. It was like making preparations to stand a siege.

With sinister rapidity I established a routine. In the morning I rose at eight, went for half an hour's walk, lingered over my fourpenny breakfast (two white coffees and two *croissants*) at the Café Biard, till the garçon had given my room its lick and promise; after which I returned to struggle with the pages of *L'Evolution Créatrice* till midday. More coffee and more *croissants*. Then I began a systematic solitary exploration of Paris on foot, or by the Métro. Never by any chance did I take a bus or a tram: that meant speaking to the conductor, whereas one could get anywhence, anywhither on the Métro in unbroken silence. I returned home at dusk and worked on till dinner-time: then, ravenously hungry, I ate all that my ticket allowed, and wandered off to the Café d'Harcourt. It took me days to scrape up the courage to advance from an outside table to one within the body of the café; and, indeed, my first visit there ended in a catastrophe which nearly scared me away for ever. I had to pay for my *café crême*, thirty-five centimes. The waiter put down my change. It never entered my head that I was supposed to tip him. I gathered up the fifteen centimes and rose to go.

Suddenly, behind my back, came a voice like the last trump, yet ending in a hiss.

'Et la ser*vice*?'

The words were, and still are, printed in my brain, but my mind was too stunned to respond. I stared at him, and felt the blush flame over me. I began to stammer: 'Je ne comprends pas.' The answer was a still more menacing:

'La ser*vice!*'

Then I understood. I fumbled in my pocket for a fifty-centime piece and hurried away, head bent, heart thumping, and sick, sick, sick.

God knows, if I were to draw a truly faithful picture of my life at this time and for years to come, how many such incidents I should have to chronicle; and that, not for their number but for the inordinate impression they made upon me. I am sure that my conscious experience in these years was altogether dominated by an abject terror of the minor cruelties of mankind. Why, why, I asked myself, should that waiter have spoken to me as though I wanted to filch his *sou*? Why should that shopkeeper look at me as though I would steal his goods? And I could find no answer. I knew, quite lucidly, that the attitude was not held towards *me* in particular. It was general as the casing air. Man's inhumanity to man had been a commonplace for countless years; and the inhumanities which oppressed me to a weary desperation were so trivial and familiar that only an abnormal person would call them by that name. Yet they caused in me a reaction that came near to physical nausea; they convulsed my being.

I suppose that, very slowly, I have grown more accustomed to this human barbarity; and it may be true, as I believe it is true, that there is less of it in England than elsewhere: in England, it seems to me, it is still, in the main, the natural approach to a fellow-man to regard him as a human being, to give him as it were the benefit of the doubt. I had not realized that distinction or its causes in those days; I was abnormal enough to experience life even in England as one incessant wincing from small unkindnesses: but in Paris casual unkindness was magnified into a substrate of sheer brutality. And it was terrifying to me.

Yet I was fascinated by it. It stood, clear-cut and menacing, for Life. So long as I could escape the clutch of its fearful cogwheels I held my breath and watched it in self-torturing delight. With an instinctive avoidance of every contact I wandered the streets, or sat in the cafés, detached and precarious. I began to divide my evenings between the Café d'Harcourt and the Closerie des Lilas, where the left-bank *littérateurs* foregathered round Paul Fort. With his big black hat, his black cravat, and his high-buttoned jacket, he dressed the part so well that I could not believe in him at all. And the more I listened to their conversation, the more glumly I grew convinced that there was no essential difference between the attitude of these men and that of Paris as a whole. They were only fancy-dress 'rebels'; but fundamentally as egoistic, and mercenary, as reverent towards the cash-nexus as the bourgeois whom it was their profession to despise. Not but what I was excited when I watched them handing round among themselves the first number of their new magazine, *Vers et Prose*, of which an impressive advertisement was gummed on to the big mirror, with a list of contributors which included everybody known to me by name among the advanced writers of France, and also the names: Havelock Ellis, Arthur Symons, and Arthur Ransome. I could conceive no more eminent distinction than to be one of the English writers in such a catalogue. But I was rather alarmed than gratified when a young Frenchwoman, who belonged more to the fringe than the centre of the company, tried to open up a conversation with me, and finally produced out of a big handbag which seemed to hold a dozen or more, a volume of poems which she insisted on inscribing to me there and then.

In truth, I vastly preferred the Café d'Harcourt, provided I could avoid the eye of my enemy the waiter. I knew by now that the correct tip for a 35c. *café crême* was one sou, and by listening sedulously I had added the correct names and prices of a dozen other drinks to my repertoire. That was all I needed to enable me to spend hour after hour in the evening in the inside of the café, watching and listening. My observation had taught me that one drink an hour was perceptibly above the average; with that consumption, and a halfpenny tip for each drink, I was fairly paying my way. My basis thus assured – so that I could stay from nine to midnight for 1 franc 25 – I settled down to become a solitary habitué.

CHAPTER X

MARGUÉRITTE

I LIKED the Café d'Harcourt chiefly because of the women there. It was at that time the chief resort of the *petites femmes* of the Left Bank, with the Panthéon and the Pascal close behind. But once at least every evening, you might be sure, each one of them would look in at the d'Harcourt. Within a fortnight I knew them all by sight. Some I liked, some I didn't; but the greater part of them were pretty. Big hats and muffs were the mode that year, and some of the faces they framed were charming indeed. Imperceptibly, I became something of a connoisseur. I had so much opportunity to study their ways, that there was sure to come the moment with each of them when I caught a glimpse of her as it were off-stage; and gradually I came to the conclusion that two or three of them were never on the stage. They were just natural. That was a conundrum to my conventional moral sense; and a positive problem when I set it alongside my conviction of the fundamental brutality of Paris. It is something of a paradox to me still.

But, as ill luck would have it, it was not one of the natural ones who fastened on me. Far from it. She was, I suppose, attractive enough in her own way, but she was perpetually on the stage, in a walking-on part, of which she made more than the uttermost. Had I been a man of any courage towards women, I should have turned aside her point-blank question: Would I pay for a coffee? And I would gladly have paid for a dozen coffees for her, if only she would have drunk them out of my company. But I would rather have bitten out my tongue than said or hinted this. So she settled herself on me. And I began to be sorry for the very thing I chiefly disliked in her – her naive and incessant professional vivacity; her pitiful determination to impress herself on the awareness of everybody.

If she dropped her bag, or overset her glass, or trod on someone's foot, she made twice as much commotion about it as anybody else; and she *would* keep swinging her leg. Desperate indeed was my desire to say to her: 'For God's sake, sit *still*, be *quiet*! Don't be a little *goose*! That's not the way to attract a man. And, for heaven's sake, don't run away with the idea you have attracted me. I am probably the one man in this café at this moment who would put up with your tricks: not because I can put up with them, but simply because I happen to be the only man here who hasn't learned to say "no" to a woman – even to a woman like you.' I kept that harangue to myself; and soon I was half-inured to the ordeal of sharing the attention she attracted. What did it really matter, anyhow? When you have been sitting silent in a café three mortal hours, the thought comes very near that nothing matters at all.

After all, who was I to put on airs, and read sermons? If she was a silly little goose, probably it wasn't her fault. And if, as I sadly surmised, I was the only man in the café who would pay for her drinks and her sandwich – why, her luck was in. I bore her no grudge. Only, for all my rapidly-developing toler-ance, I couldn't help hoping devoutly that she wouldn't make a habit of me. I drew the line at having a claim staked out in me by Yvonne: well before that point in fact, for I was polite but firm in my answer to her final question: 'Tu veux coucher avec moi?'

My French rose memorably to the occasion.

'Si tu veux boire avec moi, *bon*: mais coucher, *non*. Je suis sérieux.'

But though I had cleared that particular hurdle, and appeased her hurt vanity by offering to stand her a dinner on the following night in the d'Harcourt (which would cost me the price of twenty dinners at my own place) she had posed me a question that would not leave me alone.

Up to that moment I had had no desire to sleep with any woman; and certainly I had no desire, at that moment, to sleep with her. No doubt I was virgin and sexually timid; but I did not suffer from suppressed desire. Such adolescent fever as I had endured was overpast by the time I went to Oxford, and there the crudity of most of the bawdy talk I heard was so alien that it aroused no response in me. And, though I took good care not to show it, I was secretly bewildered by the fact that some of the men whom I genuinely liked were occupied with casual and venal amours. It was just rather mysterious to me; and I explained their behaviour to myself as a form of bravado, not essentially different from my own in pretending that I was quite *au fait* and at ease in a conversation about such affairs. But I could not account for the difference: which simply was that I found in myself a quite invincible reluctance to such experiences.

Maybe, it was the same old disposition in me; maybe, I wanted the experience, and did not want to pay the price of it. But since the price of it was precisely a plunge into that same underlying brutality of life from which I shrank so fearfully, this explains nothing. I wanted the experience of physical love; but I did not want the experience of venal fornication. Perhaps the distinction was not clearly present to my mind, but it certainly was to my feeling; and no doubt, had I been able to imagine the possibility of genuine physical love both apart from marriage and apart from venality, I should have known what I did want. Certainly, conventional morality had no hold on me whatever. Oxford had given me glimpses enough of the engaged young man writing to his fiancée on Sunday after picking up a whore in Piccadilly on Saturday. This kind of working compromise made no appeal to me. If I had to eat my peck of dirt (which I hardly admitted) I did not intend to eat it in that form.

But, in Paris, the situation had subtly changed. There was, to me, a world of difference between the d'Harcourt and the Leicester Lounge. At least on the Boulevard St. Michel there was the illusion of some sort of camaraderie between the woman and the man. Whether it was only an illusion, I could not judge; but I felt it was not. And I tried to ponder over the strange contrast between London, where the brutality shrieked aloud in sexual things, yet in the ordinary commerce of life was mitigated or concealed; and Paris, where the fundamental brutality was so apparent in the ordinary commerce of life, yet sexual things were relatively humane. Even Yvonne's 'Tu veux coucher avec moi?' was somehow clean and straightforward; one wasn't put to shame by it, or by replying to it, as one was in turning away from the nod of solicitation in Leicester Square. Above all, it was not furtive. It put an honest question, honestly.

Though I was quite convinced that I did not want to sleep with Yvonne, I knew that my refusal was not determined by some really irrelevant consideration – such as my loathing of the furtive sordidness of venal amours in London. I didn't want to sleep with Yvonne, because I didn't want to sleep with *Yvonne*. She had had no charms for me. But at the same time I recognized that if Yvonne had been somebody else, with charms for me, and had put that same simple question to me, my resistance would have been far less peremptory. It was a genuine realization. As the clear air of Paris had sharpened my blunted sense of outline, and made walking down a commonplace street a positive delight instead of a dull nothingness, so it had cleared the mists away from my own sight of myself. I knew myself a little better than I did before.

But I felt rather glum at the prospect of having to give Yvonne that dinner; glummer still in the middle of it, when, half a bottle of some near-champagne inside her, she was behaving more like a little goose than ever; and at a positive nadir of glumness when I observed that the man of the couple who had now taken the table beside us was English. As a total stranger, a sort of man from the moon, I didn't particularly mind being involved in the antics of Yvonne – perching herself on my knee, and addressing me as '*mon petit Anglais*' in ringing tones for all the café to hear; but to be implicated in this exhibition with one of my own countrymen for the interested spectator was intolerable; particularly intolerable, because I liked the look of this English-man, with his rakish bowler-hat, his blue collar, his keen shaven face, and his fresh bow-tie. I couldn't make out what he was; but he was certainly not a business-man, and one thing I knew immediately, that he was a man whose good opinion I shouldn't care to lose. Naturally, with this added inhibition, I became more boring still – if that were possible – to Yvonne; and she soon began wandering round the café, making a noisy nuisance of herself. I seized the opportunity of paying the bill and making some remark to the Englishman. We drifted into further conversation; and before my head was clear enough to know what I was really doing, I found myself plunged into an exposition of Bergson's distinction between Time and Duration. My neighbour was not an Englishman, after all, but a Scot: and a painter to boot. His companion was a buxom and charming woman, with a fresh complexion, and smiling eyes of periwinkle blue: she was an American painter. Whether she was interested in our conversa-tion, I don't remember: in fact I doubt whether my part in it was very coherent. But it interested F., and before we said good-bye he asked me to call at his studio and see his painting, which he believed to be somehow related to Bergson's philosphy. But I lost the address he gave me.

I was done with Yvonne; not more than Yvonne had done with me, when I refused point-blank to go home with her. For one ugly moment I thought she was going to make a scene outside the café: so I thrust a louis into her hand, and fairly ran. Better be a mug than face the music of *spretae injuria formae*. But I made a twofold vow: first, that I would have nothing more, of any sort, to do with Yvonne; and second, that I would not capitulate to my timid impulse to forsake the d'Harcourt for ever, for fear of meeting her. This was for me a strange accession of courage; but I could not admire myself for it. The real cause why I refused to be scared away from the d'Harcourt was that I had become really interested in one of the girls whom I have described as 'just natural'. She was one of a pair who generally appeared together and appeared to be rather attached to one another. They were among the rarer visitors: one was a good five or six years older than the other, who particularly attracted me and who, I guessed, was certainly not more than twenty. She was the taller; she had gay brown eyes and was very distinct among her colleagues by the fact that she did not wear a big hat, but a little black velvet one, with a bunch of cherries dangling about her ear. I liked her. But it never entered my head to get into conversation with her, and she never noticed me: or so I thought. Generally she sat with two Frenchmen, one a rather debonair fellow with a silky brown beard and a pleasant way of wearing his overcoat like a cape; the other a younger man of the type for which a young Englishman finds it hard to make due allowance. The silky beard, in its phase of incipience, is an unpleasant thing; beside it, mere stubble is impressive. That, of course, is the merest British prejudice. There was a time in Rome when the clean-shaven ones were the effeminates, and the *barbati senes*, who growled at the introduction of the Grecian razor, were the hearts of oak. So I was unfair to this young man; but I could not help being pleased that the girl with the cherries was always teasing him.

Then, for some days, I did not see her again. But her two cavaliers came every night, and the younger man took the opportunity of an upset glass, for which he civilly insisted on paying, to enter into conversation with me. He had sized me up correctly as an Englishman, and, as he very frankly explained, he wanted to practise his English, which was rather worse than my French. So we made a bargain that, if we happened to be in the café together, I would talk nothing but English to him for half an hour, and he would talk nothing but French to me for the next half hour. Whereupon Silky Beard announced that he wanted to come into the arrangement. That suited me well, for it gave me the freedom to listen carefully to two Frenchmen chattering together, and the right to pull them up at any phrase I did not understand. And, above or beneath all this, I hoped it would give me the chance of meeting Cherry-hat naturally.

It did; but not for a long while, or what seemed a long while to me. Probably it was less than a week; for I remember that it was on New Year's Night that I actually spoke to her. That night the inside of the café was cleared between 10 and 11 o'clock to be made ready for those who could pay to celebrate the *réveillon*. We three could not; so we began to wander aimlessly up and down the Boulevard, looking at the stalls, and wondering where we could find a tolerable café that was not given over to expensive suppers. Up and down, up and down we went: till I was hungry enough to purchase a deceptive piece of ginger-bread from a stall. It tasted like plastic sawdust – and the taste will remain with me till my dying day, for it was still in my mouth when I first spoke to Marguéritte. We had stopped to listen to the ballad-singer who used to fix his song-sheets to the railings of the Musée de Cluny. It was beside those railings that I spoke to Marguéritte. She was walking up the Boulevard, with the cherries bobbing in her hat, and her hands tucked in an astrakhan muff. Silky Beard hailed her by her name. She paused bewildered in the crowd; then she saw him.

'C'est vous?' she said to him. 'Et vous?' to his companion. But there was something faintly mocking in her voice and smile. And then to me: 'Bon soir, monsieur!' as I raised my hat.

My two companions wanted to detain her. One put his hand on her arm. But she was bent on escaping. I could not hear what they were saying to her; but she was evidently vexed, from the scraps I caught of what she was saying.

'Mais je vous dis, j'ai été malade . . . Non, je ne veux pas . . . Parceque ça m'em*bête* . . .' Then, half-relenting: 'Je serai au café, peut-être demain.' Unexpectedly she turned to me. 'Vous y serez?' I said I would. 'Alors, à demain soir.' Then finally to me: 'Au revoir, monsieur!'

I needed to be not only a better linguist, but another man than I was, to be sure of the nuance there. I would have liked to believe that the 'Alors' meant because of me. But never, in my wildest moments, have I ever been able to persuade myself of things like that; I have always been taken by surprise when I have discovered that a woman has a liking for me. My instinctive presupposition has always been that if I like a woman, the woman will not like me. It is just the same to-day, even though I have to confess that my uniform experience has been that whenever I have liked a woman it has always turned out that she has liked me. But that experience makes not the faintest difference to my expectation of not being liked by any woman I like. And, when I was twenty-one, the idea that Marguéritte said 'Alors' because of me, would have been quite fantastic. It was more than enough that she was going to be there.

And there she was; and there was I: and there were the other two. I have no memory of what we talked of. My feelers were out to discover the situation; and I was quickly convinced that she was not particularly fond of either of them. I felt that I had in her sight quite as good a claim to be sitting with her as they had. I do not know what happened then. But suddenly, there was only one woman in the world for me; and all I wanted was the knowledge that there was only one man in the world for her, and that it was I. That was *all* I wanted, veritably all. And while I was in that condition existence became a blur to me, with sudden moments when our eyes caught one another, and it seemed to me that I saw reflected in her eyes what I felt, warm, surging, unutterable and sad, in my own heart. Sad: yes, I was strangely and mysteriously sad; and the praeternatural sparkle in her gay brown eyes, when they caught mine at such moments, was the shining of a tear. *Amor: pondus.*

Verily, the weight of love bore on us then. But I did not know it. I only knew that in the midst of the laughing and the talk this warm oppressive weight would surge up suddenly and choke me when her eyes caught mine: and I could say nothing, but only turn my head away. Then someone – not I – would say to her:

'Tu es triste, ce soir?'

And I would hear, from far away, her answer:

'Mais oui . . . je ne sais pas ce que j'ai . . .'

And that would be a sad-sweet music, terribly sad, terribly sweet, echoing in my heart and bursting through my body: so that I would go back to my room, weak and heavy-laden, aching with the burden of I knew not what – promise and menace in one.

I hardly spoke to her: I could not speak. Even if there had been an opportunity, I could not have spoken. But one night we were sitting together, the four of us, in a corner of the café behind the door, and I was trying to keep up a sprightly conversation, when a rose-seller came in, and thrust her pink and sweet-smelling bunch between us. I woke out of my dream. I chose three of the loveliest half-open buds, and gave them to Marguéritte, brusquely almost, for I could not trust myself to look at her. 'I love roses,' she said and made as though to pin them on to her fur; but there was no pin. So I took the little gold pin – my only piece of jewellery – out of my collar and handed it to her. She looked at it, and gave it back to me.

'Oh, ça, non! C'est de l'or, vous savez.'

'Oui, je le sais: c'est pourquoi je vous la donne.'

'Si je la prends, je la garderai – toujours.'

'C'est ce que je veux.'

She pinned the roses at her neck.

That night I asked her to dine with me the next day. There was no question now of an expensive dinner; I took it for granted that she would be content to share my dinner-tickets. She was. Every evening I waited for her at a little café next my restaurant, and we drank a cheap apéritif together before we dined; after dinner we sat in the d'Harcourt together till close on midnight, when we walked together to the door of the house where she lodged, near the Sorbonne, and said 'Good night'. Until we met my day was heavy with anxiety; while we were together the evening was heavy with the sense of the parting to come. The even tenor of my life was completely shattered: the reality changed into two strange and different dreams – the dream when I was alone, and the dream when I was with her: hostile, irreconcilable dreams, yet both unhappy. I lived in a perpetual fever. All my native sense of insecurity was intensified a thousandfold. Not that I thought of what was to happen; I was incapable of thinking. I simply felt that in some strange incalculable way all my defences had been torn away, and I was exposed, utterly naked – to what? To life, to misery.

An evening came when Marguéritte was not at the rendez-vous. Since she had warned me that, if ever she failed, I was not to worry, but to go on to the d'Harcourt, I hurried through my dinner and went there. I watched the clock go round in a fever-dream. Suddenly, out of the dream, her friend Simone entered the café and came straight to me, and whispered:

'Marguéritte est malade . . . Elle veut vous voir . . . tout de suite.'

I hurried away, stopped for an instant to buy a bunch of the same pink roses, entered the big door for the first time, and groped my way up the stairs. She had a little room sub-let from someone else's flat. I knocked and entered.

A tiny oil-lamp gave a dim yellowish light, so that I could hardly see her, till I sat by the side of her bed. 'I wondered whether you would come,' she said.

'How should I not come, when you are ill?'

'You love me, then?'

'Oh, Marguéritte!'

'Come close to me then!'

How strange and faraway and achingly near and unaccountable it seems! I did not want to come close to her; I wanted to stay as I was, sitting by her bedside, holding her hand, feeling each separate finger. But since she would, I must. So I lay, in my overcoat as I was, on top of the bed beside her. After a little while, she turned away from me, sobbing.

'You don't love me.'

'But, Marguéritte . . .'

'Then why don't you want me?'

God in Heaven, how could I answer that question? I did not know, I do not know. She was lovely, she was desirable, and – if the word has a meaning – I loved her completely: but I did not want her. And if I had been asked what it was I wanted of her, I could only have answered: to be with her for ever.

It had not entered my head, egoist that I was, that she might have another thought than mine; and so naive was I that it did not, even now, occur to me that her illness might be a ruse. Nor would it ever have occurred to me, unless she had told me so, many days after. But now I did realize that she was asking me to prove that I did love her. It was strange to me that this should be the proof. I had lost my bearings now. All I knew was that she would be intolerably hurt, if I did not respond to her desire.

In an agony of self-surrender, I slipped off my clothes and lay in the bed beside her. Her sobbing eased, and my separateness melted away. Then it seemed I was enveloped in her tenderness. All that I had seen in her gay, brown eyes – the candour, the simplicity, the joy, the sadness – was now incarnate in her body. The warm and tender darkness swallowed me up.

Then I was called back out of the darkness, by her whisper: 'Tu es heureux?' I could not answer; I could only hold her close to me. 'Tu n'es pas triste?' I could only kiss her. Happiness, sadness – where and what were they? I was what I was not. I was renewed and reborn; but I was also naked and exposed, so that I must cling to her to cover me. And this she knew; with her body she cherished the shrinking new-born shrinking me, and her lips felt after words. 'Moi, je suis tellement heureuse . . . et j'aï tellement envie de pleurer.'

Such was Marguéritte, and such was I. Whether it was cowardice in me, who could with more courage and less fear have borne the burden, or whether it was indeed, as it at last appeared to me, a situation without an issue in which I was involved, I cannot tell. But the moment came, after months of feverish endeavour to find some way for both of us, when we parted. But it is not true to say we parted. I had not the courage to part from her; I simply ran away. Even at that moment my only desire was the former simple one – to be with her for ever. If I could have seen my way to even the barest livelihood, I would have married her. And the barest livelihood would have been enough: for she was essentially a simple country girl who would have worked and been happy without any luxury at all. But it was not in her destiny, nor mine.

For I had nothing. Apart from my scholarship and exhibitions at Oxford I was completely penniless; and, unless I could stick the course and take a degree, I could hope for nothing. I knew no aptitudes in myself that fitted me for any occupation. All my plans of a career had now dissolved into air: with them, my Cotswold sweetheart and Waterloo were now swept into the irrevocable past. Oxford itself was merely a strange and cynical dream – a ghostly place whither I must return in order to remain alive. And there was no one whom I could tell of the mysterious thing that had happened to me, and suddenly cut off all the last thin threads that bound me to my kind. How could I return to the Thornhills now, how could I even write to them? What could I say? How could I explain why I could not return? I dared not tell them the truth; and I could not tell them a lie. There must be silence between us, for ever. Yet how many times, even now, when I journey across the Cotswold country, have I paused, with my heart and mind in a sick tumult, staring at the signpost that points me towards Waterloo! A dream signpost, a dream road, swinging sheer across the gulf of years. I drive along it, I halt, I turn again. It cannot be.

What foolish, sentimental exaggeration! Was I the first poverty-stricken young Englishman to fall hopelessly in love with a *petite femme* in Paris? I was not. But if there had been ten thousand before me, what difference would that have made to me? *Es ist eine alte Geschichte;* true. But truer far the rest of Heine's verse. The one is a tale; the other is experience: and the experience was mine, was me. I know, only too well – for even the memory twenty-three years after tears me in two – in what a sick and aching fever I now lived. I could not exist apart from Marguéritte; yet with her I felt an abyss of foreboding under my feet. I dared not really think of the future, yet I was incapable of living in the moment for fear of the future, which I could not face. Yet I was not always unhappy. With her, I often forgot everything, and believed that somehow a miracle would happen: and then the only agony was that I must return to England, in a little while. Then, I shut out the real future entirely. I was content to see three months ahead: and that was a lifetime.

CHAPTER XI

LEARNING

MARGUÉRITTE had managed to get a job as a sempstress. It was not enough to keep her, even on a starvation level: nor were such jobs intended to enable girls to keep themselves. But she calculated that if I could send her regularly ten shillings a week besides, she could keep going. And I was sure that, in spite of my burden of debts, I could manage that, and yet have enough to return to Paris at Easter. I would stave off my creditors somehow, and scrape together enough to perform my promise. It seemed fantastic and ironical to me even then that if I had had but fifty pounds, I could have made Marguéritte secure for a year. But since fifty pounds was as remote as fifty thousand, I pulled in my belt immediately. Without telling her, I determined that I must, on no account, spend more than a franc a day besides my dinner; and I began to feed on packets of roasted chestnuts, which I found less sustaining than they are reputed to be. By such devices I hoped to have some few pounds in hand, which I could give Marguéritte when the day came for me to leave.

Now that she was at work, my days were all my own. My Oxford friend had arrived. He had been at an art-school some time before, and some of his artist friends lived in Paris. One of these he took me to visit, in an untidy flat, somewhere near the Quai Voltaire. G—— was a strange and brilliant woman, whose psychology was quite outside my range. She must have lived (I now think) in a condition of permanent hysteria due to sexual repression. She was a large and beautiful woman with a heavy, pale face reminiscent of the photograph of Oscar Wilde, which was tucked in her mantel-mirror. Her wit, for all its hysteria, was mordant; and her drawings, which she was always tearing up, had a touch of biting imagination, palpable even to me

She pressed me to come again the next day; and I was only too willing to have another such tea. It was a better meal than I had had for days.

So it came about that I went to see her often. It helped to fill my empty day and my empty belly; and I was naive enough to imagine that I might confide in her. Perhaps I vaguely dreamed that she might help me to the miracle of a livelihood. But far from giving confidences, I received them: or the strange things that served for confidences with her – the narration, pursued through bursts of tears and laughter, of a tense and complex psychological drama, of which the characters – fellow-artists – were completely unknown to me. Or she would overwhelm me with Wilde and Weininger. Of Weininger I knew nothing; of Wilde I had no great opinion, and I let it appear. For that I was deluged with denunciation: I was an ignorant little fool, full of Oxford airs, and completely lacking in knowledge of life. I let the flood go over my head. It was true enough. I did know astonishingly little about life: for instance, I was completely unprepared for such behaviour as hers. I did not say so: but while I silently endured her violent denunciations, I ruminated within myself that I was learning: yes, I was learning. And when the denunciation ended in a sudden outburst of weeping, and I made a clumsy attempt to comfort her, putting my arm about her shoulder, and assuring her that, so far as I could see, life was a horribly painful affair, some little fragment of my mind detached itself, and grinned ironically at the spectacle of myself, with my arm round those broad shoulders, being required to comfort the woman who had spent the last hour deriding my babyish innocence. Yes, I was learning.

The pace of my education was furious. The fever of my love for Marguéritte now became the solid background of a fabulous, phantasmagoric life. Through G——, or apart from G——, I suddenly made a host of new acquaintances. First, the characters of her drama – two of whom turned out to be the artist-philosopher and his friend who had watched my unwilling entertainment of Yvonne; then an Irishman, whom G—— averred to have ten times more genius than 'the lot of us'. Since I myself made no claim to any, it was not quite so impressive as it sounds; but I met him in a café with her and went to see him, at his invitation, in yet another untidy flat. The untidiness was much more evident to me than the genius; but I was interested to hear his cynical account of his experiences with G——. To her I merely reported that I found his genius overrated: for which I suffered another tirade against my ignorance. I endured it patiently. I now had a clue. G—— was the naive one.

Then I was involved with a strange group of men from one of the Russian Baltic provinces – all revolutionaries, all artists. I had watched them in the café a month before, and one of them had tried to speak to me in broken German; since he seemed a nice fellow – he was an enormous man with big blue eyes, a full fortnight's stubble, and an extraordinary cloth-cap – and the point of his speech appeared to be that he had no money, I had lent him a louis. After that I had not seen him again; and had given up my louis for lost. I had no grievance about it. Whatever that blond bear might be, he was not a cadger: probably he had been simply forced to go to earth. But one afternoon on entering the café I was astonished to see someone waving to me wildly. It was Ourits. There they were – he and a half-dozen of his friends – with just so many bottles of white wine on the table before them, and a large quantity of raw eggs. Disconcertingly, Ourits embraced me in a Titan hug that drove the breath out of my lungs, then all his compatriots rose and swept off their hats and I bowed in return, while he made a place for me beside him. With a childlike smile on his big face he dragged an ancestral-looking purse out of his pocket and gave me back my louis. Then, in scraps of French and scraps of German, he explained that the money which he and his friends had been expecting had only arrived that day; that they had come to the café in the hope of finding me; and that they were eating raw eggs because they had been a long while without solid food. Apparently, they lived in a sort of community, and were supported as a group by some semi-revolutionary organization which had, perforce, to put its cultural interests in the foreground. He had brought along with him some numbers of a substantial and beautifully produced magazine which was, I gathered, the organ of their national-cultural movement; and he showed me his own drawings and decorations in it, pausing as he turned the pages to point to an essay or a poem by one of the company, who, when indicated by Ourits' finger – 'grann' poète' – would rise in his seat, sweep off his hat and bow to me. There was something curiously moving in this odd procedure: one could not but be touched to admira-tion by the childlike and religious simplicity of it all. The eyes of the whole company were bent on Ourits and me while he displayed the magazines; and whenever I glanced up, I found one of them looking anxiously at me to see if I had understood. When it was all over, Ourits explained to me that the company desired that he should make a drawing of me, which could be repro-duced in the magazine – 'Ong-glais . . . ami . . . de nott-re pays'. At this they all rose, and drank down a glass of white wine in my honour. 'Ong-glais . . . bon . . . cama-rrade!'

I blushed with pleasure at this royal return for the loan of a louis; and on the morrow made my way to a rabbit-warren of tiny studios in a street with the portentous name of Rue Vercing-é-tor-ix. There I sat to Ourits on the solitary chair in the untidiest room of all. The red-tiled floor had not been cleaned for months; it was covered with a whole stratum of cigarette-ends and ash: and though Ourits' visible belongings were so few that the possi-bilities of disorder which they offered were restricted, one was not conscious of any such limitation. With his few materials he seemed to have achieved an absolute of chaos. But by this time I was prepared for it. If Ourits was content, why should I be troubled? But when he opened the top of his little stove to show me that it was so full of rubbish that it could not be lit, I felt depressed. It never was lit while I was there; and I was glad when my hours of shivering were over, and the drawing was finished.

Save for the cold, it was not tedious. Ourits laboriously told me tale after tale of the rebellion in the Baltic Provinces in 1905, in which he had been involved. He took revolution lightly, in a sense; it was plain to see that he had been baptized in it, in its most brutal forms. 'Fusillé . . . couppy la gorge' came as handy as 'a crack under the jaw' in a conversation in an English pub. I knew, from reading, something of the doings of the Baltic barons, and Ourits made them real to me. His queer combination of childish gentleness and implacable hatred of the Baltic land-owners made a permanent impression on me. I knew that he would not have spared them – no, not one; and that his heart would never be at rest until they were exterminated, like rats. For him, they were outside the pale of humanity altogether: yet, I am sure, he had as warm a heart as any man. And when, years after, the true Revolution came, and I read that the regiments from the Baltic provinces were the most reliable instruments of the Red Terror, I remembered Ourits: and understood.

Yes, I was learning. Through Marguéritte herself I met a young French writer of my own age. When we met, he handed me an elegant card:

M. R—— D——
Secrétaire de Rédaction à la revue
littéraire et artistique
'La Flamme'
Reçoit tous les vendredis de 5 à 7 heures

It impressed me deeply; and I was still more impressed by what I discovered when I paid the visit which he urgently requested to the *rédaction*. At the address (which was a small but elegant flat with no appearance of an office) I found myself plunged in a sort of family party. Whether it was that the invitation had not been seriously meant, or that I was unduly sensitive to the atmosphere of a coterie, I had the feeling that I was an unexpected and not very welcome guest. Since the conversation included me but rarely, I was at leisure to take stock of the situation; and, though I was far from astute in these matters, it was fairly plain to me that my new acquaintance fulfilled a double function. He might well have done, for the duties of *secrétaire de rédaction* were evidently not onerous. But they were doubled by those of *cavaliere servente* to the wife of one of the chief backers of the review. And I could not help speculating whether the review might not really have been the wife's idea, and the real purpose of the enterprise to provide Monsieur R—— D—— with a position in every sense convenient. For it was plain to see that the said backer was a goose: almost the Platonic idea of a *cocu* made corporeal; and equally plain that the whole coterie regarded his literary ambitions and pretensions with open contempt. That the contempt in itself was reasonable I established for myself that evening in the Métro, when I opened the volume of poems with which he had presented me; but the openness of it was singular and trying. The whole situation was cynical French farce, in real life, and I was uncomfortable to be on the stage.

Yes, I was learning. I could see the attractiveness of my new acquaintance. He was, to me, altogether remarkable: a touch of the *voyou*, a touch of the singer at the *caf' concert*, an evident streak of talent – he was (I guessed) the only one of the coterie who had any – and a truly portentous façade of cynicism, were all compactly framed within his dapper clothes. Anything less like a young English man of letters, or my notion of a young French one for that matter, was inconceivable; and I couldn't help admiring the amazing audacity with which he played his part. His cynicism enveloped everybody: if everybody else was contemptuous of the moneyed man, Monsieur R—— D—— was contemptuous not only of him, but of them, and (strangest of all) of the lady as well. But that evidently was not so obvious to the others, or to the lady, as to me. Perhaps that was due to my enforced detachment. But I should hardly have been surprised if suddenly the whole company had combined against him, and shot him out of the window into the gutter. And I suspected that he felt this himself; that he was somehow, though in a totally opposite way, as insecure in life as I was. At any rate, some current of mutual understanding passed between us; and I was left to ponder the problem of my instinctive sympathy for one whose moral code was antipodal to my own.

Yes, I was learning. And above all I learned from my Scottish philosopher-painter. At last I had been to see him and his work. I had appeared at the appointed hour for tea, and was surprised when he opened the door in a dressing-gown, with lather on his face. 'Come in, come in', he said cheerily; and straightway explained that his habit was to go to bed when he wanted to go to bed, and get up when he wanted to get up. His studio was beautiful in itself, and twice as beautiful by the order and precision in which he kept it – his floor, which he took his exercise in polishing when he did get up, reminded me of the deck of a racing yacht; and the contrast between his go-as-you-please habit of life, which was associated in my grooved mind with the bohemian disorder of which I had seen too much, and the austere yet workmanlike perfection of his surroundings, was enthralling to me. I had plenty of time to drink it in, for his shaving took him fully half an hour; and a whole hour must have passed before he was ready to prepare a tea that was exactly congruous with his studio and himself. It consisted simply of tea and brown bread and butter; but both were perfect of their kind: and, here again, the principle was that you went on with both of them until you had really had enough. Every day he went for his loaf – a long thin one, baked in a tin – to a particular shop, because this was the only 'real brown bread' to be had in Paris; and that, with good butter, was real 'fudd'. As he cut the loaf he gathered up the crisp crumbs on his knife and embedded them in the butter of each successive slice, leisurely and carefully. Then he poured his tea off the leaves into a fresh warm teapot and wrapped it in a towel. Then the meal began. I was ashamed of the amount of bread and butter that I ate; but since he insisted that it was my *duty* to go on until I really did not want to eat any more, I gladly obeyed.

F——fascinated me by his singular completeness. He made

no compromises with the world at all. He did not rebel against it; he simply ignored it. He lived in a rhythm of his own, and it was a real rhythm: and I am not surprised that I was impressed. For nothing is more rare than to encounter a man who has the strength to do this thing. I have never met another: though I have known one or two men who would have done it, if they had possessed the strength: men who imagined the condition and found it desirable. But they could not endure the necessary isolation. They needed companionship; or they needed the support of a woman. But whereas they would have envied F—— for his achievement of the condition which they secretly desired, I felt no envy, even while I admired F——, as I came to do, prodigiously. I knew now, with complete certainty, that I was a woman's man; and though I could imagine – on the strength of my new and painful experience – that it might have been better for me if I hadn't been a woman's man, that 'betterness' was purely ideal: it had no relation to any possibility existing in myself. There was that in my very composition which made it inevitable that I should be completely involved with a woman. And I think that it was the sense of this destiny, obscurely emerging into my consciousness, that made my love of Marguéritte so strangely hard to bear: somehow I felt that this warm unbearable anguish was my native element, and now that I had entered it, I should never escape again. Nor did I.

So I looked upon F—— with an admiration the more complete and pure, in that it was untinged with any envy, and unalloyed by any reservation. I knew so well that I could not be like F—— that I was entirely free to rejoice in his perfection. His qualities were to me all positive and all his own: no possibility of judgment – that he might be more of this, or less of that – entered in. Yet my attitude was not one of hero-worship; I did not exaggerate any one of his qualities. For instance, I tried very sincerely to appreciate his recent painting – he was one of the first British painters, if not the very first, to be deeply influenced by the post-Impressionists – but I had no doubt in my own mind that I preferred his earlier work. The possibility that his later development was mistaken was always present to me: but it made not the faintest difference to my admiration. Neither did the fact – and in this province I was a slightly more competent judge – that a good deal of his philosophizing struck me as rather naive. Again, it was his own, and, as he uttered it to me, with his own voice and gesture – 'But look now, Murry lad!' – nonpareil.

A clean strong reality of being was in all he said, and did, and was. Nothing in him astonished or shocked me. When he turned aside to descant on the merits of the chesterfield couch on which I was sitting beside him and remarked, quite casually, that it facilitated 'a hammer lock' for the complete embrace of a woman, it seemed all of a piece with the naturalness and wholesomeness of his brown bread. In all my life I have never met another man from whom such a remark would not have set me quivering – in these matters my reactions are instant and profound – but when F—— spoke it, there was not a tremor in me. I was left with a problem. How was it that he could say such a thing without shocking me, whereas I knew for certain that I could never say such a thing without shocking myself?

I was too thronged by new experiences to disentangle such problems and brood upon them; too raw with innumerable impacts to feel the precise weight of a single one. It was only afterwards that I realized that my friendship with F—— was only less important than my love for Marguéritte in shaping me. This came to me in actual experience as a sense of security in his studio. While I was there, I ceased to feel myself exposed and naked: the nervous nausea, the primitive sensation that I had no stomach for the fight with life, which elsewhere abode with me all my waking hours, would leave me in F——'s company. Looking back, I suppose that this was only another form of the security I had felt with Fox and Thornhill; but this was hidden from me then. It never occurred to me that these men were all of a type – one noble type – men who had, by native or acquired endowment, the courage of themselves. They were sure of their own validity. Whatever they might be in the world's eyes, they did not care. They did not waste a thought or an effort on seeming: they were content to be – precisely what they were. They were solid and whole, made of the same stuff throughout, so that one's first and one's last contact with them was always with the same substance, just as in cutting an oak tree, the saw shears through bark and sapwood and finally the heart of oak; but bark and sapwood and heart are all alike living oak.

That I cleaved to such men is now no wonder to me at all. But the wonder remains that they should have cleaved to me, or been willing that I should cleave to them. They must have seen something in me; but what it was they saw is beyond my comprehension. Or it may be that the heartfelt and spontaneous admiration I felt for them could not but elicit some return. For at least this admiration was, to some degree, what all true admiration must be, namely selfless. I say, to some degree: for obviously on the elemental plane, I was like the vine which clings, or used in Virgil's days to cling, to the elm. I was attaching my weakness and nonentity to their strength and positiveness, in order to live. But I did not know that; and God knows what I should have felt if I had known it; or, more probably, that is one of the things which even God himself cannot know: for I suspect that such self-knowledge and such a condition are incompatible with one another, and that true self-awareness comes only when one is strong enough to bear it. At any rate, in those days and for long years afterwards, my self-awareness was rudimentary. I was conscious merely of admiring them and admiring the whole of them; and every time there was the same shock of delighted surprise, never wholly free of incredulity, to discover that they were a little fond of me.

As with the others, so now with F——. I desired to be what he wanted me to be. And he not merely wanted me to be an 'artist'; but he took it somehow for granted that I was one. Now to be an 'artist', in F——'s thought and language, was not primarily to paint pictures or to write books: it was to have the courage of one's being and one's faculties in the face of the world. Not that F—— ever *said* any such thing, and perhaps such an explicit admission could never have been extorted from him (for in speech, he stood strongly for an exclusive freemasonry of artists in the conventional sense: the artist against the bourgeois), but his unguarded language and his whole behaviour told their own tale. Everybody he was interested in was for him 'an artist'. At first, I thought it just an amusing *tic* of speech in him, to be for ever talking – whether the subject was actually a railway-porter, or a waiter, or a bargee, or even a shipbroker or a solicitor – of 'this artist'. Partly, no doubt, it was a mere habit with F——; but it was a significant habit, and its significance gradually penetrated me. Anyone who was worth remarking or thinking about, any-one who manifested idiosyncrasy or character, anyone who was something, anyone, in short, who put up, consciously or un-consciously, some resistance to the disease of mechanical uniformity, was an 'artist' for F——. With such a one he acknowledged solidarity: they belonged to the same tribe. The effect of this was (though he never formulated it) that he, in his capacity of a painter of pictures, was a representative and peculiar champion of this tribe of men. If he stuck to his guns, and faced without flinching the unpopularity he knew was coming to him through abandoning his earlier and very saleable manner, he was, in his function of advance-guard, somehow clearing the way for future freedom for the tribe. Again, it followed that it was unseemly for an artist to live uncleanly or in disorder: he must embody a natural discipline of his own. His rhythm must be his own rhythm: but rhythm he must have. In other words, art was not a profession. No man could be a professional artist. By profession he might be a painter, a writer, or equally well a boxer or a bootblack; whether he was an artist or not depended on what he was in him-self. Art was a quality of being – an achievement of, or an effort towards integrity.

I repeat that F—— himself did not formulate this doctrine; nor did I then present it to myself in such terms as these. What I could and did see, manifest in him and distinguishing him from other artists whom I met, was that art implied a way of life. It was not some fortuitous faculty tacked on to a man; or if it was, it was one which imposed a moral responsibility upon him. He had to make himself worthy of it. At any rate it was plain that when an artist instinctively made that his aim, as F—— did, then his effort awakened a response in me, quite different from my response to artists of a different kind, who combined talent with irresponsibility. By such people I was bewildered and distressed; in any contact with them my own vitality seemed to be drained away. But with F—— I was always at peace in myself, and when I left him, I always felt enriched.

Enriched, not in understanding, but in being. The contact was immediate. From our long arguments and discussions nothing conclusive ever emerged, nor did I ever know precisely what we were talking *about*. I was obviously being credited by F—— with some sort of arcane philosophic knowledge; and he was particularly respectful when, at his request, I tried to expound the relation between Plato's doctrine of Ideas and Plato's theory of Art. He found sustenance in that, and I was pleased to have made some small return for what he had given me. But I think that, if I had been honest and courageous, I should have told him that it would hardly have seemed as evident to Plato as it did to F—— that his non-representational 'decorative' art was exempt from the condemnation accorded to all *mimêsis*. So far from saying any such thing, I was more than content that F—— should find some relevant meaning in my exposition of Plato; and indeed I was more than half-willing to believe that F—— was right. Since Plato at Oxford did not appear to *mean* anything to anybody, but to be at best a *corpus vile* for the demonstration of principles of logic, it seemed to me better in general, and more satisfying to me in particular, that he should be made to mean something by F—— in Paris, even though that something might be wrong.

One word was recurrent in all our strange discussions – the word 'rhythm'. We never made any attempt to define it; nor even

took any precaution to discover whether it had the same significance for us both. All that mattered was that it had some meaning
for each of us. Assuredly it was a very potent word. For F——
it was the essential quality in a painting or a sculpture; and since
it was at that moment that the Russian Ballet first came to Western
Europe for a season at the Châtelet, dancing was obviously linked,
by rhythm, with the plastic arts. From that it was but a short
step to the position that rhythm was the distinctive element in all
the arts, and that the real purpose of 'this modern movement' – a
phrase frequent on F——'s lips – was to reassert the pre-eminence
of rhythm. Since the only art with which I was even on nodding
terms was the art of literature, I was baffled by F——'s attempt to
make rhythm all-inclusive, and I listened, curious but uncon-
vinced, to his demonstrations that 'old man Kipling' was a great
hand at rhythm. In this matter F—— was not altogether convinced himself; and it was at this point that my function in life
began to be revealed. I was appointed to be the man who should
carry the new doctrine of rhythm into literature. Nor did I
demur; I was only too pleased to have a function that linked me
with F——. It was a trivial detail that I had no notion at all
what the function really could be.

For the moment I made up for that deficiency by discovering
tremendous significances for myself in the word, rhythm. They
were vague; but one of them at least was real. It was very evident
to me that F——'s own life had rhythm; and equally evident to
me that my own had none. Whereas I was borne hither and
thither by every wind and tide of circumstance, F——'s splendid
ship, with its spread of gleaming canvas, had a compass, a rudder
and a man at the helm. His being had natural laws which it
obeyed: mine had none. So rhythm came to mean for me that
essential living positive thing – whatever it might be – which I
was acutely conscious that I lacked and F—— possessed. But that
meaning was private, and I kept it to myself.

Instead, I mentioned to F—— that an Oxford friend of mine
and I had been meditating the project of starting a literary

magazine. How far the project had been serious, I do not remember at all. I was quite capable, in those days, when stimulated by a friendly atmosphere and my own desire to please, of suddenly magnifying into seriousness a project which had been in reality no more than a daydream. But whether this was actually the case now, I do not remember. Anyhow, the project became immensely serious in F——'s eyes, when I tentatively suggested that perhaps a good name for it would be 'Rhythm'. It was obvious; it must be called 'Rhythm'. And its function was equally obvious: it would be 'The Yellow Book' of the modern movement. F—— would see to it that the drawings and pictures were representative of the best; my duty was to see that the literary part should correspond.

I had got myself into a truly preposterous position. At most I possessed some vague velleities towards literature: of aptitude for it, or convictions about it, I had none – or, at best, none of which I was consciously aware. Intellectually and emotionally, my bearings were now quite lost. I had drifted at Oxford into the company of men whose taste was far more sophisticated than mine, and I had kept my end up among them, without much difficulty but without a scrap of real conviction; I was merely bent on acquiring another polite accomplishment. In the process I had lost hold of the small atoms of spontaneous and authentic literary appreciation I formerly possessed – my love of my favourite classics, my real reverence for Aristotle's and my respect for Matthew Arnold's criticism. Those – small things, but mine own – had no relation, or none that I could pause to discover, with the new objects of literary appreciation to which I now did lip-service. Those had meant something to me; these meant nothing at all. And when I was off-stage, and free from the obligation of keeping up my aesthetic rôle, I plunged with the relief of simple enjoyment into Mr. Wells' *Tono-Bungay* and his *The New Machiavelli*, which appeared at this time.

Yet, to be honest, I seem to have been forced towards literature by a process of simple elimination. That I possessed my fair share of abilities was recognized, by others if not by myself; that I was capable of hard work, I knew: yet it was quite impossible for me to settle down to the work of preparation for any recognized career. I really had tried; but sooner or later I would be overwhelmed with the sense that it was all an alien drudgery, by which some obscure but insistent demand of my own being could never be satisfied. And, I suppose I was coming more and more to feel that this could be satisfied only by literature. But the possibility of any achievement seemed so remote that it could not be my conscious goal. Even if I had seen any opening into journalism, I shrank timidly from the rough-and-tumble of the struggle; I had nothing of the self-confidence that could carry me through Fleet Street. My rosiest dream was that I might follow, at a discreet distance, the example of Walter Pater, who had been a fellow of my college, whose writings were my first college prize, and whose critical insight I admired. I might get a fellowship, and, with that security, gradually win a place for myself in the world of letters. But I knew this for a dream at the very moment that I conceived it – probably in my early days in Paris: for it made upon me the fatal demand which I knew I could never satisfy – that I should stick the academic course.

The truth is that in those days things simply happened to me. I was completely passive; the only form of activity I knew was gliding out of situations that promised to throttle me: and possibly there was a dim feeling that if I were thrust into a situation that would not throttle me, I might somehow rise to the occasion. So I suppose it was with *Rhythm*. What interests me in it – now that after twenty-three years I have at last found in myself the courage to turn its pages (for the first time since it appeared) is the gradual stiffening of its back; it did, in the course of its career, change from a completely invertebrate to a semi-vertebrate condition; and, no doubt, I changed with it. But it existed for nearly two years, and two years was a long time then.

Such was the chaos of experience into which seven weeks

in Paris had plunged me. My old protective self was broken into pieces; and there was nothing to take its place. I was intolerably naked. Many years after, F—— told me that when I came to see him I looked so ill that his chief concern was to see that I had a good meal; and I can well believe that I did look ill. Every day that brought me nearer to parting from Marguéritte brought a torment of its own, and I half-suspect that much of the eagerness with which I entered into F——'s projects derived from sheer anxiety to have something to distract my thoughts from brooding over the coming separation.

At last it came. Marguéritte and I waited, in café after café, all through the night for the early morning train. There was nothing to do but sit, clasping hands, in silence. The lumbering train began to move and she hurried off, crying. I watched her to the barrier. She did not turn. I sat down in the carriage with a heart like lead.

CHAPTER XII

DEFEAT AND DECAY

WHAT had happened to me in Paris was that I had become quite
unfitted to continue at Oxford. I was plunged into a tumult of
emotions and ideas which incapacitated me wholly for any
serious work of the kind expected of me. The tumult of ideas I
might conceivably have controlled; but to master my emotional
tumult was altogether beyond my power. Perhaps, if I could have
confided in someone with more experience of life than I had, I
might have obtained some release: but I dared not. My love for
Marguéritte was too sensitive to be exposed to the sneaping frost
of criticism, or of sympathy. I hugged it to myself, and it seemed
to eat me away.

Even her letters seemed to scald me, though after the first
bitterness of parting they were gay and cheerful. There was
something in her very spelling mistakes which would send an
aching lump to my throat; so that I was afraid to open them.
Beyond that I remember nothing. I suppose that I behaved
outwardly like a rational being. I now lived out of college.
Prompted by the obscure desire to withdraw myself, I had asked
and obtained permission to be excused part of the third year in
college which was incumbent on a scholar; and for the same cause
I had chosen to share rooms with a scholar of the year senior to
me who was one of the most isolated men in all the college. It
was a perverse and paradoxical thing to do. I did not like W——.
There were at least a half-dozen men in college towards whom I
felt a simple warm affection. Towards W—— I felt nothing of the
kind. Not that I disliked him, as many others did. His very
isolation gave me a certain sympathy for him, and I had some
respect for his abilities. But it would have been hard to single out

a man superficially less attractive than he; and I liked neither his manners nor his mind. He was the son of a dour north-country merchant, and fairly well supplied with money; but his tastes were naive and vulgar. They ran to expensive meerschaum pipes, superlative sets of razors, and thirteen guinea suits of clothes. Yet there was a geniality about him which was disarming, and a saving grace of kindly humour shone not seldom in his eyes. If W—— was by no means all that I pretended him to be, to justify my unexpected choice, he was more than others supposed him to be. And he let me alone. Whether or not he had any inkling of my condition, there was often a friendly sort of peace between us as he sat, lighting match after match, in the determination to do his duty by his meerschaum and burn the last shreds of the dottle into ash.

But the whole period has become a blur in my memory; only the vague sense of a slow but ruthless increase of anxiety abides. Even of my second stay in Paris little remains. I had more than kept my promise with Marguéritte about the money I could send her, but only by evading bills; and I looked forward with dread to what would happen in the summer. Once more, the only thing to do was to live in the present; and I never had much aptitude for that. But again the mere presence of Marguéritte could 'obliterate all consideration'. My trouble was that she was now so seldom with me. She had arranged that I should live in her little room, while she lodged with a married relation. She came to me when she had finished her work, and we had tea together. It was a Paris spring – to me always the most delicate and enchanting of all springs – and we sat by the open window looking on to the Sorbonne. She was frighteningly happy: frighteningly, I say, for there was that in her gay confidence that all would be well which filled me with foreboding, and her simple happiness made it quite impossible for me to tell her that my poor finances could not stand the strain. And the strain was so pitifully small. At any rate I had scraped up enough to be able, if I lived on bare necessities during the vacation, to leave her enough to tide her over until my return in the summer. What would happen then, God alone knew.

Now, she never stayed with me at night. It was the condition on which her married relative allowed Marguéritte to lodge with her; and Marguéritte had accepted it willingly. She was determined to break with her own brief unrespectable past. What had happened was that in her grief at our separation in the winter, she could not bear to be alone; and she had plucked up the courage to go to her only relative in Paris, and ask to be taken in. It must have been a grim interview between the wayward sister and the righteous one; but Marguéritte had won the day. On condition that henceforward she was absolutely *sérieuse*, she was reinstated in respectability: from something different, she was become the *fiancée* of a young Englishman.

He did not mind; indeed, he was glad, though he was sometimes hungry for her at nights. He was conscious, rather, of a subtler change. Something of the atmosphere of generous reckless giving which had intoxicated him in Marguéritte was gone. If he clasped her close and kissed her, eager to be lost, she would yield for a moment only: then she would remember, and draw herself away. Since he felt that it hurt her thus to withhold herself, he shrank from giving and receiving the pain. It was better not to kiss her even; better to sit quiet and talk and watch the people in the street below. But if he resigned himself to that, there would come the moment when her eyes would fill with tears, and she would beg him to clasp her close once more. In some such moment, but very rarely, they would be lovers again, but not as they had been before.

He dimly felt that the responsibility for this strained situation was being placed on him: that Marguéritte was asking him why he did not put an end to it by marrying her. She would ask laughingly why he did not take her back to England with him? Was she not willing to do anything, live on anything? And underneath the laughter he felt that a serious and simple question was being asked, and that he was evading it.

Was it not evading it to say as he did that he had no money and no prospects: that what vague prospects he might have depended entirely on his going through the mill at Oxford, and that was quite impossible if he took Marguéritte back with him? That was all true; but was it the whole truth? Could he not, if he had the courage, throw up Oxford now, and take any job that he could get? Was it not likely that he would get something – some petty ushership, some trivial clerkship? Why, anyhow, had it never really occurred to him to make a real effort to do so?

Why? The final answer seemed to be that it was because he had not the courage: because he *was* a coward. He could not face the burden of hunting for a job with no credentials; or the ordeal of explaining to those who might be willing to help him the reason why he was impelled to do a thing ostensibly so foolish. Yes, that was true. And if that was true, it followed that he did not love Marguéritte absolutely, as he had believed. And that was not all. It was not merely that he was too much of a coward to take this plunge; it was also true that, deep down, he was unwilling to take it. He was not prepared to do *anything* for the sake of Marguéritte, as he had believed. What he would do had to be something that he could do without a fatal sense of self-frustration. If there had been the opportunity of the meagerest and most pitiful job that would have helped him on his way – whatever that way might be – he would have jumped at it; but to seek and chain himself to one which would have led him out of his way was impossible. True, he did not know what was his way. Life alone could reveal that to him. But there was a simple and infallible test of what was not his way. Any occupation which did not vitally interest him, which did not engage his being, must be wrong; and not all the love he felt for Marguéritte could overcome this deep reluctance to be thrust away from his own unconscious path.

He did not think or argue these things. He was not even conscious of his reluctance. His resistance was unaware of itself; it was expressed in its own non-expression. The form of his

163

rejection of the possibilities he was rejecting was that they did not enter his mind at all; and the form of his evasion of the simple serious question which Marguéritte was putting to him, was a feeling that there was something on his side of the situation that she could not understand. She *seemed* to understand his position – after all, it had been explained at the beginning, and how many times afterwards had they not talked of it; they talked of little else – but there at the end she seemed to be somehow as uncomprehending as ever. It was not in anything she said; no one, in words, could have been more simply or sweetly reasonable than she. But her being did not, could not, would not understand.

He felt this; and he explained it to himself that conditions were so totally different in England that, with the best will in the world, she could not understand. How could she understand the complete divorce that existed between life at Oxford and the real life of England? A student in Paris was part of the living texture of the city and the nation; a student at Oxford was secluded as by the walls of a monastery. He was not being fitted for life, he was being fitted to escape life: being given a permanent bias which would for ever prevent him from mixing freely with humanity at large. He was being shaped to be a member of a caste – a caste which indeed fulfilled necessary functions in the life of society; but those functions were few and peculiar, and may be even their necessity was a mere convention. How could a French country-girl from the Corrèze understand that? He did not understand it himself; he dimly felt that it was so.

And Marguéritte had been, and was, Life to him – a living, warm, simple, passionate, generous creature, to whom his starved nature had turned because he could not acquire the habits of the caste. He could wear them well enough; but only as a garment. They had no hold upon his nature. Who, but a man unfitted for and unworthy of the caste, would have been frayed to shreds as he had been by his love for Marguéritte? The caste had a code of behaviour towards her kind. He had known what it was; as far as speech might go he had adopted and acquiesced in it. But when the crucial moment came, the garment, the code, the behaviour, all had dropped from him, and left him the naked nothing that he was. At the test he had simply collapsed, disgraced the regiment, betrayed the caste into which he had been adopted. What other than this was the reason why he could not speak of Marguéritte to his friends, and had no one in whom he dared to confide? The simple truth was that what ought to have been a nothing to him had become everything.

But not quite everything. That was the trouble. It was as though the very impact with the life in her had awakened some slumbering life in him that could not be focussed on her: as though her warmth had brought to birth in him some infant purpose that looked beyond her. If she had aroused the impulse by which he broke through the code and the caste; now that he had broken through, he began to feel stirring within him vague new obligations. Under the compulsion of her he had ceased to be quite other than himself; now, he had somehow to become himself. She had shattered a whole life-form into which he had been poured; now, he had to find his own. The tragedy of it was that the very liberation of which she had been the instrument was obscurely turning against her.

He did not know this; but in his feeling he was aware that she found him inexplicable. The impossibility which he took for granted, of thrusting himself into yet another life-form not his own, she did not take for granted. All that he had to do, in her eyes, was to do anything in order that they might live together; and since she felt that he was the kind of man who would do anything, she was baffled by his hesitation. If there had been anything about him cynical, or harsh, or even determined; if there had been in him an apparent grain of worldly wisdom, the hesitation would have been explained. But she knew he really loved her, as deeply and as truly as a man could love a woman. What was it then, that turned him subtly away from her?

She thought her own thought on this matter. Instinctively, she was convinced that it must be the pull of another love; and, since she knew it could not be the love of another mistress, she was persuaded that it must be the love of his mother. So she began to feel her way through him to the reality of his mother. Would his mother, she asked, like her? Suspecting nothing, he answered, quite sincerely, that he was sure she would. Then, a day or two later: Why did he not take her to see his mother? And at the sudden question he faltered and could not reply, struck numb by the realization that it was certain that his mother would welcome her, and as like as not contrive some way of taking her into the house until they could be married. He suddenly saw that essentially Marguéritte and his mother were the same kind of simple, tender, reckless souls: and that there would be an instant bond between them – and that he would be trapped.

It was a strange lightning-flash of grim illumination. For long months now he had been conspiring to forget his mother, and he had succeeded; and because she had ceased to be vivid and present in his mind, he had imagined that she ceased to be vivid and present in himself. And so it was that in fighting away from her, her tenderness, that threatened to engulf him, he had only fought his way back to her. Marguéritte and his mother were as one!

It happened in a moment, while his reply to Marguéritte was still faltering on his lips. She marked the hesitation; she had expected it. Then what she feared was true. It was his mother who stood in the way. 'Why did you say she would love me?' And, cunning coward that he was, he did not say, 'Because it's true', but instead wearily, wearily: 'I don't know, I don't know'. The pretence had begun. For Marguéritte, he now knew, his mother was the enemy. Far better to let her think it. The truth would be fatal. And Marguéritte had opened a way of escape for him: he would take it, he must take it.

I do not say it happened exactly thus. My memory has shirked the truth of it now so many years that it is overspread with the callousness of pure oblivion. But essentially it happened thus.

During that Easter vacation in Paris, strangely, obscurely, and at last by a culminating realization of that kind, I turned from Marguéritte. When she charged me with having changed towards her, I denied it, but I knew that it was true. Somewhere, mysteriously, a core of hardness had formed in me. If I tried to disown it, still it returned. It was not mine, it was not me, it was utterly unlike anything I had ever known in myself; nevertheless, it returned. If I drove it out of doors, and pulled the bolts upon it, when I went back to the hearth, it was there. I hated it, but there it was.

A kind of cool desperation took hold of me. One night, towards the end of my time in Paris, after dinner, when Marguéritte left me, as she always did, I had gone to the Closerie des Lilas. We never even entered the d'Harcourt now. It was a beautiful spring evening and the leaves of the trees outside were tender in the light from the café. I sat apart in a dark corner, musing and brooding in a kind of dream, till midnight. Then I took out my wallet, which had in it two five-pound notes besides some fifty francs, and paid the bill, and walked slowly away, still in my dream, down the Boulevard St. Michel. I had not walked for more than two or three minutes when I clapped my hand to my pocket: I had left my wallet behind. Back I ran. My table had been cleared. I caught the waiter who had served me. 'Where was my wallet?' He declared that he had not seen it, that he knew nothing about it. *Enfin*, if I chose to sit in the dark, on the very edge of the café, and leave my wallet, what could I expect?

I knew he was lying. But there was – or it seemed to me there was – nothing to be done. When one is faced with downright knavery – 'the mystery of iniquity' – one can only turn on one's heel, as I did, and walk away. Down the empty boulevard I went, in the middle of the cobbled road. Just one clean sweep of all my money – my fare back, the ten pounds I had saved to give Marguéritte to see her through till I returned. And then, for some queer reason, I began to laugh. *Il ne manquait que ça:* cleaned-out, and clean. Somehow they went together on that virginal spring night. I was delivered over to destiny. Still laughing, half-possessed, I wanted to know what destiny had in store. I had a big five-franc piece in my pocket: heads it would go well with me, tails it would go ill. I spun it high in the air in the deserted street: it glittered in the moonlight, tinkled on the road, and rolled firmly and decisively towards the open gutter under the kerb. Perhaps I might have stopped it, but I was spellbound. I was so astonished that I could not move. It sped on, predestined, into the abyss: and, but for some odd coppers, I was penniless.

That, I still think, was intrinsically the strangest thing that ever happened to me. I did not ponder, as I might have done, on what that unhesitating oracle meant: I was too astonished. It was a thing that I could never have imagined; yet it seemed to fit perfectly with some unknown thing that was happening to me. It was the hard, definite symbol of my true condition. That was irresponsible fancy, and I knew it; but the fancy was far more real than any knowledge. And it made me blithe. I felt that my destiny was taken entirely out of my own hands. I went home and slept soundly.

The next morning I went to F—— and, without hesitation, asked him to lend me a louis, which he did without hesitation. I spent most of it in sending telegrams to Oxford friends of mine asking them to telegraph me £2 apiece, if they could. More than half of them responded: so that by the time of my departure I had all that I lost, and a little more. But, alas, there were debts which I must pay immediately. On the day of my departure I cashed the last order – by some mistake it had been made payable only in Belleville. Marguéritte was with me. She had arranged to be with me, as before, until my train went. We dined together and sat in deserted café after deserted café. I felt sad, but quite differently sad. Everything was to my senses at once remote and distinct, as though a pane of clarifying glass had been interposed between the outside world and me – between me and Marguéritte. I *saw* her, as I had never seen her before. It seemed to me that she was more beautiful, more simple, more true, than even I had known. It seemed to me, in this strange detachment, that she was gathered to herself in the brooding peace of her own lovely soul: that, though I was all the world to her, yet somewhere, somehow, I did not matter. And in that place where I did not matter to her, I longed to matter, and I could not. And I did not know, and I should never know, whether the sentence that I could not enter into the place where she was gathered and withheld was due to me – whether in that moment, and by that impossibility, I was judged and found wanting for ever – or whether we both bowed our heads under one common award from a judgment seat far beyond us both.

We kissed, and said 'Au revoir'; and kissed again, strained close to one another on the platform. And then I knew what the anguish of love could be. It is when the blind and secret soul knows parting and the mind cannot endure it; when through love, and in love, two beings have grown apart, and cannot understand the necessity, nor admit the fact. I ached with the longing to say that I was hers for ever; to do the one simple thing that would fill her with joy and certainty. But I could not. In this no man, nor woman either, can pretend. The man who could pretend has never known the thing which he pretends. It is, or it is not; the authentic word is spoken, or it is not spoken; the gift is given, or withheld. There is no condition between. Between us, at that moment, the thing was not, the word was not spoken, the gift was withheld. There was only the bond of the aching knowledge that it had not been, and could not be.

I have called this *the* anguish of love. In my ensuing life I was to explore, more thoroughly than most men, the labyrinthine possibilities of pain that love for a woman can contain. I believe that I can say, with truth, that I have known them all; in this one regard, life can have no surprises in store for me. When, therefore, I call this *the* anguish of love, I mean that it is an anguish which comes once, but never again. No man who had ever endured it could ever suffer it a second time. Whether it is that, having suffered it, he is bound to shrink away from it; or that it is a warning that, when he loves again, he must love entirely or be perdurably damned; or that it is an experience which must turn a man into one of two for ever separate paths – of the cynic, or the lover indeed – this I do not know. But I do know that after the illumination of this anguish, there rises up in the body and soul a sudden overwhelming wave of unshakable and unshaken conviction that this thing shall not and cannot ever be again.

By such a wave of conviction I was overwhelmed as I sat silent in the train. I did not translate it; I could not decipher its meaning. I was cold, and shaking like a leaf, as though I had been bereft of the very organ that sent the warm blood pulsing through my body; or as though, at some strange touch, the fever of months had left my mind entirely to possess my body alone. My mind was cold and clear, without a tinge of sadness or sorrow or pity, 'white as a bone'; and it seemed to be saying to me, clearly and distinctly: 'Now you know, now you *know*'. And I knew that I knew, but what I knew I did not know.

I did not even know that I should never see Marguéritte again. I think that if I had known that, or rather dared to know it, something would have snapped in my being. Even to-day, fantastic though it sounds, the thought that there was once a moment when it was uncertain, when it was not a fixed and inexorable destiny that I should never see her again, unmans me; and just as I seek, instinctively, now to harden the past into a destiny, so I know that then, if the future had appeared to me as the past now does, I should have fled from it in horror. But whither should I have fled? There was no place; my imagination can discover none but the way I went. Therefore it was necessary to me that I should not know the way I was to go. And I did not know it.

Of what I had been doing in Paris during those last weeks, of what I now did when I returned to Oxford, I have no memory at all. My mind is quite vacant concerning them; completely devoid of all impress of real experience. I can deduce that I must have been busy with the new magazine, for the first number appeared during the summer term of this year 1911; but it did not become real to me until the winter. There is, in some sort, at this point, a gap in nature: an absolute breach in the continuity of my experience, which I can fill only by calculation.

By calculation, I know that I began to learn German, and to take lessons from a German teacher; that I made arrangements to go to stay *en pension* in Heidelberg; and that, to pay for this, I looked out for another tutorship, which I found without difficulty. All this must have been deliberate, though on what level of my self-deceptive consciousness, I cannot tell. But the evidence is clear enough that I was trying to hold myself away from Marguéritte; and – now comes authentic life-memory – I am certain that I concealed this from her. I was capable of concealing it from myself as well; but I believe that I was conscious of my own self-deception, and that the real cause of the hiatus in my memory is that my unconsciousness has been untiringly at work to salve, with the unguent of oblivion, a mortal wound in my own self-esteem.

Now that I can unmask the mechanism, I feel no pity towards the coward I was. I can see him, only too plainly, holding himself away from Marguéritte because he was afraid to face her: not afraid of anything that she would say or do, but of the mute reproach, the withering accusation that she would embody; afraid above all of himself who would melt to water at one glance of her eyes, yield everything, swear anything, only at length to struggle ignominiously out of the toils again. One thing alone could have saved him in his own esteem: the courage to meet her, and tell her that it was not circumstance that was parting them – but himself, alone: because he was afraid of the struggle with life with so heavy a burden; because he had been educated out of the simple capacities which would have made the struggle possible. This, and nothing else, was the cause of their parting. One atom of security, one inch of margin, one grain of real faith in his own strength, so that he could have felt that he could wrench himself free of the deadly, suffocating weight of the bare mean struggle for subsistence – and his life would have been changed. In the last resort, he was afraid, even to agony, of being dragged back to the level of existence out of which he had so painfully clawed his way: and to that fear he sacrificed his love.

That was the truth; and he dared not say it. He dared not look into her eyes and say: 'Perfect fear has cast out love' lest in that very moment perfect love might cast out fear. And God knows – it is one of the things He does know – it might have done. God knows what sudden unknown strength comes to a man who is capable of absolute honesty towards the creature he loves. The honesty that is compelled from a man by love, the complete self-annihilation that is required of a man who will respond to Love's implicit and unspoken demand for the naked truth – this is the absolute of human strength. The man who is driven to honesty by Love, knows all that there is to know concerning human life. Then he knows even as he is known; then he has discovered in himself the strength to bear the absolute of human pain.

I had not that strength; and I have no pity for myself, save in that I know the price required of me for that refusal. But the years have taught me this: that the trial from which I blenched at that moment, was the extreme trial that comes to a man. There is, and can be, none greater. If a man has once been in a position where 'perfect love has cast out perfect fear' – only once, for once is for ever – then he has conquered Life. After that victory, nothing that he is, or says, or does, can ever be wrong. The coal from the altar has touched his lips, he has been throughly purged from dross by the living fire, he has been bathed in the waters of eternity, he has achieved the purity to which all things are pure. But if a man has been in the position where perfect love might have cast out fear, but he could not suffer it to do so; if he is put to the test and he fails, then he bears the marks for ever: for even though such a man is brought to the same trial again and again, as I believe he must inevitably be brought to it, and even if at the last he conquers – and perhaps this also is inevitable, for the hound of Heaven is on his trail – still, though he be made whole, the marks of the wound are on him. He is haunted by the might-have-been. 'Nor God, nor demon can undo the done.' To whatever ultimate of self-acceptance he may come, the human pang will never be abated.

I went to Germany, a haunted and miserable man. I still wrote to Marguéritte and sent her what money I could; I pretended that I had to be in Germany, and that, so soon as my work there was over, I would return to her in Paris. At last the day came that I had fixed for my return. I did return to Paris; but I did not meet Marguéritte. I had not told her the train I should come by, and, after twenty-four hours of waiting in a Paris hôtel to find the courage to meet her, I fled to England. I never wrote to her again; nor did I read the letters she wrote to me. After some months they ceased.

> Not a line of her writing have I;
> Not a thread of her hair . . .

How long after this I was a beaten and abject man, I cannot remember. But for weeks an ashy sense of degradation invaded me – a feeling that inch by inch I was being given over to decay and corruption. I lived at home for the remainder of that vacation. It suited me now; I was a beaten man, and might as well return to the place whence I had started.

CHAPTER XIII

AVE, IMPERATOR AMORIS

In the early autumn of 1911 I began to frequent Dan Rider's bookshop in a court off St. Martin's Lane. I had been taken to it earlier in the year by F—— when he was in London, and had been invited to return. As an editor of *Rhythm* I had standing enough in the Bohemian-literary circle whose centre was that shop to please my vanity. Dan gave me a kindly welcome, and instructed me in the eminence of 'the great man' – Frank Harris. I concealed my ignorance, and, with my usual wary adaptiveness, absorbed the Faith (for it was no less) that Frank Harris was *the* greatest master of the short-story in English, and *the* greatest critic of Shakespeare. With my usual passiveness, I made no attempt to check either of these assertions; and I knew in myself no critical powers which would have enabled me to control them. About short-stories I knew nothing, except that I liked Kipling's and Stevenson's and H. G. Wells's and W. W. Jacobs's; but I sensed the atmosphere quickly enough to realize that to mention them would be a hopeless give-away. About Shakespeare criticism I knew as much as I did about Shakespeare – substantially nothing at all; but I had read and admired A. G. Bradley. He also, I sensed, was taboo – an old don, who knew nothing about 'Life'. Therefore I did not mention him.

'Life' was the *spécialité de la maison*; and 'Life' consisted, essentially, in love-affairs with women. The connoisseur and acknowledged authority in this pursuit was Frank Harris. It was accepted that his record in this vital matter (for without a comprehensive experience in this order no man could hope to be an 'artist') was incomparable and prodigious. What he did not know about love, or love-affairs – it was the same thing – was not knowledge; by virtue of his unique experience in this genre he had been able to do, what no man had done before him, namely, to penetrate the secret of Shakespeare. One master of love had had to wait for another; and at his advent the blood-less, gutless, spunkless academics – from Coleridge to Bradley – had bowed their ponderous heads: *Ave, imperator Amoris!*

All this I was ready to believe. Why not? My mind was a blank on the subject, and it might as well be filled with this as with anything else. Moreover, I met in the shop a young Oxford man whom I had never met in Oxford. He was a great light in University journalism, for he was the editor of *The Isis*. I did not read *The Isis*; but I took it for granted that it was witty, pungent and clever. A year before, indeed, the editor of *The Isis* would have been a great man to me: now, being an editor myself, I was less impressed, but still impressed enough to be influenced by the fact that he had surrendered himself entirely to this faith concerning Frank Harris. What was good enough for him, I thought, when Dan Rider told me the story, was good enough for me. I was not quite so certain when I met Mr. Hugh Kingsmill in the flesh; for though he was a cheerful, hilarious, breezy and alto-gether disarming fellow, whom I couldn't help liking, it struck me that it would be rather odd if it finally turned out that our tastes should be really the same. We were not quite of the same tribe.

But far more potent in its effect upon me than the consensus of opinion that Frank Harris was *the* great man which radiated from Dan Rider's shop, was the subtle medicine which this simple doctrine brought to my shattered self-esteem. After all, by these standards, I was not at all just the coward I felt myself to be: on the contrary, I had taken a great step forward. I was a sworn apprentice to the craft and mystery of 'Life'. My behaviour to Marguéritte was substantially how a great man would behave: the only difference was that what he would do expeditiously and confidently, I had done lingeringly and fearfully. Whatever pain I had felt was just the necessary pain incidental to initiation. Henceforward, having made this brave beginning, I would be able to enter into my love-affairs (of which the long sequence would end only with my life) with more sang-froid, and depart out of them with more – 'material'. I saw myself in a new light, indeed: instead of being abject, I was really a little of a hero. I had now in myself the essential makings of an artist. It was freely admitted, of course, that I could never hope to compare in amorous magnificence with the great man himself. I would always be a minor figure. But there was room for such minor figures as I might hope to be. There had been Dowson, on whom the great man had set the seal of imperial approval; there was Richard Middleton, of whom he spoke with appreciation. It was a defect in these men that they were compelled to take their love-affairs to heart; it prevented them from true greatness, but on the other hand it enabled them to give out a sort of a plangent minor note which was very appealing in its way.

I was particularly impressed by the example of Richard Middleton, whom Frank Harris had taken under his wing. First, the affinity of name counted for something; then, there was the unusual fact that I genuinely liked and admired his work, which I had read in *The English Review*: and most compulsive of all was the story I was told of his devouring love for a woman in Brussels, to whom, whenever he could get a little money for his stories or his poems, he incessantly returned. He was there, and with her now. Therefore I never met him, as I wished to do. Rightly or wrongly, I felt that he and I might have something to say to one another. And, when later in the winter, the news came that he had killed himself in Brussels, I felt the shock of one whom Fate has robbed of a friend.

Anyway, at this time I loved Middleton's writing with a genuine love; and I was restive, though of course silent, under Frank Harris's obvious contempt of him for being at the mercy of a woman. For, by this time, I had met the great man. To my mingled joy and alarm he had come striding into Rider's shop, with his great moustache, his shining emerald stud, his brown-strapped buckskin shoes, his straw-hat, and his grey raincoat over his arm. He had deigned to notice me, deferential and apprehensive; and had referred, with affable condescension, to my 'little magazine', which was sold in Dan's shop, and even hinted that he might not be unwilling to write something for it. Straightway I was hooked. The very next day I was taken off to lunch at the Café Royal, to be a rapt listener to his talk and his stories, and an admiring witness of his imperial manner with waiters and managers. When at the end he paid his bill by asking for a sheet of note-paper and writing on it something which (he explained to me) *made* it a cheque for £20, and received three five-pound notes in his change, I was overawed.

A few days more and I was speaking familiarly of him and to him, as 'Frankie'; and listening, spell-bound, to a plan for making *Rhythm* the rival of *The English Review*. The principal enlargement necessary to this end was the addition of some 'financial' pages. I do not think that Harris talked in this intoxicating fashion merely to capture my allegiance, which, of course, he did. He liked to build castles in the air for his own pleasure, as well as to impress such minnows as myself. Moreover, I have it at heart to say candidly that Harris never treated me badly. On the contrary, he was generous to me; he once gave me, without my asking for it, ten pounds, which was a lot of money to me, and more to him in these his latter days – I came afterwards to suspect – than the mere flea-bite he pretended it to be. And if I am told that this was done simply to impress me, I must answer that I do not altogether believe it. Harris could have impressed me at a cheaper rate. My finding is that there was a genuine streak of kindliness in Harris's nature. I believe he treated Richard Middleton generously. That this impression is a different one from that formed and conveyed by Mr. Hugh Kingsmill, who was an admirer and a friend of Harris's for a much longer period than I, is mainly due (I should say) to the fact that Mr. Kingsmill's father was a relatively wealthy man. All wealthy fathers were legitimate prey to Harris, according to his queer moral code. And, no doubt, it is uncomfortable to feel that one has been made the stool-pigeon for a raid upon one's father's

money, and an intelligible cause of resentment. But at no time
did Harris conceal the nature of his code: to get by any means
the money of the rich bourgeois, and employ a little of it to help
the poor artist. To accept that code as genuine was, of course,
to look at Harris's behaviour through very rosy spectacles.
Helping the poor artist was not at all (as he liked to persuade
himself) the purpose of his spoliation of the rich bourgeois: and
his undoubted kindness to me and to others was, rather, the
incidental largesse by which he salved his conscience. But that,
taken on the whole, he was kind to me, I am certain: and I have
not found so many anxious to play the rôle of benefactor to me
that I can afford to withhold my tribute to him. When many
years after, I heard that he was ill and wretched in Nice, and
I happened to be in a position – for the first time in my life – to
repay that ten pounds and did so, I felt truly sorry for the battered
old warrior, and wished that I could do more.

Nor have I ever been able to bring myself to criticize Frank
Harris. Somewhere in me there has always been a sentimental
tenderness towards him. If I called him always to myself 'the
old ruffian', as I did, it was a term of affection. And that sums
up my attitude towards him. I felt affectionate towards him,
and always shall. Maybe it was because there was a bond of
instinctive and unconscious sympathy between one social outcast
and another; and, indeed, I was always impressed by his bravery.
It takes real courage to stand up to the social order as he did,
with a gulf always yawning before his feet; and, so far as I know,
he always stood alone. Therefore, I respected him, and I respected his aloof and beautiful wife for the way in which she kept
her end up, and I respected Bernard Shaw for the way in which
he stood by Harris. I think, too, that Mr. Hugh Kingsmill's
clever book about Harris would have been a better one if it had
been warmed with a little more sympathy. It exhibits Harris,
but it does not understand him.

For a short time Harris was my hero. I cut adrift from him
very soon; and, with more courage than I generally displayed,

refused point-blank his peremptory invitation to become a
director of *Hearth and Home*. I was not going to be mixed up in
any way with his financial or journalistic enterprises. How
quickly I came to that decision, I do not remember; but since
Harris acquired *Hearth and Home* in the summer of 1912, and I had
made up my mind to have nothing to do with it before the régime
began, it cannot have taken very long. My defection was notice-
able: for *Hearth and Home* was staffed from Dan Rider's shop, Dan
himself being business manager, and Hugh Kingsmill and Enid
Bagnold sub-editors. Lovat Fraser's father, who was a well-to-do
solicitor, put up most of the money. And it had been so long a
subject of enthusiastic anticipation among us what we would do
'when Frankie got a paper' that I should be astonished by my own
temerity in holding aloof, if I did not remember the cause of it.

The great topic, shortly after I entered the Harris circle,
was the refusal of W. H. Smith to circulate a number of *The
English Review* containing a short-story by Harris called 'An
English Saint'. It went without saying that it was a masterpiece,
and that its attempted suppression was a supreme iniquity. It
was part of the creed. Unfortunately for my faith, I happened
in those days to have become fascinated by Stendhal – rather at
Harris's instigation – and to have begun a systematic reading
of all his works. Suddenly, in a volume of his comparatively
unknown stories I came upon the unmistakable original of 'An
English Saint'. I kept my discovery to myself, but my attitude
to Harris was changed in a moment. I did not trust him any
more; for the shock of that discovery came at a fatal moment.
I had just written and published in *Rhythm* a tremendous dithy-
ramb about him. It is pathetic in its extravagance. Here are
two paragraphs from it:

> I knew and loved the work of Frank Harris long before
> I knew and loved the man. To me, two years ago, the name
> Frank Harris meant a prince of artists too great for the people
> among which he wrote. [This was quite untrue.] But now

the name means a prince among men, a prince of talkers and critics, a prince of the lovers of life as well. It means a man whose word of praise can change the whole of life for me for months, and a word of condemnation make me cry till I think my heart would break. I cannot hope to write of such a man with the sober detachment of criticism. For Frank Harris is one of those great spirits whom I can but accept wholly, it may be even blindly, but with the security of knowledge that if I am mistaken, then life and art have no more meaning for me. . . .

It will always be the truth about Frank Harris which I shall endeavour to declare to the world. Moreover, in the next number I shall try to show exactly where and how Frank Harris is the greatest writer of short-stories England has ever possessed, and how 'Montes the Matador', 'Sonia' and 'The Stigmata' will rank among the supreme creations of art; how, as the work of Frank Harris has progressed, he has touched higher and yet higher issues, while at every stage of his achievement his work has been of its kind supreme. I shall try to show where and how 'The Bomb' is one of the greatest novels ever written in the English language. I shall try to show where and how Frank Harris is the greatest creative critic whom the world has known; how he has seen where his greatest predecessors in criticism, Coleridge and Goethe, have had but a half-vision. This is what I shall attempt to do. . . .

Frank Harris seems to have got more than his ten pounds' worth from me, after all. But it was a truly horrible position for me to be in to have discovered, within a few days of writing that, that one at least of his masterpieces was a masterpiece – of plagiarism. As my admiration and affection had been unbounded, so was my recoil. I could not write a word of the promised article on his work; nor could I offer a word of explanation why it did not appear, in the next number, or in any other.

And the man who had thus let me down was the man of whom I had said in public, in complete sincerity, that he was one 'whose word of praise can change the whole of life for me for months, and a word of condemnation make me cry till I think my heart would break'. Alas, it was the literal truth; and when I wrote those words I was fresh from the actual experience.

In the previous number of *Rhythm* I had written a dithyrambic review of Mr. James Stephens' book of poetry: *The Hill of Vision*. A poem in it which had, indeed, moved me deeply, called 'The Lonely God', I had forthwith declared to be better than Milton: a dozen lines of it were worth the whole of *Endymion*. What had happened, quite simply, was that the poem *had* moved me, where modern poetry seldom did move me, and that I declared the fact in these ridiculous terms – setting it above *Paradise Lost*, which did not then move me, and *Endymion*, which I had never really read. Mr. Hugh Kingsmill, who kept a diary during these days, has told the story of Harris's onslaught upon me for this extravagance in Rider's shop, and of my childish reaction by bursting into tears and rushing blindly out of the shop. The story is true, and set down more clearly than I could have done. And it is no fault of Mr. Kingsmill that he implies that 'my enthusiasm for Harris waned' because of this incident. But the truth is quite the contrary: because of this incident my devotion was increased tenfold. I felt that, even though I had been punished dreadfully – for nothing could have been more bitter to one of my age and nature than to be held up to savage ridicule in a circle of acquaintances – I had been punished for my good. My enthusiasm, when I had recovered from the manhandling, boiled over. It was in the number following my extravagant review of James Stephens that I wrote the far more extravagant eulogy of Harris.

This was the fatal moment at which I made my own discovery of the genesis of 'An English Saint'; and hard upon this, I learned that 'The Bomb' was practically a transcript of an actual occurrence in Chicago. Such was the condition of my feeling towards

181

Harris that I was not angry or indignant that I had been fooled, but horribly hurt at the down-toppling of my idol. I experienced in myself the truth of Nietzsche's profound remark that there is no wound to one's vanity when one's pride has been badly wounded. My pride it was, and not my vanity which suffered then. My admiration for Harris, though absurd, was single; I was prepared to make a fool of myself in public for his sake; I never doubted his absolute sincerity in the cause of Art, and believed implicitly in his own asseverations that he was a daily martyr to the cause. I was and am the kind of fool who always has to believe in somebody, or something. I had believed in Harris completely, and I had found that he had been deliberately betraying – not me, but the ideal he professed to serve, and by professing to serve which he had gained my absurd devotion. It was the end. I withdrew from him as completely as I had trusted him; and that was the reason why I found in myself the quite unfamiliar courage to refuse to have anything to do, either as writer or dummy-director, with *Hearth and Home*.

But, when I first met him in the early autumn of 1911, my vanity was soothed by his doctrine, as I have said. I was only too eager to have an excuse for believing that my behaviour to Marguéritte was not that of a coward, but of a man serving a painful and necessary apprenticeship to Life. I wanted to emulate Harris's cynicism in regard to love. I did my poor best. When I returned to Oxford, I gradually made up my mind that the right and proper way to break the spell of Marguéritte was to go to bed with another woman. Perhaps the resolve was, in part, the direct influence of Dowson-cum-Harris: for some such is the practical burden of *Cynara*. I also was to be 'faithful after my fashion'. Unfortunately, the fashion proved not to be mine at all. More my own was the desire to break down, or break in, a sensitiveness which I felt to be humiliating and ridiculous, not in itself, but in a person like myself who, when it came to the pinch, had not the courage to live up to it.

So I hinted to my friend, who had seen something of the

beginning of my affair with Marguéritte, that I was prepared for an 'adventure'. He kindly undertook the arrangements. I say kindly, with no sense of irony, for I am convinced he meant well by me, believing that I was sick and needed a drastic remedy. Accordingly, one afternoon we cycled out to a house of assignation somewhere in the countryside. On the journey, I began to feel really sick; and I do not know which required more courage in myself – to withdraw, or go on. I went on. My friend, who knew one of the girls, was cheerful and casual when we entered: I straightway fell into an abysm of depression, from which I never recovered. I was sorry for the girl, who got no pleasure out of me, sorry for my friend, whose adventure I was spoiling, and sorry for myself. It was a sordid, miserable business; and I knew long before the end of it, that if my hope of liberation lay that way, I might as well resign myself to my chains. I simply was not made for such experiences.

For some days after we were quit of it, I grew steadily more and more depressed. In about a week I felt downright ill. And then, to my horror, I discovered that I was. I had contracted gonorrhœa. I went straight to a doctor, who was stern, but reassuring: hoped it had taught me a lesson, and congratulated me on having had at least the sense to go to him immediately, and sent me to bed. As I lay in the dingy bedroom of my lodgings, staring at a wallpaper covered with what looked like pale purple beetles, I felt that I had touched a nadir: as indeed I had. Uncleanness had entered into my very vitals, and was festering there. The process of degradation which had begun when I fled from Marguéritte was now completed. From my soul it had spread to my body.

Strangely, in that period of extreme self-loathing, a sort of resurrection began. In a way utterly different from any I had imagined I was, by that experience, somehow liberated from the gnawing memory of Marguéritte. Through the unspeakable depression of my dingy bedroom, I emerged into a sort of health, with the conviction that now I did know something of my own about life.

CHAPTER XIV

ENTERING JOURNALISM

In December 1911 I entered into correspondence with Katherine Mansfield. W. L. George, whom I had met earlier in the year, had sent me a curious 'fairy story' of hers for *Rhythm*, with an enthusiastic note about her. The story puzzled and intrigued me, and I returned it saying that I did not understand it, and asking if she would send something else. After a little delay, she sent in *The Woman at the Store* which impressed me mightily, and I accepted it on the spot, in a letter which said, very truly, that it was by far the best story that had been sent to *Rhythm*. I expected a somewhat warmer reply than I received – a brief note to say that she was glad I liked the story; and would I send the proof to her in the care of her publishers, Messrs. Stephen Swift? At the same time I bought for two shillings in Dan Rider's shop a review copy, conspicuous by its bright orange wrapper, of her *In a German Pension*, which had just been published. Once more I was impressed, and this time more intimately. Whereas *The Woman at the Store* realized my vague idea of what an appropriate story for *Rhythm* should be – the most definite of its 'slogans' was a phrase picked up from J. M. Synge: 'Before art can be human again, it must learn to be brutal' – the stories that made up *In a German Pension* seemed to express, with a power I envied, my own revulsion from life; and I conceived a strong desire to meet Katherine Mansfield.

It grew the stronger because W. L. George, at whose house in Hamilton Terrace I was now a regular visitor, was rather mysterious about her. She was, he hinted, not only difficult to meet, but terribly clever. Till then, I had not thought that she was clever, in the formidable sense of the word, anyhow. I had encountered much cleverness at Oxford, and I had not liked it, for I had discovered that I was painfully inept in a scintillating conversation. My slow mind always lagged far in the rear of the explosions of verbal wit, and while I was disentangling the echoes of one such explosion, another and yet another would confound me quite. Thus, by the time that W. L. George had come to the conclusion that Katherine Mansfield and I ought to meet, my eagerness was dulled by apprehension. But W. L. George, having made up his mind, was not to be gainsaid. It was, I was now given to understand, a necessary *confrontation*.

W. L. George had an odd mind. He was never quite satisfied till he had succeeded in labelling people. Nor was he content to label them in his own mind. They were required to accept a verbal ticket. My own was fairly straightforward: I was a brilliant young 'Bergsonian'. But others were very mysterious: Katherine Mansfield was a wayward and cynical 'Mongolian'. The suggestion was that the contact between the Bergsonian and the Mongolian would produce a very rich and peculiar kind of intellectual spark. The meeting between Katherine Mansfield and myself indeed appeared to be designed as a collision: for which I was quite unfitted.

Already I felt that I enjoyed the amenities of W. L. George's house – which afterwards served Katherine as the background for 'Bliss' – on false pretences. I liked him – for his candid naivety was not unlike Arnold Bennett's, on whom he modelled himself as a literary man – and still more I liked his odd, gentle, and perceptive wife, who puffed demurely and astonishingly at a big briar-pipe; but I was uncomfortably conscious that I was regarded as a 'character', and that I was expected to behave like one. Since I had no distinct idea of what my character was, but only a hazy notion that I was required to be a sensitive and rather sardonic young 'Bergsonian', I could neither act my part nor be natural. Silent enough by habit, I took refuge in a silence that was præternatural. And this also was imputed to the credit of my 'character'.

Therefore I was, though excited, nervous and unhappy when

the evening of the great encounter arrived. Katherine Mansfield
arrived in a taxi, late. She wore a simple dove-grey evening
frock with a single red flower, and a gauze scarf of the same dove-
grey colour. She was formidable, though not at all in the way
I had been made to fear. She was aloof and reserved; and beside
her I felt clumsy. In other ways, too, I felt subtly out of it. W. L.
George always addressed her, Russian-fashion, as 'Yékaterina',
beside which my 'Miss Mansfield' sounded very provincial. In
honour of her newly-published book there was red plum-soup for
dinner – a German gourmet's dish quite unknown to me, and
equally unknown were Antzibashef and his book *Sanine*, on
which the conversation turned. Again, I was singularly incompe-
tent to take a part in the discussion on the relative merits of
French and German translations from the Russian. Katherine
Mansfield maintained that the German were altogether superior –
more conscientious in every sense.

In spite of all these obstacles there was a spark between us,
though not, I fancy, of the proper colour and crackle. In reply
to some remark of W. L. George concerning the necessity of
'starkness', Katherine Mansfield began to enlarge on the difficulty
of *simplicity* in writing; and she appealed to me to corroborate her.
When she spoke of the danger of the ever-present temptation to
'force the note', I responded immediately, because my own crude
literary efforts were dogged by a truly horrible emotional exaggeration; and I said that I sometimes wondered despairingly
whether real simplicity could ever be achieved by taking pains.
How the talk developed from this beginning, I forget; but I was
quickly absorbed in it, yet alert enough to notice, or to think
I noticed, a certain amused firmness in her dissociation of herself
from the 'character' for which W. L. George had cast her. She
was evidently supposed to be very cynical, and to be perpetually
on the point of saying very bitter and witty things. But, instead
of playing up to this part, she somehow subtly turned the tables
on W. L. George, so that he appeared rather like a kindly, well-
groomed, but not very quick-witted dog, who must be humoured

and allowed to do his tricks: the chief of which was his obvious expectation that she should do hers. But whether she really carried the stick, or ever really threw it for him to fetch, I had no idea. For he would be delighted with remarks of hers which were certainly not bitter; and, if they were witty, were obviously not said for the sake of the wit alone.

In short, she seemed to me to be altogether mistress of the situation, and I admired her quiet poise tremendously. As I looked across at her in the candlelight, with her dove-grey gauze and her scarlet flower, my eyes came to rest continually on her hands. They were small and beautiful hands; but there was something about them quite peculiar that fascinated me. It was the way she cupped them unconsciously, as if to hold some liquid in her palm. Her fingers, when at rest, were always flexed inward, yet firmly, so that her hand seemed to my fancy like a shell. And when that fancy entered my head, I had to work to keep my wits from wandering. But in the drawing-room we talked away, and I so forgot myself that I was taken aback when she rose to go, and I discovered that I should be hard put to it to catch my own train at Waterloo.

We walked all three to the end of the road to find a taxi for her. As she was getting in, she asked if she could give me a lift. I replied, decisively but vaguely, that I was going 'the other way', really because I had not money enough to pay my share of the journey. Before she said 'Good-bye', she asked me to come to tea with her; but she forgot to give me her address, and I to ask it.

That I liked her very much was certain; and, as ever, I could see no reason to imagine that she might like me. But since she had said that she would be willing to review a book occasionally for *Rhythm* I had an excuse for writing to her. Unfortunately, books for review were scarce, and I had to wait some time before anything came in that seemed worth sending to her: it was a book of poetry. By that time I was back at Oxford. Katherine Mansfield must have written to me to ask whether I knew anything about the author: for I have found among her papers what was evidently my reply to such a letter. It is dated January 27th, 1912, and begins 'Dear Miss Katharine Mansfield'. I suppose the mere fact that she did preserve that letter tells its own tale. Intrinsic interest it has none.

Shortly afterwards Katherine Mansfield left London for Geneva. She wrote to me from there in February to say that she would be in London again very soon and would give me brown bread and Russian cherry-jam for tea if I cared to go to see her. I went, from Oxford, towards the end of term. I have described the visit in the final chapter which I contributed to Miss Mantz's *Life of Katherine Mansfield*; and I must needs use the substance of that narrative once more.

It was a rainy day when I sought out her flat at 69 Clovelly Mansions, in the Gray's Inn Road. I don't know what I had expected, but I was surprised to find her in a room with brown paper on the walls, rush matting on the floor, and hardly any furniture. Conspicuously, there was no table. There was a roll-top desk with a chair, a simple divan contrived out of a camp-bed with its legs off, and a small rocking-chair, in which I was invited to sit. She served the tea in bowls upon the floor.

For a little while I felt awkward, perched uncertainly above her, while she squatted on the floor and poured the tea. But again the ice melted magically, and I found myself confiding in her not merely my ambitions with regard to *Rhythm*, but my acute and immediate problem. It was that I now felt that Oxford had become unendurable, and that I could no longer face the prospect of returning there merely to sit for an examination in which I had long since lost all interest. Yet what could I do? I was maintained at Oxford solely by scholarships and exhibitions and both my school and my college had been very generous towards me. It was my duty, I knew, to work at least moderately well and get the First that was expected of me. And precisely that was impossible. I could not work. It seemed futile, and worse – ignominious, to stay there in essential idleness. Yet, if

I left Oxford, what could I do? It was the same old story; but now I could tell it to someone who understood, and it was different.

Katherine was gravely sympathetic; and together we stared for a long while at the manifest impossibility. Then we laughed. Life was like that. 'But', she said, 'don't stay at Oxford, whatever you do. It's wrong.' And somehow that seemed to lift a weight from my shoulders and to be, in some inexplicable way, a solution of the problem which it left precisely the same as before. Yet not precisely the same. For the decision now was taken. It was no longer a question of whether, but of how.

So we parted, having arranged to meet again. Katherine came into the dark hall to see me out. When I reached the bottom of the long stairs I crossed the road and looked up to mark her rooms in memory. It was hard to distinguish them. The floors, the windows were all alike. I calculated by the staircase – four flights, and then to the left. There, or thereabouts. Was that a peach-coloured shawl I could see dimly at the window? I took the risk, and waved, and ran.

I now decided with an effort to unburden myself to Fox; and I did. I told him that I had quite made up my mind to leave Oxford, where I was doing, and should do, no good. He who had stood by me so many times before, stood by me once again. But he made no secret of his disapproval. 'I don't think I ought to help you,' he said, severely and fiercely, 'but I will go and see Spender about you when I'm next in London.'

He was as good as his word; but it did not happen so promptly as my unaided memory represented it in *The Life of Katherine Mansfield*. Among her papers I have since found a series of my notes to her written during the Easter vacation, which show that, though I had left Oxford for good, I had no job and was uncertain of getting one. I was living with my parents in a new house they had taken at 13 Nicosia Road, Wandsworth Common; and I was busy painting and staining a pleasant room allotted me for my own. Yet I had no heart in the business; I felt uneasily that I was

now making a mere convenience of my father and mother.
'Here's fun for you', I wrote to Katherine on March 26th. 'There's
a batch of verses for you. No wonder I can't do any work if my
mind's been like that all the month. Chaos is nothing to it . . .
Also, I shall probably shift from Wandsworth in April. I don't
know where. *Je m'étouffe* here. I shall come into London if I can
get a job.' That was addressed to 'Dear K.M.' and it said that
I would call in on her on the following Tuesday: which I did.
For I find a postcard written on the Tuesday night, again
addressed 'Dear K.M.', but this time, rather oddly, 'M.' (for
Miss) has been inserted afterwards so that it reads 'Dear M.K.M.'
And I think I can tell the reason from the text of the forgotten
postcard.

Dear M.K.M.
Will you suggest the day for the visit to the pictures?
They're all the same to me. I'm lunching with W. L.
G(eorge) I believe on Thursday. I feel very much as though
I want to get drunk now. I was delighted to see you, but
you musn't run away into the country yet. I am still chuck-
ling over 'the *Rhythm* set'. I'm so awfully out of it.

Yours

J.M.M.

The fact that Katherine, who kept so little, kept all these
bald notes of mine tells its own tale. But I knew nothing of what
was going on in her; and assuredly it would never have entered
my head that her plan of leaving London to live in a country
cottage, called 'Cherry Tree Cottage', Heronsgate, had anything
to do with me. I was taken aback when she sprang the news
upon me. Unconsciously, I had come to count on her presence
in London; and I was quite cast down at the thought of her
going. I felt that she was withdrawing from me; that she might
be withdrawing because of me was not within the range of my
imagination. Hence, I have no doubt, the 'Dear *M*.K.M.'; hence
the desire 'to get drunk'.

Evidently, she replied, suggesting Friday for the pictures, which I think were J. D. Fergusson's.

We met on the Friday and saw the pictures together. On the Saturday I sent her two closely-written postcards, making one continuous letter. After suggesting that we should 'fix up a day next week to lunch out, tea out, dine out, and saying surprisingly that I expected a cheque from *T.P.'s Weekly*,[1] I went on: 'Your d——d house has got on my brain. I've just drawn a wonderful picture of it in words and told a friend of mine that I'm going to live there'.

'You can run out naked in the long grass and roll, roll, right under the pine-trees, and little winds creep about and pink your body all warm; and right over the wall on the right-hand side is a deep place, all white-nettle and convolvulus, and you don't dare jump down because there must be creepy things in the water, so you wriggle back under the tussocky grass, right back to the Cherry Tree; and then you cry just out of pure joy because you know the world is made for you and you can do anything in it: and day after day you do nothing because you can do everything, and you lie on your back under the fir-tree and look right up the long tunnels and little stars just twinkle down, twiddling round and round the long barrel till they drop in your face, and they sing and you shout. My God, it's awful: and all at the Cherry Tree, Heronsgate! My God, those herons just coming on a wisp of wind and flickering over the pine-tops!

It's all because my gas lamp makes a hard steel mark on the roof below and I hate this bloody place. You'll be able to write masterpieces and won't because the windy blood is all round your heart; and I shan't be able to, and shall write absolute muck and think for an hour that it's good, and wake in the morning to know what a fool I've been. . . .

[1] This was, I think, for an article on Emile Verhaeren, which Mr. Holbrook Jackson had kindly asked me to write: my first literary earnings.

But I'm going to take you seriously. When you're swinging on Heron's Gate, you must ask me down to the tramp-room – I am a goodish tramp – and I shall forget everything for a bit. Or, if you want an expert stainer, stain all day for his food, call on me at once. And don't forget all about it.

Yours

J.M.M.

A stupid letter, no doubt; but it plainly shows what was the matter with me. I could not bear the thought of her going away without me. Until this day it never occurred to me that perhaps she could not bear it either. But the fact is that within the next ten days, Katherine had decided not to take Cherry Tree Cottage after all, and had taken me in as a lodger in her flat.

At the beginning of April Fox sent me a note to say that I was to meet him at the office of *The Westminster Gazette*, shortly before noon – the time I came to know so well, the moment when the proof of the front page leader had been corrected, the paper sent to press, and the Editor was free. I was there before my time, and walked nervously round Salisbury Square till the moment arrived. Fox, in his shaggy great-coat, was waiting for me in the lobby. Since I had not seen him enter, I might have concluded that he had been upstairs with Spender preparing the way for me, as he had been. He rushed me up to Spender's room, and with a 'Here he is!' set me in front of the most distinguished journalist of my time. His grave, serious eyes regarded me through his spectacles.

I have good reason to think of that meeting often: for on that day I became what I have been ever since, a professional journalist. But chiefly I think of it in quite another light. It was the first and last time I saw Spender and Fox together. Fox is dead; and now for many years Spender has had no newspaper to edit and control. Modern journalism has no place for an editor of Spender's kind: or for a contributor like Fox whose function it was to set and judge the compositions in Greek and Latin verse by which, among many other things, the old *Westminster* was distinguished. Those two men, met together, represent vividly to me an old order which has passed. One felt, in their presence, that it was indeed no mean thing to be a journalist: that it was not a trade, but indeed a profession, with precise and exacting standards of honour and integrity; and one also felt the dignity of Liberalism. Two humaner men – two men more liberal in the ideal sense of that now hackneyed word – were not, than these two friends. During the time I was busy round and about the office of the old *Westminster* I was to catch glimpses of most of the famous Liberal politicians in that heyday of Liberalism in the two years before the war; but none of these – not even Mr. Asquith – impressed me as possessing quite the same fineness of soul as these two men. Perhaps if I had met Lord Morley, I should have been able to salute a spirit essentially the same as theirs. But I did not; and in my scale of values Liberal cabinet ministers and even Prime Ministers have to take rank below men like Spender and Fox.

When they joined forces against me, as they appeared to do, it was hard indeed for me to stand my ground. 'After all,' said Spender, 'a first in Greats *is* worth having.' 'And why not take a year in Germany before you make the plunge?' said Fox. 'There are new travelling fellowships; the College would give you one gladly, I believe.' 'Besides', said Spender, 'it's only a matter of three months' more work.'

'But I ceased to work a year ago. I don't work. I simply read Plato over and over. I don't *work* even on him. I can't see him from the Schools point of view any more. I don't know why, but I just can't.'

And if I had been aware of what had happened to me, I could have added: 'And I've fallen hopelessly, finally in love.' But I was not aware of anything save that it had become still more impossible than before to go on with Oxford.

Somehow, I convinced them that it was so.

'Well, well, it can't be helped, I see,' said Spender. 'But

remember, there's no future in this profession. Since Northcliffe came, we journalists are doomed. I can't take you on the staff; but I'll give you what work I can. You must begin by writing paragraphs.' He opened the fresh copy of the day's *Westminster* on his desk and pointed to them

'We pay 7s. 6d. each for these. One a day is £2 5s. a week; two a day is £4 10s. – if they are accepted. Get them in every morning by the first post. I'll take what I can. And you had better look in at this time every Friday, when the books are given out for review.'

I stammered my thanks and prepared to leave. Evidently Fox and Spender had something more important to talk about. 'Just a moment,' said Spender, and sat down at his desk. He wrote a cheque for £5. 'That's in advance,' he said. 'It will be taken from your first earnings.' It never was.

I had told Katherine Mansfield of the coming interview, and arranged to bring her the result. For the next thing I remember is her opening the door of her flat to me. She was ready to go out, dressed in a tailored suit of dark blue serge, with a small cream-coloured straw-hat trimmed with a tiny bunch of gay flowers – there was something almost boyish about her. Perhaps it came from the little tailored coat, which hung straight from the shoulders. But no: it was more inward than that. She was not, somehow, primarily a woman. I was not conscious of her as a woman. She was a perfectly exquisite, perfectly simple human being, whose naturalness made me natural. With her there was no need to pretend.

'I've got a job!' I said.

Her brown eyes sparkled. 'Not really?' she said incredulously.

I nodded. It was hard to prevent my face from beaming with a stupid smile. 'Really and truly . . . Let me show you.'

She led the way into her writing-room. I took Spender's cheque out of my pocket-book and laid it before her. 'That's in advance – for work,' I said.

She seemed to be as blissfully astonished by it as I. She

clasped her hands together and said, 'I *am* glad'. And I knew she meant it. I began to explain how it had happened. 'No, don't tell me now', she said. 'Let's go and have lunch.'

As she was closing the door, she paused, as though remembering something. 'You haven't really *seen* my flat', she said and led the way in again. 'You haven't seen the kitchen.' It had a gas-stove, a white-wood table and two chairs, and a big window which she opened. 'That is my *view*,' she said. It looked out over the top of a vast forest of chimney-pots, with here and there in the distance a tall grey church-spire, almost silvery in the sunlight. No street could be seen. The noise of the London traffic sank to a low hum – no more, it seemed, than the natural murmur of the city forest, making the quiet intense.

'Do you like my view?' she asked.

'It's beautiful.'

She showed me her second sitting-room Like the first, its walls were covered with plain brown paper, and the floor with matting. There was a black grand piano and a divan. The fireplace was filled with a great bunch of lavender. On the floor was a big *pawa* shell, and a flat oval bowl of water with a green-brown lizard within.

She showed me her bathroom and her little bedroom – hardly more than a cubicle – with just room for a camp-bed and a chair; and then she had shown me everything.

'Do you like the place I live in?'

'Very much.'

'It's a good place for work, and it's not dear – really. £52 a year. It's better, don't you think, to spend the money on the rooms and go short on the other things? Better be hungry than sordid.'

We went to the ground floor of the Isola Bella restaurant and sat with our backs to the window. We were alone, save for the proprietress who served us. Then I told the story of the interview. Katherine listened. Half-way through, 'I like your Fox', she said. At the end: 'Let me look at that cheque again.' I produced it. She studied it.

'I don't think I've ever liked the look of a cheque so much.'

'Do you know', said I, 'I think you are in some way responsible for this?'

'Me?'

'Yes. You see, I think you clinched it in my mind. If it hadn't been for that talk of ours, I might never have tackled Fox.'

She pondered this. Her beautiful hand, cupped like a shell, moved slowly on the table. 'I wonder . . . I would like to think so.'

CHAPTER XV

KATHERINE MANSFIELD

My life at Oxford was ended. Though I had not openly disgraced myself, it had been a failure. My first year, indeed, had been idyllic; but ever after I had been straining at the leash. A conviction had steadily grown within me that Oxford was 'unreal'; and though the forms assumed by my efforts to escape its unreality was dubious, the increasing strength of my feeling was not. Its roots, though I did not understand it then. were social. The life I lived at Oxford was the life of a relatively rich young man: yet I was in fact an extremely poor one, and I was always conscious that if I was to continue in this kind of life after my time at Oxford was over, I must deliver myself over to a career. The choice before me, if I wanted this kind of life to continue, was really very small. For either I must earn my own living immediately, or I must seek some further endowment. And that reduced, in fact, to the simple choice: either I must remain there as a Fellow, or I must enter the Civil Service. I spent many hours dreaming how different life would be if I had possessed two pounds a week of my own for a few years, so that I might stand back and take a breath and make a real decision.

I was restive under the sense of economic compulsion. Though I liked the ample way of life at Oxford, it was not so precious to me that I was prepared to commit myself to a career in order to maintain it. Though I liked the feeling of being rich, I did not dislike the feeling of being poor, provided that I could be poor in my own way. And I truly believe that, if the most meagre security had offered itself, I would have. married Marguéritte and cheerfully said good-bye to all my 'prospects' for ever. Oxford was 'unreal' to me, because it was an abnormal interlude in the continuity of my own life. It need not have been. If I had been ordinarily concerned with a career, with 'getting on in the world', it would not have been. It was my own fault that it was. But I felt that I had received all that Oxford had to give me when I knew by experience that I could move easily and unremarked in any walk of society, and when, further, I had finally made up my mind that, although life at Oxford itself had had an intoxicating charm for me, nothing on earth would induce me to stay there.

That, I know, was much less than just to Oxford; but to be just at twenty-two is more than human. But, even now, I think it was a right instinct which set me struggling against the influence of Oxford. I was struggling, blindly and foolishly, against a charm and a tradition which took a stronger hold of me than most young men. It was a heritage into which I had had to fight my way, and I knew better than others of my age how rare and singular it was. It was impossible for me to take Oxford for granted. I had no right to Oxford; and the queer fact that I never felt myself to be an interloper there, and that I had taken on *le ton de la maison* as though I had been born to it, only heightened my sense that my time there was a gift of the sort bestowed in fairy tales – more than three years of changeling royalty granted me by a djinn – to which, if I accommodated myself completely, either the pain of awakening would be intolerable: or, still worse, I should not awaken at all.

For I knew, though I was only too ready to forget it, that life and life at Oxford were utterly different things; and, obscurely but obstinately, the feeling grew in me that my business was with life. Yet I was terrified of life; and, as I have shown, my attempts to take the plunge into it were pathetic. They left me raw and quivering. Yet, no matter how devouring was my desire to seek shelter and safety, I was always involved again. It was as though, against my own will and the bias of my composition, I had been cursed with 'an experiencing nature', in some minor sort. My 'experiencing nature' was not of the willing, eager kind. It was of the timid, hesitating sort, that is drawn into life against its will and its desire. All it did was to venture a curious and reluctant finger into what Amiel called 'l'engrenage terrible de la responsabilité et la souffrance humaine': only to be drawn in body and soul. But that curious and reluctant finger was me.

There was nothing decisively my own either in my drift from Oxford, or in my drift towards literature. Though no doubt it is true, as I have said elsewhere, that by the time I left Oxford, I had the desire 'to be a good writer', that desire itself was fortuitous. I had drifted towards literature simply by avoiding other occupations, or by edging myself out of currents which would have swept me away from this vague thing which I called life, which I longed to avoid, yet which if I did avoid, I knew I should go a lifelong hungry man. My struggle against Oxford was simply the struggle to avoid my avoidance.

Now at long last it was finally over, and my mind was instantly busy to contrive myself another shelter from life. I would take a solitary room in London, and live like a hermit. I had no idea what I might hope to earn from the *Westminster*; but I thought that I might reckon on thirty shillings a week. I would take a big, clean room at not more than ten shillings, and live on a pound: and I would write – poetry. If I lived in that frugal, satisfying way for four or five years, I thought that I would be able to write some good poetry. Perhaps I might have done, though it is safer to conclude that I should never have done, for my plans were scattered at birth.

I had arranged with Frederick Goodyear, my senior college friend, who had taken on the duty of writing the manifesto-preface to the first number of *Rhythm* (and thereby saved that number from being quite nugatory on the literary side), that he should meet Katherine Mansfield, whose work in *The New Age* he admired. So, one night soon after my interview with Spender, we dined gaily together at the Dieppe, where dinner was 1s. 3d. We sat on and on, talking and laughing together. Goodyear's laugh was memorable; and ten years afterwards, Katherine,

thinking back to this same night, perfectly described its quality –
'a kind of snorting laugh, ending in a chuckle and then a sudden
terrific frown, and he got very red.'

'Whatever you do,' said Goodyear when I told them that I
had begun to look for a room, 'whatever you do, don't live at
home. Living at home has been the ruin of me,' he said ruefully.
Then he laughed his laugh. 'I have a parent,' he explained to
Katherine, 'who *will not* kick me out. Why, he's *glad* when I
drift back home to sponge on him again. And so, of course, I
do. The duty of a parent is to kick his offspring out, wherein if
he fails, then it is the duty of the offspring to kick himself out. That's
the law of life, which whoso offendeth, it were better for him to
wear a sky-blue suit and be an advertising agent – as I am about
to be.'

We were incredulous.

'It's true. I am already. Only the suit isn't ready yet. I
have in my care the advertising of the Stepney Progressive
Furnishing Company. You two are artists; you are effete. In
me the great twin streams of the *Zeitgeist* converge – Advertising
and Hire Purchase. The man who is the advertising agent for a
hire purchase company is the New Machiavelli. Wells has missed
the bus this time. *Ecce homo!*'

Katherine enjoyed Frederick Goodyear. He belonged to a
tribe she knew. He was a born Pa Man. After this evening they
became great friends.

We three stood on the pavement of the fountain in Piccadilly
Circus. It was a lovely spring night, and a pale moon was
shining. Nobody wanted to go home. We were happy together.

So we walked round and round.

'I shall begin hunting for a room to-morrow', I said. 'Not
more than ten shillings a week.'

Goodyear approved. Then silence fell again. It was easy to be
silent in that evening and that happiness.

'I have a suggestion to make', said Katherine airily. 'Why
not take a room in my flat? There's the music-room. I hardly

ever use it, and I certainly don't need it. We could move the piano. You can have the use of the kitchen and the bathroom. And I won't charge you ten shillings, because I shall have two rooms and you only one. Would seven-and-six be too much? I think it will suit you better than anything you will find at ten shillings.'

I could hardly believe my ears. She could not be serious. But Goodyear took it coolly enough. 'That's a damned good idea!' he said.

There was another silence. We walked round once again. Then we had to say good night.

'Do you really mean it – about the room?' I asked her.

'Of course. Why ever not?'

'Then I should like it very much.'

'Go-ood!' she said, in a small, cool, flute-like voice. Then: 'When will you come?'

'Whenever you like.'

'Well . . . let's say Thursday . . . Thursday afternoon. I'll have everything ready by then. Do you like eggs?'

I said I did. She gave me her hand, holding her body back and her other hand on her hip. '*Auf wiedersehen*', she said, and flitted across the Circus towards Shaftesbury Avenue. I watched her white hat disappear in the dusk.

'So that's K.M.,' said Goodyear.

On the Thursday – it was April 11th, 1912 – I arrived at 69, Clovelly Mansions with my belongings. Katherine was dressed, as before, and ready to go out. But she showed me my room. The piano had been shifted, and in its place by the window stood a deal table with a bright blue strip for a tablecloth, and on it a vase of catkins. A cupboard had been emptied to make room for my clothes, and there were shelves for my books. The little divan was in its old place; but now it was a bed. She gave me two keys, the big one for the hall door on the street below.

'I have to go out now. You will find your tea in the kitchen. And there are sardines and things for supper, if you want them.

You'll find everything there. I hope you will be comfortable. Now, I'll say "Good night" – Murry!' and she disappeared.

I worked hard and painfully at my paragraphs for the *Westminster* after tea. They did not come easily. I had to tear up fully a dozen before I had produced two which seemed tolerable. Then it was past ten, and I was tired. I went out to post them, and went to bed.

In the morning I was awakened by a knock at the door. 'I've finished with the bathroom,' said Katherine's voice. 'And your breakfast is in the kitchen.'

There I found the table laid, and a kettle boiling. Brown bread and butter and honey, and a large brown egg in an egg-cup. Fixed between the egg and the egg-cup, like a big label, was a half-sheet of blue notepaper, with this inscription: 'This is your egg.· You must boil it. K.M.'

Thus I became Katherine Mansfield's lodger. For weeks we went our own ways, meeting only when work was finished. Then at midnight we would have bowls of tea and bread and butter on the floor in front of Katherine's fire and talk till two in the morning. We always shook hands before we went to bed.

Occasionally, I had to work very late. My first important piece of work for the *Westminster* kept me up all through the night. I had a telegram in the afternoon summoning me to the office. Spender put two newly-published German volumes in my hand: *Deutschland und der nächste Krieg* by General von Bernhardi. Could I do two columns on them for the next morning's paper? Since I believed that it was the duty of a journalist never to refuse to do anything required of him by an editor whom he respected, I replied that I could, and took them away. I was no adept at 'gutting' a book, nor did I ever become adept at it; and my German was poor. I read on steadily from 2 p.m. to 6 a.m. before I had mastered the substance of those two volumes, and could address myself to the ticklish business of making my review of that exposition of blatant Pan-Germanism accord with the *Westminster* policy of doing nothing to exacerbate Anglo-German relations. Since I was now a regular reader of the *Kölnische* and the *Frankfurter*, I knew that the views of the *Westminster* were regarded in Germany as semi-official – *offiziös*, as they called it – because of its close relations with the Liberal Government; and I couldn't help smiling rather wanly at my semi-official self, with a head full of nothing but ache, trying to make up its mind whether the egregious von Bernhardi was to be treated seriously or not. At last my article, with the title 'The Ethics of Realpolitik', was finished, and I took it by taxi to Salisbury Square. And there, in the paper, it was two hours afterwards, unaltered, two columns full of it. Then, with the pleasant feeling that I had won my spurs, and the still pleasanter one that I had earned four guineas, I went to bed.

I gradually became a sort of jack-of-all-trades at the *Westminster*, and so eager was I to take and do as well as I could any job that was offered to me, that it was not till after some weeks that I woke up to the fact that I was in danger of becoming a Liberal political journalist. True, if I was anything at all, I was a Liberal; but truer still that I was not, and did not want to become, anything at all. So once more I began instinctively to edge myself away from the chance of a career; and once more I had the uncomfortable feeling of disappointing the expectations of one whom I admired, and to whom I owed very much. Unfortunately, there was none too much room for me on the literary side of the paper, where Miss Naomi Royde-Smith was in control, and the two reviewers senior to me were Walter de la Mare and J. D. Beresford, against whose claims my own were obviously trifling; and I had to content myself in the main with doing an omnibus weekly column reviewing fat and rather insipid books which were not worth more serious notice. There was one very real consolation about that rather depressing occupation; it left me with a fine pile of books to sell.

In fact, instead of the 30s. a week I had expected, I found myself earning an average of £5 a week. It was a pleasant discovery; but the fine point of it was blunted by the simultaneous discovery that *Rhythm* was heavily in debt. I was a complete ignoramus about printing and publishing. When the printers, who were also the publishers, told me to print 3000 copies, I took their advice supposing it to be disinterested. Now, at the end of a year, I realized the full beauty of the system of 'on sale or return'. Orders were not, as I had fondly imagined them to be, real orders. Of 3000 copies printed of the several issues not one-sixth part had been really sold. It was I who had really 'ordered' them; and it was I who had to pay – something well over a hundred pounds. It was a colossal blow; the heavier in that, out of my fool's paradise, I had announced that *Rhythm* was to become monthly instead of quarterly.

Since it had been agreed between Katherine and myself that we should edit the magazine together, we were faced with a pretty problem. Should we bring the magazine to an end? Obviously, it was the only practical thing to do. But, alas, we were not practical. Now that we were working together we sincerely felt that great things were before us. And there was, besides, the question of prestige. Katherine had broken with *The New Age*; she had been presented with a kind of ultimatum, calling upon her to choose between the two journals, and she had chosen *Rhythm*. It was intolerable to our pride that at this moment we should suffer the magazine to fade out. And we were not without hope that, if only we changed the publisher, things would be different. So, with Katherine's allowance of £100 a year, and my own uncertain earnings of £5 a week, we shouldered the burden of a magazine which we knew was losing £20 and which actually lost more than £30 a month.

We were happy. We cut our expenses down to the bone. We fed at the cheapest of cheap restaurants, and even persevered, until our stomachs could stand it no longer, at a meat-pie shop, where a pie was a penny, potatoes a halfpenny, and bread a halfpenny – twopence in all for dinner. It was false economy, for we found that we had to go to the near-by public-house, The Duke of York, to take the taste away. But we were happy. We discussed everything on heaven or earth in the small hours of the morning by Katherine's fire. I expounded my new conviction that falling in love was a complete mistake; I told her the whole story of Marguéritte; I told her of my sordid and miserable assignation at Oxford, and its sequel: and together we brooded on the meaning of my painful history. Then, as though waking out of an unhappy dream, I said gaily: 'You see, I had given up hope that this kind of thing could be.'

'What kind of thing?'

'Why, being as we are – you and I.'

'And what do you think we are?'

'Well . . . we're very fond of each other, and we aren't in love.'

'No, we're not in love. And it *is* nice. But what do you mean by being in love?'

'I mean feeling the kind of thing I felt for Marguéritte. Now what I feel for you is the kind of thing I felt for Marguéritte, *before* I fell in love with her.'

'You mean: before she was your mistress. As soon as that happened you fell in love with her, and that . . .'

'That spoiled everything, somehow.'

'I wonder why?' said Katherine.

I also wondered why; but I did not wonder deeply. Not that I wanted to deceive myself, or her. But I clung to the simple solution. My love for Marguéritte had been spoiled by the fact that we became lover and mistress. That satisfied me: for it seemed to fit with the fact that I was perfectly happy to be with Katherine, as we were. I did not want to be her lover. And no doubt I felt that I had not wanted to be the lover of Marguéritte.

I was a strange creature. Assuredly, there was little indeed of the conquering male about me; and all my life I have been without experience of those 'torments of physical passion' which, in French novels, the reluctant mistress is supposed to inflict upon her lover; and to which in the end she capitulates out of pity. I am afraid I do not much believe in them; and I certainly have no patience with a woman who should capitulate to a lover solely out of pity for his torments, which (if they *are* real) a man would be ashamed to plead. What man wants to be loved out of pity? And if the answer is that the man who pleads his torments does not want to be loved, but simply to possess the woman physically, well, the woman ought to know whether she wants to be possessed or not, and not indulge her vanity with a lot of nonsense about yielding to pity. In fact, I suspect that the 'physical torment' is merely an age-old gambit in the stupid art of seduction. It is a double appeal to a woman's vanity; and the woman who succumbs to it deserves all she gets.

I know, only too well, the ache of desire to hold one's beloved in one's arms again, to break through the devilish space of physical separation and all the infinite possibilities of disaster which that devilish space contains; I know, also too well, the ache of desire for the moment of oblivion that a woman's body can give to a man, when the burden of life is too grievous to be borne: but those aching desires are not physical torments. Of the torment of physical passion for its own sake, I know nothing. Perhaps it is merely an accident – the happy accident, if such it be, that whenever I have loved a woman, I have discovered that she loved me. If it is so, I am more fortunate than I know: for I am glad to have escaped those 'torments' which seem to my imagination so ignominious.

Anyhow, it is true that I did not want to be Katherine's lover. Or if I did, I was unconscious that I did. And the way I suppressed my unconscious desire, if it needed suppressing, was to be very clear and positive, as I was, that sex spoiled love. That is a clumsy way of putting it; for I also firmly believed that sex without love was an ignoble thing. The truth is, I suppose, that I was by now afraid of sex, simply because I had been badly hurt by it. I had suffered mentally and physically, and wanted to forget. Moreover, I believed that I was perfectly content to remain as I was. It was marvellous to me to have Katherine as my companion. I could talk to her intimately in a way I had never talked to anyone before. We trusted one another. Her wings had been more badly bruised than mine, because she had more bravely flown against the bars; but we seemed to share the same secret conviction that there was, somewhere to be found, a better way of life. And we both felt that, if only we could keep together, we should discover it. We were on the threshold of a new country.

Those were golden days. But somewhere in myself I was afraid of my own happiness. It seemed by its very nature such that it could not last; and I was half-terrified of doing anything to disturb the loveliness. And so it was that I made the odd reply over which, in after years, Katherine and I would sometimes laugh and sometimes cry, because it set a piece of our living past before us. We were talking gaily, seriously, and happily together on the floor in front of Katherine's fire. I sat in an old blue fisherman's jersey, nursing my knees, with my back against the corner of her roll-top desk; she, with a bright orange scarf over a little black velvet jacket, was kneeling by the tea-bowls. I had been musing aloud on how long our happiness would last. 'It seems', I said, 'as though it ought to last for ever.' But things never did last for ever; and I never had the feeling that happiness would last for ever, or even last long. Something would happen. A gust of wind would come and blow me from my anchorage. 'I wish', I said, 'I had finished with women; but I have an awful, sinking feeling that my affair with Marguéritte is only child's play to what they'll put me through.'

That was true enough: that was how I felt. Katherine pondered it.

'But why won't you *believe* that this will last for ever?'

'Pour toujours? Do you know I'm frightened of believing that; I'm frightened of the very word. I always hear something saying, when I begin to believe those things, "The little fool, the little *fool*!" '

There was a long silence.

'You haven't much faith, have you?' said Katherine.

'Have you?'

'I sometimes think that I am a perfect little mine of faith: only I'm not quite certain what it is I believe in.'

There was another long silence, so long that it seemed hard to break.

Then Katherine abruptly said:

'Why don't you make me your mistress?'

I was surprised, and not surprised, all at once. There was nothing in myself to give a direct, spontaneous answer to that simple question. And though it was simple, it was strange. As though I should ever dream of *making* any woman my mistress! If she had said: 'Why don't you let me be your lover?' it would have been different, and I might have been hard bested. But the question was strange and remote.

I did not say all this to her; I merely had the confused feeling that the question was strange and remote, by reason of its words. By its strangeness, it boded change. And what there was was far too precious to be exposed to change. So I lay on my back on the floor and pondered. Then at last – Katherine always reminded me of this – I raised both my legs in the air and waved them about, and said:

'I feel it would spoil – everything.'

'So do I,' she said.

Months afterwards Katherine told me she was bitterly hurt by my reply, and that she wondered that I had not noticed that her 'So do I' was bitter, too. It had meant: 'Since that is how you look upon my surrender, it would indeed be fatal if I were to surrender. Thank you for enlightening me.' But I seemed (as I was) impervious to all that meaning, and when we had said 'Good night' and she lay thinking it over in bed, she couldn't help seeing those waving legs of mine before her, and smiling at them: and then, she told me, she came finally to the conclusion that I was a very odd, and very charming person, indeed.

Odd – yes. I myself have been forced to the conclusion at the end of forty-five years of life that I am an odd person. The

charm is quite beyond my comprehension. And, were it not that
this legend has dogged me persistently and painfully, it could be
safely left to sleep. But, unfortunately, time and time again, both
men and women, whom I thought to be my friends, have made it
a capital charge against me that I possess some mysterious
'personal charm': to which they succumb, and then cherish
resentment against me for my behaviour to them. This has
happened so often and so strangely that for whole periods of my
life I have been miserably torn by the conviction that either my
friends were mad, or I was. Nor have I ever found any solution
to the mystery.

Anyhow, I am quite certain that Katherine was never
bothered by any mysterious and illegitimate 'personal charm'
about me; any more than I was bothered by her 'personal charm'.
She was a woman simple and lovely in all her ways. Yet there is
no doubt that she was regarded by many of her acquaintance as a
rather icily perfect, remote and forbidding figure. Undoubtedly,
people tended to be 'afraid' of her. I don't know why, unless it
were that she shrank, very vehemently, from conventional and
superficial intimacies, and was terribly alert to any kind of moral
slovenliness. She had also an uncanny knack of spying out any
inward emptiness, and she made pretentious people uncomfortable. Thus, from the very first encounter, she was suspicious and
critical of Frank Harris, though she 'enjoyed' him vastly as a sort
of super-Dickensian figure. She would never have dreamed of
trusting him. Yet she made no effort at all to undermine my trust
in him; that would to her have been an interference, and unpardonable.

From the first to the last Katherine appeared to me a totally
exquisite being. Everything she did or said had its own manifest
validity. I do not think it ever entered my head, at any time, to
criticize her in any way. And certainly for a very long while I
was secretly astonished that she should have chosen me. Yet life
with her was so natural, and so naturally my own, that it seemed
that there must be some hidden congruity between our natures;

and that idea, which I must needs accept, was at once self-evident and bewildering.

For mine was a fundamentally diffident and unformed nature. I was aware of nothing in myself that was indefeasibly me. My shrinkings and my expansions, my goings-out and my comings-in, were simply things that happened. It was not I who wilted away from this person, or stretched out towards that one: I, if I was anywhere, was a disembodied spirit who watched these occurrences with surprise or alarm or acquiescence. The queer thing was that with Katherine all this was changed. At a touch, she elicited some sort of unity in me. With her I felt free and careless, gay and confident, as though the immense accumulation of an artificial self, which had been gathering about me ever since I could remember, were suddenly lifted from me.

All this I do not profess to explain, but merely to describe. My self of the days when I first met Katherine Mansfield is far more distant from me than I could easily convey. Yet, in my own belief, I remained substantially the same person until her death. As at the beginning, so at the end; I was real with her, and with no one else. Now, and for many years, this strange condition has changed. For better or worse, I have the sense of being the same person wherever I am, whatever I may be doing: the queer sensation of being a kind of wraith in nearly all my contacts and occupations has left me for ever. I can say for ever, quite resolutely, because I am convinced that it will never return to me again.

Again, I do not profess to understand this thing. I merely record that it was so, and that I am making a simple statement of fact when I say that all my real life, from this time onward till Katherine Mansfield's death, was my life with her. The rest was, indeed, a dream. There may be occasion, as I make my way onward through this narrative, to modify the absoluteness of that statement under the urge of re-discovered memories. But at this moment it seems to me to be absolutely and exactly true; and I am certain that, even if it should need to be modified, it is substantially true. The whole of the ensuing story, until Katherine's death – the story of ten years and a half – is to be read in the light (or it may be the darkness) of that declaration. It is for others to understand, if they are interested to understand: I disclaim all pretention to do so.

I suppose that it might be simply explained by saying that for ten and a half years I was in love with Katherine. That, of course, is the simple truth. But other people have been in love for ten and a half years without undergoing experience of this kind. And, I am sure, Katherine herself had no such experience. Yet, when I have written that, I hesitate. Perhaps, indeed, she did have *some* such experience; but I am sure that this absolute division between my life with her – *with* her, not in the corporeal sense, but in the meaning of all that part of my life which centred on her – and my life without her, was peculiar to me. It derived from some peculiar conditioning in me: perhaps from the extremity of my fear of life, and the consequent extremity of happiness I felt in a life wherein was no fear.

CHAPTER XVI

HENRI GAUDIER-BRZESKA

THE public-house to which we used to go to take the taste of the meat-pies away was The Duke of York in Theobald's Road. The landlady there had taken us to her bosom, and convinced herself that we were a boy and girl turn on the music-halls, 'resting'. Perhaps the combination of Katherine's velvet jacket and orange scarf, and my blue fisherman's jersey was responsible for this fixed idea: but fixed it was. All our efforts to dislodge it merely strengthened her conviction. She was positive that she had seen us in our act. At length, finding that denial was unavailing and that the notion gave her pleasure, we tacitly accepted the rôle, and Ma was mightily pleased.

'I know what it is, my dears, to be down on your luck,' she would say, with a heart-warming smile, and insist, when we had finished our drinks, on standing us another. This she did every night; nor did she ever allow us to stand her one in return. She had an easy escape, for she was obviously pregnant, and had the serene and secret happiness of a pregnant woman.

Her husband, Len, was rather a trial to her. He was a long thin man with a passion for one single tune on the gramophone: 'Rolling down to Rio,' which he would play over and over and over again. That was harmless enough: more of a trial to Ma was his incessant journeying to race-meetings, from which he returned always with the same reply: 'Just cleared my exes.' Then, while he disappeared to have his supper, Ma would whisper: 'Cleared his exes – don't you believe it! He's always down on the day: and by more than his exes, believe me.' They were a queer couple: he, long, lugubrious and taciturn, she confidential and cheerful. Yet they were evidently fond of one another; and he seemed to share his wife's liking for us.

The habitués of the saloon-bar were a collection, in the main, of kindly and faded solicitors' clerks, copyists and engrossers: not improved by the addition of a fat man with an insatiable appetite for telling obscene stories. The legal fraternity had a taste that way, too, but they drew the line, definitely and audibly, at the fat man's idea of a joke. Their bawdy talk was kindly and witty: his was neither. Besides these there would be a shop-keeping couple or two, sedately drinking stout at the round tables. And there was Lil.

We took it for granted that Lil was a prostitute, though we never saw her leave with a man. There was something tremendously impressive about Lil. One would never have dreamed of saying that one liked her: she was altogether too remote. No matter how inclusive might be the gaiety in the saloon-bar, she was never involved in it. Yet she was Lil to everybody. The name was not meant, or felt, to be a familiarity. Everybody said to her 'Good-evening, Lil' when they entered; hardly anybody said a word more to her during the evening. It was a convention of the place to ignore her – out of a kind of deference, as though she were there *incognito*. Yet if by chance she was absent, the first question asked of Ma was always: 'Where's Lil?' And a great part of the evening's conversation would then be spent in wondering what could have happened to her. Was she ill?

All unconsciously Lil played a crucial part in our lives: and the manner of her strange influence was this. I had been given for review by *The Westminster* one of Dr. Wallis Budge's translations of the Egyptian sacred books. Since I knew nothing of ancient Egypt, I was reading it with great care, and, since Katherine was out, I had been working on it all the afternoon. In the book recurred continually the phrase: *the Boat of a Million Years*. Suddenly, in the silent flat, the phrase became real to my imagination. I described the experience in the introductory chapter of my first book, on Dostoevsky, when the experience was a good many years nearer to me than it is now:

'I think I should have passed it safely, had it not been that the phrase was repeated many times. Suddenly, each faint impression united in my brain and *I saw the boat*. I was cold with horror; it was as though my very spirit had frozen. I dared not move: I dared not look out of the window, for I knew that all that lay outside would be old and cold and grey. I remember that I wept bitterly, and sobbed; the involuntary action seemed to rouse me again to physical life, and the moment was over.'

The moment was over, but not the effect of it. The cold about my heart remained. Perhaps half an hour afterwards Katherine came in.

She noticed instantly that something was wrong. 'What *is* the matter?' she asked anxiously.

'Nothing . . . it's nothing.'

'Oh no, it isn't nothing. I can see that something *has* happened.'

So I tried to explain the desolation which had suddenly descended upon me: how a sense of the futility and insignificance of all human things before the infinite process of the years had seized me with a grasp almost physical. It was as though some inward part of me which had been warm and living were suddenly cold and dead. She listened; and then took hold of my hands, and said:

'Murry, I *love* you. Doesn't that make any difference?'

It did make a difference. But, as before, we lived our separate lives. We kissed one another good night instead of shaking hands. Yet I could not rid myself of traces of the same cold ghostly fear. An icy wind from nowhere would blow upon my soul, against which I was powerless.

One night we were in The Duke of York together. The saloon-bar was half-full, and the gramophone was playing 'Rio', when suddenly the same icy wind blew upon me. But not from nowhere. It came straight out of the great mirror, where I caught sight of Lil looking intently at the reflection of her own face. Probably she had looked at herself many times before, and probably I had seen her do it. But to-night it was different. She

was looking at herself as at a stranger in whose face she was trying
to discover something. And the stranger's face in the mirror
was white and old; and the eyes in the face were dark fathom-
less caverns, reaching back, back. Lil could not take her own
eyes away from those eyes in the mirror. They had laid some
spell upon her. And well they might.

I did not know that Katherine was also watching Lil;
neither did Katherine know that I was watching her. When we
spoke of it afterwards we discovered that each had wanted the
other not to see. When I rose from my high stool to go, long
before the usual time, Katherine had followed eagerly, thankful
that I had escaped the vision.

Neither of us had escaped it. All our lives long this remained
the most vivid of our experiences together. Yet I do not believe
that either of us spoke of it again after that night. As we passed
down the mirrored corridor to the street, I said, as carelessly as
I could: 'Did you notice Lil?' 'I did', said Katherine. But even
on that night we said little about it, though it occupied all our
thoughts: there was nothing to say. We sat on the floor together
by the fire, and hardly spoke.

Lil's face in the mirror brought us finally together. Against
that vision – and all its meaning – we knew we must hold
together for *ever*. It had been part of the understanding between
us, since we had acknowledged that we did love one another,
that it might not be permanent. That night, as we clasped each
other close, and sat silent before the fire, we knew that we were
bound together for ever. That night, for the first time, we slept
in each other's arms.

Had Katherine been free, we would have married the next
day. We were not to be legally married for nearly six full years.
Katherine's husband refused to take divorce proceedings against
her. They were begun and dropped. It seemed to us monstrous
that the caprice of a husband should thus prevent us; but it may
be that there were excuses for his conduct of which we were
ignorant. And, assuredly, we did not care for the reasons for

215

which we ought to have cared. It was the practical unpleasantness which concerned and exasperated us. Almost immediately we set about looking for a home in the country, where nobody would know that we were not man and wife.

Before beginning our search, we went to Paris for a few days: chiefly because I wanted Katherine to meet my hero, F——, and I wanted him to give us his blessing. He did so with a will: he put his hand on my shoulder with a smile, while Katherine was looking out of his studio window. 'Well, Murry lad, you know my views about marriage and this art-business; but if ever a couple ought to be together, it's you two.' No doubt, he said it out of mere kindness, but his frank approval meant very much to me, and to Katherine. I had talked so much about F—— and of my admiration for him that it would have gone hard with us both if there had been a trace of hesitation to his welcome. But when he, who read little, spoke out his delight in her story, 'The Woman at the Store', our cup of happiness brimmed over. Katherine and F—— became fast friends thenceforward. Six years afterwards, F—— was the witness to our marriage, and Katherine gave me for a wedding-present one of his pictures, which she saved up to buy.

But that was far ahead: half-way through our life together, when the shadow of death was visible. I think of those few days in Paris in the full spring of 1912 as of a brief interlude when we

> thought there was no more behind
> But such a day to-morrow as to-day
> And to be child eternal.

That was our honeymoon. When we returned, troubles came thick upon us. First, *Rhythm* was becoming a heavy drain on our resources. It was plain that we must either bring it to an end, or find someone to bear the burden. Katherine had a brilliant idea. Stephen Swift, her publisher, believed that in her he had discovered a genius. What more appropriate than that she should persuade him to take over the magazine – the medium by which he would discover more geniuses? She was confident that she could persuade him; and when Katherine was confident, it was impossible to believe that she would fail. Nor did she. Stephen Swift immediately agreed to her proposal, and took one astonishing step further: of his own initiative he suggested that we two should have a salary for editing the magazine: £10 a month. And he clinched the bargain by handing us a cheque (which was duly honoured) for four month's salary in advance. It never occurred to either of us to demand an agreement in writing; but, if it had occurred to us, we should certainly have brushed the suggestion aside as churlish, in face of Stephen Swift's generosity. The next number of *Rhythm*, the first of the new monthly series, appeared in a blue cover with Stephen Swift's imprint.

Next, I was under a moral obligation to my college and to Fox to sit for my Schools at Oxford in a month's time. It was already mid-May. During the whole of the year I had done no work for the Schools at all; and now I was so immersed in journalism, and in the increased business of *Rhythm*, that it was impossible even to give that last month of feverish preparation of which I had dreamed. It was no use even to pretend to work, and I decided that it was better not to. Much better, I said and Katherine agreed, to take the risk royally and not try to conceal my absolute ignorance of a full half of the books I was supposed to have read. So we gaily decided that we would make a holiday of my taking Greats. Katherine and I and Gordon Campbell would settle in rooms on Boars Hill for a week together, while I descended daily into Oxford to let the examiners do their worst.

Gordon Campbell was a barrister friend of Katherine's, of whom I had grown very fond. He was an Irishman of great ability, who had a romantic passion for the country of his birth. He took refuge in the Celtic twilight from the sordid but profitable necessities of the Parliamentary Bar. With this long lugubrious face, his conspicuous white spats, his inseparable umbrella, his rich, forlorn and melancholy voice which quavered off, on the least provocation, into a dreamy recitation of Yeats' poetry:

To fight God's battles in the long grey ships . . .
Rose of all roses, Rose of all the wor-rld . . .

with all these, Gordon Campbell was a delightful man. I have
no doubt he still is; but he is Lord Glenavy now, and I have not
seen him for years. Anyway, he was not faithless to his creed.
When the Irish Free State was established, he threw up what
would certainly have been a very lucrative career at the Parliamentary Bar to do his share in creating the necessary new Civil
Service of Ireland. And he is now an unobtrusive but essential
pillar of the new régime.

But at this time he was chiefly to me a man to whom I could
talk my heart out. I was, in every respect, far younger than he;
and when I first met him I was shy. But since he made no bones
about accepting me, and genuinely took my 'marriage' with
Katherine as a natural thing, and, moreover, appeared to regard
me as a person of some potentiality, I became more deeply
attached to him than I knew. Anyhow I could imagine nothing
more certain to take the unpleasant taste of the Examination
Schools away than to go with Katherine and him to Boars Hill
So that was settled.

The third trouble was more soul-destroying. It concerned
my parents. For all my waywardness I was deeply attached to
them. Even though I felt that it was inevitable that a chasm
should have opened between us, I was sorry that it was there.
I was sorry, too, that I had so grievously disappointed my father's
ambition for me. But now that it appeared that the end to my
Oxford career had not been quite so ignominious as it had
promised to be eight or nine months before, and I could claim
that my failure had not been absolutely unmitigated, since I had
managed to establish myself as a journalist, it seemed that there
might be some friendly relation between us. And, characteristically, the possibility of a happy reconciliation between my parents
and me blossomed into a simple certainty under the influence of
my love for Katherine. That seemed so abundantly and astound-

ingly right that it at once justified and obliterated all that had
gone before. When they met Katherine, they could not fail to
see that there had been method in the madness of their son. It
had not been for nothing that he had disappointed them.

I say to myself now that all this confidence of mine was naive
and deluded. Indeed it was; but that does not alter the fact that
I was wholly surrendered to it, or that, when it was shattered, it
shattered me. With this naive expectation of harmony and happiness, I arranged that Katherine and I should visit my parents at
Wandsworth one Saturday afternoon, when my father was at
home. That visit was a grim experience for me; and what it was
for Katherine I dare not, even now, imagine. A curtain of ice
was between us. To my sharpened senses everything stood still
and frozen in that suburban drawing-room; and bitten in my
memory is the picture of my small brother, then about nine years
old, bewildered and frightened by the inexplicable tension, not
knowing on which side of the barrier to range himself. Perhaps
he was the most wretched of us all.

Katherine and I escaped. We returned home in silence.
I was completely humiliated, and deeply grateful to her for not
turning upon me with the question: why had I exposed *her* to
such an ordeal? So overwrought was I that I should certainly
have burst into tears. Now that I am middle-aged it is easy for
me to see what a fool I was, to have dreamed that the manifest
rightness of our love for one another could have prevailed over
my parents' horror at the situation of their son, in love with and
living with a married woman. But then I was a fool. I suspect
that I am still a fool.

But this miserable visit was not the end, nor the worst. One
afternoon, perhaps a fortnight after, there came a ring at the
door of the flat. Katherine went to open it. Suddenly I heard
her cry: 'Jack!' I rushed to the door, and to my horror found my
mother and my aunt trying to force their way in. They were
both frantic and hysterical. For a second I was on the point of
being physically sick. Then I got a sort of dream-command of

myself. There was nothing to be done. By main force I pushed my mother and my aunt outside. To this day I can hear myself saying, in a voice not my own, 'Go away, you women! Go *away!*' Then I locked and bolted the door and turned to Katherine. Her face was white as chalk, and she was shivering as with an ague. I simply picked her up and laid her on the couch, covered her with a rug, and sat by her side, and listened to the battering on the door. My own heart seemed to go quite still, as if I was dying.

That, I know, is not a pleasant incident either to remember or record. Why should I rake it out from oblivion? For one sole reason: that this narrative is concerned with the truth, and there could be no truth about my life which did not contain that incident. But why try to tell the truth? That I do not know; I do not understand the nature of the obscure impulse which compels this effort after the truth of my own life. But I do know this: that, as Lawrence said, 'it is terrible to be young': that there is no suffering to be compared to that which comes to the young, and the naive, and the innocent. And it is precisely such an impersonal malignity of things as I then experienced which bites so deep. If I could have hated my mother at that moment, it would have been far easier for me; but I could not. I loved her, and I knew that she, timid thing that she was, was acting heroically out of her love for me – she wanted to save me from perdition – so that I even loved her for what she was doing. And though, as I have said, I acted unhesitatingly, the stress of the subsequent conflict was acute. It was nearly three years before I saw my mother again; and then, I am happy to say, she became one of Katherine's most single-hearted admirers. In her will, Katherine bequeathed to her her most valuable single possession – the fur coat which she bought a year before her death.

But I could not then foresee that sad and happy sequel. For the moment, all that I knew was that out of the simplest loyalty to Katherine I must cut myself off absolutely from all communication with my family: which I did. It cost me something, and the hardest part of the price I had to pay was not the severance from my mother (because deep down I knew that the bond was unbreakable) but the severance from my small brother. He had been always my faithful esquire, who believed in me implicitly; and I grieved bitterly over the thought that his faith in me had to be destroyed.

What with this inward convulsion, my new and pretty arduous work as a journalist, our new responsibilities for *Rhythm*, it surprises me in retrospect that I even managed to sit out the examination at Oxford. I did better than I feared. I was at least viva'd for a First on the strength of my essays on Plato; and perhaps, had my Ancient History been less palpably shocking, I might have pulled it off. However, I was more than content with a tolerable second, and, having taken my degree, believed I had done with Oxford for ever. I did not see the University again till 1921, when Sir Walter Raleigh (to my equal surprise and pleasure) invited me to give a course of lectures in the English School on 'Style'.

It was about this time that I met Henri Gaudier-Brzeska. He had sent some drawings to *Rhythm* which had impressed us greatly, and we invited him to come to see us. He wrote to ask: Might he bring his sister with him? We gladly agreed. They came along one evening to supper, he with a big portfolio under his arm. Straightway, the four of us plunged into an animated discussion, so that Katherine and I forgot all about the *pot-au-feu* for supper. We were recalled to reality by an unmistakable smell of burning. It was indeed a tragedy. For Katherine and I were very hard up – the strain of paying off the deficit on the first year of *Rhythm* was exhausting – but what was worse, we knew that the Gaudiers were living practically on starvation-level. Our *pot-au-feu*, which was substantial, had been prepared to give them a substantial meal. This famous *pot-au-feu* was instituted by me, after we had decided that to continue with the meat-pies would make us ill. For a few days we lived on snippets of ham bought from a tiny general shop behind the block of flats. One day I asked the shopman the price of the knuckle from which all the saleable ham had been cut. He looked at it with an appraising eye, and said 'Sevenpence'. I bought it on the spot, for I knew that there was more than a shillingsworth of ham on that bone, and a day's good soup from the bone itself. Katherine was impressed by my knowledgeability in these matters, and still more impressed when, with the aid of two pennyworth of mixed vegetables, I produced enough good soup to keep us going for two whole days. After that I entered into a permanent arrangement with the shopman to take from him two knuckles of ham every week.

But the special point of the *pot-au-feu* for the Gaudiers was that the knuckle was used as it came from the shop, with all its meat upon it. That it should have been burned was an unmitigated disaster. However, the Gaudiers declared bravely that it did not matter; and, since we were all hungry, perhaps it did not. Anyhow, we topped up – to use Katherine's word – with plenty of bread and cheese and lashings of coffee, and soon were lost in talk again; or rather, lost in Gaudier's talk. For, as he told me afterwards, he had decided instantly on seeing me, that I was the man in whom he must confide absolutely. And it was not many minutes before he told us that Sophie was not his sister, nor Gaudier-Brzeska his real name. We could do no less than tell them in return that we were not really Mr. and Mrs. Middleton Murry. 'What did I say?' said Henri, turning radiantly to Sophie. Naturally we pressed to know what he had said. And Sophie explained. It was not that they had guessed that we were not married; but from something in our letters, Henri had surmised beforehand that we four were destined to become intimate friends. The discovery that we were two pairs of unmarried lovers had made it a certainty.

Assuredly, if destiny had been kind, we should have become bosom-friends; indeed, for a short space we were: the shortness of the friendship and the manner of its dissolution were tragic.

The irony of the disaster would have suited Thomas Hardy, though, strangely enough, when I came to know Hardy, the story had passed clean out of my mind. However, before we parted that night, Gaudier had told us the full story of his life, and of his meeting with Sophie. This last was a truly beautiful story; but since it has been told already, it is not my business to tell it again. Nor could I tell it as it would need to be told, or re-told – as it was told to us that night, with the life-worn Sophie eagerly interrupting to correct Henri on every tiny point of detail. My heart melted towards her. It was all so precious to her, and it was all, because of that, so beautiful. They were a lovely and a noble pair.

It was settled that, in order to eternize the birth of this new friendship, Gaudier must immediately model my head, and I arranged to go to sit in his room at Chelsea. Then, as we parted, he suddenly seized me in his arms and hugged me and kissed me. I was quite unprepared for this; and the violence of his embrace left me breathless. I was embarrassed, as I always am, by any physical demonstration of affection, and I had the uneasy feeling that I had unwittingly awakened in Gaudier a kind of passion that was incomprehensible to me, and therefore alarming. I was acutely conscious, too, of the immense physical strength in that lithe body of his; and far away on the edge of my mind passed a sort of presentiment that it would need but little to set him murdering instead of hugging me.

But in my own way I took Gaudier to my heart. His passionate simplicity had crashed through all my defences; and I was convinced, in the simplest possible fashion, that he was a genius – in the true sense: a man with a daimon. I have never felt this with any other person except D. H. Lawrence. They are the only two men whom I have immediately recognized to be of a different *kind* from myself. I have made brief contacts, at one time or another, with many of the famous figures of my time – at any rate with those eminent in art or literature – but with all of them, save Gaudier and Lawrence, I have felt that the difference between them and me was one of degree only: but with these two it was a difference of kind. By no imaginable perfecting of my elements could I have become a creature of their tribe. And if I were required to distinguish what it was which thus set them apart from me, and from other men, I should say it was a kind of profound animal spontaneity, but not on the animal level. They were complete human beings, but with the grace and poise and quickness of an animal in *all* their human doings. Lawrence in the act of writing, Gaudier in the act of modelling, were at once totally concentrated, and totally uninvolved, like a cat who, from total intentness on the capture of a bird, can in a flash subside into total indifference. Indeed, from the beginning one image of Gaudier took possession of my mind: the image of a panther, crouching to the ground, almost one with the earth, sinuous, swift and strong.

Like Lawrence, Gaudier had a pretty complete contempt for all contemporary artists, which did not strike me as overweening. In virtue of their daimon, both of them had the right to be thus contemptuous. My acceptance of this did not mean that I accepted their judgments as right. For aught I knew Gaudier or Lawrence might be wrong; but I felt that I could not challenge their opinions except from an immediacy of conviction equal to their own. With Gaudier I was never in this position. For one thing, our friendship was 'brief as the lightning in the collied night'; and for another I never have been able to acquire intense convictions in the matter of art as I have in the matter of literature. Except in the province of architecture, plastic art has never been more than a matter of liking with me: but in literature, though slowly and painfully, I have come to feel that the significance of certain things is overwhelming – a question of life or death. Since I had no such convictions concerning art of any kind when I was friends with Gaudier, I listened with interest and without opposition, to his complete dismissal of all modern sculpture. As I watched my head being transmuted into something strangely like, and strangely unlike me – strangely unlike in that it became

massive, heroic, hieratic, the head of a sort of brooding demiurge[1]
– I was quite prepared to accept his right to give judgment.

The room in which I sat for him was almost entirely bare.
There was a bit of a bed, in which the springs were more conspicuous than the mattress, perhaps a couple of seedy deck-chairs,
and a scrap of matting on the floor. Sophie would be sitting on the
bed. And Gaudier, while he worked, intent and swift, would tell
me about the book that Sophie was writing. I never read this
book. While our friendship lasted it was not yet in a condition to
be read; but I understood that it was the complete story of Sophie's
life. Anyhow, Gaudier declared that it was marvellous. About
that I felt rather sceptical. Not that I did not believe that Sophie's
life-story was marvellous; but I had the uncomfortable feeling that
Sophie was not the one to tell it. The mere mention of the book
agitated her visibly; and at the same time she obviously loved that
it should be mentioned. She was, I thought, far too involved in
her own writing for it to be good, and I came to look forward with
apprehension to the moment when the manuscript would be in a
condition to be submitted to Katherine and me. I feared that
honesty and dishonesty in our judgment would be alike disastrous.

Already there were potentialities of discord. Katherine admired and liked Gaudier; but for Sophie she felt more pity than
affection. She told me that she was afraid of Sophie, as of the kind
of woman who would fasten her tentacles round her and suck her
dry. And I, at least vaguely, understood what Katherine meant.
There was something hungry and avid in Sophie, as if it were a
void in her incessantly seeking to be filled. She was eager both to
confide in Katherine and for Katherine to confide in her: what
Gaudier and I were to be to one another, Katherine and she
were to be to one another. That, even I knew, would never work.
If the four of us were to be friends, there could be no such pairing-
off. Katherine did not mind being confided in particularly; but
she was adamant against confiding. Why should she confide,

<hr>

[1] An account of the destruction of this head is in Mr. Brodzky's book on
Gaudier-Brzeska.

when she felt neither need nor impulse to confide? The notion of swapping intimacies as a sort of game, or at least a self-indulgence, was completely repugnant to her at all times. Sophie sensed this resistance in Katherine.

Katherine and I were still intent on our plan of finding a hiding-place in the country. The Gaudiers were enthusiastic about the idea. They would be able to come for week-ends. And Katherine and I were happy in that thought. There should be a place for Gaudier to work. Then he insisted that he must pay his share. But that was obviously out of the question. The week-end fare alone would be as big a burden as he could possibly carry – probably bigger. And so it proved. For the house we found, and fell in love with, was at Runcton, on the Selsey side of Chichester – a 'cottage' indeed, but a 'cottage' in the Jane Austen sense of the word: a very pretty small house, which we could have for £40 a year. Since we were already paying £52 a year for the Gray's Inn Road flat, and *Rhythm* was now no longer to be a burden, we felt that we were justified. And we had fallen in love with it. As we stood in the long, low dining-room and looked out on the walled garden, Katherine dropped her head on my shoulder: 'It's lovely; it's *our* place.'

At this moment, had we been thoughtful creatures, we should have hesitated. We should have said, first, that it was *too* lovely: and must undoubtedly conceal a snare – what Katherine called 'the snail under the leaf'. Second, we should have said that it was too far away, for though the distance suited us well enough, it could not suit the Gaudiers, who could not afford to travel as far as Chichester every week-end. But we did not hesitate. We had signed a three-year lease before we saw the Gaudiers again. 'All the better,' said Gaudier, when he heard how far it was. 'Sophie will *live* there – it will do her good: and I shall be able to come every week-end: even if I have to walk.' To that, we could say nothing; or we had not the courage to say anything. But when we reached home, Katherine cried. 'It's our house,' she moaned. 'Our first house, our wedding-house. I can't bear the idea of anybody else *living* there. They could come at the week-ends and be welcome; but all day and every day – no, it's too much.'

We kept silence, and set to the business of furnishing our house. With our added £120 a year, with Katherine's £100 a year, with my earnings of £5 a week, it appeared that we were moderately secure of £450 a year. So we went off to Maples,' and completely furnished the house on the hire-purchase system. Further, Katherine engaged an ex-soldier to do everything about the house. We then transferred our lease of the flat, arranged for the removal of our few things, of which the chief were our books and Katherine's grand piano, told the Gaudiers it would take us a month to settle in, and departed for Runcton.

All through August we painted and stained and polished. The month was nearly over. Rather sadly Katherine wrote to the Gaudiers to say that all was finished; and that Sophie could come at any time she pleased. Her room was ready. And a charming room it was. Katherine, having made up her mind that there was no escape, had done her utmost to make a beautiful room for Sophie: at any rate, if she was to live with us, she should be happy – if that were possible.

Gaudier's reply was dumbfounding. Neither he nor Sophie, he wrote, wanted to have anything to do with us any more. They had learned what utter traitors we were. As for Jack, they neither of them believed that he was actually bad; but since he was completely under the thumb of Katherine, who was bad through and through, it came to the same thing. Fortunately, they had found us out in time. He, Gaudier, would have nothing more to do with *Rhythm* in any way. We were to send him back whatever drawings of his we might have, and we were to lose no time in paying for those which we had reproduced.

This was completely incomprehensible to us. After trying to make head or tail of it, we could only conclude that someone must have been telling lies about us; and Katherine wrote him a gay little note to say that, unless he had gone completely mad, he must give some explanation of his astonishing letter. The reply came by return. It did give the explanation, and the explanation was astonishing. There had been a tragedy indeed.

On the Saturday before, he wrote, he found that his impatience to see the new house was intolerable. So he had made up his mind to pay us a visit. Since he could not raise the full fare, and did not want us to offer to pay, he had decided to take the train half-way and walk the rest. Since he had not known how long it would take, he had not warned us of his coming. But he had arrived, and come in by the garden gate (which was well to the side of the house). As he approached the house he had heard Katherine and me talking, while we were hanging the curtains in the big room in front. The windows were wide open. He had heard Sophie's name mentioned. And the sudden impulse to hear what we were saying about her had come to him. He had crept close to the house wall, crawled under the window, and listened. When he had heard what Katherine was saying about Sophie, while I made some half-hearted defence of her, he had gone straight away, resolved never to see us again, for ever.

It was terrible. We remembered that we had been hanging curtains on the Saturday afternoon at the open window, and that Katherine had been talking about Sophie. She had said nothing cruel, and nothing untrue: merely that she was quite sad that the good time of our being together alone was coming to an end, and that now, with Sophie's coming, everything was going to be spoiled: that she did not, could not really like Sophie. She couldn't make herself like a person. With Sophie, she never had any impulse to go out towards her, but only to shrink back. She felt that Sophie wanted to drag her into a morass. I had listened glumly, and rather with the idea of encouraging Katherine than speaking the truth about Sophie, had said that I thought she had been badly treated by life, and that, once she had the chance of a real rest in the country, she would grow calm and peaceful again.

It was terrible. We thought of poor Gaudier there by the window, having come in all the passionate simplicity of his heart to his chosen friends, dusty and tired – he had walked nearly thirty miles – but brimming with happiness at the thought of the glad surprise with which we should welcome him: and hearing what he heard. And we were overwhelmed with misery. The damage was irreparable. We knew it, and made no attempt to reply. For either Katherine would have had to maintain the truth of her criticism of Sophie, which would have hurt again, or to withdraw it all, which would at best have landed us in a new falsity – neither could Gaudier have believed it. I returned to him such of his drawings as we had; and I saw him but twice again before his death.

Thenceforward, Gaudier became an almost malignant enemy of ours. Nor could I be surprised at that; but I was surprised by the meanness of his suspicions. It thenceforward became a matter of faith with him that Katherine and I were making an enormous profit out of *Rhythm*, by obtaining contributions and drawings for nothing. He knew that, in fact, this was absolutely impossible; but he needed to believe it, and he did. I do not understand this curious capacity to believe every kind of turpitude of a friend who has disappointed you. It is quite alien to my own nature. My own experience is that if a man has been my friend, it is a psychological, or spiritual, impossibility for me to believe him really base. But I have to confess, sadly, that this simple law has been quite in-operative in the case of some of my own friends. There seems to have been no possibility of a mean in their attitude to me. Either I must be enthroned high on a pedestal, as the man of men, the one and only understanding friend, or, when that brief apotheosis was over, I must be held completely vile, and capable of every iniquity. I appear to have loomed in their eyes as a kind of Satan: at one moment a Prince of Glory, at another on the burning marl. It happened to me so often that, after many painful years, I hardened myself within, and came to take no more account of it. I simply ceased to desire or to seek friends.

But the process of this self-hardening was painful. What I have called Gaudier's 'malignity' towards me was my first real initiation into it. I had, as I have said, returned to him all the drawings of his which we had; but I had forgotten a thin purple book of poems by Jehan Rictus, which he greatly admired and had lent me. Gaudier, at the time of our rupture, said nothing about this, and I forgot it. But some two months later, when our life at Runcton was at an end and we were in London again, he wrote me a savage letter which treated the retention of this book as a sinister crime. Unfortunately, I could not find it. After two quickly succeeding removals (one of the catastrophic sort) a thin purple book was naturally hard to find. Moreover, I bitterly resented his attitude – as though I had swindled him out of his last shilling. So I dashed out to the post office and bought a postal order for 2s. 6d. – the price of a 3 fr. 50 book in those far-off days – and wrote to him coldly, suggesting that this trouble was simple to mend. He had only to order another copy, for which I enclosed the money. But, in my agitation, I left the postal order out of the letter, which I rushed out to post immediately. When I came back I found it on my table. So I put it in another envelope, and posted it later in the day. The next morning I received another savage letter to say that he knew me so well by now that he was not surprised that I had 'pretended' to send him a postal order, with the deliberate intention of not sending it. It ended with the usual abuse and a curious postscript to the effect that though I was vile beyond imagination, Katherine was yet worse; and he was sure it was she who had put me up to this trick. That was the last letter I received from him. Not a word of apology when he received the missing postal order, as he must have done, by the next post. And I had, and have, no doubt that he convinced himself that I had sent it only when my 'trick' had been unmasked.

It may seem childish to record an episode so trivial. But it had a deep effect upon me; for by this time I was well nigh overwhelmed with disaster. And possibly the whole episode of which this was the fantastic and sordid conclusion was of hardly less importance in Gaudier's own life than it was in mine. He suffered, I think, as badly as I did; and the experience may have had something to do with the savage *je m'en fichisme* which was characteristic of him and his utterances in the brief succeeding years of his life and work. For I am quite certain that Gaudier was very different from the strong, implacable, steely man he gave himself out to be. At heart he was extraordinarily sensitive and tender; even sentimental, in the good sense of that word. The Gaudier who was friends with me – and while we were friends we were very intimate friends indeed – was a very real Gaudier. I do not presume to say he was *the* real Gaudier; but I am quite certain that he was not a fictitious personage, an assumed character. What happened I think was that, in contact with Katherine and me, he gave free play to an element in his nature which, in his hard struggle with life, he had suppressed perforce; and when he thought he discovered that we had played him false he closed down like a vice upon that element in his nature which, he felt, had exposed him to intolerable pain. For it does not need much imagination to understand that the pain he must have suffered under our window at Runcton was intolerable. Henceforward, that side of his nature would be revealed to Sophie alone.

Much the same process was happening to me. For I suffered also under what seemed to me then his motiveless malignity towards me. I could and did understand that he was deeply and perdurably hurt; but I could not understand why he should treat me as a kind of *canaille*. It seemed just monstrous and unendurable: and, as I have said, this final blow came at a moment when I had already more than I could carry. I turned more and more to Katherine.

CHAPTER XVII

RUNCTON COTTAGE

WE moved into Runcton Cottage in August, 1912; by early November we had been driven out again.

We had furnished the house by hire-purchase. We had our soldier-servant, who swindled us right and left and was dirty beyond imagination. We were staggering under the shock of the experience with my mother and with Gaudier. Our blithe confidence was well on the ebb. A strange feeling of precariousness now began to invade us, while we lived in that beautiful house, with its sun-dappled rooms, its walled garden, and its medlar trees, as though it were a kind of stage-scenery that might be removed in the twinkling of an eye. As between ourselves we were happy; but now with the sickening sense that this happiness was only snatched from the jaws of a devouring element, and that we held each other as it were upon a little island of sand which the tide was eating away. At this moment, and perhaps for this cause, a deep desire to have a child took possession of us both; and, wonder of wonders, it seemed that this desire was to be realized. We scarcely dared to breathe about it, so sweet and secret and agonizing was our desire. Dimly we felt that, if only this would happen, we should be secure against all that might assail us. Then, the scenery might go. What would it matter? We should *be*, in a way in which we were not.

How was it, I ask myself when I try to recapture the feeling of those autumn days, that two beings such as Katherine and I should have been a prey to a subtle sense of our own unreality, as though we were only a kind of dream-children, haunting the house we loved, not living in it, not consubstantial with it? Or as though the house, and the salt-marshes before it, and the pasture-fields

232

behind, were merely remembering us, or evoking us, out of some beyond? I do not understand how this should be; but that it was so, I know. We were encompassed by an aching sense of effort to become real, and we knew it did not lie within our power to decide this issue. It trembled in the balance of the Gods. Somewhere, a long and delicate struggle was being waged about our destinies. And sometimes we had faith and were brave, and sometimes we disbelieved and were afraid.

All the while, we were condemned to be passive. Things were happening to us. While we dreamed, the waking life went on: and there was no conjuncture between them. Whether this conjuncture should be, or not, depended on the birth of a child. We spoke of him, we named him – Dicky was his name – we thought of him, hid him in the garden, astonished him with flowers; but, as yet, he had only the same kind of reality as we. Let him but be born, and he would break through the veil that we could not penetrate. And often in the evenings, when the scent from the magnolia tree by the door would come in soft waves through the window, it would fill us with a kind of agonizing premonition that neither in any house made with hands, nor in any country of this earth, nor in any child of our bodies, should that which was between us find an abiding-place. In the half-dusk, by the window, at such a moment, I could see Katherine's eyes brimming with tears.

But mostly we believed, or tried to. And things happened. Suddenly a Slavonic friend of Katherine's came to England, and being penniless, came to us, with two big black trunks full of books and manuscripts, for he was a writer. Once again, we resented this intrusion upon us, not personally, but as an unkind stroke of fortune, that would not suffer us to be alone. We made him welcome, though he was a burden to our purse as well as our spirit. In the solemn autumn evenings the house would echo to his forlorn Slav songs, and once more we would be spell-bound by a sense of the precariousness of all things human and lovely. At this time, too, we were enchanted by the verses of Walter de la Mare,

233

whom we now knew, and whose little book *The Listener* appeared
at this moment.

> But words are shallow, and soon
> Dreams fade that the heart once knew;
> And youth fades out in the mind,
>   In the dark eyes too.
>
> What can a tired heart say,
> Which the wise of the world have made dumb?
> Save to the lovely dreams of a child,
>   'Return again, come!'

We read his verses to one another, and we felt that he shared our
secret, and our sadness; but, if only we were granted a child who
might dream our dream anew, nay, embody it and make it prevail,
as we could not – all would be well.

Friends – new friends – came to stay with us: Eddie Marsh,
the generous, who would gladly have taken us under his wing, I
believe, if we had been the kind of people who could be taken
under a wing at all; Rupert Brooke, the debonair, who told us
with a gay laugh macabre and horrifying tales of old women in
lonely houses being devoured by their own cats, and of strange
and sinister happenings among the Lithuanian peasants, of which
he was making a play; and our own Frederick Goodyear, boisterous
and blushing and brilliant. Rupert Brooke and Goodyear,
Katherine and I tramped miles over the salt marshes in the dusk,
singing the choruses of Goodyear's innumerable songs. Eddie
Marsh was not with us then. He came alone; and hoisted me
upon his back, so that I stood on his shoulders, to gather medlars
from our tallest medlar tree. And even to-day, whenever I think
of Eddie Marsh, I think of that moment when, elegant and
immaculate, he made me clamber on his shoulders as though it
were the most natural thing in the world, and stood firm while I
picked the bright brown fruit, while the smoke from a fire of
leaves curled lazily about us.

But these were only ripples in our pool of silence; even while our friends were with us. they merged into our dream. Nothing, it seemed, could break it; nor was it broken when the crash came. We did not wake from a dream into reality: the dream changed sickeningly into a nightmare. At the moment when our hope of a child seemed on the brink of certainty it was gone, and gone for ever. And at that moment we were hurriedly summoned to London. The publisher of *Rhythm* was bankrupt, or on the point of bankruptcy, and the printers had seized upon the fact that they had been given no notice of a formal change in the printing order, to make me responsible for everything. The publisher had increased the printing order; but he had done it in my name. I owed them £400. Four hundred pounds! It might as well have been four million. And the salary on which we were depending to pay for the furniture was no more.

The devastation was complete. It was so complete that it was almost a comic relief to return and find that the soldier-servant was drunk, and making a maudlin confession of theft. He had taken what few portable valuables we had – a couple of watches and the like – sold them for a few pounds, backed losers with some of it and drunk the rest. We were too defeated to be angry. 'Oh, go away!' we said, 'and don't come near us again.' But we were not alone. There was V——, the Slav, walking up and down the long drawing-room, as though in travail of some impossible solution to our disaster, singing his melancholy songs. It was a sort of comfort to know we should not be required to 'lend' him any more money. But we had a good deal yet to learn about the expectations of a temperamental Slav.

There was nothing for it but to try to clear up the wreckage. A good angel appeared. A village woman, whose husband had heard our soldier-servant boasting at the public-house about the way he was 'doing' us, came to the door to ask if she could help. Mrs. Bean talked to Katherine so kindly and motherly that she came crying into my room, where I was doing desperate arithmetic to discover whether anything could be saved. 'There *are* good people in the world,' said Katherine. There are. For the fortnight that remained to us, Mrs. Bean, with her smile, her grey alpaca, and her instinct for doing the first thing first, was the rock on which we rested. With soap and water she conquered the disgusting dirt of the kitchen, she plunged the batman's filthy bedding into a great tubful of suds, she saved our money and she saved Katherine's health, she fed and cosseted us – all out of the kindness of her heart. For no cause at all she made us, who were nothing to her, her everything. Only she could not abide the 'foreign gentleman'. She had no charity for him.

Meantime, we had decided that our position was hopeless; and that the only thing to do was to make this clear to everybody concerned. I wrote to the printers to say that I did not regard the debt as mine at all: that it was completely beyond my capacity to pay, and that I had no intention of trying to. They must do what they liked. And I wrote to Maple's to tell them that the salary on which I had relied to pay for the furniture had now disappeared, and that they must take it all away. There remained the question of *Rhythm*. It now had a certain small but regular sale. It was suggested to us by Martin Secker that the printing could be done more cheaply and he kindly offered to publish it for us. At the same time Eddie Marsh gave us £100 to carry on, and suggested that he should pay a small salary, through us, to Wilfrid Gibson to act as assistant editor. H. G. Wells, Lord Dunsany, Gilbert Cannan, Filson Young, Frank Swinnerton, Ford Hueffer, and perhaps others whom I am sorry to have forgotten, helped us, whether with money or contributions, to keep afloat. Probably it was not worth the effort either for them or for us. But it seemed so then.

Then came a man with a bowler hat and yellow gloves and a writ from the printers; and after him another to seize what little of the furniture was our own. We watched the sand-island dissolve beneath our feet. Then, with our trunks, our clothes, and our books, we said Good-bye to Runcton Cottage. It was Mrs. Bean's turn to cry now; and she did.

We gave V—— some money to fend for himself, and took a single room in Chancery Lane at 10s. a week, which we furnished with one camp bed, two chairs and a packing-case. It was now mid-winter, and we were pretty miserable. We tried to sleep two in a camp bed until we ached insufferably, and one of us dropped on to the floor. This we endured until the next cheque came from the *Westminster*; it was small enough – for the turmoil had played havoc with my journalism – but it enabled us to buy a larger bed.

For the moment we temporized with the old printers, by arranging to pay them off at the rate of £100 a year: £8 6s. 8d. a month. It was a foolish thing to attempt to do: it meant that the whole of Katherine's allowance was paid straight over to the printers every month. Certainly we should have saved ourselves a good deal of hardship if we had done what wiser heads advised us to do – namely, file a petition in bankruptcy. After all, this debt was not morally ours at all. But we had no heroic intention in thus pinching ourselves intolerably; the simple fact was that we were terrified by the idea of bankruptcy. We engaged a solicitor to try to make a composition with the printers for £100, which someone offered to find for the purpose. The printers were adamant; they seemed to be under the same illusion as other people at this time: that we were really quite well-off, and if only they pressed us hard enough, they would get everything. The futile negotiations went on for some weeks, at the end of which the solicitor presented us with a staggering bill for a further £22, and left us precisely as we were before.

In the meantime we had exchanged our miserable bare room for a little office-flat at 57 Chancery Lane. We had painted on the ground-glass door in big imposing letters: R H Y T H M : *Editorial Office*, and, in accordance with Eddie Marsh's plan, invited Wilfrid Gibson to be assistant editor at the salary of £1 per week. No sooner had we settled in than we were forced to find room for our Slavonic incubus, who by this time appeared to regard himself as our dependent for life. Ever since the break-up of our home at

Runcton we had been supporting him. He was, indeed, nominally our lodger at 15s. a week; but since his method of paying this sum was to borrow from us at the rate of 25s. a week; we were not notably profited. By the time that we ceased to keep a reckoning he owed us more than £40, and when we finally plucked up courage to declare that we would support him no longer, we had not merely to move again in order to get rid of him, but to 'lend' him a further £15 to make him go.

Rhythm had become at last a *succès d'estime*. Gradually, most of the prominent writers of the younger generation had gathered round it: Gilbert Cannan, Hugh Walpole, Frank Swinnerton, Lord Dunsany, James Stephens, Walter de la Mare, Rupert Brooke, Lascelles Abercrombie, Wilfrid Gibson, J. D. Beresford, Max Plowman, and finally D. H. Lawrence. There was, one felt, a fresh breeze in the air. This was the moment at which the first collection of 'Georgian Poetry' was made by Eddie Marsh, and published to the general applause. But there was a subtle difference between the tone of *Rhythm* (which owed its very existence now to Marsh's generosity) and the tone of that famous volume, which may have been simply due to the fact that Katherine and I were in control of *Rhythm*. Moreover, my own position as editor, though it was accepted cheerfully enough by the contributors, was really rather equivocal. I was by far the youngest, and I had done nothing. All the others had at least won their spurs, published volumes, and had some measure of reputation. I had none; and, to judge by my own contributions, I did not deserve any. Though I was indeed slowly improving, I was far too deeply involved in what were to me shattering experiences to participate directly in the general feeling of confidence that was in the air.

What that was like to one who did participate in it can be gathered from this passage from a review of *Georgian Poetry* which D. H. Lawrence wrote in the last actual number of *Rhythm*. (It existed for three more months under the changed name of *The Blue Review*.) Said Lawrence:

'This collection is like a big breath taken when we are waking up after a night of oppressive dreams. The nihilists, the intellectual, hopeless people – Ibsen, Flaubert, Thomas Hardy – represent the dream we are waking from. It was a dream of demolition. Nothing was, but was nothing. Everything was taken from us. And now our lungs are full of new air, and our eyes see it is morning, but we have not forgotten the terror of the night. We dreamed we were falling through space into nothingness, and the anguish of it leaves us rather eager.

'But we are awake again, our lungs are full of new air, our eyes of morning. The first song is nearly a cry, fear and the pain of remembrance sharpening away the pure music. And that is this book.

'The last years have been years of demolition. Because faith and relief were getting pot-bound, and the Temple was made a place to barter sacrifices, therefore faith and belief and the Temple must be broken. This time Art fought the battle, rather than Science or any new religious faction: and Art has been demolishing for us. Nietzsche the Christian Religion as it stood, Hardy our faith in our own endeavour, Flaubert our belief in love. Now, for us, it is all smashed, we can see the whole again. We were in prison, peeping at the sky through loopholes. The great prisoners smashed at the loopholes for lying to us. And behold, out of the ruins leaps the whole sky.

'It is we who see it and breathe in it for joy. God is there, faith, belief, love, everything. We are drunk with the joy of it, having got away from the fear. In almost every poem in the book comes this note of exultation after fear, the exultation in the vast freedom, the illimitable wealth that we suddenly have got.'

In another sixteen months the European War had broken out. Talleyrand once said, 'Qui n'a pas vécu sous l'ancien régime n'a pas connu la douceur de vivre.' Something like, I imagine, could be said of the years immediately before the war. And though, for personal reasons, I did not participate like Lawrence in this general exaltation, I was conscious of its existence. I knew at least that it surrounded me; and, in the intervals when I ceased to be the prey of an agonizing sense of insecurity, I too was affected by the feeling of confidence, of faith in the future, which was general among my coevals at that time.

But my feeling of insecurity went pretty deep. It was, in its origin, peculiar to myself, as this narrative has shown I had had, from the beginning, an altogether peculiar fear of life. There must have been, I suppose, some original shrinking sensitiveness in myself as a little child; but this had been inordinately increased by my social instability. I was for ever passing into new social environments, and being compelled to adjust myself to them. I had a perpetual sense that I was required to live, as it were, on false pretences; that I, a creature without a background, was deceiving others into believing that I had the same background as they. And yet it was unmannerly and outrageous to do otherwise. If they were content with me as I appeared, and indeed was, why should I disturb them with unwelcome confessions? It would have been somehow boorish in me to insist that I was a 'self-made boy', as it was in the industrial plutocrat to insist that he was a 'self-made man'. After all, I was not hiding something essential, but something irrelevant, from the judgment of my friends. I was I; it was myself they knew.

But the trouble was that, all at the same time, I was not I. Though I had become the creature of my new environments, I never had the simple confidence of the member of a definite social class. 'Give me a standing-place and I will move the world', said Archimedes. I had no desire to move the world, but even for my modest purposes (whatever they were) I needed firm ground beneath my feet. The simple substitute for this unconscious social confidence which I lacked was the adoption of a recognized 'profession', the incorporation of myself into a definite society within society. But I could not stay the course. My own little daimon would not suffer it. It was not to that end that I was born: not to that end had I undergone this succession of social metamorphoses. But what might be my true end, that I did not know at all.

None the less, I had had glimpses of it. Gradually, there had emerged in me a devouring desire to love and be loved. I had tasted the condition as it were afar off; then I had drawn nearer to it; at last, with Katherine, I entered into the fullness of it. It was overwhelming. The essential insecurity which haunted me was at an end: here, in her, was my security, my rest, my peace. Now I could be, and was, known even as I knew. Now there was nothing, nor would be any more, to conceal. And this condition, even as I entered into it, I knew was the only possible condition of life for such a one as I. Herein, alone, was fulfilment and peace.

But so far from having achieved a condition *in* life, by this all-satisfying love, it seemed that I had found a beatitude outside life altogether. By a single stroke, one whose competence in the sheer struggle for life was always ridiculously small, had been bereft wholly of the faculty. If I approached life in the spirit of this love, wherein I lived and moved and had my being, the outcome was disastrous. If I took people at their word, as I could not help doing, I was involved in catastrophe. If I trusted that the manifestness of our love would, as I felt it must, overcome all prejudice, the result (as with my parents) was pure agony. If I believed that what we were must at any rate lift us free from all suspicion of bad faith, I was straightway exposed (as with Gaudier) to a hostility which set every fibre of me trembling. My life was now clean divided as by a knife: on the one side, the security of my life with Katherine: on the other, the insecurity of my life in the world. Both seemed absolute. And the one had been the cause of the other. It was the completeness of my security with Katherine which had brought me to the final knowledge of the completeness of my insecurity in the world.

And our tremulous halcyon life at Runcton had been an epitome of the knowledge which had begun to dawn in me. In its ominous opening, its secret and intimate disappointment, and its final disaster, it had expressed the absoluteness of the incompatibility between our life and life. The appearance of the writ-server, in his bright yellow gloves, had been a sort of cynical epiphany. He was not unkind; according to his lights he was friendly and affable: indubitably he meant well. But his familiarity, as he leant upon Katherine's grand piano, making it thereby indescribably his own, was a revelation. His well-meant kindness was only a more devastating comment upon our dream; as though, in a twinkling, the scenery of a play were swept away, and only a good-natured stage-hand were left between the ugly tackle and the footlights, saying to the children: 'Yer didn't believe that was real, did yer?' A devil might be more terrifying: but he would at least belong to the same order – of imagination. Though he annihilated the form, yet he would have confirmed the essence. But our visitant turned our dream, at a touch, into sheer hallucination, and revealed us to ourselves not as victims, but as fools.

It was the sense of our return to London as an unmitigated defeat that, more than any other motive, determined us, once more against all common sense, to keep *Rhythm* in being. So long as it remained, we could persuade ourselves that our defeat was unessential. If *Rhythm* also had been swept away, at that moment, there would have been nothing between us and the naked knowledge of our own complete foolishness. Probably, it was in the instinctive effort to ward off this evil day, that we flung ourselves, with redoubled energy, into the effort to keep the ship from sinking. Day after day we went out to canvass for advertisements, and if, as we occasionally did, we succeeded in getting one, we felt for a moment that we had actually won a tiny victory for our 'idea' over the world's inertia. But Katherine was far braver at this unholy task than I. Whereas one rebuff would incapacitate me for the business for the rest of the day, she would persevere till she had gone through all the names on her list. Still the strain of it told upon her; her heart began to 'flutter': and we decided that she at least must give over for a time and go to live in the country.

CHAPTER XVIII

CHOLESBURY AND LONDON

GILBERT and Mary Cannan had become good friends of ours. Gilbert had been attracted to *Rhythm*, and had come to visit Katherine and me at the very beginning of our life together. Not only had he worked hard to help us with the magazine, but he had adopted a kindly protective attitude towards me in particular. Perhaps we struck him as oddly *farouche*, for it was he who gave us the nickname of the Two Tigers, which – hardened first into Tig, then softened into Wig – was the origin of my name for Katherine till the end of her life. With his stick, his pipe and his shaggy dog, Gilbert would stride over from Kensington to Gray's Inn Road, sit silent in a corner and smile an inscrutable smile.

We liked him and we trusted him, though we found him hard to understand. The centre of him seemed to be totally withdrawn and impenetrable, but by no conscious effort of his own. And I was far too timid to make any direct inquisition into that in him which baffled me. I was far too conscious, besides, of his kindness to me to risk disturbing a relation which struck me as curiously though beneficently one-sided.

Therefore, when the Cannans, who were making ready the Mill House at Cholesbury, suggested that we should take the cottage next door to them, we responded eagerly. The cottage was, in reality, a semi-detached red brick villa; but Mary Cannan, well-practised in such transformations – indeed, a born 'interior decorator' before it became a profession – convinced us that it could be made to look beautiful inside at least. And its situation on the very edge of the Common was indeed magnificent, and the fare was cheap. So we suggested to Gordon Campbell that he should go shares in it for the summer. He agreed. That brought the rent down to three shillings a week each. And once again we settled in. Katherine stayed there permanently – permanently, in a very relative sense, of course: in the space of two years she and I moved house (house, also, in a very relative sense) no less than thirteen times – while I worked in London from Monday till Friday, when the review books were given out at the *Westminster*, after which I fled. It was a good arrangement: only I, unfortunately, was in no condition to play my part. I was scared to be alone.

In retrospect it seems fantastic; but there is no doubt that at this time – the spring of 1913 – I was really terrified of what Gaudier might do to me. His malignity had caused a sort of convulsion within me, and I believed him to be the kind of man who might do anything. And now, to complete my consternation, I learned that he had formed an offensive alliance against me with the woman-artist, G——, whom I had known in Paris. I had been the witness of her hostility towards an artist who had been her friend, and I knew what to expect. Either of these antagonists alone would have filled me with apprehension, in alliance they struck panic into my heart.

The origin of Gaudier's grievance against me, I knew and understood; the cause of G——'s animus was a mystery. But the basis of their present alliance was a common pretence that I had exploited them, as artists. Since I could not suppose that they seriously believed this to be true, their behaviour to me seemed to proceed from a motiveless malignity. I am not surprised that I was scared by it. Indeed, it is only after many years and much experience that I have come to a full understanding of this incomprehensible episode. Within a few years, it is true, I had a glimmering of the emotions that were working in G——, but the case of Gaudier remained mysterious. For why was his hatred directed against me? On his own confession, it was not I, but Katherine, who had dealt the blow. Yet his hostility to Katherine was merely theoretical and perfunctory. In the same breath he made her responsible for all that I had done, or left undone, and proclaimed that all my iniquities were committed at her instigation; yet it was me, and me alone, that he threatened with revenge. It was me that he proposed to kill.

Whenever in after years, I thought about this queer business – which was seldom enough, for I preferred to raze it from the book of memory – I put this contradiction down to a sort of chivalry. Since he could not seek revenge upon Katherine, he was going to wreak it on me. It was, indeed, an odd reversal of the passionate affection he had evinced for me; but the explanation seemed good enough. But I now believe I was completely obtuse in my conception of Gaudier's attitude towards me. And since a like misconception was to play a considerable part in a more important relation to my life (that with D. H. Lawrence), it behoves me to dwell upon it here. In the case of Gaudier, it was only when I read Mr. Ede's *Savage Messiah* that I realized how naive had been my assumption that Gaudier's relation with Sophie was exactly parallel with the relation between Katherine and myself.

I confess I am out of my depth in this matter. But I have since come to believe that in both Gaudier and Lawrence there may have been some kind of sexual ambivalence, and that this may have been intimately connected with the quite peculiar impression of natural genius which both made on me. (I should make it perfectly clear that I am not at all attributing to them what is generally understood by the word homosexuality.)

Were it not that the phrase could be misunderstood, I should say that I have loved more than one man in the course of my life. By my reckoning, I loved Gaudier and Campbell and Lawrence at least, and I should be inclined to add a half-dozen more; but the idea that this love could have had any physical manifestation was, and is, incomprehensible.

But Gaudier was different, and I did not know it. I was surprised by his sudden passionate embrace, to which I have referred. And I have come to the conclusion that his later conduct towards me, which I found so inexplicable and frightening, yields to the explanation that it was the spite of miscarried love. Every now and then I would receive from him some mysterious and menacing epistle to say that he was preparing his revenge. I forget how he signified to me that he had entered into his alliance with G—— for this purpose; but I know I was given due warning. And, I confess, now that I was alone, I lived in fear and trembling; I felt that they were capable of anything – quite capable, at least, of creating an uproar in the block of offices where I lived, and accusing me of all manner of crimes for all the world to hear. I locked and bolted my door in the evenings and refused to open it. They came once or twice together and hammered in vain.

But late one afternoon they took me by surprise. Unsuspectingly I answered the knock. There they were. They brushed past me.

'Now, we've got you,' said Gaudier.

'So it seems. What do you want?'

'All sorts of things. We've come to pay you out.'

'Very well. Fire away.'

'I should like,' said Gaudier, squeezing his fingers together round an imaginary throat, 'to throttle you. But you're not worth murdering. But you're going to pay me for the drawings of mine you published.'

At that my indignation got the better of my fear. I was trembling, but I managed to speak quietly.

'You know, perfectly well, there never was any question, or any possibility, of your being paid for your drawings. And what is more you know that you were only too anxious to have your drawings published for nothing. You know that *Rhythm* has never had any money at all. It's been Katherine and I who have paid for *Rhythm* – two hundred pounds.'

'You're a dirty liar, as well as a dirty thief!' said Gaudier.

'It's you who are the liar, and you know it.'

We glared at one another, and the next moment I was aware that two drawings hanging framed on the wall had been suddenly snatched down.

'Are you going to pay?' said Gaudier.

'Certainly not. I haven't any money to pay you with. And, if I had any money, I would never dream of paying you.'

Then I felt a stinging slap on the face. Gaudier laughed. I tried to look as though nothing had happened.

'Have you finished?' I said.

'That's enough – for to-night,' said Gaudier. 'But we've only begun.' And they went away.

How it had come about that Gaudier and G—— had joined forces I do not remember. The real cause of G——'s animus, I came to suspect long afterwards, when my naivety had given place to a certain awareness, was that she felt I had slighted her, and she had been unable to forgive me. But at that time such simple, unideal notions never entered my head with regard to women. I was twenty-three; and I was very much in the condition of Keats, at exactly the same age, concerning women.

> When I was a Schoolboy I thought a fair Woman a pure Goddess, my mind was a soft nest in which some one of them slept, though she knew it not . . . I thought them ethereal above Men . . . Insult may be inflicted in more ways than by Word or Action – one who is tender of being insulted does not like to think an insult against another. I do not like to think insults in a Lady's company – I commit a Crime with her which absence would not have known. – [*Letter to Bailey, June 18th*, 1818.]

But I was much less awakened even than Keats, who wrote those words when his eyes were being opened to the reality of women. He was writing of a past condition; but his past was my present. That a woman with whom I was not in love could resent my loving another was inconceivable to me. That G——'s strange behaviour might be due to such an elemental cause was not even a remote possibility in my mind; it did not enter it at all. I took it for granted that there must be some real justification for her behaviour. And, since I could find none, and I knew that the justification she alleged was completely preposterous. I was utterly bewildered. My universe had gone mad.

It was not, as I say, till long afterwards that the true solution dawned upon me; and then characteristically, it was during the effort to write a novel in which the still mysterious G—— was one of the chief characters. And when I realized the depths of my own 'innocence', I was overwhelmed, first with a kind of shame, and then with a wave of pity for G——. For truly in my 'innocence' I had treated her terribly. Under her eyes, almost, I had fallen in love with Marguéritte; and, when that had come to its end, again, under her eyes almost, I had fallen in love with Katherine. Inevitably, I had been negligent in friendship.

But in May, 1913, when the combined onslaught of Gaudier and G—— was made upon me, I knew nothing. I was simply devastated by what seemed to me an outburst of insane hatred. Among my letters which Katherine kept is one written to her, immediately after they had left.

G—— and Gaudier have just been. Of course, I am not worth a twopenny damn now. I've been crying out of sheer nervous reaction. The old story shrieked at me, plus some Gaudier lies and venom. I can't do any work now. I'm just good for nothing. I don't know, but all this business simply does for me, darling. – I'm crying again now. O God! It'll be all over when you get this; but somehow it's upset all my notions of what's right and just in the world. Am I a villain? Why can't somebody stand up and say I'm not? I can bear anything almost. I'd be as poor as anything willingly but this kind of thing I cannot stand. God, is it all a joke? Or am I simply lying to myself when I say that we have struggled and fought for *Rhythm*?

Oh, I shall be all right. If you see Gilbert tell him, as he loves me and thinks me straight, to crush that woman when he sees her – or I shall kill her. I'm not crying any more. Before they came I was happy and thinking how glorious the weather is, but now I'm a bit skew. But it won't last much longer now I've had a good cry.

I love you – but suddenly this beast has fouled everything.

A hysterical letter, truly; but containing the truth of my feelings as I remember them. This happening did, finally, 'upset my notions of what was right and just in the world'. My faith in the world had been worn pretty thin before; now I had none at all.

Therefore I found the separation from Katherine imposed on me during the week very hard to bear. Alone at Chancery Lane I felt like a naked outpost in an enemy country. There was plenty going on in London, but it did not touch me at all. In one letter to Katherine, I give a list of my day's visitors ('all at different times', I note, with an obvious touch of resentment) Richard Curle, Frank Swinnerton, W. H. Davies, X-M. Boulestin, Arthur Ransome, Dominic Spring-Rice. The reason for my resentment was that I had my journalistic work to do, and found it well nigh impossible with a stream of callers. They were welcome enough, indeed they were all kindly and friendly people, who could not be expected to know that the office of *Rhythm* was an office only by courtesy, or ambition; and that it was in reality the only place I had to live and work in. Still less could they be expected to understand that I was living in a condition of nervous tension. My letters to Katherine are full of the devious contrivances by which I tried to get an uninterrupted hour. Had I been, as a year before I had seemed to be, in receipt of some small salary for my work as editor of *Rhythm*, the life would have been far less burdensome; but as things were, my whole day was wasted as far as the business of getting a living was concerned. And I had to strain unduly to accomplish the journalistic grind necessary to bring in the £6 a week required to keep the ship afloat, for we were still paying the £8 6s. 8d. a month to the printers, which completely engulfed Katherine's allowance.

The truth was that I was working far too hard, and in a way that was exasperating to my nerves. The hours I spent in receiving callers, I knew, even as they were being spent, were the hours in which I could have been doing work of my own; and I had begun to desire to do work of my own. Instead of that, what little 'leisure' was left me over and beyond the editing of the magazine, and the reception of my visitors, had to be given up wholly to a barren kind of journalism. Since my callers were all relatively free men, I felt the contrast acutely. 'I'm going to supper with Rupert [Brooke] to-night', I wrote to Katherine, 'because he's going off to America in the morning; it's all very silly, but a free meal is fascinating.' In that the touch of my resentment is plain to see. There was nothing at all silly in Rupert's going to America, or in his asking me to a parting supper; that indeed was kind of him, as he always was to me. The touch of cynicism was simply due to envy; I was a slave and he was free. This envy makes an unpleasant undertone in most of my letters. _____

> Gordon [Campbell] was miserable a bit last night; but I can't help envying him all the money he earns. He has two more cases; and I'm trying hard to write my column for two guineas. It's funny . . . I'm all tired now. I don't want to begin writing a review; and I don't dare not to. I feel I should like just one big real holiday without thinking, just lying in long grass and swimming in a soft sea and pushing an old boat off.

That one long big holiday was to elude me for a long while yet. It did not come until the second year of the war, when I escaped with Katherine to Bandol in the south of France. Then for the first time since she and I came together I took a good deep breath. Together we daffed the troubles of the world aside. And Katherine wrote *Prelude*, which is a masterpiece; and I wrote a book on Dostoevsky, which is not. None the less, it is an effort at real criticism – and the first real writing of mine. It was the golden moment of our life together.

But that was far ahead. Now, and for many months to come, I was struggling under a weight too heavy to carry. And no one, save Katherine and Eddie Marsh, gave me any credit for carrying it. On the contrary, because I did manage to keep the ship afloat, it was taken for granted that I was comfortably off. Now that I look back, the supposition seems entirely reasonable. For it was quite preposterous that I should conduct myself in this fashion – keeping an unpopular monthly magazine in being, and letting my working-day be swallowed up by it – without any financial resources at all save those I laboriously earned. It must have been hard, even for those who were kindly disposed towards me, to believe that such a situation was real. Thus, for example, D. H. Lawrence, whom we now met for the first time, was astonished when he heard from Eddie Marsh that the reason why we had not kept our promise to visit him at Broadstairs was that we had not the money for the railway tickets. 'I thought it was stupid', he wrote, 'because you seemed so rich'. And stupid it was, I suppose, though it never struck me in that light, at that time.

Now that I am older, it is easy for me to see that our desperate and exhausting efforts to keep *Rhythm* and *The Blue Review* alive were foolish in the extreme. But then it seemed quite different. Over this magazine Katherine and I had met; it was the purpose for which we had first joined forces. From the complete wreckage of our affairs, it alone had survived; it was the one evidence that our disaster was not entire. And, again, the very vehemence with which we were assailed by our enemies stiffened our determination to maintain it. Its collapse would be to them an occasion of triumph too bitter for us to bear. At all costs we must fight the ship to the last.

It was, I think, during this time that I succumbed to a sort of nervous tension which became habitual with me for many years. The elements of it had always been in my composition, but during these months it conquered me completely. Now, everything was done at an acute strain. Even my letters to Katherine bear the marks of having been written *entre deux trains*, as the French say. And though she urged me constantly not to take things so hard, I cannot see what else I could have done, short of making a clean sweep of my encumbered life and beginning all over again.

It was a tremendous relief to escape to Cholesbury, and there, even though much of my time was taken up with reading books for review, we were often riotously happy. Gordon Campbell taught us to play poker, and Mary and Gilbert Cannan were bitten with the passion. Nobody ever won or lost more than two shillings; but it was a desperate, uproarious gamble that sometimes lasted three or four hours on end. Hysterical and exhausting hours, of which most were spent in helpless laughter. For Gordon turned all the familiar poker terms – and a good many new ones which we invented – into a sort of Rabelaisian cipher. And the delirious point of the situation was that while he and Katherine and I were initiate into it, Mary Cannan was utterly uncomprehending and innocent, and Gilbert half-guessed what we were after. Gordon would make one of his præternaturally solemn and shocking remarks; Katherine and I would explode; Mary would stare at us as though we were mad; and Gilbert become contorted between a laugh and a frown. And Mary's innocent bewilderment, and Gilbert's uneasy effort not to arouse her suspicions, were so funny that we could only explode again and again. 'What *is* it, Gilly?' Mary would say in plaintive exasperation. And that question, and Gilbert's ensuing embarrassment, would send us into a final hysteria.

Yet, behind all this lay a tragedy, which we dimly sensed, and which our instinctive effort to implicate Gilbert in our joyful and harmless Rabelaisianism was an attempt to remedy or avert. Though we liked them both, and for Gilbert we had a particular affection, we had come rather dimly to the conclusion that Gilbert's devouring interest in ourselves was the outcome of an essential life-starvation. He was trying to live the sensuous, simple life, from which he had cut himself off, vicariously. But the more intimately we came to know him, the more baffled we were. There was a kind of inward vacancy in him that was almost frightening; and after a while, even his prodigious literary fluency seemed to be a symptom of disease. And one came at the last to a queer vague and grandiose megalomania in him which, had it not been painful, would have been comic. It was so sublime, and so pathetic. Undoubtedly, some profound inward conflict was eating away his vitals. Our well-meaning efforts to involve him in our spontaneous sculduddery were a mere tinkering with his condition. When the final crash came, some years afterwards, at a time when there was no more contact between us, we were not surprised. Early in 1918, shortly before his insanity, I met Gilbert by chance in the Adelphi. He had just returned from America, and he talked strangely of the magnitude of his own exploits there. The encounter was disquieting. It was not that Gilbert had *changed*; he was merely more intensely what he had been three years before. But now, I felt, he had finally lost contact with reality. His childish self-absorption and vacant insouciance, at a moment when the reality of the war was at its grimmest, was terrible to behold in one naturally so generous and kindly as Gilbert Cannan. I fled, miserably, from the stare of that wild unseeing eye, with the certainty that I should never encounter it again.

But much had happened to me by that time; principally I had acquired some small grains of confidence in myself, so that I could, as it were, pit my own reality against Gilbert's and judge him accordingly. But at the time of the poker-orgies at Cholesbury, I was incapable of grappling with him at all. He was simply a friendly and mysterious being. When I was unself-conscious and happy, I could simply laugh with him; but if I really thought about him I was completely nonplussed. He was in the first flight of the novelists of the younger generation, who were generally held to be – and in this order – Compton Mackenzie, Gilbert Cannan, Hugh Walpole, D. H. Lawrence, with Frank Swinnerton for *proxime accessit*; he was a writer with a real and

253

growing reputation: yet he was somehow puzzlingly unreal, as it were but half-embodied. And if I tried to talk seriously with him, as I sometimes did, the conversation evaporated away into nothingness. So he became merely a piece of the odd furniture of my life. Whereas I was unreal to myself, and apparently real enough to other people; he appeared to be intensely real to himself and unreal to me.

Fortunately, at this moment, to replace my own efforts at recollection, there is the opening entry of a Journal which I now began, but found it impossible to keep up. It is dated from Cholesbury, May 29th, 1913 – the exact period of which I am writing now – and is, on the face of it, an authentic record of my own self-knowledge, or self-ignorance.

I intend to use this book to record, as regularly as my increasing indolence will allow, what I think rather than what I feel. Now that I am 23 I notice in myself an increasing lack of capacity to co-ordinate my thinking, which proceeds, I imagine, from 2 causes (1) that my memory is less reliable than it was, (2) that a slipshod habit of reading (for the purpose of writing so many words of the most superficial criticism) at least eight books a week, has overwhelmed any gift I may have had for real critical reading. On second thoughts I consider that reason (1) is only a minor manifestation of reason (2). Though I hope within two years to be able to give up most of my more repellent journalistic work, I think that if I can form the habit of keeping a notebook of the results of any thinking in which I may indulge from time to time, I shall be able to overcome my difficulty in remembering, and ultimately improve both my memory and my power of criticism beyond what they were before the degeneration began.

I shall try to be absolutely honest with myself and, like Stendhal, 'not tell myself any lies through vanity'; yet at the very outset I am faced with the reflection that the immediate cause of my writing in this book is vanity. I have been reading

Stendhal's *Vie de Henri Brulard* lately; and I recognize that the value of that journal to those who wish to understand the greatest novelist who ever wrote can hardly be expressed. I can hardly say yet (*sic*) that I expect to be a second Stendhal; but I do expect when I die to have written something – as time goes on I am more and more convinced that it will be a novel, or novels – which will last, and I think that if I and posterity ever decide that I have written something permanent, this journal will help them (and me) to understand a young man who as yet hardly understands himself.

Now that I have written 'I expect when I die to have written something that will last' – is it vanity? Is it just a touching piece of self-deception? Or do I really think that this is true? Honestly, I am compelled to say that it is true. I do not mean that I think I have any genius. I do not think that I have a suspicion of anything of the kind. I am certainly not clever (e.g. Chesterton's writing – I have read but little – astounds me by its cleverness, which I could not even dream of imitating. Again, Katherine's conversation, her power of seizing the essence of persons and books and expressing it with just that touch of caricature which seems to put the thing in its right place, is an object of incessant admiration to me.) I never say a clever thing – or at least what wit I do show turns almost invariably upon bawdy subjects, on which I am more *spirituel* than most. I have not written anything which a good man would even (take the trouble to) spit upon. If I take stock of my production during 2 years, it amounts to £400 worth of journalism, by the yard, 1 sketch *A Little Boy* (*Rhythm:* Aug., 1912) which had something really imagined in it, 1 story *The Squirrel* (*Rhythm:* Dec., 1912) which was good in a sentimental Kenneth Grahame kind of way, 1 or 2 pieces of criticism better written than thought, a letter to the *W.G.* upon 'The Coin of Literary Criticism' which was fairly well thought, badly written, and attracted no attention – and I suppose a good part of the editing of *Rhythm*, which was a failure, and *The Blue Review* which may well be another. There's not much in this – less even than I thought. Why in God's name do I believe I am going to write something which will last?

(1) I know that such gifts as I have lie wholly in the direction of *writing*, which I use in almost mechanical sense, as tho' writing were a kind of motor reaction by which I instinctively satisfy my need of action. This is an ambiguous statement of the case, however. It suggests something too physical, whereas in fact the physical effort of writing very often prevents me from recording a thought, and almost always from writing a letter. On the other hand the satisfaction that I get only comes from the piece of writing that I have thought out thoroughly and often with great effort. However, this satisfaction is my greatest pleasure; and this is why I said that my gifts lie wholly in the direction of writing.

(2) I know that my contemporaries – older than me for the most part – who enjoy a certain reputation already, are not really very good, D. H. Lawrence always excepted. They are better than the ruck, because they are more serious. There is not much captation of the crowd in them. But they are all essentially minor. I know quite certainly that I could write *now* something bigger (if not so technically accomplished) than any of them; but I must fight through my money troubles first. More important, I know that I am not yet ripe to write. Technical accomplishment is of the greatest importance, and I need to study the great novelists with the closest critical attention – Stendhal, Flaubert, Dostoevsky, Turgeniev (whom I make a practice of running down through pure ignorance).

All this has been parenthetical. *La Vie de Henri Brulard* set me off. The other immediate cause of this activity is Samuel Butler's *Notebooks*. I have only had time to glance at them during the last months; but S.B. in that way said things in plenty worth saying because he put them down when he had thought them. A thought: like Heine's lyrics, often comes clean 'like a spit out of the mouth'. If you trust to memory, its edges become rounded, and what might have been a diamond is only a dirty pebble. It must be recorded at once. It does *not* want to go back for another dip in your mentality and be subdued to the neutral colour your mind normally takes on. Moreover, a thought once evolved will always be pregnant with suggestion for the thinker of it. It may even go to make the steel-frame of a masterpiece.

Now, I think I have given in some detail the circumstances which gave rise to this note-book, as honestly as I am able to at the present moment.

In reconsidering – a particular subject also helped the suggestion of a note-book. Reading Mr. Philip Snowden on *Syndicalism and Socialism*, a sane but completely uninspired book, I was carried away by the statement of the Socialist ideal. Now, for the most part, except when I put on the political *cothurnus* for the *W.G.*, I don't worry in the slightest about Social Reform. I am not so sure that I shall be so indifferent in the future. However that may be, the problem which suggests itself is: What is the true attitude of the artist towards such ideals and their movements? Stendhal was an admirer of Napoleon, even a Radical in thought, but he abominated the proletariat. I cannot find the place, but somewhere he is explicit on his sympathy with popular aspirations and his *horreur du bas peuple*. This to me seems unsatisfactory. What is the real relation of the artist to social thinking? Could a man be a great novelist and a genuine Socialist, or does not rather the seclusion demanded by the artist preclude any pre-occupation with social matters? Artists – the bad ones – generally claim to be an aristocracy, and found their Chelsea Bohemias, and talk shop at about the lowest level of human intelligence. Others spread over everything a milk-and-water humanitarianism, absolutely sickening and false to reality. (G.C. is completely ruined by this.)

Wells – Shaw might be said to have combined the two; but I doubt it. Shaw is not in the running as a *creative* artist; and Wells at his biggest writes a social tract instead of a novel. Still, there must be some solution. I must try to think it out.

On the next day, apparently, I tried to talk the question over with Katherine but to no satisfying issue. Katherine, I record, 'agreed with me that two totally different (and seemingly incompatible) sets of values were necessary for the creative artist and the social reformer. The social reformer treats men as units, 1, 2, 3, universally. The artist is, above all, interested in the individual: that *something* which separates him from other men. But otherwise, the S.R. is concerned with external economic conditions of the individual's existence; the artist with his inner spiritual existence'. My final conclusion was that there seemed to be 'no reason why an artist should not have unit-values when reasoning, and thus support actively measures of the social reformers which serve to give freer play to human individualities'. But I did not think that it was possible to embody this kind of propaganda *in* creative writing. 'As Katherine says, the writer must have "innocence of intention". André Gide puts it well, of Stendhal: "Il n'affirme proprement rien".'

I had not re-read this 'note-book' since it was begun in 1913, and it was with a curious shock of surprise that I found the first entry – the earliest extant record of the workings of my adult consciousness – ending in this attempt to examine the relation, and the possibility of combination, of the socialist and the artist: and I could scarcely believe my eyes when I read that at twenty-three 'I was carried away by the statement of the Socialist ideal'. For hitherto, I had been under the firm impression that I had been, up to 1930, indifferent to such things. Certainly, I had been indifferent at Oxford; and certainly I was for many years afterwards. But it so happened that my life, until a few years ago, was in the main an effort to carry a personal burden which held my eyes fixed to the path I had to tread. I dared not look around me for fear of stumbling beyond recovery. And to this may be due my own complete forgetfulness of the fact that my first preoccupation is essentially the same as my last.

But that was not the reason why I have copied this first entry of my journal. As I say, I had no notion that it ended in this unexpected fashion. What interests me in it is the queer combination of naive and extravagant self-confidence, with radical scepticism concerning my own powers and distrust of my own capacity for self-delusion. But chiefly it makes on me, who may be over-kindly disposed towards this remote young man of twenty-two years ago, the impression of a real attempt at intellectual honesty. Preposterous as his claims may have been, they are put forward with a certain integrity. He does not seem to be trying, desperately, to convince himself. Whatever apparatus of self-criticism he possesses he has brought into action. If what remains is preposterous, it is not only preposterous and nothing more.

But preposterous it was. Why on earth, on the strength of a very complete surrender to Stendhal, should I have imagined that I was one day to be a novelist of achievement? Whatever ambiguous kind of literary monster I have become, it is certainly not a novelist. True, I was to write three novels in my time; but they were merely my blundering way of learning – as always by hard experience – that I was *not* a novelist. Lawrence, even at this time when we barely knew one another, had a far clearer notion of my own capacity than I had, when he told me: 'You must stick to criticism'. And, if I had possessed any power of estimating my own work, the succeeding entries in the note-book should have been conclusive. They are better than I imagined I could do at twenty-three; but there is not a trace of the novelist in them. They are purely critical.

When I cast about for the reason why this strange delusion should have possessed me, I find it first in the fact that the air was full, in those days, of the achievements of 'the younger novelists', and that I knew that the only quick way to emancipate myself from the sheer drudgery of journalism was to write a moderately

259

successful novel; and, still more important, that the road of advance in criticism for me was barred.

In July, 1913, *The Blue Review* came to an end. After three months it was evident that it could not pay its way; and Katherine and I were no longer quite so innocent as we had been. We had no intention of piling up another load of debt. We already owed Martin Secker some £30 for printing, which we had no prospect of paying. So we accepted the inevitable without overmuch regret.

My debt to Secker turned out to be a godsend in disguise. Since there was no other way of clearing it off, he eventually accepted my suggestion that I should write a book for him – on Dostoevsky. I don't think he would have given me the commission in different circumstances; and indeed I was rather surprised that he accepted the proposal, even as the only way of realizing something on a bad debt.

CHAPTER XIX

PARIS EXCURSION

IT was during these early months of 1913 that D. H. Lawrence entered into our life. His letters suggest that there had been some coincidence. In December, 1912, he was wondering, in a letter to Edward Garnett, whether *Rhythm* would take any of his stories; and a month later he mentioned that Katherine Mansfield had sent him a copy of the magazine, asking him for a story, which he straightway agreed to send. Yet another month, and he was writing that 'it was a daft paper, but the folk seemed rather nice'. A daft paper it was indeed, though I don't remember that he ever told us so.

At the end of June the Lawrences came to England, and called to see us at Chancery Lane. It was a bright sunshine day, and Frieda's lovely fair hair glowed under her panama. We rode in a bus to have lunch together in Soho, and Frieda was surprised and delighted to catch Katherine and me making faces at one another. For Lawrence and she had formed the curious idea that we were wealthy and important people: the kind of people, I suppose, who finance daft magazines. We liked one another, and when it emerged, as it quickly did, that Katherine and I were not married, and that Katherine like Freda was waiting to be divorced, it began to appear (as with the Gaudiers) that we were made for one another.

They invited us to go down and see them at Broadstairs, and we promised to go; but when the day came, we had no money for the journey. When that was explained to Lawrence by Eddie Marsh, he thought it was stupid, 'because I seemed so rich and because I could earn so much more than he could', and sent me a reproachful letter. Probably it was true that I could at that time earn rather more than he did; but since we were still struggling to pay our debts and to maintain a magazine, it meant nothing. We were perpetually hard up. But shortly after we went down with Gordon Campbell to stay the week-end. We bathed together in the dusky evening, and feasted sumptuously on beefsteak and tomatoes. Lawrence gave us a copy of *Sons and Lovers*, which we read in the train returning; and I can still remember the impression of warm rich darkness which the opening pages of that great novel made upon me.

Lawrence was a really new experience. I was quite unprepared for such an immediacy of contact. In an astonishingly short time he knew all about me: all, at any rate, that I could tell him, and no doubt a good deal more. He seemed straightway to be taking charge of my affairs, unravelling the tangle. He had no sympathy with our feeling of depression at the decease of *The Blue Review*; on the contrary, he assured us that it was a good riddance, and he was very insistent that we should seize the opportunity of breaking away from England and coming to live beside him at Lerici in Italy. We both needed, he said, a thorough rest. With our debts and our magazine we had been working ourselves threadbare, all for nothing. We must turn over a new leaf.

It was not merely that the prospect was in itself alluring – for life at Lerici, as Lawrence described it to us, was one long enchantment – but we were in danger of being swept clean off our feet by the intensity of his concern for us. It was churlish to reply to that by calm consideration; but equally it was impossible to make the definite promise to go. For such money as I earned wholly depended upon my being in London, and I knew, if Lawrence did not, that no editor would dream of sending me books to Italy to review. If we had followed Lawrence's advice, I should have had to live on Katherine's allowance: and that seemed to me quite intolerable. My position and his were entirely different. He was an independent creative writer, who wrote what he liked and sold what he could, and could operate from anywhere. I was simply a young reviewer. It is quite probable that he thought that my position was more august than his own, very much as

Thomas Hardy, even at the end of his life, inclined to believe that the London editors and critics were more important people than himself.

So we left it that we would come if we could, with the clear idea on our side, at least, that the chances of our being able to come were exceedingly remote. But Lawrence had re-kindled in our minds the desire to get out of England. The problem was to find ways and means. Now that *The Blue Review* was ended, we joyfully gave up the rooms in Chancery Lane and established ourselves in a big block of flats at Barons Court, called Chaucer Mansions, and I set myself to earn all the money I could. By this time I was working for the *Daily News* as well as the *Westminster*, and now that I was free of the burden of a monthly magazine, I had plenty of work and plenty of time to do it. I found myself earning some £12 a week. It was the zenith of my career as a book reviewer; and I believe it was possible only in the brave old days before the war for a young and anonymous book-reviewer to earn so much. Certainly, it was hard work; but it was not degrading work: and after the strain of the last eighteen months it was almost a relaxation to live quiet and uninterrupted with a pile of books on my table. I began to relapse into the student which, perhaps, I am by nature; and I began reading on my own again.

Since Stendhal, I had discovered nothing. Now, I discovered Milton – and above all Milton's prose. The magnificence of the *Areopagitica* overwhelmed me. I read it again and again, and always with the same peculiar and surprising result. Something in me melted, and I wept at the beauty and majesty of the phrasing. This was a new and mysterious experience: and, indeed, it has never exactly recurred to me. For, though I have grown, if anything, more and more susceptible to certain kinds of writing, it is to something over and above sheer beauty of diction that I respond. My response is rather to the experience that is distilled into the words that move me: or, more exactly, to what Robert Bridges magnificently defined as the poet's supreme power 'of concentrating all the far-reaching resources of language on one point, so that a single and apparently effortless expression rejoices the aesthetic imagination at the moment when it is most expectant and exacting, and at the same time astonishes the intellect with a new aspect of truth'. But the power of Milton upon me at this time was not of this order at all. He revealed no new aspect of truth to me; he overwhelmed me simply by the majesty of a pure beauty of language. Probably because at this time this was the highest response of which I was capable, it was shattering to me. And it perplexed me. For it seemed that Milton's mastery over me was beyond my conscious control. The only experience to which I could liken it was my response to certain passages of Plato, whom I accordingly began to read once more.

Even at this time, I was a person who could not rest until he had rendered to himself some account of his deepest experiences, and much of my thinking was occupied with the attempt to find some explanation of the extraordinary disturbance which Milton and Plato produced in me. This was, for me, no mere intellectual exercise. Something within me, which I did not understand, responded to something without, which also I did not understand. I could not call it Beauty, for that was the name I gave to many things which had no such unbearable power over me. Assuredly, if I had had anything of a religious disposition in me, I should not have hesitated to call the unknown thing in me which responded, my soul, and the unknown thing to which it thus responded, my God. But such ways of thinking were alien to me.

I expressed my perplexity in a curious poem which I called 'The Critic in Judgment'. I have never read it since it was published, until this day. It seems to me a better poem than I feared: its blank verse has merits which I certainly did not expect to find. But chiefly it interests me by the seriousness of its intellectual mysticism. One thought is sustained throughout: that beyond the world of sense and change, there is an eternal Beauty, of which memories or premonitions haunt the soul of man, and to which he is compelled to aspire. This eternal Beauty, avowedly

unutterable, is figured forth in the poem, in the songs of three
Voices, of which any one may serve as example. Here is the Voice
of the Sirens:

> Faint with the perfect circling of the Sun,
>> Faint with the mountain-tides that heap the Zones,
> But Spirit-prompted, Man doth journey on,
>> Marking the stages with his bleached bones,
>>> To seek the lips that singing
>>> Awoke his drowsy soul
>>> To prescience of the goal,
>>> And ever secret ringing
> Faint prime and fainter vespers bid be strong
> And fervent in remembrance of the Eternal Song.
>
> Beyond the clashing rocks and moaning seas
>> There lies a land all golden: quiet winds
> Tremble to fairy music in the trees
>> No winter prisons fast or spring unbinds:
>>> In no birth-pangs unfolded
>>> Each leaf and bud and flower
>>> At his predestined hour
>>> Is in an instant moulded
> To bloom eternal, vaulted in a shrine
> Vocal with secret praise of the one flower Divine;
>
> Whose petals by their self-spun Destiny
>> Poised in the extreme of motion ever fret
> Invisible; and thence a harmony
>> Most blinding-clear transpires, whereby is set
>>> The lesser harmony
>>> Of the enshrining leaves
>>> And the circumfluent waves
>>> From the still silver sea
> In sacred modulation inward rolling
> Their might majestical, the one Supreme extolling.

And by this Music doth the Primal Fire
   Govern its circuits through the ambient space,
Whereto all things created must aspire
   And seek by wandering to our final grace
      Who guard the dim sea-portal
      Whereby the seekers come
      To their desirèd home,
      Where vision immortal
Illumes their eyes, search-blinded, to disclose
The unutterable beauty of the Living Rose.

I do not copy that in any illusion concerning its poetic merits: it is no better and no worse than the poem as a whole. It interests me, not as poetry, but as evidence of the kind of thought that haunted me at this time. Haunted, I say advisedly; for the upshot of the whole poem is that, although these intimations of Eternity have meaning, their meaning cannot be translated: they are intimations, and no more. Neither by adventure, nor by love, nor by thought, can the Eternal Beauty, if it exist, be apprehended. It is not a goal at which the soul of Man arrives; it is not a finality beyond himself. What causes the mind of Man to entertain the idea of Eternal Beauty is the effort of life within him to be purer and nobler than it is. The Absolute is a mirage. It is the projection of the desire of man for harmony within himself.

This, so far as I can now decipher it, is the meaning of 'The Critic in Judgment'; but inevitably in such an interpretation the original emphases are subtly changed, to accord with a later conviction. What chiefly strikes me about the poem is that, although the thought of an absolute and eternal Beauty is repudiated in it, the praises of that Beauty are far more convincing than the repudiations; and that there is a curious strain of stubbornness and egotism in the Critic's insistence that he will be the architect of his own harmony. This is oddly manifest in his rejection of the voice of Love, which puts forward the Platonic argument that earthly love is a means of ascent towards the heavenly. To which the Critic replies:

> Nor . . . would I choose
> My end an alien divinity:
> But self-discovered, self-appointed mine,
> Struck out from my own metal, by my fire
> Fined, nor with any foreign principle
> Irrevocably blent. My destiny
> I know not. This I know. My soul-strings I
> First stretched to earliest discord unresolved.
> I seek the key tormented. I will be
> The master of my soul's lost harmony.

Once more I make no claims for it as poetry; it is adduced merely as evidence of what I was. It seems to me now a pathetic piece of bravado, but as a document it is genuine enough.

Whether or not there ever had been any harmony in my soul, there was none now, and I was painfully aware of it. I wanted something to surrender to, and I could find nothing; and to me the peculiar interest of the passage is that it reminds me that I was, in a sense, rebellious even against the love that bound me to Katherine. Even to her, I surrendered unwillingly. I wanted to guard my own personality against her. Against what in her I wanted to guard it, I have now no idea; and I doubt whether I had any then. I am sure that I had no idea what it was that I wished to guard. But an impulse of resistance and withdrawal had grown up in me, which was intimately connected with the curious intellectual mysticism with which I was afflicted. This intellectual mysticism was not altogether spurious; it was indeed my main sustenance. But I fed the fire of it with a certain perverse assiduity.

I was verily a poor thing: for I felt myself to be Katherine's inferior. I knew I was her inferior in many ways, but I could have accepted them all save one. She had an immediate contact with life which was completely denied to me. No matter where she was, or how she suffered, she was a part of life: she lived in the moment, and responded entirely to experience. With me it was very different. It would be almost true to say that nothing was real to me until my mind had grasped it. It would not be quite true, because there was one great breach in my apartness, the breach made by my devouring love for her. And it was so devouring, I think, precisely because with her alone I lived, through her alone I felt that I had contact with life. Yet though it was a devouring, it was not a jealous love. If she had seen fit to leave me, as more than once she did, I should have held my peace, because deep down I felt that I wanted her only so long as she wanted me. If she ceased to love me, that was the act of God, or the fiat of Destiny: I should not cease to love her, but still less would I seek to hold her to me.

Maybe – though I do not believe it – it was because of some corresponding sense of the precariousness in the tie which held us, that I felt the need of building up some citadel of the soul in which to withdraw; or that I felt that I was so compacted that if I were to surrender wholly to my love for her, and it were once withdrawn, I should be left completely naked. But I think the instinct for seclusion and separateness was primitive in me. Perhaps it is primitive in every man: so that, the more completely in love he is, the more he feels the necessity of withdrawing into his own masculine solitude. I call it masculine, because it was, in my own case, certainly connected with the desire for the friendship and society of men. My intellectual mysticism, if it deserves the name, had been largely developed from converse with men, living or dead; and I felt that it belonged to the man in me. Probably Katherine did also, for she was never very sympathetic to it, whether because such motions of the mind were intrinsically alien to her, or because it was the recurrent theme, in one form or another, of my conversations with Campbell and Goodyear.

Anyway, it was the natural bent of my own mind, which was always poorly furnished with sensuous perception. If it was a

J. M. M., Frieda Lawrence and D. H. Lawrence at
Shelwood Terrace, 1914

vice, it was one of which I could not easily rid myself. My weakness was that I indulged it overmuch. Not that I did this deliberately. The mere fact that I was working hard at the uncongenial business of journalism, while Katherine was free to work as the spirit moved her, made me the more eager to be at something of my own, if only to assure myself that I existed. And when I attempted something of my own, inevitably it became a very thinly disguised record of the intellectual perplexities that were uppermost in my mind. For, though I was vaguely and uncomfortably aware that the thoughts of my mind were not me, I was totally at a loss where to look for myself if not in them. I was compelled to substitute an intelligence for an individuality, if I was to credit myself with an individuality at all.

Like other victims of their own nonentity, I put the blame on to my circumstances. If only I were free from the drudgery of journalism, I should begin to flower. If only I could escape from England, I should be different. In late October 1913 I wrote in my journal:

Stendhal says a man never changes after twenty-five. It may not be true, probably isn't – but I feel as though this, my twenty-fifth year [my twenty-fourth, in fact], were all-important. I just feel it. Unless I change my way of life, cut myself off from this supervacuating journalism, there'll be nothing left worth freeing at all. This year will be really critical. I shall either write something, or be no good, self-confessed. When I think about starting to write, I succumb to a lethargy of impotence; partly because I'm tired, partly, because writing well (i.e., with some thought behind) is truly a tremendous effort for me. At present, mentally, I'm staking everything on getting abroad at Christmas for some years. It's curious how I have a childish and implicit faith that, once across the Channel, inspiration will run free, thought be profound, and words come back to the speechless. It has become a very potent symbol – perhaps a purification by water. There it is, anyhow. I wonder if it's any more than crying for the moon.

Truly, the faith was childish; and it was characteristic that I both held it and was sceptical of it, and that I managed to conceal from myself my own knowledge that it was not going abroad, but how I went abroad that mattered. If I could have taken a real plunge, my dream of freedom might have come true. Certainly, being what I was, congenitally timid of life and with a profound distrust of my own capacities, it would have been mere madness to go abroad and trust to make a living by writing books, when the only book I had to write was in payment of a debt. But what I might have done was to go on working for another six months until I had saved enough to keep us abroad for a year. That seemed to me impossible, because the harder I worked the more eager grew the desire of both of us to escape from an intolerable existence. Lawrence had offered a simple solution: that we should both go to Italy and live on Katherine's allowance. Probably it was a wise suggestion, but to me, with my notion of gentlemanly behaviour, it seemed fantastic; and I am very doubtful whether, in like circumstances, Lawrence, who was so scrupulous of his financial independence, would have acted on his own advice.

Italy was out of the question. It must be somewhere where I could make a small living. The choice was between a very meagre lektorship in a German university, and some small journalistic job in Paris. Of the two Katherine was in favour of Paris, of which, since our 'honeymoon' there in May 1912, she had the happiest memories. I smiled ruefully at Lawrence's lordly suggestion that I should arrange with the *Westminster* to supply it with two columns a week; it showed his complete ignorance of my journalistic standing. I had already been disappointment enough to Spender by fading out of the political work of the paper; I was frightened even of telling him that I wanted to go abroad: that I should ask him to give me work to keep me there required a courage or an impertinence that I did not possess.

So I scratched an introduction to the editor of *The Times Literary Supplement* and, with what seems to me still a most surprising boldness, asked him to allow me to send him reviews of French books from Paris. My courage was not more surprising than his reply: for, instead of turning down the request out of hand, he said he would do his best. That was my first meeting with Mr. Bruce Richmond. No literary man ever found a more generous editor, or more constant friend, than I in him.

I was so excited that I could hardly tell the news coherently over the telephone to Katherine. We set about our preparations instantly; and with our customary fecklessness arranged to spend £25 of our savings in having all our worldly goods transported to Paris. Then came the grim job of breaking the news to Spender. It was about the moment that Northcliffe acquired a controlling interest in *The Times*, and Spender connected my new appointment (which was not an appointment at all) with the new régime. He warned me very seriously against putting my trust in Northcliffe, and ended by saying that he would not fill my place on the *Westminster* for three months, 'in case something happened'. I felt myself to be a great-siz'd monster of ingratitude.

Accordingly, early in December we went to Paris. In three months we were back again, completely defeated, all our money gone, and the furniture we had paid £25 merely to send across sold desperately and comically for less than £10. Once more by a brave gesture we had succeeded only in making ourselves ridiculous.

We began with the usual high-flying confidence. Furnished rooms in an hotel would not do, at all. We must have a flat. We found one at No. 31 rue de Tournon, which, though it was next door to Foyot, was less than £40 a year. But Messieurs Boiffard et Debladis – such were the splendid names, with moustaches to correspond, of the estate agents – insisted on references. That was a blow. We knew nobody of the sort.

F—— was in the South of France, and R.D. was in no condition to be a reference for anybody. I murmured to Messieurs Boiffard et Debladis that I was working for *le Times*. Ah, then it was quite simple; *le Times* had a bureau in Paris. All that was required was a letter from the bureau.

There was no escape. I, who had hoped in the course of a week or two to summon up courage enough to call at the office and apprise it of my humble existence – for well I knew that the Paris correspondent of *le Times* was little less than an Ambassador – was now compelled to go to ask for a reference. I sat patiently one morning in the waiting-room while the concierge in a green-baize apron dusted round me, I sat humbly in the sanctum while the Correspondent, smoking a big Turkish cigarette in a long holder, wondered what I should find to do for *The Times* in Paris. I also wondered. A forlorn sense of my own futility and insignificance enveloped me. I felt that my reference was a charity, to which I was not entitled, as no doubt it was.

From that moment onward gloomy misgivings, which I could not dislodge, settled upon me. They were quickly realized. I had been told that I might write a leading article on Stendhal for *The Literary Supplement*. I toiled at it for a fortnight, and it was returned to me. (I have it still: and I have never yet found the courage to read it again.) It had been arranged that I might submit a series of six critical articles 'On the Present State of English Letters' to the *Westminster*. I wrote them: they also were returned. I began to be really frightened: frightened of being left stranded, and more deeply afraid that I was no good.

Then it was dismally cold – with that intense, searching cold which Paris darts upon the unsuspecting Englishman. We tried every conceivable combination of French fuel in French fireplaces and succeeded only in reminding ourselves that in England fires were warm.

Our money began to dwindle with a terrifying speed. One inroad on it is comic enough to be recorded. My French friend, R.D., eager to consolidate his own precarious position, introduced me everywhere as *le correspondant littéraire du Times*. It sounded, as it was meant to sound, imposing; and I was received with deference into a little circle of French journalists which gathered after lunch at the Taverne du Panthéon. One or two of them were on the staff of well-established journals, but the majority led an ambiguous existence. One, for instance, was part-time secretary to M. Tardieu, the politician; another was a sort of Aunt Emily in a *bien-pensant* family paper called *Le Foyer*; yet another, I guessed, was not totally innocent of connection with the drug-traffic. Anyway, the kindly president of the assembly, M. Albalat of the *Débats*, took me aside one day and warned me that in Paris all were not journalists who professed to be.

My friend R.D., who was hardly a pillar of respectabillity was nevertheless a writer born. Though he was compelled to live by his wits, he had a touch of genius which has since proved itself. He conceived the excellent idea of writing an article for me to translate. It went without saying that the *correspondant littéraire du Times* had the entrée into the English reviews. Like a fool I did not disabuse him, but said I would do my best: it was quite *possible* (I said) that his article would be accepted. In a couple of days it was done and handed to me. In another day, possibility of acceptance had changed in his mind to certainty. Yet another, and he was asking me for an advance. Weakly and resentfully, I handed him 100 francs. I was saved the labour of translating his article; but I kept away from the Taverne du Panthéon.

My earnings had dropped from £12 to a doubtful 30s. a week. To keep ourselves afloat at all, we had to give up paying Katherine's allowance to the printers. And straightway the bankruptcy proceedings began. Since I could not afford to go to London, I ignored them. Katherine and I stared gloomily at the situation. Suddenly, at the beginning of February 1914, I received a letter from Spender, telling me that the post of art-critic on the *Westminster* would shortly be vacant, and that if I returned, I could have it. In any case he thought I had better go to London and see him. It is hard to understand why I did not give a whoop of joy and gratitude; but I can find no trace of either in the letters which I wrote Katherine from London, and which she preserved.

Partly this was because I was instantly involved in bankruptcy proceedings which frightened me; but chiefly it was because our pride had received another mortal blow. Once more we had to confess defeat; and something more than our pride was defeated. Though we were terribly disillusioned with Paris, we had made a home there. All our precious belongings, which represented the solidity of our life, were settled there: and if we returned to London we should have to leave them all behind. We had been to see Boiffard and Debladis, and they would release us from our agreement only on condition we paid an extra quarter's rent. We dared not argue, because the reputation of *le Times* was involved. But it meant that our last penny was gone. So we decided on a clean sweep. We would sell everything we could sell.

I say 'we' by anticipation: for although at my interview with Spender I asked for a fortnight to think it over and discuss it with Katherine, I straightway borrowed £5 and went off to buy myself some new clothes which, but for a coming change in my fortunes, I certainly could not have afforded. They consisted of a new pair of shoes, a black overcoat, a double-breasted dark jacket, and a pair of pepper-and-salt trousers. These, with a bowler hat and a monocle, comprised what I supposed to be the appropriate attire of an art-critic; and they cost precisely £5 16s. 6d. I had long cherished an ambition to wear pepper-and-salt trousers, which Katherine encouraged. Nevertheless, I had yet to persuade her that the return to London was inevitable.

I scouted round, as best I could, for work that might keep me in Paris. I called on *The British Review*, in vain: at *The Nation* office I found that Massingham was in Egypt. I went to publishers to propose myself as a reader of French books. Fisher Unwin received me kindly; but I could see there was no depending on that. I reported all my efforts to Katherine, and tried to overcome her reluctance to return. 'Don't you think' (I wrote) 'that we had better try to exchange our flat for a year with somebody and meanwhile work here in London till we've got some money to fall back on, and then if we see a fair chance, clear off to Paris for good?' It was the giving up of the home that was the bitter pill. I concluded grimly: 'One thing we *cannot* do – that is, *move* in the real sense of the word. Even if our pride would allow it, our purse won't'.

I was staying with Gordon Campbell at Selwood Terrace. That was very fortunate for me, for I asked his professional advice concerning the papers from the Bankruptcy Court which I had ignored. He consulted a fellow-barrister who was an Assistant-Receiver, and was told that the one thing for me to do was to go and see the officials immediately. If I did, they would be very nice to me, as the bankruptcy was obviously not my fault: if I did not . . . So straightway I went off, with my monocle and my pepper-and-salt trousers, to Carey Street, and it was – to my astonishment – precisely as Gordon's friend had prophesied. The official treated me as the injured party. Perhaps it was demoralizing to be made to feel, as I was, that bankruptcy is a gentlemanly accident. But I don't think I was demoralized. My ancestral horror of not being able to pay my way was increased rather than diminished. But certainly the kindness of the officials then, and a month later the sympathy of the Receiver who publicly examined me and hauled my implacable creditor over the coals for pressing me inordinately for a debt which was not morally mine, made a deep and enduring impression on me, coming fresh from the minor bureaucratic tyrannies of Paris. In Carey Street were securely laid the foundations of one minor conviction, which has remained with me all my life: that the apparatus of English government – what we Socialists call the State machine – is humane and civilized beyond any other in the world.

Anyhow I returned to Katherine in Paris full of admiration for my own country. I had been kept in London much longer than I intended to stay, and the empty flat had begun to get on

275

Katherine's nerves. She devised complicated barricades, behind which she passed sleepless nights. By the time I returned she had conceived a hatred of the flat which ten days before had been her precious 'home'. No persuasion was required; she was ready to leave it instantly, and her fondness for 'a clean sweep' and no delay made her reject my suggestion that we should try to let it furnished. Since we had barely enough money to pay for the removal of our books alone, there was nothing for it but to try to sell our furniture. But the French dealers were contemptuous of our few sticks; they took a glance, snorted 'Pas de grandes meubles!' and went vindictive away.

So we called in R.D. Surely it was worth something. He agreed that it was, and set about disposing of it among his friends, in return for an English armchair which he coveted. But there was a recalcitrant residue, of which our divan-bed was the nucleus. It was the day before our departure, and it was also Mardi Gras – by no means a day for selling things. Suddenly R.D. had an inspiration, and bade me follow him – on a strange journey into the underworld: for as we went down the stairs, he explained to me that 'he always believed in *putains*'. His idea, I gathered in wide-eyed astonishment, was that the brothel-keepers would know the likeliest dealers, or, better still, offer to buy the things themselves. So with my pepper-and-salt trousers and my monocle, I trotted after him in a dream across Paris and back again. After him I dived into strange warrens, stood with an assumed indifference in ante-rooms, being stared at by the women and staring in my turn at the inscription LA MAISON EST OUVERTE TOUTE LA NUIT seen backwards through a glass door, till the hieroglyph was printed on my retina.

I have sometimes wondered why R.D. took me with him. I was no earthly use, I never spoke a word, and I was acutely miserable. Perhaps he was experimenting to discover how far *le phlegme anglais* would go; perhaps he was merely making copy for one of his exotic stories. He was something of a connoisseur in bizarre sensations. I had been taken by him before to desolate brothel-bars in forlorn suburbs, with that queer tired atmosphere of dingily commercial vice, which he was himself to render so impressively in his novels, and which sorted so well with his own queer faded ivory face. But this last experience was too much for my weak stomach. 'Everything has been strange, and horrible, and *false*', I wrote in my journal. 'Even R., Frenchman, noticed what I was feeling. Soon after I got home, the *patron* of the last brothel came with the pianist to offer 100 francs for the things. They went into our bedroom and flung our bedclothes about. I *loathed* them.'

Such was our macabre farewell to Paris. But that was not all. Early that morning our concierge had died suddenly, died, so to speak, with his feather-duster in his hand. Concierges, one feels, are like old soldiers: they never die. Since we had to depart on the morrow, we could have no respect for this unnatural event. We bumped our furniture down the stairs while Madame Lefebvre and her gossips wailed audibly below. Past cure, past care: in the full consciousness that Madame looked upon me as worse than a Turk, a pagan or an infidel, I clattered my clumsy burdens out of the grim Balzacian house into the carnival street below, to the tune of 'C'est dégoûtant'? Meanwhile Katherine was in the flat, writing this unfinished letter to a friend. I have kept it ever since as a reminder of our fantastic departure.

Dear ——

Everything is packed of ours – the book-packer is here now and we are waiting for the man to come and take away the furniture. Grimy and draughty and smelling of dust, tea-leaves and senna-leaves and match-ends in the sink, cigarette ash on the floor, you never saw an uglier place – now – or a more desolate. The clock (sold, too) is ticking desperately, and doesn't believe it's going yet, and yet is hopeless. Jack, in a moment of desperation, has sold even the bedding . . . Yes, I *am* tired, my dear, a little, – but it's mostly mental. I'm tired of this disgusting atmosphere

of eating hard-boiled eggs out of my hand and drinking milk
out of a bottle. It's a gay day outside. What we shall do
till the man goes, I can't think – very little money, and
we both don't want cafés. Oh, how I love Jack! There is
something wonderfully sustaining and comforting to have
another person with you, who goes to bed where you do and
is there when you wake up – who turns to you, and to whom
you turn.

The dear little toilet set is on the same table with me – all
packed into the basin. I have been talking to the book-
packer. He is tall and more graceful than anyone I have
ever seen. He wears light blue woollen shoes, and has never
worn boots since he was 'tout p'tit': that's why he walks so,
doesn't seem to put his feet *down* at all, but has a delightful
sort of swaying stride. I have given R.D. a few souvenirs –
the egg-timer which *charmed* him and some odd little pieces
like that. The guitar has gone, and the candlesticks – except
the dragons. I have an idea I shall find the *femme de ménage*
has taken something really important before I go. She was a
little too gushing and grateful to be innocent, I'm afraid. . . .

It was true. The *femme de ménage* had taken Katherine's
overcoat. And so my resolve was accomplished. We certainly
did not '*move*, in the real sense of the word'. We escaped.

What remains to me of that strange interlude in Paris beyond
what I have recorded? A glimpse, late at night, in the Café
Weber of a tall slim man in black with a sickly yellow face: that
was Marcel Proust. A glimpse, in full daylight, through the
windows of his little shop in the rue de la Sorbonne, where the
Cahiers de la Quinzaine were sold, of a man with a pince-nez set
awry on his nose, tying up a parcel: that was Charles Péguy.
I admired him, and admire him still. If I could have my way
(I dreamed) that is how I would live: publishing my friends'
works and mine in a little shop with my own hands – keeping the
books, taking the cash, tying the parcels.

CHAPTER XX

REGARDLESS OF THEIR DOOM

It was in March 1914 that we returned thus ignominiously to London. 'You don't know what you are', Lawrence had written to me four months before. 'You've never come to it. You've always been dodging round, getting *Rhythms* and flats and doing criticism for money.' It was true enough, but not very helpful. The difficulty was how to discover what I was? And Lawrence had nothing to suggest in this regard. I was capable of conducting all kinds of intellectual examinations of myself – indeed, I was too fond of the occupation – but they led nowhere. Practically, Lawrence's advice had reduced to this: that I should live on Katherine's small allowance and lie fallow. It was probably good advice; but it did not speak to my condition. I was quite incapable of living on Katherine's money, even if it would have supported us both: my code did not allow it. But whether I was indeed the kind of man who could not do these things, I cannot say. The intrinsic me and the conventional me were indissolubly mixed. All that I really knew was that in joining with Katherine I had been myself: at that moment I had had no thought of code or convention. But that moment was unique.

'You want to be strong in possession of your own soul', said Lawrence. And that also was true. But I had not the faintest notion of how to achieve this condition. Half by instinct, half through sheer inertia, I had refused to shape myself to any of the life-patterns that had been offered me; and even now that I was embarked on the profession of letters, whenever any reasonable security came my way, it was not long before I threw it over. Yet as soon as I had thrown it over, I wanted it again. I wanted to be independent; yet I was completely unable to maintain myself in independence. And for what did I want to be independent? I did not know. Did I really want to write? I could not say. Time after time, I asked myself the question in my journal: all to no purpose, for my knowledge of myself was entirely intellectual. If I said, as I did, that I wanted to write something worth while, straightway there returned on me a wave of suspicion that all these anxieties of mine were merely superficial. It was by accident only that they took this form. By accident, I had drifted into writing; I might have drifted into anything else, yet the same malaise would have been there. I wanted not to write, but to be.

Don't be a child', said Lawrence. 'Don't keep that rather childish charm. Throw everything away, and say, "Now I act for my own good, at last".' To hell with the childish charm! I thought, as I read and meditated his letter. There the damned thing was again, for ever dogging and disconcerting me. Who was this charming child? Where was he? What was he? If I could have grasped him, I would have wrung his neck; but he was impalpable and invisible.

'Perhaps you will come into possession of your own soul', said Lawrence, 'when this affair of you and Katherine has gone crash'. That might have been true, because statements of that kind are always bound to be true in some sense. A crash between Katherine and myself would have been infinitely the biggest happening in my life: an earthquake which was bound to reveal some unknown stratum beneath. But I might just as well have turned upon him and told him that perhaps he would not come into possession of his own soul till the affair of him and Frieda had gone crash. There would have been an equal truth in it.

Now Katherine and I were in London again, with our books and our clothes and nothing more. We took a furnished flat from a friend in Beaufort Mansions, Chelsea, for two guineas a week and stayed there (on money borrowed from Gordon Campbell: for we had none and my earnings as art-critic had not begun) while Katherine looked for rooms we could afford. I was now an art-critic. I worked hard at the National Gallery in the effort to put a little order into my vague and untidy knowledge of painting, and toiled away at a novel I had begun in Paris, which was eventually published as *Still Life*. But Katherine could settle to nothing. All that she wrote she tore up immediately. 'I long and long to write,' she wrote at this time, 'and the words simply won't come.' And the squalor of the rooms she visited preyed upon her. We had decided that we could not afford to pay more than 10s. a week for two rooms and a kitchen; and the choice in Chelsea at that price was not generous. If the rooms were tolerable, the smells were not. We consoled ourselves by walking along the Embankment and envying those who inhabited the lovely houses in Swan Walk, 'white with flowering pear-trees in the gardens and green railings and fine carved gates'.

At last we settled ourselves in two rooms and a half off the Fulham Road, with two chairs and two tables, and a big mattress on the floor. It seemed auspicious that the day we entered in should be the private-view day at the Royal Academy: for that meant three long articles in the *Westminster* and the beginning of a reconstruction of our finances. I had been staring at the pictures all the morning, and was puzzled to find that they began to swim before my eyes. I got home, feeling hot and ill, and had to go straight to bed. It was pleurisy. I managed to do the articles and Katherine took them to the office. When I was on my legs again, at the end of a week, Katherine promptly went down with it herself. The first symptom with her was that she suddenly dropped into a chair, white and unable to speak, her heart was galloping so. I was terrified. When the heart-attack was over, I went off to fetch the doctor – Croft-Hill was his name: I give it *honoris causa*. He looked askance at me, for disobeying orders, but when he heard my tale drove me back home, put Katherine to bed, gave me a kindly lecture for not living more comfortably, looked after Katherine till she was well, and refused to send in a bill.

In my new capacity as an art-critic, I had to educate myself as I went along. An exhibition of early English water-colours

281

meant for me a day in the Print Room and a day at South Kensington before I could write with any confidence; and it was a godsend to me when, for example, a show of Sir William Richmond's paintings of Umbria enabled me to escape with a pleasant little dissertation, full of quotations, on Propertius's images of the Umbrian countryside. Such was an evening paper in the brave pre-war days! On the whole, when I read through my old art-criticism, I find it not too bad; and, in particular, I take credit to myself that I was from the beginning a zealous champion of Mr. Walter Sickert's painting. I was very proud when one day Mr. Clifton of the Carfax Gallery told me that Sickert wanted to meet me, because he thought my criticism of his exhibition by far the most interesting he had had. And when I met Sickert, and he invited me to his studio, 'I like your criticism', he said, 'because it *is* literary, and doesn't pretend to be anything else. What's the use of you – or any other critic – pretending to know about painting? You don't, you can't, or you would be painters yourselves, and not even a painter can write intelligently about the *painting* of a picture. And I'm glad to see you don't fall into the modern trick of abusing the Academy. There's as high a proportion of real painting, genuine craftsmanship, in the Academy as in any other gallery.' I am glad to think that Mr. Richard Sickert is now R.A.

Not that it was any particular virtue to discover Sickert and Steer (for whom my admiration was also great). As I reminded myself in one of my articles on the fifty-first exhibition of the New English Art Club, Mr. George Moore had written an essay on the ninth exhibition – twenty-two years before – in which he chiefly commended the work of those two painters. But since the Post-Impressionist exhibition at the Grafton Galleries the critical fashion had changed. Sickert could hardly sell his pictures at all in 1914; and the prices even of Steers were surprisingly low. There was an auction-sale at this time of modern works to provide some sort of memorial for Spencer Gore: for fifty pounds one could have carried off a half-dozen first-rate modern pictures. Seeing that barely two years had passed since I had seen an authentic Cézanne offered in the Boulevard Raspail for 125 francs, this was perhaps hardly remarkable. Cheap as good pictures were, they were entirely beyond my means. My only treasures were a half-dozen of his etchings which Sickert gave me, and which were stolen in the following year.

I am glad to discover, too, that in spite of my disastrous quarrel with Gaudier-Brzeska, I praised the beauty of his Marble Faun. But though I enjoyed criticizing pictures more than I did criticizing books, it was always for me a sort of *tour de force*: better still than the actual work of doing the rounds of the galleries, I liked browsing away in the National Gallery, or the Print Room, or South Kensington. And I conceived the idea that I might rid myself of the worst of my financial worries by joining the staff of a public gallery. It may have been Mr. Charles Aitken who put into my head that a good way to begin would be to become the Director of The Whitechapel Art Gallery, which was shortly to be vacant. Anyhow, for a time, I indulged pleasant visions of myself sedately earning my living in this fashion. My school-friend, 'Porky' Allen, after long waiting, had at last secured a post in the Ashmolean; and it seemed not a bad way out.

For, in truth, I was weary of the precariousness of journalism; I was tired of the business of worrying whether this or that was 'in', and of reckoning up my columns – or inches – to find out what the monthly cheque would bring. I was coming to the conclusion that one might honourably sacrifice a good deal for some kind of security. But always, when it came to the point, I jibbed. Some other form of security would strike my fancy: I was even tempted by the offer, which came to me in some way I have forgotten, of a post in the Imperial Library in St. Petersburg. Behind all this restlessness was the fact that Katherine and I were miserable. We had been three months in the Chelsea rooms, when the Lawrences returned to London, in July, 1914. We were annoyed with them, I remember, because they delayed in coming to see us. Our pride was very sore, just then.

Katherine was fretted by her inability to write, and I was discovering, by painful experience, that I was not what I had imagined I might be – a novelist. And worse than anything, we loathed our dingy rooms. That night, after we had given the Lawrences supper, Katherine unlocked her heart and told them how much she detested the dirty staircase, the common w.c., the smell of unwashed socks and cabbage-water that clung perpetually about the dark varnished hall. I listened with gloomy resentment. When the Lawrences had gone, I upbraided Katherine for 'betraying us' by revealing how much we hated the rooms: and we had a horrible quarrel till one o'clock in the morning.

The coming of the Lawrences had brought our discontents to a head. Our fortunes were at a nadir; theirs at zenith. Methuen had offered £300 for Lawrence's next novel, and naturally they felt gay and confident. Frieda in particular was glowing at the prospect of having some money to spend in the shops. Katherine, who had never had any money to spare since she met me, felt it badly; and I felt it even worse. For naturally, I felt guilty, and because I felt guilty towards her, I was the more vexed that she had given us away. We ought, I said, to have kept up appearances in front of the Lawrences. That they should pity us was intolerable.

Our quarrel cleared the air. We woke the next morning determined to find some different rooms: we would even go to a pound a week rather than endure the Chelsea flat any longer. At that decision, Fortune seemed to smile on us: for no sooner had we begun the old familiar search than we found the whole upperpart of what appeared a charming little house in Arthur Street. It was almost too good to be true: three charming rooms, two attics and a kitchen, and a whole tree of our own at the back. We took it on the spot, and went straight off to a friendly decorator, who had helped us before, to tell him to distemper the walls.

The next morning a mysterious note came to us from the decorator: Would we go to see him at once? We went. At first he was so politely elusive that we were bewildered; but at last, taking pity on our obtuseness, he disclosed the secret: BUGS. And we had signed the agreement. I remember how I waited by a bookshop in the King's Road, while Katherine went, at the decorator's instigation, to the pock-marked, evil-smelling agent to ask if he would guarantee that the house was free from vermin. No, he said, it was an old house: he couldn't take responsibility.

We wandered up and down a cul-de-sac behind Chelsea Town Hall, debating what to do. We knew enough to be aware that we could not really be bound by our agreement; and if we had been sensible people, we would have thrown the whole thing over. But we were not sensible people. All the joy would be gone out of life if we did not have the little house with its two attics, its two studies, its common room, its kitchen and its bathroom, all with old-fashioned windows and fine doors, and its beautiful stairs with two windows glancing out towards a transparent greenness – only a tree hiding the kitchen of the Cancer Hospital, it is true, but wonderful. And Katherine, who declared it was the first time she had known me passionately concerned about a house – by instinctive consent we blotted Runcton from our minds as a painful memory – was swayed by me. We decided to take the risk. The decorator did his best without any confidence: and we moved. It cost us eight shillings to move.

We slept in an attic, and the beasts attacked us. We had first-hand experience of the curious sense of defilement which these loathsome vermin can engender. We could not sleep. We went gloomily down to our kitchen in the middle of the night to make ourselves tea, and extract the full savour of a characteristic situation: 'the snail under the leaf'. When, at last, determined to escape squalor, we had found a lovely little house that we could afford, Fortune put bugs in the wainscot. 'Let's imagine that we are Russians,' Katherine said. 'Or in training for Russia,' said I, for the Imperial Library at St. Petersburg was still in the offing. And then we began to laugh, ruefully indeed, but unmistakably. It was such a comic epitome of our experience.

With paraffin and petrol and sulphur we waged war against the enemy and in a little while demoralized him so that we could sleep; and we breathed no word of our tribulations to our friends. For already, by reason of their unremitting vicissitudes, the Murry-Mansfields were in danger of becoming a standing joke. In spite of everything, we felt better in our little house, and more inclined than before to enter into the happiness of the Lawrences at their forthcoming marriage. Before, it had been too much of a strain on our disinterestedness: for beneath our superficial discomfiture that they were prosperous and we were failures, was the much more real misery that, whereas they could get married, we could not. Katherine's husband had withdrawn his petition for divorce; and we were entirely at his mercy. Though we put a bold face on it, the disappointment was no joke. We took no delight at all in being moral rebels, we both wanted very genuinely to be married to one another, and we were not even 'advanced' enough to believe that there was nothing in a ceremony. On the contrary, we believed that there was a good deal in a ceremony, and when at last the ban was lifted four years later, and we were married, we were very solemn about it indeed.

Perhaps it is those who have known what it is to live together unmarried who really do feel solemn about marriage; for they have known more nakedly the reality of the bond that binds a man and a woman. Precisely because they are, conventionally, free to leave one another, they know how closely they are bound. And, as I remember it, Lawrence felt solemn about his marriage, when on July 13th, it took place at a Registry office somewhere behind Harrods. Katherine, Gordon Campbell and I were the witnesses. Though we were envious, we were unfeignedly happy, because by this time we had come to look on the Lawrences, equally with the Campbells, as our closest friends. And Katherine was really moved when Frieda, on a sudden impulse, gave her the wedding-ring of her former marriage. Katherine wore it ever afterwards; nor would she change it even when we married. She was buried with it on her finger at Fontainebleau.

The Lawrences were staying with the Campbells at Selwood

Terrace, the home of the homeless, and their tiny drawing-room was our chief meeting-place. This was the first time I had been with Lawrence for long together, and I had my first real taste of an experience that was pretty constant throughout my relation with him – a feeling that I did not really understand what he was 'driving at'. At this particular moment his novel *Sons and Lovers* had been discovered by some of the Freudian psycho-analysts, who were enthusiastic about it because it exemplified some of Freud's main theses: and Dr. Eder then called more than once on Lawrence to discuss the doctrine, when I happened to be there. I was, as usual, quite ignorant about Freud; I knew his name and the significance he attached to dream-symbolism, also the word *Traumbedeutung*; and that was about all. But I was bewildered by the tone of the discussion. I could not understand why the matter should be taken so seriously, as though it were one of life and death. When Dr. Eder was gone, Lawrence would take me to task for my insouciance and my scepticism, and imply that I in particular ought to be very concerned about the Freudian theory. I felt that I was being indicted, rather unreasonably, for not taking SEX seriously.

I was, indeed, quite incurious about my complexes and my repressions; and I could see no good reason why I should get bothered about them, supposing that they existed. The dogs were asleep, as far as I knew, so why not let them lie? Moreover, I hadn't the faintest notion of how to make them bark: they had no visible tails for me to pull. No doubt a psycho-analyst could have set them in motion; but why should I consult an analyst? On the sexual side of my being, I felt normal, positively commonplace indeed. The specific problem of sex had never been a reality in my life, and never would be. Yet Lawrence seemed to feel, and to be anxious to make me feel, that this immunity of mine was wrong, and that somehow I was evading reality and behaving irresponsibly. That attitude was perplexing: for I did feel that, in comparison with Lawrence, I was somehow evading reality – but my evasion was not in the province of sex at all. On the contrary, it was precisely there that I felt myself on firmer ground than he. And though I was aware, from his books and his conversation, that he had vastly more experience of sex than I, I did not feel that he had come to any better conclusion than myself – if one as good.

Neither Katherine nor I could really understand Lawrence's point of view in the matter. He appeared to think that we, simply because we had nothing to correspond with his intense and agonizing sexual experiences, were flippant about sex. And that we rather resented. If we were abnomal, our abnormality lay in the fact that we were unusually happy as lovers, and we felt that, in this one thing, we were a good deal happier than Lawrence and Frieda. To have this vaguely imputed to us as a crime seemed rather extravagant. Perhaps neither of us fully appreciated quite how fortunate we were; it struck us as quite exorbitant that Katherine should be regarded as a butterfly and I as a child, merely because our sex-relation was exempt from agony. We tended to retaliate by making fun of Lawrence's Freudian entourage – a game which Katherine played like a master; but it only confirmed Lawrence in his suspicion that we were flippant about the Holy of Holies.

This was unfortunate, for there was growing up a real affection between the four of us. But the gulf between us was real. We could not enter, by imagination, into the core of the Lawrences' experience, nor they into ours. When we talked seriously together, it was almost always at cross-purposes. 'By pretending a bit,' Lawrence wrote in his last letter to me, fifteen years later, 'we had some jolly times, in the past. But we all had to pretend a bit – and we could none of us keep it up.' That is partially true; but it is the terrible truth which comes from a finally isolated man: for every human being has to pretend a bit in any relation with any other human being. When the last atom of pretence is gone, remains only the final loneliness of death, or of God.

Anyhow, in those days, we pretended as well together as we ever did. There was a world where we met and were happy

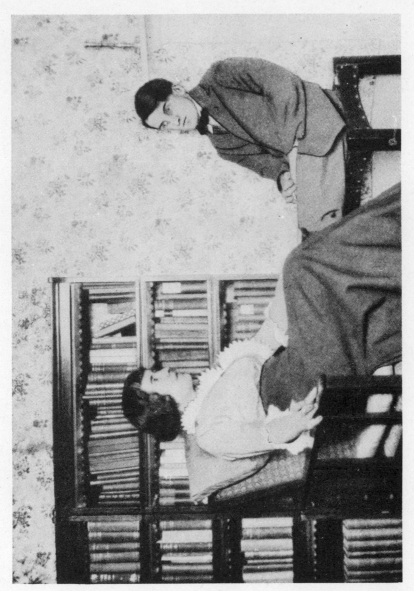

K. M. and J. M. M., October 1913

together; and there were two worlds where we never met at all: on both sides our intimate lives were sealed from one another. What glimpses they had of ours, and we of theirs, were alike incomprehensible. Nor, I think, could it have been otherwise. But in those days we were more conscious of the world we had in common, than of the worlds which we held, and which held us, apart. They were the halcyon days immediately before the outbreak of the War.

One odd episode is vivid in my mind. The Lawrences were making many new friends: chief among them Mrs. Carswell. A colony of these new friends lived in Hampstead. We, who always had the jealous idea that the Lawrences made new friends too easily – a not unnatural jealousy, considering how deep an inroad Lawrence made upon one's intimacy – were a little suspicious of the new Hampstead galaxy. But one day Lawrence and Frieda returned from the heights with the announcement that there was to be a picnic on the Heath, and that we had been specially invited. There was no help for it; obviously we must go. So on a beautiful afternoon, in late July, Campbell, Katherine and I with the Lawrences took the tube for Hampstead. All went well until we reached the Hampstead Station. We emerged in good order, and began to advance up the steep road immediately opposite – Holly Bush Hill. We three hung back a little, so that the Lawrences were well ahead. Suddenly, there was a piercing cry of 'Lawrence!' and we had a hasty glimpse of a young lady, clad it seemed in a kimono, rushing with enthusiastic arms outspread down the hill. 'Good God!' said Campbell. 'I won't have *that*!' said Katherine. With one accord we sped down the hill, round the corner, and fled. The lady from whom we fled in such panic discourtesy is now Madame Litvinov.

When he returned home Lawrence was very angry, though he had to admit that no one had seen us in flight. But, as he reasonably complained, we had made him look a fool. He had turned round to introduce us, and we just weren't there. Katherine tried to mollify him by explaining that it was not deliberately done; and that she simply had a horror of effusiveness. If she had been able to prevail upon herself to stay, she would have spoiled the party by her aloofness. Like her own Kezia, she could not bear things that rushed at her. Moreover, there is no doubt that we were very exclusive: we had the Campbells and the Lawrences, and desired no other friends. On the rare occasions when we received an invitation which we could not evade, as to a party in Church Row at the house of H. G. Wells whom we genuinely admired, or to a literary at-home at the house of some editor who had power over us, we endured it in misery. What Katherine wrote of one such occasion might serve for them all. 'A silly, unreal evening. Pretty rooms and pretty people, pretty coffee, and cigarettes out of a silver tankard. A sort of sham Meredith atmosphere lurking . . . I was wretched. I have nothing to say to "charming" women. I feel like a cat among tigers.' Still less had she anything to say to forward women. Whether she was the object or merely the witness of the onslaught, she withdrew behind her defences. And I gave her no assistance during these ordeals: I sat mute and glum and, as she once put it, as though I were suffering from sea-sickness.

The difference, in this respect, between us was that, whereas Katherine had great social aptitude, I had none. Katherine's method was to retire always in good order to her citadel, with her rearguard in constant action, and the enemy under close and critical observation; mine was precipitate retreat. But each alike had no use for mere acquaintances. We wanted friends with whom we could be at our ease; of these we had one or two, and we desired no more.

The party I have mentioned at the Wells's was a tremendous undertaking. Lawrence had a new dress-suit, his first one, and he insisted on wearing it. He had curiously rigid ideas of polite behaviour. I was rebellious about this, and wanted to go in grey flannels; I was quite sure, I said, that not all the guests would be in evening dress, and even if they were I didn't care. Again Lawrence was annoyed with me: I was letting him down again,

So I agreed to wear a dinner-jacket. That called for a good deal of improvisation, for though I had a clean boiled shirt, I had neither studs nor links: but with Katherine's help, a few pearl buttons and a piece of wire, I managed to make myself presentable. Then I had to go round and tie Lawrence's tie for him.

Now Lawrence, who looked his lithe and limber self in many kinds of attire, did not resemble himself at all when locked into a dress-suit. Though there was a slight improvement in this matter with the years, it was only slight; and to the end Lawrence in a dress-suit was hardly more than a caricature of Lawrence in his habit as he lived. While I tied his tie, I was acutely conscious of this, and was on the point of imploring him not to wear it, on the pretext that it looked too new. But something warned me that he would take such advice in bad part, and that this initiation into the dress-suit world was for him a serious and ritual affair, my attitude towards which would be construed as another example of my fundamental flippancy. So I held my peace, and tried to make his bow-tie a little more dashing – in vain, for Lawrence had bought the kind of bow-tie which I associated with nonconformist parsons – excellent in its place, but very incongruous on Lawrence at that moment. I struggled with it; but no matter what bold innovations I endeavoured, it relapsed into decorous nonconformity, demanding to be completed by an upturned eye and a Bible. And I, in my turn, began to be annoyed with Lawrence, for allowing himself to be turned into this unnatural exhibition. The author of *Sons and Lovers* had a perfect right to go to a party in his pyjamas, I thought to myself, rather than appear as a callow acolyte of the Reverend Mr. Stiggins. And when I remembered that it was to abet this travesty that I was sporting links of pearl buttons and ginger-beer wire, I felt exasperated; and particularly exasperated with Frieda, for being totally unaware that her husband looked silly. She had the blissful habit of being completely preoccupied with her own appearance; yet, oddly enough, she would submit herself entirely to be dressed by him, and he did it well.

So, once more, we had 'to pretend a bit'; but that evening we got no jolly time for our pains. We were a forlorn and somewhat irritable procession by the time we reached Hampstead. The only thing to do was to make a thorough joke of it all, which Katherine was inclined to do; but in his panoply something of the stiffness of his shirt and collar seemed to have entered into Lawrence's moral being. He became the puritan he looked, and he frowned upon Katherine's ill-timed gaiety. Inevitably, the party was a miserable affair for us all, and, as we returned, Lawrence was apocalyptic in his denunciation of H. G. Wells, who had nevertheless been very decent, and genuinely pleased to meet him. But when Katherine pointed out that one or two of the effusive ladies had had, on that evening, not much of their effusiveness to spare for him, but had lavished it on H. G. Wells, his anger fairly boiled over. This discreet insinuation that he had been letting himself down touched Lawrence on the raw. And on that journey home H. G. Wells had to suffer for it.

It seemed to me always that Lawrence showed to ill advantage with his social 'superiors'. He who was the perfection of naturalness and spontaneity with the peasants of any country was (unless my observation was quite mistaken) self-conscious, ill at ease, and perceptibly over-eager in aristocratic company. And I remember that about this time Katherine returned one night from a party at Lady Ottoline Morrell's very indignant with him for making himself cheap, and confessed that she had reacted by behaving icily to Lady Ottoline. Since this was so marked in him, I have sometimes speculated – naturally to no result – in what way he was influenced by the fact that Frieda was a Baronin von Richthofen. That the influence was considerable, I have no doubt whatever; but precisely how it worked, I can only conjecture. But when I was told years after, by the original of one of the more striking women characters in *Sons and Lovers*, that Frieda's rank was of tremendous significance to Lawrence in the days when he first met her, I was not altogether surprised to hear it.

CHAPTER XXI

RUMOURS OF WAR

THE assassination of the Archduke Franz Ferdinand was to us no more than a headline in the newspapers. Lawrence was going to his home at Eastwood, then on to the Lake District for a walking tour with an Englishman whom he had met at Spezia, and then returning to Italy. Katherine and I had arranged to take a holiday in Cornwall, at St. Merryn, where the local school-teacher had let us her cottage. Its discovery was due to the Beresfords, who were always our good friends, and we were delighted at the prospect of a fortnight near them.

When we said good-bye to the Lawrences, at the very end of July, it was in none of our heads that a European war was imminent. It was outside the range of possibility. It is true that I had reviewed Bernhardi's book, *Deutschland und der nächste Krieg*; but that had been a mere intellectual exercise. More serious had been a glimpse of French recruits entraining at the Gare de l'Est, and the obstinacy with which a Prussian fellow-lodger of mine in a Heidelberg *pension* had insisted on playing game after game of chess with me until he beat me. He was a portent. I made no pretension to be a chess-player, and accepted his invitation to a game out of civility. As bad luck would have it, I beat him. Then night after night, when I wanted to be in a boat on the Neckar, I had to let him challenge me. If I tried to put it off with excuses, I was given to understand without any ambiguity that I was afraid of being beaten. That put me on my mettle, and I went on beating him – or rather letting him beat himself, for he was so nervously intent on putting the Englishman in his place that his play became childish. At last, in order to get free from an intolerable *corvée*, I had to lose on purpose, which I did so clumsily that I was afraid he would see through it. But no! And then, to crown it all, I had to submit nearly every dinner-time to a homily on the weakness of the English character compared to the Prussian. Had Herr Murry not experienced how Prussian *Hartnäckigkeit* always won in the end? Herr Murry had indeed, but not quite in the sense that Herr Schniebel meant. But Herr Murry kept that politely to himself.

Herr Schniebel had been a portent; but that was three years before, and Herr Murry had forgotten all about it. Besides, now, in Frieda Lawrence, *geboren* von Richthofen, he had met quite a different type of Prussian: more authentic than Herr Schniebel, indeed in a sense almost the 'idea' of a Prussian. For her father had won the Iron Cross in the war of 1870, and had been the first German military governor of Metz after the peace. And Frieda's stories of her girlhood in Lorraine, in the sunshine and the ripening orchards, among friendly French peasants, recalled the atmosphere of *Dichtung und Wahrheit* rather than the tension of Saverne. No, emphatically European war was not to be numbered among the possible horrors of existence.

Nevertheless, one evening Elliot Crooke, a scholar of my college at Oxford a year junior to me who, having just commenced journalism, had formed the habit of coming round to Arthur Street in the evenings, brought with him the staggering news that the threat of war was really serious. He was an officer in the Special Reserve, and he had received orders to report at a depot either that night or at an early hour in the morning. Anyhow, he had come to say good-bye. Since Crooke was the very opposite of an alarmist, incredulity was stifled. Moreover, he was a historian and something of a student of war. Whatever he did, he did thoroughly and well, and he had taken his training in the Special Reserve very seriously. He was under no illusions; he sincerely hoped it would be a false alarm. If it was not, it would be a horrible business.

Katherine liked Crooke better than any of my Oxford friends save Goodyear (who by this time had disappeared to India). Crooke's quiet seriousness and gentle charm attracted her greatly; and that last evening together made a great impression on her.

The night was sultry and the streets were quiet. Desultorily, we talked on till midnight with hushed voices, as though we were in a cathedral. We did not turn on the lights. There was this strange, new, ominous thing hovering about us, and the warm gloom kept it friendly. Still more Katherine and I were moved that Crooke had to come to spend his last evening with us. His kit and sword were in the hall below. I was overwhelmed by the sudden realization that Crooke had a deep affection for me, which I felt I had done nothing to deserve. Perhaps I had: I don't know; but at that moment I could remember nothing. It seemed to me that this quiet and loving farewell was a sort of grace dropped from Heaven.

The talk drifted to the extermination of the human race: an inopportune subject, it might seem, but it was not without its peace that evening. Sooner or later – it appeared – life would be insupportable on the earth. There would be a final epoch when the ice-caps would slowly close down on the equator, and human history would end. And yet, though this was thinkable, it was unimaginable. Or was it? Were there not aeons and aeons of pre-history buried in an undecipherable past? And was recorded history essentially more intelligible? What was the *meaning* of this convulsion that was upon us now? To that we had no answer; and we said good-bye. We never saw one another again.

On the next day a fever of unrest had entered into Katherine and me. We drifted about London, bought newspapers, read them in tea-shops: in the evening we swirled with the crowds from one embassy to another, were caught in strange momentary eddies of mass-emotion, and flung aside, bewildered. We were neither for war, nor against it. To be for or against a thing, it must belong to one's world; and this was not in ours. Of this queer, heart-racking drama we were the apprehensive spectators. Life, which had already brought us such great surprises, had now dumbfounded us altogether. We stood, clasping hands, by the railings of the Green Park, late at night, while a Highland regiment – someone said the Black Watch – marched to the station, and our hearts were big within us, hot with the sadness and the beauty of their ordered going.

The next day Hugh Kingsmill came to tell me of his doings. He had discovered, somewhere in Putney, a cyclist battalion of the Middlesex Regiment that was enlisting men. Why should I not go too? And Kingsmill's cheerful holiday face, combined with the cycles, seemed to put a more human complexion on the event. So off I went, and took my place in a queue of some hundreds. I wanted to explain to an overworked and perspiring sergeant that my affairs needed some tidying up, and that I should not be ready for at least a week; but he was past listening to any rigmarole of mine. 'Foreign service?' I nodded. He gave me something to swear and to sign, and handed me a piece of yellow paper: 'Pass out till medical examination.' And I was an enlisted man.

'Pass-out . . . medical examination.' On the way home, the first rang ominously in my ears. So I was not my own master any more. I just had to hang about till they pulled the leash on my collar. That was a cooling thought. And just when I was counting on a holiday in Cornwall. Katherine would have to go alone. She refused point-blank. Either we went together, or she stayed at home. Anyhow, if I wanted to pass that medical examination, I had better have a holiday first, for no doctor would pass me as I was. So off I went to Putney to explain. There was no doctor to be seen. I must wait at home till my turn came, and they would let me know.

At that I grew restive and contumacious. I was not going to wait about, and I was going to have my holiday. So I went to the doctor who had taken care of our pleurisies a couple of months before to put the case. I was a little disconcerted to see a sword in his hall. What if he were a military martinet, with the same fixed idea as the Putney sergeant-major? That was a grim prospect; but there was no escaping now. I told him what had happened and what I wanted; and I was overjoyed to see that he thought it reasonable enough. He tapped and sounded me.

'You should have taken your holiday before, young man', he said. I was far too pleased with the consequences of the verdict to worry about the verdict itself. He wrote a note. 'Give them this', he said. 'That will put you right. Eat plenty of Cornish cream. And come and see me again when you return.'

By this time, feeling that my hardly-won freedom was still precarious, I was determined to take no risks. I would not take that medical chit in person, but send it, and be well on my way to Cornwall by the time it arrived. But I could not forbear to have a look at it first. It said that I had had a severe attack of pleurisy, that I now had a tenacious catarrh, and ended: Query T.B. I have good reason to believe that that conjectural diagnosis was mistaken; but it was repeated more than once afterwards in circumstances when I was inclined to pay more attention to it than I did then.

Then, I simply welcomed it as a release from my overhasty enlistment. I wanted the opportunity to take stock of the situation, and to discover, if I could, some more substantial motive for action or inaction than a mere surrender to the tide. But I could discover none. There was always the same sense of the lack of any vital connection between myself and the war. One Sunday afternoon, before we left for Cornwall, I had been to see my mother and father for the first time since Katherine's disastrous visit more than two years before. The war had at least brought this outward reconciliation between myself and my parents; but it seemed pretty hollow that day. For I was astonished to find that my father, who had been an ardent Radical and a pro-Boer, had made a right-about-turn. Lord Northcliffe and the *Daily Mail* had always been right. His eyes were opened to the devilry of Germany, at last. And the first consequence of this opening of his eyes was that he swallowed, for gospel, every tale of German brutality; while the Tsar of All the Russias, who was wont to be my father's bogy-man, had suddenly become a great Crusader against the infidel. Whatever I was, I was not that kind of patriot, and I gently suggested that it was not easy for an Englishman to

297

understand how the Germans must feel, caught in the vice of a
Franco-Russian alliance, with an open frontier either way. I was
made to understand that, if I wanted to remain friends with my
father, there must be no more talk of that kind; and that, unless
it were self-evident to me that the whole population of Germany
ought to be sold into slavery, I was no son of his. The night before
I had listened to the crashing of the windows of an inoffensive
German barber in my street, by a drunken and foul-mouthed
mob, and I had felt sick; I was not prepared to meet the same
mentality at home. Whatever the rights and wrongs of the War,
one thing was certain to me: that it was a tragedy for civilization.
And, although I did not know whether the position taken by
Lord Morley was justified, I felt a sort of cold and weary misery
at the manner in which my father abused a statesman who had
once been his idol, for sticking to the principles for which he had
idolized him.

I made my way forlornly back to Chelsea. At Clapham
Junction a special edition of *The Times* on a single sheet was being
sold excitedly. I read it on top of the bus on that grey and sultry
afternoon. It was the story of the defeat of the English expedition-
ary force. It seemed circumstantial enough, and the emotion
of the writer, if overstrained, was genuine. Something dreadful
had happened. Suddenly, I realized how naively and completely
I had taken it for granted that the English would be victorious.
My universe was falling to pieces.

Yet in Cornwall, the whole thing became remote again.
Though I stared every day at the Beresfords' *Times* and watched
the thick black line of the German advance draw nearer and
nearer to Paris, it was with a kind of abstract fascination. The
Germans would capture Paris. Very well. What then? My
imagination could make nothing of it. Would the Germans go
on and on till they reached the Atlantic? What then? Was
anything greatly changed when Napoleon's armies over-ran
Germany, or when in 1870 the German army over-ran France?
What difference had it made? What difference would it make

to-day? One thing, even I knew, was certain: that you could not keep an alien nation in subjection by military force. Sooner or later you had to withdraw.

The War, I decided in Cornwall, was not *for* anything – for anything of importance to me. If it was a war for Democracy, Democracy had found a strange defender in the Tsar of all the Russias. Even I could not believe in that. For small nations? What about the Poles? A war to end war? Wasn't that the object of every war? No, the only reason for the war that I could see was that there had, for some cause unknown to me, to be a war; it was as senseless and as necessary as an outbreak of the plague. I could not work up any moral indignation about it, any more than I could about an earthquake. Sooner or later, I supposed, I should be engulfed in it. I hated the idea; but there was nothing to be done about it: but I wasn't going any more to meet the trouble half-way.

That was an inglorious attitude; but, essentially, it did not change, so far as my personal self was concerned. War-resistance, conscientious objection – these were not for me. To be genuine, they demanded a depth of political conviction which I did not possess, nor ever came near to possessing. Perhaps, if I had met some of the few men who were really imbued with the true moral conviction of absolute pacifism, they might have influenced me. But the 'pacifists' I did meet completely sickened me of the tribe. Perhaps, though eminent, they were a poor sample. At all events, one of the few things of which I was certain was that I had nothing in common with them. Meanwhile, in Cornwall, we lived on cream, and blackberry jam and eggs, and wondered how long the money would last. I was earning nothing at all. Literary journalism and art-criticism had disappeared in the deluge. Now there was only Katherine's money; and in order to live on 35s. a week, it was necessary that we should cease to pay £1 a week for rent. And we were determined not to return to squalid ten-shilling rooms in London.

So, we spent most of our time at St. Merryn looking for a

small cottage in Cornwall. By some instinct we turned south, and hunted down the Truro River, and in the parts about Fowey and Polperro – but all in vain. When our time was up and the schoolmistress had resumed possession, we returned to London, and straightway left it again for a furnished cottage (again at 10s.) near Rye, and again we resumed our search. Summer was ending, and the nights were drawing in. Though we vastly enjoyed ourselves scouring the countryside, we found nothing. Yet we were very happy. Now that there really was no work to do, I was freed from the prickings of conscience, and could share Katherine's money without a qualm. Our very primitive cottage at Udimore, which was no more than a wooden shack, satisfied us, and had we not known that it would be uninhabitable in the winter, we should have stayed there.

As usual, when we were happy, we began to compose verses against and about one another. Two have survived. Katherine's describes an episode in my house-hunting. Somewhere in the outskirts of Rye we had come on a derelict building with the legend 'Estate Agent' upon it, and in a dusty window a list of properties to be let: one of which was obviously meant for us. It was a still late summer afternoon, steeped in sunshine. The broad street was deserted; 'the very houses seemed asleep'. War was inconceivable.

Inside the office, I saw an old man at a desk. I knocked at the door. He made no reply. Through the window, we stared at him again. He was certainly alive: he was actually writing something. I marched boldly in, with Katherine behind me.

That deaf old man
With his hand to his ear –
His hand to his head stood out like a shell,
Horny and hollow. He said, 'I can't hear';
He muttered, 'Don't shout,
I can hear very well';
He mumbled, 'I can't catch a word;

I can't follow!'
Then Jack with a voice like a Protestant bell
Roared – 'Particulars! Farmhouse! At 10 quid a year!'
'I dunno wot place you are talking about',
Said the deaf old man.
Said Jack, 'What the HELL!'
But the deaf old man took a pin from his desk, picked a piece
of wool the size of a hen's egg from his ear, had a good look at
it, decided in its favour and replaced it in the afore-mentioned
organ.

Thus was I discomfited; and thus did Katherine celebrate
my discomfiture. But I had my revenge. Our cottage at Udimore
was on a hill. To get our milk we had to decend sharply through
some fields towards the river Brede. Katherine proved to be an
unreliable emissary. She said there was a bull in the path;
but her bull was a cow. So I triumphed over her accordingly.

> 'There's nothing so fine as the country,' says Tig.
> 'A windy hill with the sea below,
> And shock-haired trees in a shining row,
> Waving over the silver thread
> That's really a river. Overhead
> Armies of birds like a black rain falling,
> Wheeling in company, bugles calling
> From general birds to birds of the line.
> That's what *I* call the country. It's fine. It's fine,'
>   Says Tig,
>   But she's talking big.
> It's only a cow. 'Well, I can't stand cows,'
>   Says Tig,
>   Feeling small,
>   'After all,
> They're stupid, with horns – and nobody knows
> What a stupid beast with a horn might do
> To me. Of course, they won't touch you.

301

You're stupid, too.
But if they see
Clever people like me,
It's different. I tell you I want my tea.
I don't care a button about the sea,
Or the hills,
Or the birds,
Or the streams.
It's no use your looking so angrily.
I *like* the cows; but they don't like me.'

As ever, when we were entirely by ourselves – forgetting and forgotten by the world, we were entirely happy. It was the business of maintaining some connection with the world which frayed us: whether it were maintaining relations with our friends, or, in my own case, trying to find some job of work. It would have been hard to find a man and woman better suited to living on a desert island than we two. But with the world of social responsibility we were singularly unfitted to deal. We were for ever incurring rash obligations of every sort that were quite unnecessary, and which we struggled in vain to fulfil. We were incessantly changing our 'home' and always losing heavily by each change. Unlike the Lawrences, who were the only people with whom we could compare ourselves, we disliked intensely the idea of being 'impermanent movables'. We liked modest possessions, and we were for ever acquiring a few, only to lose them again. Since we never could afford the places or the things we liked, in a sort of desperation we would attach ourselves, with far too solid bonds, to those we did not like, until the moment came when we must wrench ourselves free.

It is difficult to explain; but we were somehow conscience-stricken by our own irresponsibility. I was more a prey to this feeling than Katherine; but Katherine suffered from it too. We felt that it was wrong to be so unattached as we were to society, and even to our own friends. We were fond of them, but we could get on alarmingly well without them. And ever and anon, I would be overwhelmed by the sense that this was an unnatural and unregenerate condition, and react violently from this wicked isolation, and Katherine would seem to approve.

CHAPTER XXII

THE COTTAGE ON THE LEE

So we were always plunging from isolation and happiness into society and sorrow; as we did now. Our time at Udimore was over, and we returned to London. There we heard from the Lawrences that they were established in a cottage not far from familiar Cholesbury, and we were invited for the week-end. Here, for the first time, we met Koteliansky, who had accompanied Lawrence on his walking-tour in the Lakes and who quickly became Katherine's fast friend. Here, too, we had our first experience of the desperate quarrels which were raging between Lawrence and Frieda, and instinctively, like all his friends, we ranged ourselves on Lawrence's side, without any real understanding of the situation. But it was evident that Lawrence was exceedingly unhappy. Probably Frieda was, too; but she had a more immediate power of recovery than he. Two things were preying on him together: one was the War, the other his struggle with his wife; the two strains seemed to be making a sick man of one who, on his return to England, had looked radiantly well. Since we still had our winter home to find, and Lawrence seemed anxious that we should live near by, I began my search on my bicycle again, and found the Rose Tree Cottage, at the Lee. It was the best part of three miles across the fields from the Triangle, where Lawrence lived; but it was now mid-October, and since there seemed nothing better, we decided on it.

We spent ten days at the Lawrences' cottage, walking backwards and forwards every day to clean and decorate our own. Lawrence was distinctly ill and had grown a beard (whereby I inherited his excellent razor and strop), yet he insisted on sharing in the painting. Or rather, thinking that I was too slow, he took the brush out of my hand and laid on in a kind of berserk fury.

304

On October 26th, 1914, we moved in, without enthusiasm. It went against the grain to return to a part of the country where we had lived before.

Then began three months of fairly close association with the Lawrences, of which my memories, though extensive, are miserable. None of us was happy, but though the unhappiness of the Lawrences was much more spectacular than ours, ours also was real. The times were out of joint. There seemed so little to cling to. Perhaps the Lawrences and we might have been stronger separately. Together, we seemed chiefly to brood on a world gone mad. One night, I remember, there was a knock on the door of the shed where I worked and Lawrence came in. He said nothing, but sat in a chair by the stove, rocking himself to and fro, and moaning. I thought that there had been another quarrel with Frieda, and I felt it was futile to attempt to comfort him. Their struggle was beyond me; I was out of my depth. But on this night, it turned out, there had been no quarrel. Suddenly Lawrence had been overwhelmed by the horror of the war and had made his way across in the dark. That was all. I can see him now, in his brown corduroy jacket, buttoned tight up to the neck, and his head bowed, radiating desolation.

Another night also is vivid to me. Katherine and I had been invited to a supper of roast veal. Everything had gone well; the crocks and the saucepans had been thoroughly well washed, and we were talking gaily enough, when there was a mention of Frieda's children, and Frieda burst into tears. Lawrence went pale. In a moment, there was a fearful outburst. Ominously, there was no physical violence. Lawrence, though passionately angry, had kept control; and it was the more frightening. He had had enough, he said; she must go, she was draining the life out of him. She must go, she must go now. She knew what money he had; he would give her her share – more than her share. He went upstairs, and came down again, and counted out on the table to me sixteen sovereigns. Frieda was standing by the door, crying, with her hat and coat on, ready to go – but where?

I had often said to myself that it would be better that Lawrence and Frieda should part; but when the crucial moment came, it seemed unthinkable. Indeed, at that moment I knew it was impossible, and ceased thereafter to indulge that facile illusion, for I felt that Lawrence could not survive that severance. He looked terrible. Yet at that time I was very hostile to Frieda. I accused her, in my journal, of 'squandering his nervous energy', and accepted without criticism his own charge against her that she played the traitor to him, by turning backwards towards her children. 'I do not understand why L. goes on with it', I wrote – 'not *really, intimately* understand'. That was true enough. I understood nothing about their relation at all. And the more Lawrence tried to explain it to me, the more ignorant I became. There is in my journal a puzzled note of a doctrine which Lawrence expounded to me concerning the necessity of a 'dual mortification', which he explained by saying that 'very often when he wants F. she does not want him at all, and that he has to recognize and fully allow for this'. It was all outside my experience, and in taking Lawrence's side I was rushing in like a fool where an angel would have feared to tread.

That night I put all the blame on Frieda; it seemed to me that Lawrence was perfectly right in telling her to go. And at the same time I knew it was impossible; still more, that Lawrence would never forgive me if I helped her to go. And beyond this, I was afraid that it would end merely in Frieda coming to our house, and turning it into a sort of anti-Lawrence camp. That I was determined to prevent. But this mixture of motives in my head made me terribly self-conscious; and though I was completely sincere in my effort to reconcile them, I felt that I was playing a part. Instead of being able to say, quite simply, 'Look here, you two, this is impossible; you cannot get on without one another', I found myself swept into a kind of theatrical harangue. Instead of being spontaneous, I was deliberate and calculated. I was listening to and criticizing every word I uttered, judging its effect. And some part of me stood coldly and cynically aside, asking whether indeed I meant well, and condemning me for hollowness and hypocrisy. If I truly meant well, could I be feeling what I did? Still worse, how could words, uttered in such fashion, be making the impression which I saw they were making, upon such a one as Lawrence? True, I was straining myself to the uttermost, but like an actor, not like a man; and I was completely exhausted when it was over. But I had succeeded. I had won over Lawrence completely, and he and Frieda were smiling together before we left.

I was bewildered by my own achievement. Katherine had said nothing while the scene went on. As we walked back, she said that she could not speak for sheer astonishment at my performance. Neither then did I understand it myself, nor do I now. But whereas now it is merely incomprehensible, then it troubled me. It was, I suppose, only an extreme case of the strange dislocation of the personality from which I suffered. I had no 'proper self'. I was loosely compacted of a consciousness, and an unknown; and there was no vital relation between them. How deeply it troubled me many scattered entries in my tedious journal might witness; but there is one which is curious enough to be re-copied here. I do not profess to understand it; but it is evidently an attempt to record a momentary closing of the pitiful fissure within my being.

Sunday, November 23rd, 1914. I know I shan't be able to write about this intelligibly, because I know it's the biggest thing that has happened to me. (Even words seem strange now, and my pen will not form them.)

Gordon [Campbell] left for London at 8 o'clock. An hour before I had been reading my poem [*The Critic in Judgment*] to him. Katherine seemed to me rather distant and antagonistic during the time supper was being prepared. I felt exceedingly remote, listening to Gordon asking her questions about the novel I am writing, as though it and I were somehow strange and incomprehensible, apart from me. Gordon had praised the poem, and that too was strange to me, as though he had praised something foreign, with which I had no concern.

We did not wash up the supper things after he had gone, for we were sorry that he had gone at the moment when we seemed to be getting free and close to each other. We had been talking during supper of our *selves*. Gordon said he always wondered how much I noticed, that he sometimes thought I noticed nothing, but that he could never say so positively, because I might suddenly produce something to show that I had. He himself (he said, when I asked him) had no vivid memories of places, only of moments when some word of another person had revealed his own composition to himself. Katherine described her own power of noticing as searching through leaf after leaf of a wood and finally discovering what she sought – the word of perfect significance.

When Katherine and I drew up our chairs by the fire, I was still feeling aloof from her. I asked her, 'Do you know anything of your *self*?' She answered: 'I have been, for the last weeks since we were down here, exploring my self. I have thrown away all kinds of foreign matter and left my self, so that I do seem to know a good deal about it.'

I said: 'I know nothing about my self. I realize it at this moment. The poem and the novel have fallen right away from me, and left me nakedly with my self. And now that I am thus, I feel that I know nothing of it. It is undefined and indefinable. I have no means of approach to it. It is an eternity away.'

'I too feel that,' she said. The strange thing is that this was the first occasion on which she had said that she felt the same as I felt, and *I believed her*.

I cannot remember the exact words we spoke henceforward, but since I must put them down, lest the memory of them should fade away, I must try to represent them.

Katherine: 'That is what most people feel about their selves, the stage before this. To have realized your self as something apart and unattainable, and yet to have reached to it, that is our, the artist's, business.'

J.M.M.: 'But I feel that I have no tools with which I can attack it. I see it just as a ball, vaguely outlined, in front of me, and I am millions of miles away from it. I am, it seems, at this moment, communicating my observations of it to you, a third person. It tells me nothing of what I am to do to draw closer to it. I feel that I might make the supreme effort for two weeks to do nothing in which my self did not directly participate; yet after that it might just fall apart, and leave my actions dropping, dropping down into an abyss.'

Katherine: 'That was how I felt while you were reading your poem. I could not listen to it, at least distinctly. I was dropping, dropping. But do you feel that you have ever been your self?'

J.M.M.: 'Never. I could only be my self, after this moment when I have realized the abyss between. Before that, I have at times been free of foreign matter, and lost my self-consciousness, but no more.'

Katherine: 'I have been attempting to be my self since I was a child. I always wanted "to get down to my self" when I was seventeen. From twenty to twenty-four, certain moments of music, a tree waving outside, seemed to take me to my self. I realized by their contrast with me at other moments that there was a self to get at.'

J.M.M.: 'Isn't that a lie? I mean: didn't those moments just have a kind of ultimate quality? It was more real perhaps, but neither by contrast, nor positively, did it suggest anything about your self.'

Katherine: 'Yes, I don't think I am being really honest. I wonder what kind of quality it really was?'

J.M.M.: 'With me a kind of loneliness, a being carried far distances away, perhaps.'

Katherine: 'Mine was an Alas! I don't know how else to

put it.' (The word 'desiderium', I remember, passed across my mind, but I said nothing about it.)

J.M.M.: 'But this feeling of mine now, as I speak, is something quite different, new, something I have never felt before.'

Katherine: 'For me, too, if I am absolutely honest.'

J.M.M.: 'My self is utterly remote and unapproachable. It has suddenly thrown off, passed clear away from, all its acts, and has just shown me that they are not its acts.'

Katherine: 'Yet I feel that there is something which acts on behalf of the self.'

J.M.M.: 'But do you feel that what acts "on behalf of" is sure of its instructions?'

Katherine: 'Not at all.'

J.M.M.: 'I feel now that there is no possible communication between me and my self. I *see* it, so plainly. It is like a great smooth wall – a side, rather – neither up nor down, nor to the right nor to the left, can the end of it be seen; and I am a tiny speck in front of it, looking in vain for a foothold.'

Katherine: 'I see it like a misty river flowing out of the beyond into the beyond, and I am like a little figure running in the mist on the bank, knowing that there is a bridge to be found, but not knowing for the mist whether to go right or left.'

My journal continues:

That moment of the two pictures is quite definite in my memory. After that they seemed to obscure the reality I had been seeing up till then. The pictures obtruded whenever I tried to look beyond them. I asked Katherine if it was the same with her, and she said 'Yes'.

But the vision had already gone. I remember asking her: 'Can you hold this moment?' and that she replied, 'No, I can't', having first said, 'Yes'.

Then as the intensity began to slowly subside, we talked about what had happened. Katherine said that the wonderful thing was to have been with another person when the greatest thing of all had happened. I do not remember what I said, until I asked what she felt, and told her that I had a sense of an infinite beatitude descending upon me. So, she said, had she.

By that time I was clearly conscious that something *positive* had happened to me. Before that, though I was acutely conscious of the sudden lifting out of time and space, I felt rather that it was *negative* and that in it remained a tinge of the despair at the inaccessibility of the new-found self with which it all began.

There is the record as it stands. I can make but little of it to-day, save that out of the very intensity of my awareness of the separation between my consciousness and my unknown self there came to me, and strangely to Katherine also, some kind of intellectual ecstasy.

I say, strangely to Katherine also, because she was always rather hostile to my tendency towards what I have dignified by the name of 'intellectual mysticism'. It does not really deserve the name; and it would be more accurately called a queer kind of intellectual sensationalism, because there was an indubitable element of self-indulgence in it – a kind of private drug-taking. It is all a little mysterious to me now; but there is no doubt that sometimes my intellectual experiences, or my efforts towards a kind of intellectual imagination, ended in overpowering sensations. And in some of these odd adventures, Gordon Campbell was my sympathetic companion. Sometimes I followed his lead, sometimes he mine. Thus, this very 'ecstasy' of which I have preserved the record seems to have begun with my reading to Campbell a poem born of the same sort of 'ecstasy'. And elsewhere in my journal at this time I note that I am worn out 'partly because my mind has been assaulted by an extraordinary mental excitement aroused by Gordon'.

I had a profound admiration for Campbell at this time; partly because I was very fond of him as a person, and partly for a less excellent reason: namely, that I set immense store by these intellectual 'experiences'. My natural bias towards an extreme condition of self-consciousness had received a powerful stimulus from my reading of Dostoevsky; and it had been still further stimulated by the closer acquaintance with Lawrence which had now begun. For I reacted vehemently away from what I felt to be his unnatural submersion of himself – a man – in the Woman. This is not easy to define; and indeed it can be described only in terms which anticipate the development of Lawrence's own philosophy. Rightly or wrongly, it seemed to me that Lawrence did not serve Frieda as a person, or an individual, but as a sort of incarnation of the Female principle, a sort of Magna Mater in whom he deliberately engulfed and obliterated himself. And I felt a morbidly fastidious aversion to this. It produced in me a kind of nausea. Thus, I felt an acute unease when, during a whole evening, Lawrence sat trimming a hat for Frieda. Or, on a different level, I was made uncomfortable by Lawrence's declaration made to me while he was writing *The Rainbow*, that 'he was conscious of Frieda's participation in his work, to such an extent that it depended upon her active goodwill'. My comment on that is revealing.

'It is very curious [I wrote in my journal], for K—— and I work best in complete isolation, mental and physical. Doubtless a negative condition of good work is hitting it between us; but in the positive sense, no.'

That, as it turned out, was by no means true; and, in fact, at this time I was incapable of good work, even by my own standards: and precisely at the moment when I did become capable of it, some sort of fusion between Katherine and myself had occurred. Nevertheless, there was a deep distinction. Whereas the fusion between Lawrence and Frieda was (so to speak) infra-personal, that between Katherine and myself, when it came, was supra-personal. We were distinct beings, who surrendered to one another as distinct beings, when we did surrender. But Lawrence seemed to merge himself in an impersonal Woman, and often to regard his wife as a sort of prophetess and instrument of the 'blood-consciousness'.

Though I have become much less intolerant of that conception than I used to be, I must confess that it still arouses in me a pretty elemental feeling of hostility. At that time I reacted away from it very vehemently. And the form my reaction took was to set an exaggerated value on my masculine and intellectual relation with Campbell. An extremity of self-consciousness, such as I attained with him, seemed to me to be a condition possessing positive value, and something to be guarded jealously against feminine usurpation. Hence came the plain confession, in that record of my experience shared with Katherine, of my previous scepticism of any claim of hers to have experienced the same intellectual emotions as myself. A good deal (which it has cost me an effort to rescue from oblivion) is concealed behind the curious phrase: 'The strange thing is that this was the first time on which she had said that she felt the same as I felt, and *I believed her.*'

Whatever the experience we shared that night actually was, there is no doubt that it was momentarily overwhelming: all my 'ecstasies' with Campbell paled before it. It undoubtedly was 'the greatest thing that had happened to me'; and the essential part of its 'greatness' was that it was shared by us both. It may seem fantastic, but I cannot help surmising that this experience was somehow antithetical to the Lawrences', and that just as Lawrence instinctively merged himself in the pre-mental world of Frieda, so Katherine, by a like 'unnatural' effort, momentarily merged herself in this post-mental world of mine. That the effort was unnatural in Katherine's case I have no doubt, because she almost immediately reacted away from me with determination, as though I were a kind of intellectual ghoul, as in fact I was, though I did not know it. After this, for some months, she definitely turned away from me. I was freezing the warm immediate life in her.

Her hostility to this morbid apotheosis of self-consciousness on my part is evident in this account from my journal of an evening with Lawrence.

313

Tuesday, November 18. Lawrence was here last night, without Frieda, who had had an attack of the children and had quarrelled with him. Therefore we had a good uninterrupted talk. Lawrence's ideas are rather difficult for me to get hold of, because he uses all kinds of words in a curious symbolic sense to which I have no clue. But I find him really interesting and very congenial.

Lawrence sat in the little black chair on the right of the fire. Katherine was on the hearth, on a cushion. Occasionally she shielded herself from the fire by holding out her red silk scarf on her arm. I was in the blue chair, mostly silent, trying to attend to Lawrence, and then, when I had made myself attend, trying to understand him.

It started with Dostoevsky. Lawrence was all against him for his humility and love. It was the search for the Absolute everywhere, as though all individuals might at the last be reduced to a common ether. I retorted that the love was but a means of ascertaining the individual quality of the individual ether, in the sense that it made communication possible. Katherine was quite violent in condemnation of Dostoevsky's 'open house for foolish people'. Lawrence was even more explosive. 'Humility is Death. To believe in an Absolute is Death. There are no Absolutes.' Katherine was eager in agreement with this. I wanted to ask her what she meant, but wisely refrained.

From that we passed to an idea which Lawrence attempted to explain when last he was here. The history of human consciousness has been the history of two successive ideas – the idea of Law, and the idea of Love. Each has reached its extremity, the latter nowadays. Each is true, and false; and the way of Life is a balance between them. L—— is fond of the Orestean trilogy as showing the balance of both qualities.

After my fashion I suggested that the two things were better called: the condition of Being and the condition of Knowing. He accepted this, rather to my surprise, for I am never quite certain whether I have understood him. But if he really meant this, I can see his point about the balance between them. He has a confusing way of calling them the Male and the Female principles – I forget which is which. But I think that what he is getting at is the fundamental difference between the two attitudes – Man a tiny part of the universal system, and Man as knowing and comprehending the whole system in himself: *aliter*, Man unconscious, a root-tip of the general Life, and Man conscious, the knower of means and end.

The trouble is that the second is rather difficult at first sight to connect with Christianity. But I think it does. The Christian bond is *conscious*. 'Leave father, mother, sisters and brethren and follow me!' It is a passing away from the great unconscious physical ties to conscious and voluntary ones. From The Tables of the Law to the Sermon on the Mount. Life, real life, is the discovery of a balance, a living harmony, between the conscious and unconscious principles. Allow, satisfy, shape the one by the other. That is the problem. I do not think it is different, essentially, from my old business of soul-harmony; but it was very hard to understand what he meant.

We also talked about the sensuous nature. L—— accused me of a lack of it, which is probably right, and of an intellectual contempt for it, which is most certainly wrong. I feel certain that that part of me was terribly stunted by my Father. It worries me profoundly that it may have been irreparable. But Lawrence surprised me by a far more passionate indignation against my Father than I had ever been able to summon up myself.

The account is apposite to the tension between Katherine and myself which I have been seeking to remember. Her joining with Lawrence against me in his fervid denunciation of Dostoevsky is an indication of the strain. For her view of Dostoevsky was far different from his. What hers naturally was is to be seen from her notes upon Dostoevsky in her journal. But to Dostoevsky as Campbell and I used him, the arch-hierophant of intellectual self-consciousness, she was so hostile that she preferred to side with Lawrence at his most violent.

And, at a deeper level, the record is more apposite still. That conflict between the Male and Female principles (which I found it so hard to grasp) was precisely what we were embodying then. Campbell and I, with Dostoevsky for our prophet, were extravagantly asserting the Male principle, of Knowing and self-consciousness and mental 'love'; Lawrence and Frieda were asserting the Female principle, of Being, of self-mortification and blood 'law'. While Katherine was distraught between us. She believed in neither the one nor the other in these extreme forms: she disliked equally the dominion of the Female, or the physical, and the dominion of the Male, or mental. And she, for her part, really did embody something of the poise and true balance between them which was an idea or an ideal both to Lawrence and myself.

That seems to put Lawrence and myself at this time on some sort of equality. Nothing of the kind is intended. It is no fault of mine that my life tended to shape itself henceforward into the pattern of an antithesis to Lawrence's. This was my first intimate experience of him; and there is no doubt that it took on both sides the form of a simultaneous attraction and repulsion. I was overwhelmingly attracted to his sensuous spontaneity, and I was just as violently repelled by his actual submersion in, and his ideal exaltation of, undifferentiated Woman. Beside the richness of the former, I felt how poor a thing I was; but in respect of the latter, I felt myself to be more a *man* than he. I felt that no man should succumb to the dominance of Woman as he did. But my reaction was 'impure', at least in the scientific sense. It was not merely the healthy reaction of one who felt that this self-submersion in the Woman was wrong, as I still feel it to have been, and as I believe the whole pattern of Lawrence's life proves that it was, but it was combined with the impulse to 'compensation' of one who was forced, in comparison with Lawrence's rich spontaneity, to recognize the poverty of his own instinctive nature. I took refuge in my tower of 'intellectual mysticism', not merely to vindicate the essential apartness of the Male from the Female, but at least equally to confirm myself in the sense of some superiority to Lawrence – to save myself from the peril of being annihilated by him in my own estimation. However jealous and grudging may have been my conscious acknowledgment of his superiority, nay his difference in kind, as an instinctive being – and my journal contains some amusing evidences of that – I knew it well enough. I turned to my intellectualism to preserve my self-esteem; I counterposed it as a value to the value I knew that Lawrence pre-eminently possessed: my intellectual 'experience' to his sensuous 'experience'. And it was characteristic of me that I did not counterpose to Lawrence's my own value, but rather that of Campbell. An entry in my journal is illuminating.

> *Tuesday, Dec.* 22. Why is it that G[ilbert] C[annan], clever writer though he is (for which I envy him), and D.H.L. (in a less degree) always give me a feeling of absolute unreality in their books? I can only think it is because they have fixed ideas. D.H.L. may come to others; but I have a notion that there is no hope for G.C. I think that I have no ideas at all.
>
> Why do I find nothing in my generation? Is it because there *is* nothing? or is it because I have not the eyes to see something even if it were there? I find it impossible to believe this. The clever and futile E.M.F., the clever and homunculous G.C., the crack-brained, sex-obsessed D.H.L. (tho' of him I hope) – are these really as negligible as they seem? And isn't it funny – a confession of incompetence – that I see in Gordon Campbell, the successful barrister who makes £1800 out of a single case, a finer than them all, not in their own way, but on a different plane, only to be attained by me of known contemporaries? All these things are constantly tumid in my brain. Isn't the mere fact sufficient to damn me?
>
> Or again, look at it in this way. Katherine, who has written

317

better stories than G.C. or D.H.L. have ever written in their lives, and better than they are ever likely to, thinks of these men as I do. Is that a kind of unconscious suggestion from me, or a desire to defend me in my own estimation? The idea is ridiculous.

Perhaps Gordon was right after all, when he said that it was good that I was started young, for otherwise I should have been impatient of the creaking of my own brain, and have given up long before I had bored my way with infinite labour out on to the other side of the beyond. Somehow, he does believe in me. I think he is honest. And he believes in my most empty, incredible moments. That does mean a great deal. For I believe in his belief in me, more than I do in myself.

Claudite jam rivos pueri; sat prata biberunt.

It was Campbell whom I set on a pinnacle, that he might haul me out of my own sense of nothingness. But I was at least conscious of what I was doing. To some extent I understood the mechanism that was at work within me. That it could continue to function in spite of my own self-knowledge and my scepticism, showed that it was more than a mechanism. Indubitably, it was: in the mingled yarn of my relation to Campbell there was at least one strand of deep and genuine affection. I desperately wanted him to 'believe in me'; but that, in the last resort, was because I admired him so much – and what, above all, I admired in him was a kind of extreme integrity. I felt about him that, if ever it came to the pinch, he would not spare me because he was fond of me. Ultimately, it did not matter to me whether Lawrence 'believed in me'. We were too different. Even if Lawrence were to declare his faith in me, it would be meaningless to me: as, when he did, it proved to be. And, alas, ultimately, it did not matter to me if Katherine believed in me. Truly, if she had disbelieved in me, it would have been terrible and annihilating. But her belief in me had no positive effect on one of my sceptical composition. I knew she *had* to believe in me, while she loved me.

For my desperate disease there was no remedy save the slow and painful birth of some immediate sense of my own validity. And now circumstances began gradually to converge upon me and to compel me into the isolation in which alone this sense of validity could be found. First, Katherine inevitably began to turn away from me. She had to escape the devastating miasma of my self-consciousness and self-distrust. When the division between my consciousness and my self had reached the point of ecstasy, and she had shared it, she was bound to turn away. If that was the point where we were to be really united, then life together was truly impossible for us: it was indeed a union and ecstasy of death – such as Lawrence strove to express in the relation between Gerald and Gudrun in *Women in Love*. But I did not know this, then. My consciousness, on the contrary, told me that this was the beginning of our true union. But my unconsciousness knew better. For as soon as she began definitely to turn away from me, I accepted it as inevitable.

Katherine was profoundly unhappy at this time. Week after week, she strove with herself in the effort to write, in vain. The difference between us here was that she had experience of true creative spontaneity, whereas I had none. I could toil on and on, with my laborious and self-conscious novel, analysing my own inward life to immobility, with no particular expectation that writing would, or could, be anything other than an effort; but for her there was no such limbo condition. She wrote either well, or not at all. And in these days, and for months before and after, she wrote not at all. She finished stories, only to tear them up again. She felt remote and indifferent to the dream which Lawrence and I indulged of escaping to an island. The 'sad little house' oppressed her; and she cherished her own dream of escaping from her oppression to some more vivid life, which she thought she found in the letters which my French friend, R.D. wrote me. In a word, Katherine was in rebellion.

She wanted a life more natural to herself than what, in her diary, she called her 'three years' idyll' with me. She wanted, or thought she wanted, money, luxury, adventure, the life of cities. I had no complaint to make; it seemed to me fair enough, for I knew myself to be a sad companion. And though Katherine told me little of what was passing in her mind and heart, I was not ignorant. And I was disinclined to urge any claim upon her; indeed, I never felt that I had any claim upon her. If she was tired of me, as she seemed to be, that was destiny; and if, by reason of the kind of life she was compelled to live with me, the fountain of inspiration dried within her, she had good cause to look else-where. It may be that she was woman enough to be chagrined by what may have seemed my indifference – though, indeed, it was nothing of the kind – but I always was, and always would be, man enough to ask nothing of a woman but what of her own motion she could not help giving. My virtues were few enough; but that was one of them. I believed in Love, though I could not achieve it, and I believed that Love was, by its essence, free.

Only in one small matter do I find that Katherine was, at this time, less than fair to me: when, in her diary, she complained that 'J—— didn't want money, and wouldn't earn money'. I had very few opportunities of earning money; the few I had I took. But I stubbornly refused to get myself completely enmeshed in journalism as I had been a year before. I never was one of the purists who will not sully their artistic soul by doing a job of work; but the kind of work I would do had to have some interest for me. Even money – of which I knew the value better than Katherine – could be bought at too high a price.

By Christmas, 1914, I think, it was understood between us that we were about to part. The ostensible reason was that Katherine wanted city-life, and I did not; but the fact was that she believed she could see an escape from her unhappiness, while I saw none from mine. Moreover, she had been suffering badly from arthritis. From all her woes she imagined she had found a deliverer in R.D. I was dully aware of it, and sufficiently sensible to make no attempt to disabuse her, although I was curiously certain that she was deceiving herself. I was certain of very few things at that time; but one of the few was my knowledge of the essential Katherine. I knew that there were two Katherines: one cynical, but wonderfully brave, ready to risk anything for the sake of an 'experience', and to keep smiling when it failed her. I had met Katherine in such a moment of reaction, and since I was neither cynical nor brave, but rather a simple and sentimental and self-conscious young man, she had found a sort of peace with me, in which the other Katherine, who was truly childlike and sensitive like a child, had had time to breathe. And if I had been more firmly based in my own self, able to give the lead and set the course for both of us, her cynical self would not have got the upper hand again. But I was a broken reed to lean on. Because I knew that I did not depend on her – it was part of my disease that I did not – I did not understand that she did depend on me.

But I knew, perfectly well, which was the real Katherine; and I was not finally dismayed when I understood that she had reached the conclusion that her three years' life with me had been a charming but irrelevant idyll. In this, at least, I knew better than she; and I had, in my heart, a core of faith that she would return. But my attitude puzzled the Lawrences. That Christmas the Cannans gave a great dinner-party at the Mill House (at which we were to eat a roast sucking pig, but unfortunately no one could carve it). After a gloomy beginning, we all drank more than was absolutely good for us, and began to act plays. After two had been performed, Koteliansky was seized by an inspiration; and kept on coming to me urging that we should produce 'a play within a play'. For a time I was too muddle-headed to take it in. But suddenly my brain cleared, and I understood, though whether I understood it as Koteliansky intended, I have no idea. Anyhow I set a play in motion which was a dramatization of the actual situation between Katherine and me, and in which Mark Gertler, the painter, was cast for the part of my successor. Not unnaturally I acted my own rôle with considerable conviction; and so did Katherine, for when the third act was under way, she suddenly refused to obey the scenario, which ended in a reconciliation with me, and insisted on staying with Gertler. Then there was a psychological explosion. Lawrence indignantly interrupted the drama, hustled me aside, and asked me with intense and passionate severity: 'Was I blind?' If not, how did I dare to expose myself? 'It's not as though we didn't love you . . .' But I was not blind at all.

Koteliansky was, at this period, by far Katherine's most understanding friend. She had met him for the first time at the Lawrences' cottage two months before, and almost instantly a warm friendship had sprung up between them. Whereas Lawrence and Frieda, though genuinely fond of her, were in their different ways very critical of her, it was a maxim with Koteliansky that Katherine could do no wrong. Since as he once put it, she 'had a greater talent for being just a human being' than anyone else in the world, his attitude was that her talent should have all the scope it demanded. Whereas Lawrence's attitude to her is summed up in my memory in the slightly bewildered, slightly shocked exclamation: '*Kath* – erine!' which I heard so often on his lips, Koteliansky delighted in her 'wickedness'. His sympathy was altogether with her in this time of stress, and he stood firmly by her. The Lawrences' sympathies were rather with me, and I found them embarrassing. I simply could not feel that I had been treated badly.

But, in truth I was becoming a lonely person. I knew Katherine was preparing to part from me, and was only awaiting the ways and means. The Lawrences had decided to leave Buckinghamshire for Viola Meynell's cottage at Greatham, which they did in mid-January, so that one of my chief solaces – day-dreaming with Lawrence of the island, Rananim, to which we were all to escape from our various miseries – was taken away from me. Immediately after this came the greatest blow of all: the end of my friendship with Campbell. It happened very simply. He was to have come down for the week-end; he did not come, nor did he send me any message to say why he could not come. He 'left me in the lurch', as the comic song used to have it, and again according to the song: 'Lord, how it did upset me!'

Indeed, it had come at an awkward time: for on the very day that he was to have come I had had to face as quietly as I could Katherine's definite decision to leave me. 'We talked of London,' she wrote in her journal on January 31st. 'Jack understands that I want to live there and apart from him. It is true.' In fact, I understood more than that. She was not merely leaving me, but leaving me for someone whom I knew better than she did – well enough to know that it would be a bitter disillusion for her.

To this day I do not know whether Campbell stayed away deliberately: chose this as the best way of ending a relation which was, in the sense I have tried to describe, unhealthy. But undoubtedly the rupture – for to me it was a rupture and a final one – came upon me like a thunderclap; and I suffered – as much as I was capable of suffering. I can well believe that, unconsciously, as the bond between Katherine and myself wore thinner, I was turning more and more of my affection towards him, and that it was all for the best that he did what he did. But I was terribly hurt, and I tried to salve my wound in an unrhymed poem, which I have kept faithfully by me ever since, not for its merits – it has none – but to remind me of what I felt. One forgets so easily, and I did not want to forget.

> My soul went forth among men;
> It toiled along their roads
> And stood before their doors.
> They spoke hard words to it,
> And gave it many blows and sent it to toil onward.
> And slowly the sun went down
> And my soul sped more quickly.
> The twilight came, and it was near to darkness.
> The hedges were dim shadows
> And the dim shadows were strange men.
> But when the darkness was wholly gathered
> My soul espied a light
> And gladly hastened on.

It stood before the door, and knocked.
A man opened to him.
'I am a traveller', said my soul, 'a weary traveller.'
'Here is bread', he said, 'and money.'
My soul ate the bread, and put the money in his purse,
And waited still before the door.
'What more would you have?' said the man,
As he came forward into the light.
'No more' said my soul.
'You have given me all you have.'
But my soul came hungry away
And now, returned, he sits beside me,
Beside the embers of a dusty fire,
While the wind echoes in the chimney overhead.
'I am hungry for love', he said.
I know not whether it be he or I that weeps before the fire.

I was alone now, with a vengeance. At this moment
Katherine's brother came to England from New Zealand: and
the first thing he did was to give her money enough to go to
Paris. That was a bitter blow to my pride, or my vanity. What
I should have loved to be able to do, or rather the gesture I was
eager to make, was as easy to her brother as it was impossible for
me. It was bitter to me to reflect that Katherine looked upon me
now as the man who 'didn't want money and wouldn't earn it'.
Worse still, I felt that even her memory of the good time we had
had together – 'the three years' idyll', as she called it now – was
being blotted out by the recollection of a New Zealand past, in
which I had and could have neither part nor lot. My own past
was such a poor threadbare thing to look back to. With all its
many bitternesses life with Katherine had been the beginning of
life indeed for me. Now I knew, or thought I knew, that it had
not been so for her. What had been life itself for me, though for
some strange cause it had dwindled away, had simply been a
charming, boyish interlude for her.

I felt pretty cynical; I even felt that it might all have been different, if I had not been so wretchedly poor. And with that thought my bitterness fairly overflowed. I welcomed the onset of one of the violent influenza colds that have dogged me all my life. It seemed to deaden me into a sort of numbness. On February 12th I wrote in my journal:

> Recently, and consequent remotely on Lawrence's departure, and more closely and directly on Gordon's affair, I have been very depressed. I have felt completely isolated from the world, and too appallingly sensitive. My nervous apprehensions of contact with people have become a nightmare now – a curious mixture of hate, envy, contempt, the idea that I have failed, and that I am not valued, has made London lately pretty well intolerable to me, and me intolerable to Katherine when I am with her in London. But, perhaps under the influence of this indisposition – there is a real pleasure in such minor illnesses – I have forgotten it for a while. Nevertheless, I feel absolutely unsafe unless there is a hole into which I can crawl.
>
> Katherine hopes to start for Paris on Tuesday morning at 8.30.

On Monday, February 15th, I went with Katherine to London, and I noted the next day that 'she was very happy and excited in the Café Royal, where we met for a few moments after she had got her passport safely; and it is curious that I wasn't jealous of her happiness nor inclined to wet-blanket it'.

CHAPTER XXIII

SEPARATION

'I FELT like an oyster without any shell, and the world was just hard rocks.' It is hard to recapture the feeling which lay behind that sentence in my journal. The agonizing sensation is gone, and gone for ever; but in those days it was continual. I did not understand it; it seemed to me merely the dominant element in an unhappy idiosyncrasy, as though I were a freak of nature. But now that it is past and far away, I believe that I begin to understand.

I had been uprooted and unrooted in my early boyhood. I had no organic connection either with the class from which I had been taken, nor with the class into which I had been thrust. Obscurely, I knew this when I compared myself with Lawrence. At the core, he was still a Derbyshire miner's son, drawing unconscious strength from a social and instinctive solidarity with his 'people'. I had no people; I belonged nowhere. And Lawrence, sensing this in me, declared at one moment that 'Oxford had done me harm', or at another, that I had no sensuous nature and that my father had ruined it. One night, as I have said, he surprised me by denouncing my father with a passionate indignation far surpassing anything I could ever feel. It was unjust to my father, who had done his best, and could not know what subtle impoverishment of the instinctive boy his best inevitably involved; but Lawrence's indignation was a warm rain to my heart; and on that night were planted in it the seeds of an affection for him which, whatever the world may say, was more intense and enduring than I have ever felt for any man.

But that was my trouble. Precisely because I had no people, I was beset by an unconscious urge towards a peculiar intensity in my personal relations. In these alone my isolation was overcome.

Only when I was surrounded by the safety and warmth of an
intimate personal affection could I breathe freely, or suffer myself
to be off my guard; and probably, it was my instinctive and unconscious effort to create this atmosphere which was the cause of
the deceptive childish charm of which I was so often accused.
And this, I can see now, was unfair to my friends, for I never
uttered my desire – how could I, when I was unaware of it? – and
how could they know that I was spinning about them the threads
of an affection so tender and agonizing that a casual negligence
would break my heart? And how could Lawrence understand that
when he insisted, as he did, on the necessity of a relation beyond
the personal between us, he was not only speaking a language
which I did not understand, in those days, but hurting me deeply
by seeming to repudiate as worthless the only kind of affection
which I had to give, or wanted to receive?

I would have been most happy to live alone with Katherine,
and I sometimes have dreamed that, if our desire at Runcton had
been realized, and we had had a child, much of the subsequent
bitterness of life would have been spared us; and I have thought
that the angel of the grace of God came very near to us in those
subtly anguished days and that even now through the years I can
catch the beating of his wings as he departed. For my experience
has been that it is only with my children that I have gained that
simple sense of 'belonging' whose absence eluded and tormented
me so long. And that, it seems to me, might have come to me in
those distant days when Katherine and I longed for a child with a
single motion of our hearts and none was given. With the birth
of that simple primitive bond, whose powers and virtues I have
come to learn, I believe that the morbid intensity of my desire for
personal affection would have abated; and I should have known,
in my own fashion, the reality of that condition after which Lawrence was groping when he spoke of a bond 'beyond the personal'.
For that, strangely enough, is what I have found in my bond with
my children. With them, *I* am not. That in me which might seek
to establish a jealous affection or an exclusive claim simply does

not exist in regard to them. The bond needs no keeping and no care; it matters not one jot to me whether they recognize it, it is there, just as the earth on which they tread with lighter feet than I is there.

But these are dreams of what might have been, and they have value only in so far as they may convey to others something of the indefinable anguish of my condition. My soul was, indeed, 'hungry for love', and its hunger was of a kind that was not satisfied, nor (if I had known it) ever could be satisfied in the way I sought for satisfaction. The intense exclusive affection which I dumbly desired was something which must, I now believe, have in it the seed of its own death. I do not believe that it is deadly, in the sense that Lawrence declared it was, with that characteristic vehemence which makes a half-truth of a whole one. For there is a difference between deaths: there are deaths which are deadly, and deaths which are life-giving; and, though it is my experience that the extremity of personal affection has in it the seeds of death, it is my experience also that the death which it contains is the death of life. 'Except a corn of wheat fall into the ground, and die . . .' By its own nature, the extremity of a personal affection cannot endure; none the less its inevitable destruction is creative. It is, by the divine nature of things, impossible that one should succeed, as I blindly strove to do, in 'belonging' through the sheer intensity of a personal love; but it is through the shattering which this intensity alone entails, that one like me comes to 'belong'. And this, which is truth to me, is but the parable of physical love writ large, or if not large writ in characters to be read by the spiritual eye. For as, in the natural order, the self-destroying intensity of physical communion has its outcome in the birth of a new creature, so in the spiritual order the self-destroying intensity of 'love', which attains that intensity only where the outcome of physical birth is divinely denied (divinely, I *mean*), has its outcome in a new spiritual birth. That is my faith, or my experience: for, fortunately, there is no distinction between those things for me. And what is that, again, but the vindication of Keats' conviction that 'every passion, in its sublime, is creative of essential beauty'?

But, alas, these things were for long years to come beyond my knowing. I did not know that I was seeking in personal affection the sense of 'belonging' that was denied me; nor did I understand the compulsion by which, when what I sought was withheld, I shrank into myself with a sense of intolerable hurt, which I could not salve by accusing those who 'failed' me. I had no sustaining sense that I was right and they were wrong. On the contrary, what small conviction I had in this matter was that 'free as the wind is love'. If those from whom I looked for it did not feel it, or felt it otherwise than I desired, that could be no fault of theirs. I was cut to an awkward pattern that seemed to have no counterpart, and I was divided between the longing for the climate in which I believed I could unfold, and a desire to live completely in the isolation which seemed to be my destiny. Moreover, I would react from the one into the other with a speed which was baffling even to myself.

When circumstances forced me naked into the open, I would try painfully to create the atmosphere for myself. Thus, at my most forlorn moment, when I was with Katherine in London, waiting for her to leave, filled with 'hatred, envy and contempt' of the world beyond, I wrote this in my diary:

Coming away from Koteliansky to the train on Thursday night, I stood in the bus close to a woman and a man. The woman wore spectacles and looked robustly efficient; but I did not really notice either of them until I saw the man's hand terribly shaking. His hand was clenched, as a child clenches its hand, without the thumb, which was loosely and extravagantly curved. When I saw the woman slowly hold out her hand to cover his, I realized that he was paralytic. Then I looked at his face. The eyes were soft and grey, the upper lip covered by a full white moustache, while the lower lip seemed small and deep. It was the lower lip that impressed me, though I cannot remember how it impressed me. His nose was straight, fine and sensitive, the cheeks sunken a little, but not gaunt; rather, they were shaped. He wore a large black felt hat and flowing tie, very much as Colonel Cody or an odd Methodist parson might have done. But this man not only looked more beautiful than any man I have ever seen, but also made his clothes more beautiful. His eyes seemed to be hungry, moving slowly, steadily looking out to something beyond me. He looked as though he had been hurt by life and crucified. He reminded me somehow of an older R.L.S. – more spiritual and more beautiful.

On Tuesday night we stopped in the Richelieu after dinner for coffee. Three men – a 'cellist reading the *W.G.*, a pianist in a curiously cramped attitude but somehow gentle and serious-minded, a fiddler, small black face and long hair, very keen, beating time with his foot upon the ground and reading the score while the pianist softly played difficult parts in the intervals – made music. A woman sat by the fire. She might have been waiting. Sometimes I had a fleeting idea that she was desperately waiting – but it would not remain. Her hair and eyes were dark, her face full, and her eyes were set wide apart so that she had something of a Chinese appearance. She held her hands in a muff, and her head was bent a little sideways. Though she looked at me for a long while, there was nothing particular, no direction in her look; I could have sworn that she was listening to the rise and fall of her own breast, which was apparent even to me. She wore a cream-brown coloured coat and skirt with a wide, ordinary collar of lace. I enjoyed that place, and that woman made me feel very calm. I might very well have fallen in love with such a one. How surprised I was when Katherine remarked on her beauty to me! I replied that she looked like a Manet woman.

SEPARATION

There, as I understand it now, the spider, at his moment of extreme isolation, was spinning his threads again.

The Lawrences had asked me to go and stay with them at Greatham, and after a day alone at Rose Tree Cottage, I made my way thither. The floods were out, and I had difficulty in finding my way from Pulborough in the dark. I splashed on miserably, aching all over, for my influenza was raging. Lawrence bundled me straight into bed and kept me there for two days, looking after me as though I were a child. But on the third day he opened fire. He said, to my bewilderment, that my friendship with Campbell was the cause of Katherine's leaving me; that in our talk we left her out in the cold, and that I had no one to blame but myself if she resented it, and turned elsewhere for what I would not give. I stared at him dumbfounded, with the feeling that he was talking about some other person. But that was not all. He told me then that Campbell had said to him a week before that, 'those intelectual probings between Murry and me were the most regrettable part of each of us'. That was a right-and-left with a vengeance. If those things were true, then I was completely ignorant of myself, completely unconscious of my own actions. That it might have been so, I could not deny; for it needed a far more certain knowledge of myself than I possessed to deny it point-blank. But if it were true, it was meaningless to me; nothing in myself responded to the intimation.

At such a moment – and this was neither the first nor the last of its kind – I felt dazed and baffled, and, when I pondered it, weary and hopeless. Whether Lawrence was right or wrong, it came to the same thing in the end. Either I knew nothing about myself, or he knew nothing about me: and it didn't matter which it was. Whether the gulf was between me and myself, or between me and him, the gulf was there. It was as though my ecstatic vision had been true; as though the I that knew and thought and was were a mere illusion, and a third person inhabited my body, of whose existence and acts I learned only from the report of others: and now the reports seemed to coincide. With what Campbell had said, Lawrence agreed, and if that were true, why should it not also be true that I was responsible for Katherine's going? The pattern was perfectly coherent; only it was not mine. It was the pattern of some mysterious third person.

And all the while I stayed at Greatham, when Lawrence spoke deliberately of and to me, it seemed as though it was of and to this third person that he spoke. When we were simply doing things together – cutting and laying linoleum was the great occupation then – or when he was, as it were, musing aloud with me for audience, all was well between us. But when he consciously sought for *me*, expecting response from me, the same uneasy bewilderment would return. The person to whom he spoke was not there: I must impersonate him.

There was in this nothing deliberate. We were at cross-purposes. All I wanted from Lawrence was the warmth and security of personal affection. Up to a certain point he also wanted that between us; but his consciousness resented it. What his consciousness required was an impersonal bond between us: that we should be servants of the same purpose, disciples of the same idea. At that time, ideas and purposes meant nothing to me. Persons were everything. And, until the time came much later when I had an idea and a purpose of my own, in my relation with Lawrence I shifted back continually to this emphasis on the personal, which was the bias of my being. But when, as now, we were intimately together, I felt that Lawrence was making a *personal* appeal to me to follow him *impersonally*. The two things which he so passionately strove to separate were inextricably entangled. Whatever he may have thought, I knew that a simple acceptance of his ideas was not at all what he wanted. At that time he was meeting people far more important than myself – Bertrand Russell, for example – who had developed ideas which, Lawrence believed, were pretty much in accord with his own. But I was made clearly to understand that this intellectual agreement was of no consequence because of the disparity of being between them. In my case, Lawrence seemed to grant that there was some correspondence of being between us, and even to be glad of it. He seemed to think that there ought to be intellectual agreement between us, or that it was natural that there should be; and he strove to obtain this from me.

I was eager to give it. But I could give it only by an effort which (I felt) robbed it of all value. I was like a woman instinctively humouring her husband by accepting his arguments and principles, although in fact they are quite indifferent to her; but, unlike a woman, I was uneasy about it, and sought desperately to convince myself that I really did agree. But I knew what the experience of intellectual unison was: I had had it with Campbell. But there was nothing of the kind between Lawrence and me. If at moments I did convince myself, it was with a sense of strain and in a mood of induced exaltation. Whereas I had been quite naturally at home with his former plan of escaping to the island of Rananim, and crystallized my daydreams about it as freely as he did his own, now when he strove to enlist me under the banner of Revolution I was out of my depth. The only sort of revolution I could naturally understand, was the revolution necessary to change the world into one in which I could be unafraid. That was the enchantment of Rananim for me: on that island I should have had no need to fear. As Lawrence put it, it was to be 'a community established on the assumption of goodness in its members, instead of the assumption of badness'.

That was well enough; I had understood it, or I had thought I did. But now the conception had changed. The bond of the new society must be impersonal: it was to be soldered by the melting-down of personality in surrender to some great and all-inclusive religious purpose. Each was to be 'the angel of himself in a big cause', and this 'angel of himself' was mysteriously to arise out of the acknowledgment and fulfilment of the 'animal of himself'. Now, it seems, I can see a pretty deep meaning in Lawrence's creed, as he tried to impart it to me; but I also see that it took a peculiar colour from his own experience. Two elements at least had gone to make it, of which my ignorance was total. One

333

was an instinctive, infra-personal sense of solidarity with men – the true, deep, gregarious experience, which Lawrence had known as a child and longed to renew, which he simultaneously desired and repudiated; the other was a curiously intense preoccupation with 'the animal of himself', which fascinated and repelled him. Lawrence, it should never be forgotten, was a Puritan, and even something of a Manichee.

My ignorance, compared to his, in this matter has never vexed me. It may, of course, be due to some shallowness in my own nature that I have never felt any conflict between the animal and the angel in me with regard to sex; but I do not believe this. It is due, I imagine, rather to that extremity of the desire for personal affection of which I have spoken. Sexual love, for me, is the supreme tenderness, wherein animal and angel are one. I can understand that it might, in the experience of another man, be quite otherwise, as it certainly was with Lawrence; but this understanding is abstract and intellectual only.

It was inevitable, therefore, that Lawrence whose patterning was so largely shaped by his sexual experience, should be in one fundamental matter at least incomprehensible to me. A revolution which was partly to be based on the individual's acknowledgment of 'the animal of oneself' was bound to mean something different to each of us – extraordinarily different in fact. For whereas the acknowledgment of the animal was meant by Lawrence as a kind of bloody but beneficent death to the angel, it could mean nothing of the sort to me. Nor could I conceivably understand the subtle process by which at this time he made the communion of physical love into a sort of sacrament by which he participated in the horror and destruction of the war. This strange identification, if I had understood it, would have seemed to me perverse and malign: indeed it disturbs and repels me now. If it is profound, and beyond my comprehension, I must bear with my limitation.

Lawrence was to expound this doctrine a few months afterwards in *The Signature*. I did not understand it then; still less did

I understand while it was in embryo at Greatham. If a purgation of that kind was necessary to enter the new Jerusalem, I was for ever debarred from it. To the infinitesimal extent of my understanding I resisted it instinctively. But I equally resisted the other and precious element in Lawrence's doctrine – the overcoming of the personal in a bond of elemental solidarity with men. Of this also I must say, with a sense of painful confession, that I did not even understand it. Once more, it was completely outside my experience. I repeat, the only bond I knew, or recognized, was personal. Yet precisely because the personal bond between us was precious to me, I was impelled to agree with him. I could not imperil it by disagreement, even if I had the knowledge or the courage to disagree – and I had neither – for the personal bond between us was (I supposed) far more precious to me than to him. I was one who, having no connection with his intrinsic self, sought for the evidence of my own validity in my friends' opinion of me. If Lawrence were to reject me now that Katherine and Campbell had rejected me . . . it was unthinkable.

Instinctively, I set myself to be what he desired. Here is one record of how it was done:

Saturday, Feb. 21. In the evening we talked – about the Revolution. Lawrence said it was no more use writing novels; we had first to change the conditions, without which either people would not hear, or our novels be only a tale. At first, though I agreed, I felt an uneasiness: whether I were playing the hypocrite in agreeing; I even wondered whether I was merely trying to cling on to his skirts because I knew he was a proven writer with a tried audience. But then I knew that I was independently on the same track. I said my novels [*sic*] ended with the characters more perfect, but outside any real conditions. They would not fit any more. I said also that I began with an assumption (even in matters like sex and morality) which was beyond obtaining conditions. He agreed and said: 'What novels we could write, if we wrote of the

335

whole good we knew, instead of the good that may be in this world!' We loosely planned a scheme for publishing weekly pamphlets in which the Revolution should be expounded by us individually.

Lawrence, after expounding *The Rainbow*, said that he felt that he would write one more novel, and no more. He was sad, because he was a forerunner, like John the Baptist before the Christ, whose place it was to give up and surrender. He asked me when, in normal life, I thought that a man came to wait for the coming generation. I said: When he reached the outer edge of the innermost circle within which he knew that his own true achievement began and ended.

'So I suppose my achievement begins and ends with preaching the revolution of the conditions of life – why not?'

He said that he felt that he was clumsier than I. My lack of clumsiness, I said, was largely nervelessness.

'Yes, there is a lot of inertia in you, but that is valuable. Your effort somehow seems to be purer than mine.'

'You have more strength.'

'Yes, of a certain kind; but less, again, than you of another kind.'

Lawrence seemed sad, and in the mood of believing that I was somehow to succeed him. I said how much calmness and happiness I had gained from him during the last six months – since the war began – that he was the only man I had met whom I felt to be definitely older than I, that we made a real combination from which something, I felt, must come. He said that when we four were together he felt that the new conditions, the new vitality really *were*, and that, if we had not met down in Bucks, he would never have believed that it might be. I said I looked forward to the fight: that a hole should be made in the sky that was bearing down upon me. 'I hate it,' he said. 'It will be such an awful scrimmage.' He

was thinking of the men whom he would have to try to move;
but, even though agreeing, I did not feel it badly. I do feel
young.

He asked me during the evening what I thought was a
man's desired end. I said: 'To be free.'

'But that is only a condition.'

'No,' I said. 'That is because we look upon freedom as a
negative thing – a clearing away of barriers – but when the
barriers are cleared away, freedom is something beyond – the
establishment of immediate contact with other free souls, the immediate response in *activity* to their contact, instead of an addition
of a tiny compartment to our knowledge – an activity which
we cannot measure by any activity in which we now indulge.'

'A leap in the dark,' he said.

He said a few words about the Revolution, as to means –
nationalization of land, industry, railways. Very well – but
we hadn't thought it out, and there wasn't any need to think
it out . . .

The relation between us of which that entry is the record was
unnatural. It was preposterous that Lawrence should lean on me,
as I felt he was doing. Not that I was not glad that he turned to
me in this fashion – I was glad, exalted even – but I was being
thrust into a false position. Compared to him, as I naively said, I
did feel young. What was experience to him, was words to me.
No doubt I tried to express what I really believed; but I had no
real beliefs. There were things I thought I believed, and that was
all. I had nothing but desires. By far the chief among these was
the desire to live in a warm atmosphere of love. At this time it
existed between Lawrence and me, and I would do anything not
to break it. If he was sad, as he was, and wanted encouragement,
I would give it him in the way he wanted it. And, I suppose, the
genuine if selfish affection I had for him quite obliterated in himself all sense of what was forced and fictitious in my reflection of
his ideas.

Nevertheless, I am puzzled. I cannot understand what was in his mind when he said that my effort was somehow purer than his own.

That night his words were quite incomprehensible to me; and now I can only guess at his meaning. Since the relative 'purity' of my effort derived from my inertia, which, he thought, was valuable, I connect it with a certain obstinate reluctance in myself to separate my faith from my experience. Years afterwards, when in complete forgetfulness of Lawrence's judgment on me at twenty-four, I have tried to define to myself the peculiarity of my own life-pattern, I have found myself saying, again and again, that it consists in my having gone forward, 'only when I have been driven'. My inertia has, indeed, been extreme; and for years it was a torment to me. It seemed to me that I was completely lacking in personal initiative, even in personal courage. Whatever I could escape from, I would somehow escape: but not boldly, not with any defiant challenge. I slithered out of the encounter, evaded, not repudiated, the imminent obligation. Principles I had none, faith none: simply a blind instinct that this was not for me, this way not mine. Thus, whereas Lawrence pitted something against the War, opposed to it some faith in virtue of which he was determined not to be involved in it, such determination was quite alien to me. To me the War was a pure nightmare, an irruption of some strange and inhuman order of existence. For the scattered moments when I was in some sense myself, I ignored the War, simply because anything that I could call myself and the War could not co-exist in my consciousness; and when, as I eventually did, I succeeded in turning the face of my consciousness towards the War, I passed straightway out of myself – into a true ecstasy. But for the most part I existed in a tormented lethargy.

Lawrence, on the other hand, repudiated the War, because he had some deep sense of kinship with the War. It is perhaps hard to explain; but it was so. The kinship was two-fold. He had the sense of primal 'blood-solidarity' with his 'people'; and he had something subtler – a sort of blood-lust, a desire for destruction. I remember his saying that he would like to kill one million – two million Germans – for letting loose this horror of mechanical death upon the world. And it was not at all a rhodomontade with him; one felt that he meant it, that somehow he wanted a terrible revenge. It was mysterious to me, and frightening, as though he hated this War only because it was not war enough, and was in some sort a further frustration of the animal rather than a satiation of it. It was partly in the name of essential war that he repudiated this grim parody of war.

As Lawrence's determination was beyond me, so was his position. It was then, and is now, completely alien to me; but I had nothing positive to put against it. It was but one example of my inertia compared to his, but it is typical. It was not until the War closed round me, and thrust itself into my intimate personal experience, that it became a reality, or what I call a reality; and then it became not a reality that I could oppose, whether by principle or faith, but one which I must 'accept'. To make that sentence meaningful I should have to explain what I mean by 'acceptance'. Assuredly, it is not, as it may sound, a passive thing; it is, in my experience, a pretty grim happening, a most painful self-obliteration. All that I can positively say about it, in this connection, is that it does *happen;* one has no choice or initiative. One takes that path because there is no other to take: one is driven.

In that peculiar sense, I can, after all these years, admit that there is truth in Lawrence's judgment that my inertia was 'valuable', and even see a meaning in his judgment that, in consequence, my effort was somehow purer than his own. It was to suffer singularly little contamination by my own will. And it may have been that Lawrence, at this moment, was conscious of this potentiality in my inertia (of which I was quite ignorant) because of what seemed to him my peculiar attitude to Katherine's departure. In a crude, youthful, naive sort of way which had its own bitterness, I had 'accepted' that. Lawrence certainly was mystified by that attitude of mine. He veered about between blaming me and blaming her. If I was stubborn against the former, I was still more stubborn against the latter. There was, and could be, no 'ought' in love. Here again, my experience spoke against Lawrence's, and here I felt on firmer ground. For, in this matter, I knew what I felt, and in this matter, what I felt was what I believed: no other belief was possible to me. And I could honestly say that I would far rather Katherine had left me, than that she should have stayed against her inmost inclination.

Suddenly, I received a telegram from Katherine to say that she was returning and would be at Victoria at 8 a.m. on the next day. I went up to London to meet her. She was strange, her hair was cut short, and she was aggressively defensive. I was not to imagine that she had returned to *me*. She had come simply because there was nowhere else to go. She didn't want to see anybody. I could see that she was bitterly disillusioned, and I felt sorry and longed to comfort her. But I did not know how. It was manifest that any comfort I might try to give would be only a clumsy irritation of her wound. We were constrained and miserable, and Rose Tree Cottage, where we returned, was like a grey prison. On the next day she was ill, and she began to talk to me. She said that it had all been the result of a remark I had made to Campbell two months before, and she astonished me by giving the exact date, the 18th of December. I had apparently said on that day that I did not know whether Katherine was 'more to me than a gratification'. By that I was dazed. That I some-times had made odd, half-cynical remarks to Campbell I knew; but I was inwardly positive I had never said that to anyone. Yet the words were vaguely familiar. So I pressed her. How did she remember the date?

'If you want to know, I *read* it in your little red book.'

It was an unwritten law between us that we should not read one another's note-books. That Katherine should have broken it was a portent; and I knew instantly that our severance was not

340

the result of her reading that. Whatever had happened, had happened before; and the reading of my note-book was the result of the happening. And I said so.

'I'm sorry for writing that, all the same; but I'm not ashamed of it. I do wonder about things; and I suppose I wondered about that. But what I wonder, and what I am are different things. You know that.'

But she was in no mood to admit so much. We were millions of miles apart. I wandered about the house like a ghost, doing what I could for her; but knowing that, had she not been crippled by her arthritis, she would have taken no service from me. It was a strange, nightmarish time; but the barb of the strangeness was an utterly new and altogether unnatural sensation that she was wrong, and I was right. This feeling of right and wrong between us had never been before, and that was bad enough; but that, when it came, the right should be with me was intolerable. For a feeling of right was no companion of mine. It was forced upon me, simply because Katherine felt she was wrong.

My hatred of Rose Tree Cottage grew intense. I compared it with the beautiful cottage in which I had stayed with the Lawrences at Greatham; and I cursed its sordidness. Its damp had made Katherine ill, and its squalor had made her wretched. I determined, once more, to find rooms in London. Katherine was still convinced of the necessity of Paris for her. She must stay there until she had written a book. I was only too anxious to agree with her. But before she went back she would help me to look for rooms.

The sort of weary truce between us deepened into peace. The Lawrences were urging her to go to Greatham, and I expatiated on its beauties. She hesitated for a day or two, and finally decided. As soon as that decision was taken, she became herself again. Something hard suddenly melted in her. On March 8th she was still in rebellion. 'My God, *what* poverty!' she wrote to Koteliansky. 'So I write about hot weather and happy love and broad bands of sunlight and cafés – all things that make life to me.' But on the Saturday, March 13th, when she had reached Greatham, she wrote me a letter, gay with drawings of Lawrence, herself, and me, of anemones and catspaws, and a cake which Koteliansky had brought to Greatham:

My darling Bogey,

I came here by a fly with a man with a black patch on his eye. It was a most complicated journey. I kept thinking of 'my wandering boy' and the journey in the dark that you told me of, and when we took the 10th turning my hand flew out to you. It is a very nice cottage and I feel like you that ours is sordid in comparison. This bathroom, this thick white distemper, and a fire in one's bedroom all dancy in the dark!

The country is lovely – sand and fine hills – daffodils in flower – violets and primroses in plenty – and on the marshes this morning there were almost as many sea-gulls as we saw in Rye.

I am sitting writing to you, and Frieda and Koteliansky are talking. My brain is wispy a little . . . My Bogey, I am very near you and I feel very free in my love. I do love you, you know, dearly, dearly. I want to talk to you.

The downs so free are lovely, but I cannot walk quite there. I am *much* better, the air is so good. And the hot baths with sea-salt – very sumptuous!

If I were quite alone and writing to you, I should say something different. I want to tell you something about myself, but I hardly know what it is – against the others talking. I expect you know better than I do. I have a notion that your intuitions are almost angelic.

Of that order my intuitions certainly were not; but I did know, quite clearly, that Katherine's second going to Paris which happened a few days later was quite different from her first. Whereas the first might have ended, so far as any conscious knowledge of mine could serve me, in our parting for ever, concerning the second I felt completely secure. She needed the inflow of rich

342

sensational life. After a long period of painful sterility – the *agonie ennuyeuse* of Keats, which is the lot of every spontaneous writer – she had begun to work again. She had written *The Little Governess*, and she hoped that under the stimulus of the vivid visual life of Paris, the fountain would flow freely. She had endured an English winter, which was always a burden to her spirit; and this winter had been the worst. The gloom of the war, Lawrence's depression, my own self-isolation, our extreme poverty – during one whole month, I remember, I earned less than three pounds – our dismal cottage, and her own physical illness, had been like a prison. For long afterwards the memory of lying, unable to move, in a camp bed, while the rain slowly dripped through the leaky roof of Rose Tree Cottage, was her symbol of misery. From it all she had reacted desperately, and gulled herself into an imaginary love-passion which had collapsed at the touch of reality. Now she wanted to return to Paris for a different cause, and (I suspect) partly to prove to herself that there had been something more solid in her former motive than a day-dream.

'I cannot write my book living in these two rooms,' she wrote to Koteliansky just before she left. 'It is impossible – and if I do not write this book, I shall die. So I am going away to-morrow to finish it. Then I promise to come back shorn of all my wickedness. It is agony to go; but I must go.' She was not exaggerating. This time she did not *want* to go to Paris; but she felt – truly enough – that it would help her back to her writing vein, while another long period of frustration would drive her to rebellion again. And, though she did not write her book, or rather abandoned so much of it as she did write, her warm, gay, brilliant letters of this period are witness that life was bringing her the 'flow' again.

Meanwhile, I got great satisfaction from painting and preparing our new rooms at Elgin Crescent. I took a simple pleasure in making them beautiful against her return, and considering how little money there was to spend, I did it pretty well. Since we could not afford to have our bits of furniture removed from

Rose Tree Cottage, it had nearly all to be done again. I bought the scrubbiest pieces of furniture if I saw they were soundly made, knocked them to pieces and reconstructed them, crudely but effectively; and I paid for it all by living chiefly on porridge and bread and butter. In the evenings Koteliansky would come round with a generous supply of Russian cigarettes and we would work together translating Tchehov and Kuprin – a speculative venture, for we had no publisher. But in the main I lived entirely to myself, not unhappily, for when Katherine was happy I was never ill-content. There may even have been a grain of truth in her wry contention that that was what I really liked – to put her on the shelf, make sure she was happy, and then be quite happy myself thinking that she was. It was at this time, I think, that she coined the description of me as 'a monk without a monastery'.

Anyhow, in less than a fortnight, I had an unexpected letter from her brimming with gaiety and love, in which she declared that she was coming home immediately – a full five weeks before the appointed time. 'My work is done,' she cried, 'my freedom gained.' I was delighted. If I had had more sense, and more money, I would have sent her a telegram of rejoicing. But, as she once said, I never understood the importance of 'the enamelled spoon' in love. ('The enamelled spoon' plays a great part in a story by Anatole France; it is a beauty, a luxury, an extravagance, which the woman desires more for its very prodigality than for itself: and the moral is that a year of cheeseparing, lit up by a flash of splendid extravagance, gives more sustenance to the soul of a woman in love than twelve solid months of comfortable moderation.) But at that moment, when I was making do on about a pound a week, long telegrams to Paris were beyond my horizon, even if I had realized that her sudden gesture of love was of a kind that demands an immediate response. It was a fragile, evanescent unfolding of the petals that a breath of cold air would furl again. The letter is before me as I write; the very soul of Katherine dances on its pages. The handwriting is

quite different from that of any of the others; it flows and ripples
like the waves of a sunny sea.

> If this throws you into a fury (it dances on) do not attend me
> à la gare – or come and don't recognize me, or something.
> Ah, Bogey, be glad! Such a *good* Wig is coming back with
> money in her pocket, too – for I have lived MOST CAREFULLY.
> But what with Bugs and no gas and a heart full of love and
> fun – I cannot cannot cannot stay alone. So there you are –
> Do my letters arrive all safely? I write every every day – I
> am very silly ce soir – drunk on a black coffee – dearest – I
> believe – that life is fun – and I'll take up my leg and walk.

But, as was so often to happen in our life, the letter she received
from me hard upon this was three days old, and more or less in
tune with hers of a week before. The breath of cold wind came,
and the petals furled. The frost is in the handwriting, too.

> I got very sane after I had written to you yesterday – I
> wish something in you didn't make me feel a 'silly' when
> I want to write at full tilt. It's because you never do; you're
> such a guarded and careful little Bogey – and so frightened
> that I shall 'make a scene'. I won't, dear. I promise you. I'm
> not *at all* sure this afternoon whether I'll come on Wednesday
> [March 31st] or whether I'll wait a week. Perhaps I'd
> better wait a week. If I *do* come, I *won't* wire; if I *don't* come
> I will wire. It's a fair toss-up. Yesterday, I sat in a little parc
> and played with the idea with a *sou*. The *sou* said every time
> 'Yes, go', but that was yesterday. And this morning again
> your calm letter, as though we were 'seule pour la vie', shook
> up against the apple-cart . . .
> Things are so changed now – you and I still love each
> other, but you haven't the need of me you had then and
> somehow I do always have to be 'needed' to be happy – I've
> expressed that abominably – and it's not even quite true,
> for what I call your need of me was more or less an illusion

345

on my part – you're an amazing person in the way you can accept just so much and no more. No, I'm beating about the bush and not really saying what I want to – *and* it really doesn't matter. But I do wish my tall pale friend [Lesley Moore] were here to walk with and sit with. You're not the slightest use – for it doesn't come natural for you to desire to do such things with me. It's I who plead like 'une petite pensionnaire' to be taken out on Saturday afternoon, or to a music-hall . . .

Good-bye for now, my dear. Hanged if I know whether I'll see you on Wednesday or not – If I do wire that I am not coming, you might send me that £1, just to reassure me, will you?

Oh, Bogey, dearest –

                                                                    Tig.

It was not unfair – there was the same strange inertia in me as a lover as in all my other doings – but it hurt horribly. I have few virtues, but one of the few (if indeed it is a virtue) is a horror of inflicting pain upon another. And time after time, by such a malignant accident as this, I hurt Katherine. It was the memory of these stupid sufferings which made us vow, again and again, never to separate. But separate we always did in the end, at first by choice, then by compulsion, and the stupid sufferings went on. Beneath the malignant accident was the truth that I did not need Katherine in the way she then believed she required to be needed. But, as she truly said, that was not what she meant, and what she did mean was not easy to express. I did not need, as she did, someone to share a marvellous faculty for living in the instant; I had no such faculty. My instinctive motion was not outwards, towards life, but away from it. And, in a different order, I was self-sufficient in some odd and partial fashion. It was not, as she would sometimes hint, that the idea of Katherine was more important to me than the reality. But perhaps it was true that the feeling she awakened and kept alive in me was more

important to me even than herself. *Et amare amabam.* It was love
I loved.

No telegram arrived, and no further letter. So I went very
early to the station to meet her. I waited with the agony of a
lover at his first tryst, and while I waited I wrote this:

An hour and I shall see you. Delicately
A light will pass across your wakening eyes,
That will be smiling, steady, saying to me:
'There was no parting, all those days were lies.
I left you on the instant.' I will hesitate
Whether to kiss you, but a second gone
Since last we kissed; decide when all too late;
Then wonder would a year of love atone.
You, knowing my mind, will smile and touch my hand.
Or did you touch it then? . . . Ah, no, an hour,
A leaden hour, that will not understand,
But moon-faced mocks me from the tall clock-tower
And will not lock the door upon the band
Of devil-doubts that hold me in their power.

CHAPTER XXIV

THERE WAS A LITTLE MAN...

ON August 24th, 1914 – not three weeks after the outbreak of the war – Katherine and I had composed and solemnly signed the following document:

> Resolved that, so soon as we can rid ourselves of our present engagements in London, we will take a cottage by the sea in Cornwall or Devonshire, and there live on whatever money we can get without forcing ourselves to do anything we do not like: that this shall be our first and only care henceforward.

Jack
Katherine

A year afterwards and it had come to nothing. The superficial cause was that, after a time, Katherine reacted both from poverty and country isolation; but the deeper cause was the one which Lawrence had diagnosed two years before, the lack of any bottom in myself, in which Katherine could anchor.

I had no purpose; I served no God. The war had made it clear, and my contact with Lawrence had made it clearer still. He was striving to unite a few people – of whom Katherine and I were the youngest – in service to an idea of religious and social revolution. And all of us, in our various ways, were recalcitrant. Lawrence defined the evil in us all when he wrote concerning Bertrand Russell.

> What does Russell really want? He wants to keep his own established ego, his finite and ready-defined self intact, free from contact and connection. He wants to be ultimately a free agent. That is what they all want, ultimately . . .

For Russell, this was a definite philosophy; he was, in the full intellectual sense of the term, a philosophical anarchist. And since his ideas were fully developed, the clash between him and Lawrence was not long in coming. For Lawrence wanted 'a unity in religious belief, which leads to action'. We were to be centred 'in the knowledge of the Infinite, of God', and work from that centre. At that point I lost my bearings. I could see that Russell's was not what Lawrence meant by a religious belief, and that it was really the antithesis of such a thing. But that did not help me to understand or share in Lawrence's. I scraped up courage enough to be honest with him.

> Murry says that the spirit matters, but that an idea is bad. He says he believes in what I say because he believes in me; he might help in the work I set out to do because that would be believing in me. But he would not believe in the work. He would deplore it. He says the whole thing is personal: that between him and me it is a case of Lawrence and Murry, not of any union in an idea. He thinks the introduction of any idea, particularly of any political idea, highly dangerous and deplorable. The thing should be left personal, each man just expressing himself.

Indeed, I could get no nearer to any sort of religious faith than a belief in persons – not an abstract belief in the sacredness of the individuality – but a belief in concrete, individual persons, to whom one was united by a bond of affection. At any rate that was real to me; and I knew the difference between a real feeling and an abstract creed. I could feel that Lawrence's creed was not abstract, and that it was a living reality to him; I had not, as he thought I had, a deliberate resistance against it. It was just incomprehensible to me. The simple clue was missing.

So, during the summer of 1915, Lawrence's plan of a group united in belief and action was reduced perforce to a resolution to establish a little centre in London where those who cared to hear might come to hear Lawrence expound his views, and to issue a little magazine in connection with it. To the magazine Katherine and I were to contribute, and I was to be its technical editor; but the lectures were to be Lawrence's affair. Chiefly for this purpose, the Lawrences were to move to London and live in Hampstead. To be near him, and not too near, we looked for rooms in St. John's Wood – which was Katherine's favourite part of London; and at last, greatly daring, we rented what seemed to us a charming house, No. 5 Acacia Road. Its antecedents were of the sort that Katherine liked. The man from whom we took it was one of those majestic literary persons who used to flourish on the fringe of the theatre, adapting plays and the like. This one informed us that he was also the biographer of Sir Henry Irving. We were duly impressed, and he was gratified. Indeed, he behaved in a properly regal fashion about those treacherous things called fixtures. Before him, the house had been inhabited (so the daily woman told us, who was also a fixture, and a reliable one) by an opera singer of some repute, who used to swallow a large number of raw eggs.

The 'aspegs', as Katherine called them, were excellent. A lovely pear-tree was in the garden, and something not unlike a lawn, where we decided to play Badminton, and sometimes played it. At the top of the gabled house was a beautiful attic-room which Katherine made her own. From its window we stared at the first Zeppelin sailing over London; it so excited us that we forgot to put out the lights behind us, and were harried by special constables, doubly suspicious of us because the innocent Koteliansky was our frequent visitor. Katherine's brother, who had finished his training, came there often. From there he left for France, and thither a few days afterwards came the news of his death. That was the end of No. 5 Acacia Road for us. Katherine felt she could not live in it any more.

But, leaving aside the bitter ending, my memories of No. 5 are kindly. There was a gracious atmosphere about that stucco house in which Katherine seemed to flourish. Lawrence and Frieda liked it; and it was here, one evening in October, that he brought down in alarm a copy of the *Daily News* containing a dangerously hostile review of *The Rainbow* by Robert Lynd. Lawrence scented the danger, and sat mute in a chair while we read it. But we had nothing to say. We neither of us liked *The Rainbow* and Katherine quite definitely hated parts of it – in particular the scene where Anna, pregnant, dances naked before the mirror. That, Katherine said to me, was 'female' – her most damning adjective – and an apotheosis of the 'female': a sort of glorification of the secret, intimate talk between women, the sexual understanding of the female confraternity, which Katherine could not abide. But whereas Katherine in a sense understood the book and hated it positively, I could not understand it at all. I disliked it on instinct. There was a warm, close, heavy promiscuity of flesh about it which repelled me, and I could not understand the compulsion which was upon Lawrence to write in that fashion and of those themes; neither could I understand his surprise and dismay that the critics were out for his blood. As far as mere feeling went, I felt with them. I happened to be friends with Lawrence, and Robert Lynd didn't: that was about the only difference.

Our simple solution of the problem in those days was that Frieda had an excessive and altogether unfortunate influence upon Lawrence's beliefs and his work. Whenever Frieda announced to us that something which Lawrence was writing was magnificent and wonderful, our hearts promptly sank; when, in Lawrence's presence and with his evident approval, she told us that such and such a chapter was really hers, we felt uncomfortable, and in secret sighed and shook our heads. Was sex really so important, could it be? Or was it important in that particular way? Wasn't it somehow much simpler, omnipresent certainly, but omnipresent invisibly like the casing air? And didn't Lawrence make of this pellucid ambience a fog?

With those thoughts in our minds, and those feelings in our hearts, we were not, and could not be, much support to Lawrence. It seemed to us that the same taint, the same over-emphasis had

351

invaded his philosophy. Animality was an absolute, spirituality was an absolute; they contended with one another, murderously and mysteriously, and we could make nothing of the obscure struggle between them. Although we thoroughly entered into the fun of taking a little room in Fisher Street, off Red Lion Square, and the adventure of running a magazine with Lawrence, the very title which I proposed for it, *The Signature*, was meant to be an indication that we took no responsibility for one another's creeds. Lawrence was the big gun; he had a message, and he could preach it. We busied ourselves with getting the room ready. An old account-book tells me that we paid 22s. 6d. for a desk and 7s. for chairs, 10s. a week for rent and 7d. for paint and a brush. But, so far as I remember, neither Katherine nor I attended a lecture meeting: that was not our affair.

Naturally, Lawrence sought more enthusiastic support than we could give, and often when we went to his little ground-floor flat in the Vale of Health, we found the room full of new faces. Perhaps jealously, we did not like them; but if they had a better understanding of Lawrence's doctrines than we, it did not make them any more loyal. Philip Heseltine – 'Peter Warlock' – who came to the fore at this moment, later brought a libel action against Lawrence; and he and another of the new admirers (now famous) were guilty of the indecency of holding Lawrence's poems up to public ridicule in the Café Royal on the night when Katherine snatched their book away, as it is written in *Women in Love*.

These weeks in London must have been a lonely and a wretched time for Lawrence. He hated London pretty badly at all times; but now the suppression of *The Rainbow* and the fiasco of *The Signature*, which he naturally took to heart more than we, must have made it intolerable. But at this moment Katherine was overwhelmed by her brother's death, and I with the new separation which it made between us. Here was a grief in Katherine which was beyond my power to assuage, a whole world of memory and experience which I had no power to enter, and I

352

felt outcast. Lawrence was full of his plan to escape to Florida, in which I could not share. I could see no prospect of making even the smallest living in America, and I was more possessed than ever with the necessity of maintaining my own independence. The only possible escape for me was to a place where I could earn £2 a week. In the South of France this was possible, since by this time I had made a small place for myself as a reviewer of French books for *The Times Literary Supplement*. To the South of France Katherine and I accordingly decided to go. So I presented myself once more to a recruiting office, for the sole purpose of obtaining a certificate of rejection. We made over our house to some Russian friends of Koteliansky, and prepared to depart.

As Lawrence had composed his philosophy for *The Signature*, so had I tried to compose mine. As he had been compelled to break off in the middle, so had I. But *There was a little Man* . . . contains, I suppose, as complete and faithful an account of myself as I was capable of giving in the autumn of 1915. Therefore, since it is inaccessible, I must give some account of it here.

It opens with an attempt to convey the feverish resistance of my personal consciousness to the War. It had become impossible to ignore it any more. Now, every month brought the news of the death of a friend and coeval of my own.

The War has assailed me in my consciousness. Men I knew, of my own age, have met their death. Every time the news of such a death has come to me, I have been plunged for hours, even for days, in a cold despondency of horror. Yet the horror was not for them, but for me; not of their death, but of my own. They were like me in their ways, not wholly like me – some of them little enough – but something like, for they were, or had been, my friends. They desired to achieve something out of their lives beyond the mere extension of comfortable existence. They were like me in that, which was the chief matter: and when they died, I died with them, for a minute or an hour or a day. I died with all that I dream of and struggle for

353

unachieved. Their achievement was snuffed out with their life. Can it be so light and unsubstantial as that?

I could suppose two reasons why my similars had entered into the War: one, a passionate love of their country, of a kind of which I had no experience. I loved my country, but I did not love it passionately; I loved it in so far as it afforded me freedom to work out my own justification. Or they surrendered to a wave of mass-enthusiasm, such as had passed over me also. Then I had been overwhelmed by the desire to be quit of all responsibility for myself, and to lose the burden of my identity by becoming an obedient part of a great machine. But immediately I had felt that, if I had surrendered to it, I should have betrayed myself.

Was that only a coward's rhetoric? Was I merely afraid of death? This was the question. And this is how I answered it.

I know that I am afraid of death, and yet to me there seems a vast difference between this and to be *merely* afraid of death. For death is terrible to me only because it means that nothing of my deep desire will be satisfied, or my purpose achieved. Without a consummation my life is barren and meaningless. Death now would be not a consummation, but a stupid discordant finale interpolated by some malignant fool.

But this deep desire, on the reality of which this self-vindication all depended – what was it? I called it 'the achievement of art'. But what was that? What was the meaning of the phrase?

What is it then, this urgent desire to create art in words? It is not a desire to manipulate words for themselves? I have no pleasure in that, for words come to me always with labour. They, and their beauties, are to me no end at all. They are no more than the means by which I may express something which I feel an imperious need to express. What is this thing?

It is not beauty. Whatever beauty may be, it has no intimate existence in me. I can appreciate what is called the beauty of a vase, a picture, a poem or a face: yet, though I admire it, I cannot make it mine. It is set over against me. I am here, and there is the admirable thing. I can bring it no nearer to me. I do not even desire to bring it near and make it mine; for it does not profoundly affect me. It is independent and complete and repels me from itself, like a polished wall of steel or stone.

But there are faces and pictures and writings which attract and do not repel me. They allure me, and that which allures me in them is somehow akin to that which I desire to express in words. They awaken my active sympathy. I *feel with* the soul which expressed itself thus and thus, which shows in the face, the picture, or the writing. Yes, only that interests me deeply which I can understand as the expression of a striving soul. Then I feel with another soul. It does not mean that I feel or have felt the same things as the other soul – but I am conscious that I might have the same feelings. I recognize in them an intimate, personal possibility.

What then is this personal possibility in me? It must be that which is most intimately true of myself, for only that which others found inwardly true of themselves could appeal to me as possibly true of myself. Else how could I recognize it for true? There would be no bond between it and me.

Thus the vague phrase 'the achievement of art' hardens down to the meaning: the achievement and expression of personal truth. But personal truth? What is that?

It has a common and familiar ring, as though a man might at all times produce at summons some item of personal truth. Yet to me this is the hardest of all things to hold: so seldom does it emerge into the life a man lives. He works and rests from work, eats and sleeps, and all the while his truth lies dormant, hidden beneath the weight of the action and reactions of a life that is not life, but an ugly and laborious means of living; and even when the seals are broken and the great stone rolled away, and he finds himself careless in the

355

presence of one of those very few whom he has proved his friends, how seldom does he succeed in urging out one single word of his truth! He is compacted of numbed faculties and inhibited desires; he cannot breathe the atmosphere of his unused freedom, and he is content to feel between himself and them some current of silent understanding and some assurance that not the words he says will be taken for his own so much as the tone in which he speaks them or the smile with which he gives them: which is an acknowledgment that the intimate truth exists in him to be taken on trust, for it cannot, save at the rarest moments, struggle into the spoken word.

Does it then reduce finally to paradox? Could the personal truth of 'the wavering spirit and the little body which was me' be no more than the yearning to achieve it? If it was a paradox, it was not an empty one. Something was hidden behind it.

To seek art and express personal truth is an activity particular to me, in so far as I believe that I shall achieve more of my truth through this activity than another will of his own. But it is only part of a larger and more general activity of soul. I try to imagine myself completely achieved: and in that joyful consummation the expression of my truth seems to sink back into oneness with an harmonious whole. It tyrannizes over me no more. It is the aspect which my life bears for an hour, a week, or a day; but its other aspects are manifold and each no less desirable. It is the very condition of their being that they should be desirable, for whatever I should be doing, I should be freely doing. And that, I suppose, is the end and meaning of it all – free activity. I should be freely doing.

There follows a kind of pæan to Freedom, evidently written with some emotion, though the Freedom it celebrates is more abstract and intangible even than Shelley's Liberty, and this is followed by a painfully self-conscious repudiation of my own

enthusiasm, and, more significantly, by evidences of a real con-
fusion of mind, until at last the thread is picked up again by the
declaration that Freedom is of two kinds – negative and positive.

The freedom of the free man and the freedom of the slave –
these are two. The slave is defined by his bondage, the free
man by his aspirations. The slave is free when his material
fetters are broken; the free man is free when his aspirations are
suddenly linked to his own heart . . . For freedom is of the
spirit and won by the spirit; and whether he be bond or free,
the slave is the captive of the life that is but a hard and ugly
means to living. But the free man when in the spirit he
touches the hem of the garment of the spirit's freedom, leaps
beyond life to living. He is free, and by his freedom frees all
men. The freedom of the slave frees no man, not even himself.

I confess that I barely understand it; but I think it is a clumsy
surmise of what seems to me now the simple notion of reintegration
into unity. That notion was very, very remote from me in those
days, and if, for a fleeting moment, I had a bewildering glimpse of
the possibility, I can understand the turmoil of my own mind, and
my own despondent accusation of myself for 'mistaking giddiness
for ecstasy'.

I took refuge from this scepticism in the assertion that clear
ideas are inadequate to ultimate beliefs. The ideas which have
endured are those least like ideas: 'Freedom, Love, and their offspring Immortality, which is the outcome of the denial of Freedom
and Love in this life'. Art – or what I, in my own very private
language meant by the word – was based on the belief that
Freedom and Love must be attained in this life, and on the
conviction that personality is paramount. Thus it was opposed
to the idea of Christianity, which was then incomprehensible to
me. For, I said, 'Freedom cannot be conceived save in terms of
life, and life cannot be conceived save in relation to the physical
and moral harmony which is its implanted form'. Thus, I
continued to fumble after the notion of unity and integration.

357

The freedom of a free man is infinite. Thereby he attains to be a vehicle of the free spirit; and the infinite he touches is not sterile and endless, not without bound and void, but truly infinite, controlled into harmony by its own inward principle. Thereby his every act is become a note in the music by which life and the reluctant universe are governed. Then he lives, and is a man and life is justified in him, not by suffering and mutilation, but in the plenitude of a living soul.

At that, once more I began to doubt lest it was only rhetoric after all, and declined into the depths of depression – a whole week of it: of 'hours of utter unbelief, when it seems not that belief has failed me, but that I never can have believed'. At last, it seemed to me that I had found the cause of this. The very intensity of the search for 'personal truth' was 'an exaggeration of deliberate thought upon free living at the cost of free living'. It defeated itself, for 'the laborious definition of vague personal truth affects the soul; and the soul rejects that which honest thought discovered'.

With that apparent demonstration that I was engaged upon a task inherently impossible the portion of my self-examination that was actually printed in *The Signature* came to an end. It continues in manuscript, and becomes – to me at least – more interesting.

Therefore I must say that the personal truth of me is true only *if I myself am true*. (Define more) I am a living thing that strives after its final form of self-disciplined activity, which is Freedom. I pause in the effort and survey myself, looking back on the road by which I have come. The chart I draw and the account I give are true and valuable in so far as they are seen to depend for their meaning on the future achievement of more perfect form. Of that more perfect form I can say that it will be the least my own of all things that I call mine; for the present imperfection of my truth resides most clearly in that which is most evidently me, above all in the fever of my impatience to achieve. With that incessant fretting stilled, what will remain of the personality which I so jealously defend? Of the man who fixes his eyes upon one single end and is insensible to other beauties, envious of others' outward freedom, fiercely and unjustly critical, childishly anxious to find the worth of his seeking recognized by others, impatient of delay? Such am I. He who seeks the greatest freedom is of all men the least free; and I am Freedom's slave. I am a slave as the needle of a compass is bound to the magnetic north.

But when the pole is reached, then that which is separately mine will fall away. For in what does my individual consciousness consist save in the sense of obstacle? Suppose a seed breaks open underground and strives upward toward the sun. On the soil above its head is laid a stone against which, for a time, it seeks in vain to force a way. In that thwarted aspiration it knows itself. The uneasy sensation that the full activity of life is denied to it would be the pinnacle of the flower's self-consciousness. So with a man. His knowledge of himself is knowledge of a hostile world. His actions are not his own. His own self-governance is undermined from every side, so that by the pressure of the forces of the foreign world he is shaped into a mechanism. His consciousness of that invading mechanical tyranny is his most acute sense of self; for then is self most different from all other and most reluctant to it. Then he says: 'I am I', and proclaims his separateness from life. Only thus can he keep the flame of his life alive.

But, however loudly he proclaim, and however jealously he hold his hands around the flame to guard it, it is then that it is nearest to extinction. A man's soul then may be compared to a walled city which is most keenly conscious of its own separate existence when it is hemmed all about by besieging enemies. Its goings-out and its comings-in are controlled by an alien power. But when the siege is raised and free movement once more begins, the jealous sense of separateness begins to disappear; the city becomes one with the countryside once more. So the consciousness of particular personality gives way to a consciousness of universal personality. The individuality that was shaped by limitations, those limitations once removed, becomes an infinite principle of free activity, infinite because governed by its own inward design. Achieved, I am no longer for me, but for the world, and in myself I harbour the infinite which is the goal of all the finite imperfections of the world we know.

There at least I seem to have been on the verge of a real truth. But how, I asked myself, could those limitations be removed? Was that not a contradiction in terms? Alarmed, apparently, by the precariousness of my own thought, I tried to make it concrete. Was not a man's inevitable struggle for subsistence a limitation? How was that to be removed?

It was no use waiting for a change in the machinery of government, though it was the first duty of government to assure men subsistence. The limitation must be broken down by the individual man; he must make his means of subsistence subservient to his own free activity.

The world says: 'I will give you meat and drink (at monopoly prices) on condition you become a little wheel, a little crank, in my great machine. When you are worn out, of course I shall have to scrap you, but if you are a sensible man and choose to forego every desire, every leisure, every freedom, and every delight, you may be able to accumulate sufficient to keep you in the same state of happiness until you die. Perhaps you won't need a great deal of money, because you won't be likely to live long'.

So says the world; and men accept the beautiful arrangement.

But why should they? Why shouldn't they refuse to come

in, or being in, come out? Why shouldn't they say, 'We will work when we like at what we like, go where we will and when we will'?

They would starve? I do not for one moment believe it. A man who determines to be free of the mechanical restraint of economic laws (which, of all laws, were made only to be broken) and is resolutely careless whether he is middle-class or lower-class or no class at all, and careless for his children after him, is not likely to starve. He will find something to put his hand to cheerfully. . . .

That was my rather facile solution – a simple desertion of machine-civilization by individuals; and I optimistically antici-pated that the majority of the four million men engaged in the War would refuse to return like lambs to the industrial slaughter. I hoped that 'the something like a revolution' which would ensue would not be one of 'those pallid affairs called economic revolu-tions, whose only effect seems to be that things are perceptibly more monotonous and tyrannical than they were before'. I wanted a real revolution, real chaos. The risks of chaos seemed to me far preferable to the certainty of being ossified in the machine. That was the horror of the War: it had not brought the chaos which was prophesied beforehand. 'Chaos indeed! It is the last thing anyone thinks about. Everywhere they cry, like a lot of parrots, "Organize! Organize!" And I suppose we are being organized, and shall be organized until we have reached the seventh heaven of organization.' Life had nothing to do with organization. Organization was a means of man's wrestling with the material world, and from this very fact a cessation of his wrestling with himself. I rejected absolutely, as a silly notion, the idea of bringing back to the individual a pride in his work in a machine-civilization. That was gone for ever.

Stand at any street corner and watch the first twenty men that pass you, with their occupations written over them – bus-conductors, bus-drivers, newspaper-boys, greengrocers' men, milkmen: then try to think how they could conceivably find a pride in the work they have to do. The notion is sheer foolishness. What you must say is that both in the system as it is and any future system based *on the same elements*, work must be regarded as a period of sleep, unconsciousness or death, preparatory to a period of leisure which is life.

But how can such leisure be life? For this leisure is not a state of doing what you want to do, but of doing what you have to do: namely, to get rid of the ill-effects of a long time spent in doing what you hate. Was there any remedy? It seemed to me that there was none. 'Those who acquiesce, acquiesce; those who rebel, rebel.' I was one of the rebels.

But the thing against which I rebelled, with a morbid vehemence, was the absence of a human relation between men. It seemed to me that the whole *business* of life was brutalizing. In the smallest and most casual interchange – buying in a shop, asking the way of a stranger – I looked hungrily for some friendly warmth, some kindliness. A purely commercial relation was horrible to me; still worse, it was terrifying: in it emerged the reality from which I tried to hide myself, the universal and fearful assumption that a man who had no money had no being. He was less than a slave; he was nothing. From that reality I fled in abject terror, and a convulsion of impotent hatred. I knew perfectly well that, because of this, I should never have the courage to take the path of individual rebellion. It was inconceivable that I, who suffered agonies in an ordinary business transaction, and would sign anything only to escape from the atmosphere of bargains and contracts, should ever dare to let myself become dependent on the kindliness and decency of men. I believed that one man's need should be an all-sufficient claim on another's superfluity; but that I should assert the claim for myself was fantastic. One day of disappointed expectation would kill me.

In my morbid fashion, I seethed with hatred of this bitter

world of the cash-nexus. I felt that its members despised me, and
I loathed them. One casual contemptuous word in such a contact
would set me trembling for hours. I felt that they recognized me
instantly, as their enemy and their prey.

They band themselves against me, for I am their evil –
something that, though they bind with covenant and seals,
one upon another, will yet evade them. For I *will* evade
them. What have I to do with them? They have made me
from the cradle up to be the slave of their duties, their right
and their law. They have branded my very soul with the
mark that shall prove me theirs. They have had their
victory over me before I knew that there was a victory to
be won, or that I had a soul which I might one day call my
own. They fashioned me that I should be a citizen of the
meanest city that life has yet, through all its ages, devised,
wherein to starve one's nature and to make dead all that
really lives, is a title to honour and to power.

But they do not really hold me. I am become, in part,
my own. . . .

These most noble citizens, these glorious fruits of the well-
trained tree, these very corner-stones of the great house of
Liberty – these shall never be forgiven – never, never! The
words of Christ are precious to me: assuredly in this they
comfort me. 'Verily, it were better that a millstone were
hanged about his neck and he drowned in the depths of the
sea, than that he cause one of these little ones to stumble.'
And what is the searching, aspiring, eager, trembling human
spirit but a little child born out of the womb of time? The
child of all children – and this they have made to stumble.
To stumble! It has gone about the walls of the prison they
have built for it, beating its tender hands against the iron
door, weeping and sobbing till no sound could come up
from its swollen throat. They have kept it in darkness till it
could not see, kept it in silence till its ears could not hear.

And then they have brought it forth into the free sun and music and spaces of the world, the sun it cannot see, the music it cannot hear, the spaces it cannot run over, being maimed; and they say, 'The world is yours', and to the world they say, 'Here is another *man!*'

It is emotionally exaggerated, yet it expresses something which was constant in my feeling in those days. Its very impurity, the ill-concealed identification of myself with 'the aspiring, trembling spirit of humanity', is characteristic. Characteristic, no less, is the ever-recurring doubt of my own implicit claim to have transcended my own personality.

But it is not I any more. I am now but the unworthy vehicle of the free spirit, which has stirred in me. We have begun our progress to the infinite which is man.

'The infinite which is man.' I love the sounding words, but in the straining of my mind towards it, there comes a moment when that infinite is empty and not full. I seem to have passed beyond the things of life, and I hug the thought to my brain, and it is nothing. I can neither plunge myself into it, nor pass beyond it, for it is void.

But it is my mind which has made it void. My tyrant consciousness has made a pale ghost of a living reality, a consummation which must be lived into, and cannot be thought.

Then, I think more clearly than ever before, I put to myself the question which tormented me continually, with a torment which even those who knew me most intimately – Katherine and Lawrence and Campbell – found incomprehensible.

But how shall I escape the tyranny of my mind, here and now? I cannot escape. I can only wait until another passion than that which drives me on to make this chart of my soul takes possession of me. Then the hard clear line which seems to separate my mind from me dissolves away There takes place within me a new contact which is not unfertile. Now the sounds of voices in the garden beyond my window do not irritate me. They sink into a warm and pleasant cloud which bathes me wholly. I am no longer different, and desperately sensitive of my difference, from that which is outside me. I am in it, and it is in me.

And so my soul narrows and expands in unceasing movement. It expands and pervades my physical being and I am one, and in myself I feel the infinite which is man. It narrows and hardens and walls itself against all outward things, and in the fret of my impatience to think my freedom and my universality, the walls grow broader and higher. Desperation follows, and an empty giddiness. The thoughts of my brain no longer are distinct. They sink before my soul's eye like a point of travelling light into the curtains of visible darkness, and are lost. And when they are lost, by the very tenseness of my mind to hold them, I despair as a man who knows himself utterly cast out of heaven.

Yet even then I do not doubt this truth which I have found. How can one doubt a truth discovered except by the apprehension of another truth, however dim? It may not be apprehended by the mind; it may sweep up from the downward spaces of one's being. But it is there, set against the truth that one has found.

Nothing is set against my truth. Either that is present to me, or nothingness; and this nothingness has no quality of being of its own. It is no more than my not-truth. It is the feeling in me that the truth, as I hold it in my brain, has grown empty, resolved into a circumambient void.

Therefore not even in these most awful moments does my truth cease to exist. Its existence is the very sure condition of my knowing that these moments are terrible. Should I weep over the absence of my lover, if there were no lover at all?

So is my doubt not doubt at all, but the deep sadness for

an absent me. It is as though the resplendent I whom I bear within me, the I who am perfectly achieved and governed only by the music awakened by my full response to all that is within me and without, suddenly left his habitation empty. But there are no devils that can enter into the swept and garnished room. The devil is the emptiness itself.

And not even the emptiness itself should afflict me, were it not that I am impatient for my own fullness. I should say, 'I am empty and void. Well, let it be'. I should believe, as even now it may be I believe, that there are the precious seasons of the fallow field, and wait calmly till they brought forth once more. But I cannot rest. Some power urges me to drag, by main force, what I have lost from the whole of me back into the mind which is part of me.

So I diagnosed my disease, and sought to comfort and reassure myself. It surprises me now to discover that there were moments when I felt confident in the possession of some truth; and most surprising that I understood the nature of these moments, and experienced – or thought I experienced – my truth as a condition: a condition of unity within my discordant self, and unity with the world outside me. For this comes perilously near to whatever truth I was ultimately to apprehend, and was at least an intellectual premonition of the simple creed by which I have come to live. Evidently, the pattern of myself has changed less than I believed.

My trouble seems rather to have been that I was altogether incapable of 'a wise passiveness'. I was as though pursued by my own thoughts – 'their father and their prey'. I could dream of self-forgetfulness, I could even arrive by thinking at a realization of the necessity for it; but the thing itself I could not achieve. It visited me but fitfully, and then in waves of intense personal affection, which left me more desperately aware of the hostility of the world than before. All I could do was to formulate in abstract terms what I somehow knew to be the conditions of

366

salvation – the content of the vague concept of Freedom with which I had begun.

I see as the end of human life the achievement of an active harmony whereby our actions and thoughts and passions shall be so truly our own that they will belong to all men. We shall be without defences, because our strength will not need them. We shall be persons in the profound sense that we shall have transcended our own personality, and all obligation and constraint will pass beyond itself and become the natural desire for the full satisfaction of harmonious impulse.

I do not imagine that one day we shall achieve this condition and be thereafter blessed. We shall hate, we shall fear, we shall love, we shall desire; but we shall not fear our fears or hate our hates, for we shall *know* that the things we fear and hate are evil things; and we shall fear and hate them with all the intensity of a lively soul.

I do not understand the meaning of the final sentence in the first paragraph above; but the drift of the passage I understand, and approve.

I have quoted this old manuscript of mine to weariness, simply because it contains a more truthful picture of myself at this time than I could possibly draw now, and because it enables me to see more clearly than I could see it before the nature of the conflict between Lawrence and myself, which, though it still remained a conflict between friends, was now acute between us. The tension between spirit and flesh which was, for him, the reality of human life, and the key to the cosmos itself, was non-existent in my being and did not enter into my thought. The struggle for me was entirely different; it was to overcome the complete mental hypertrophy which threatened me. My 'consciousness' had nothing whatever to do with what Lawrence meant by 'spirit'. To spirit, for him, belonged conscious love, which was, for me and in me, instinctive. That, and a kind of corollary hatred, were the only instinctive motions I possessed, or which possessed me. All that he meant by 'blood', by the pre-mental awareness and response, was completely hidden from me; it did not speak to my condition at all. And when he implied or asserted that my only instinctive motions, my only moments of escape from the tyranny of my mental consciousness, were themselves the very quintessence of the mental consciousness, I was truly bewildered.

Not long afterwards, when Katherine and I were together in Bandol, and happier perhaps than we had ever been or were ever to be again, I was made aware, in a way that penetrated even my obtuseness, of the gulf between us. I had told Lawrence, before leaving, that I was at last going to write my book on Dostoevsky, which had been so long delayed for the good reason that I found I had nothing really to say about Dostoevsky. But this time I was determined either to make up my mind about that strange Russian who fascinated and perplexed and stimulated me, or for ever hold my peace. I would not, because I could not, 'make' a book about him. (I have never been able to 'make' a book about anything, or anybody.)

Lawrence promised to meditate his own opinion on Dostoevsky and to write some notes for me. In my condition of mental indigence concerning my subject, I was more than ordinarily grateful. But it so happened that, owing to the illness that seized him that winter, he was unable to write them until the spring. By that time I had read all Dostoevsky's major books over three times, first with a glimmering of comprehension and finally with an altogether unprecedented flood of illumination. Suddenly the whole thing had fallen into pattern; and I was, for the first time, the victim of the strange sensation of being hardly more than the amanuensis of a book that wrote itself. To a person of my peculiar composition such an experience was an inward revolution. For the first time in my life, I had the experience of certitude. It was no question of my opinion of Dostoevsky; I had no opinion of Dostoevsky: and if I expressed any personal opinions about him in the book, they were certainly exaggerated and probably wrong. All that had happened – I speak, of course, of my sensation only – was that the objective 'pattern' of Dostoevsky had declared itself, through me as instrument.

Precisely at this moment, when the book had written itself, Lawrence wrote and sent me his notes on Dostoevsky. To my consternation I found them completely incomprehensible.

1 He has a fixed will, a mania to be infinite, to be God.
2 Within this will, his activity is two-fold:
    (a) to be self-less, a pure Christian, to live in the outer whole, the social whole, the self-less whole, the universal consciousness;
    (b) to be a pure, absolute self, all-devouring and all-consuming.

That is the main statement about him.

Lawrence invited me 'to translate this into my own language'. I could not do it; my language had no equivalents for such ideas, and the ideas themselves were such that, by no exercise of my imagination, could I take hold of them. To this day, I am unable to connect them vitally with Dostoevsky. But now, at least, I realize what escaped me then, that this 'pattern' which Lawrence found in Dostoevsky was an exact replica of the 'pattern' he had put forward, with no thought of Dostoevsky at all, in his essay in *The Signature*. The (a) and the (b) of his 'main statement' about Dostoevsky are precisely the forces he had embodied in the Unicorn and the Lion; the Crown (which was the title of his essay) was simply the equipoise of tension between these polar opposites.

That was Lawrence's creed, which I could not understand; but what was mine? Perhaps in its own way it was equally incomprehensible. Behind the long confession of faith which I have summarized lies a kind of moral mysticism, which I had somehow derived from Plato, and which had been greatly strengthened in me by Milton. My notion of Freedom came from Milton; my notion of Harmony from Plato: but for me they were simply identical. And these notions were by no means intellectual. They were intimately associated with, and derived their potency from, the strange condition of mind which Plato and Milton had first induced in me and which afterwards I sought by my own ways. This was a kind of ecstasy. I cannot recapture it now; I can only remember that I seemed to be merged in a kind of divine 'understanding', and to be touched by a 'sorrow more beautiful than beauty's self'. But this condition appeared to have nothing whatever to do with my ordinary life; and the effort of my mind was to discover some possible relation between them.

The magic word was Harmony. In the novel on which I was labouring at this time, a character who is obviously a transposition of myself, meditates concerning this same word, Harmony: 'Yes, that was the word. The very word was mysterious to him. It had for years, even of *his* life, been dear to him. Seldom had he any glimmering of its meaning, but there were days when it had passed from being merely a word to a symbol of something remotely seen, infinitesimally apprehended.' This evidence tallies with that of my confession of faith; and I can only conclude that I regarded the ecstatic condition of seeming to participate in a universal harmony as somehow premonitory of a condition of harmony within the human being.

Indubitably this was my faith, or my aspiration. Whether it was more than an intellectual possibility to me, I cannot say; but even if it were only that, the fact remains that as an idea it aroused a very deep emotion in me. This condition in which a harmony of the universe should be apprehended, not by an ecstatic but a harmonious man, was the hidden God whom I was seeking. Mixed inextricably with this was the pursuit of the only sublunary peace I knew: the peace of human affection. Yet this very thing seemed to make my ideal of inward harmony chimerical. Human affection was no more than a tiny island in a hungry and devouring sea: it was repudiated by the world of things. How then could one hope to achieve harmony in a soul beset at once by the need of love, and the realization that love was impotent?

That, I think, is a fair, if charitable, account of the perplexity that gnawed at me. It is more coherent than anything I could have put into words at the time, and certainly than anything I ever said to Lawrence. Anyhow, deeply imprinted on it all he would have seen the mark of the Beast – the mental consciousness. It was the only one I had – a poor thing but mine own. But even in the simple human matter of love, I had to ask myself whether his way was really better than mine. By this time, Katherine and I were well aware of the fearful conflict between him and Frieda. Was that really the ideal of love between a man and a woman? Was it not rather that Lawrence's genius compelled him to make a virtue of his own necessity?

CHAPTER XXV

ISOLATION

IN the middle of November 1915 Katherine and I forsook No. 5 Acacia Road, and made for the South of France. We knew nothing of it. Neither of us had been farther south than Paris. So we stayed for a few days at Marseilles to take our bearings. It was full of troops, French, African, Indian, English. Every morning we were awakened by the clatter of horses and mules and guns over the cobbles – a sort of Lord Mayor's Show, with which it was impossible to believe that one had any connection. And the treacherous southern sunshine deluded us: soon we had what we came to call Marseilles fever.

However, we scouted as far as Cassis, of which we had heard as a lovely place – to be fair to Cassis, in summer. It looked lovely on the day we visited it, and we arranged with the hotel. But on the day we arrived, we could hardly see the station platform for dust. A mistral was raging. The bus clattered and swooped, we shivered and remembered glumly with what care we had chosen a room with four windows and hardly any wall. We looked through the gauze shutters on to the forlorn plane trees and wondered why we had come. Even the fire in our room, if it cheered us and gave us innumerable cups of tea, depressed us equally by the knowledge that we could not afford it. And, besides, we had imagined that the South of France was a sort of first cousin to the South Sea Islands (for which indeed it was our substitute) and that one never needed fires.

The fortnight for which we had covenanted at Cassis was a further education into reality. Katherine, whose gay humour generally made such situations bearable, was still brooding over her brother's death, and I was outcast and disconsolate. We walked forlornly over the rocks, round the point, and sat together. Katherine began to weep quietly, as though she would never stop. 'Can't I do *anything?*' I said. She shook her head. What was she weeping for? Not any more for her brother, I think; but for the disappointment of her hopes – it was the snail under the leaf again.

I found it unbearable and resolved to return. Katherine would not; the idea of London was hateful to her, and she was convinced that she could not write there. However unbearable France might be, it gave her back (she said) her power of detailed vision. Therefore she would stay awhile; but we agreed she could not stay in Cassis. So I went exploring until I found Bandol, which was so attractive that I half-repented my resolution to return. We migrated to the Hôtel Beau Rivage – an altogether different kind of place, warm and friendly, where we spent three days together. The nearer it came to my going, the sadder I became.

Why was I returning? Three weeks later I myself could not say, because my conscious and declared motives were not my real ones. I was returning, I told Katherine, because out of England I felt like a fish out of water and because I was determined to continue *The Signature*, even if I had to print it myself. I had even formed the definite plan of taking a studio and setting up a small printing-press in it for the purpose – a plan in which Katherine acquiesced. But that was merely the itch for activity to fill my own emptiness. Beneath all this was my feeling that the death of Katherine's brother had cast a shadow between us. Though I was with her, I was isolated from her, and I could not bear it: for then my isolation was complete. From that isolation I fled precipitately. That it was sheer cowardice, I have no doubt. I simply *could* not face isolation. To escape from it, I conjured up visions of a friendly England or self-forgetful work with my hands. Indeed, any illusion would do that would for a moment conceal my own nakedness from myself.

That I was leaving Katherine to isolation did not occur to me. Nor, indeed, was I. That was the trouble. For she had her brother. He, though dead, was far more real and near to her than

I was now; and that was anguish to me. Yet I never spoke of it to her. A mixture of foolish pride and genuine tenderness made me dumb. I could not confess how unbearably it hurt me to have my place in her heart taken by another – even though he was dead, and her brother, it made no difference at all; except the difference that I felt that I must not make it a grievance against her. Only once, I remember, when we were sitting together by the sea, and Katherine was crying, I burst into a fury of anger against her. Straightway, I was horrified by what I had done. That was like me, then – to regard as an unpardonable cruelty what was in fact the thwarted expression of a real upheaval of my soul.

For now, indeed, I knew what jealousy was, though I could not confess it either to myself or to Katherine. My condition was completely changed from what it was at the beginning of the year, when Katherine had left me. Then, I know not why, I had no real fear, and never dreamed that my place in her heart would ever be anyone's but mine. But now I was afraid, and more than afraid. The incredible and ghastly thing had happened; the barrier which I had believed could never be between us was there.

At least I imagined it was. But I was mistaken. No sooner had I reached England than I realized – what I never could realize – that Katherine was dependent on me. For in a day or two came letters bewailing that I had not written, though I had; and soon after, the news that she was ill. It was the sickening pattern which I was to come to know so well. A brave parting, a day or two when each retained something of the presence of the other, then the realization that there were veritably hundreds of miles between us, then –

Ah, but I wanted you to-day (she wrote). To-day I have longed for you. Have you known that? Can I long for you so and you not know? It's a terrible thing to wonder over. But I am so bound up in you that 'us' is become a kind of separate and loving being that I cannot bear to part with and cannot

374

understand why it should ever really leave me. Only pretend and then come back laughing into my arms – dearest – dearest.

Then the anguish of separation had begun, the terrible feeling that our love was now totally at the mercy of an alien world. What did it matter that I wrote religiously every day when suddenly I received an account of her illness that broke into this?

Oh, that postman is a tortoise, a detestable tortoise, half a tortoise – for I am hot and he is slow. (Bogey, I am an awful little cod. My bed is going to my brain. Now I'll wait for your letter till I go on.)

Later. I did wait with a vengeance. At half-past 3 I rang the bell. 'Le courrier – a-t-il déjà passé?' 'Ah, *oui*, Madame – une *bonne* demi-heure.' 'Merci bien!' But when she had gone I confess I turned to the wall and cried bitterly. . . .

Then, the next day, this:

To tell you the truth I feel exhausted now as though the sea which has been tossing me so rudely has thrown me on a flat rock. Of course, I do not want you to write if you do not 'feel' like it, but you are a strange being, Jack, and you have hurt me terribly. You were so sure I would be lonely in this quiet room. But once away I suppose you 'forgot'. However, I *don't mind now*.

And this, in the same letter:

I have opened my letter to say that now another day has come and again I have no news. I am sending the maid with a wire this morning, for I cannot but believe there is something terribly wrong. I do not deny that to-day I am *dreadfully anxious*.

Oh, Jack, I appeal even to your imagination as a novelist – do not leave me like this without news. It is so cruel – cruel. I weep bitterly as I write, but if you do not answer my wire I shall weep no more but face the fact that – no, I can't write it. Ever since Sunday my hope has been for letters and I've

375

not had one. Your silence makes me ashamed to so let you see my heart – and its need of you. I am still in bed.

First, I was stunned by the malignity of fortune which seemed to have engulfed my letters; then in a fever of anxiety I rushed to the French Consulate to have my passport *visé* again only to find on the next day a letter to say that a batch of my letters had arrived, and that she was feeling better now. This sickening alternation of anxiety and relief paralysed me.

My reappearance in London was mildly astonishing to Lawrence and Koteliansky who was (I wrote to Katherine) 'full of amazing theories as to why I had gone and why I had come back – but, as usual with theories, they didn't seem to have anything to do with what I was feeling'. But Koteliansky, as always, was paternal and kind. He thoroughly disapproved of my taking up my abode in a five-shilling attic in Devonshire Street, and insisted that I should get on with the business of finding a studio for Katherine and myself, for it had been agreed between us that so soon as she had 'broken the ice' with the writing she had in mind (which was eventually to be *Prelude*) she would return.

Goodyear, who had gone to the war, returned at this moment on leave. He slept the night on my attic floor, and went the next day with me to see the Lawrences. I had been to see them the day before. Lawrence reported, in a letter to Katherine, that I didn't look well, that I had told them of my dreadful experience in France, and was *very* chirpy. 'At the present I am not very much in sympathy with him, so I won't say any more about it.' I, on the other hand, reported to her:

I think that Lawrence was really and truly pleased to see me back again. I feel that he is very fond indeed of you and me – and that he feels that we are the only people who really care for him in the way he wants to be cared for. Our going away had depressed him very much; already – I have been to see him twice – I noticed that he is much more cheerful. Kot is also happier.

376

The contrast is piquant; but, having regard to the event, I don't think I was far wrong; neither, of course, was Lawrence when he declared, in the same letter, that 'Murry irritates and falsifies me; he makes *me* false'. It was another manifestation of the incessant conflict between my morbid emphasis upon the personal, and his equally morbid repudiation of it. In his desire to get beyond the personal, he misesteemed it in thought, though not in act; because I had at best only an intellectual conception of anything beyond it, I clung to it desperately.

From my cold attic-room I shifted, after a few days, to a furnished room in Worsley Road, Hampstead, where I paid 9s. a week and 7d. a day for my breakfast and listened to my landlady's story of her daughter's death, after five months' pregnancy, through an attempt at abortion.

> She fell down of an 'eap. She ses, I know I'm going to die, she ses. She 'ad a Roman figger – a real Roman – I suppose you know what that is, sir – round – she didn't look as though she 'ad 'ad one already – and if she 'ad only been a bit taller, she'd a bin a puffic figger . . . She was spoiled, that's wot *she* was. And when she got married – 'e was a first-class air-man, red and *silver* wings 'e wore on 'is sleeve – she didn't get all she used to 'ave. 'E was short with 'er. Give it over – all your dancin' and mucking about – and so she pined, fair pined. She never cared about 'ow the money was flyin' – she wasn't used to and 'e didn't like it. And there she was stuck down in the country in 'Oo, and goin' to 'ave another. You got to stop it, 'e ses, and that's 'ow it begun. . . .

The world seemed stranger than ever as I listened. Was anything to be made of it? Except the folly of my daring to put 800 miles of sea and land between myself and Katherine. But there it was. I was afraid of the South of France: I had been so naked there that the memory of it frightened me. And I had persuaded myself that Katherine hated it as much as I did, and that she really was as anxious as I to return to London

377

again, when her grief for her brother was past, and the work which was to purge her memory was begun. But in the depth of her depression she had written to Lawrence. She wrote to me about it.

> By the way, I wrote to Lawrence the other day a wild kind of letter, if I think of it, and not fair to 'us'. You understand? It was just after I had been in bed and without letters and I had a fit of positive despair, when life seemed to me to be absolutely over – and I wrote rather in that strain. I only tell you because when I have read your despairing letters to your friends, I have always felt that you betrayed us and our love a little, and I feel if you should see mine (don't, for it's nothing, and the mention is making it a mountain) you might feel a little the same. I am sorry I wrote it. To tell you the truth, I feel that our happiness rests with us and with nobody else at all, and that we ought to build for ourselves and by ourselves.

But that was afterwards. What happened was that at the very moment that I received her agonizing letters, Lawrence received his. When I went, distraught with anxiety, to the Lawrences' for a moment of peace, instead of comfort, a spate of denunciation was poured over me. I wrote to Katherine.

> I went to the Lawrences' for an hour. They had got your letter to-day. They did not show it me. I didn't ask to see it; I couldn't look at what you wrote to anybody else – and perhaps you told them not to show it. But Lawrence went for me, about you, terribly. Had I been alive, I should have been hurt; but I'm not alive to-day. I'm just numbed. He said that it was all my fault, that I was a coward, that I never offered you a new life, that I would not break with my past, that your illness was all due to your misery, and that I had made you miserable by always whining and never making a decision; that I should never have left you there. I do not know how much of it is true – perhaps all, perhaps nothing.

I can't really think about it, though I try. To me we seemed to be so happy together even when we parted. It breathed out of your first letters.

Do you just treat me as a child? Do you make your letters seem happy to deceive me? Do you just pretend to be happy in order to make me happy? And what has happened – is it that you were unhappy all the while and now do not care to conceal it any more?

Perhaps I am just blind. Lawrence says to me that your superficial happiness never deceived *him*. I don't know what to answer, except that he never knew you. . . .

I know that your brother's death was terrible, and that the pain tugs at your heart for ever; but I trusted that even then we should be yet greater lovers than we were. And now I think that was all my brutality, my insensibility.

My self-accusation went too far. The thing was elemental. Lawrence was far astray; yet he, who had suffered such agonies from Frieda's affection for her children, might have had a glimpse of what Katherine's engrossment in the memory of her brother meant to me. But I never spoke of it – I was hedged about with ultimate reticences of a kind that Lawrence never knew, and save for the faint mention of it in this letter I never hinted at it, even to Katherine herself. It seemed a kind of sacrilege. To be jealous of a dead brother – what a condition! So would the world say, and so did the little gentleman in me who had the world's values. To the best of my ability, I obeyed him and concealed my hurt. But it was there. Because I was ashamed of it, it did not the less exist. But what no one, perhaps not even myself, could have guessed was the practical effects of my isolation: how defenceless and refugeless I now felt myself to be; how totally unable to endure the contacts of a strange country, a new plunge into that 'business of life' which, at the best, was torture to me; how desperately I had fled to safety: with what excuses I had gulled myself. It never occurred to me that, beneath all her armour of

379

courage and waywardness, Katherine might have the same
desperate need of me, as I of her: and when she uttered it, I was
struck to the heart, as by a sudden revelation. That we should be
together was all that mattered – all.

Of all this, as was natural, Lawrence had only a glimpse.
As ever, his denunciation merely confused me. I had no grievance
against him for it, for I was aware that he was, at this time, almost
desperately attached to us. We represented something that was
precious to him; and even though I bewildered him as much as
he did me, beneath his exasperation I was conscious of a pleading
and hungry tenderness, as though he could not bear to let the
thing that was between Katherine and me escape from his life.
There was a tantalizing potentiality of self-sufficiency about us
which fascinated him, and gave him the desire to rivet us to
himself. He was trying hard to attract us to his plan of emigrating
to Florida. As I interpret it now, he was seeking in the idea of
community a satisfaction for an emptiness in his personal life,
just as I was seeking in the idea of personal relation a satisfaction
for an emptiness in my communal life. And just as he repudiated
the idea of personal relation, so did we the idea of community.

He has given up his flat, as from Wednesday next (I wrote
to Katherine on December 19th), then he is going to his home
for Christmas, and then – well, I have to go to J. D. Beresford
this afternoon and see if there is a cottage for him in Cornwall.
At all events, he is going somewhere into the country. But
he still talks ardently of Florida, having somehow gathered
together one hundred pounds: and he expects that I should
find as much again. But I have learned, I think, that Florida
is a state of mind, not a place – so I don't commit myself,
and wait till the crisis has passed. However, they are both
extremely nice to me, Lawrence of course in particular.

My refusal to commit myself, and a spice of wisdom in the
realization that underlay it, must have been trying to Lawrence.
I am not surprised that I irritated him. But what he meant by

380

saying that I 'made him false' I can only conjecture. Probably it was that, in spite of himself and his doctrine – 'I don't want a personal relation with him; he is a man, therefore our relation should be based on *purpose*: not upon that which we are, but that which we desire to bring to pass' – he found that I did involve him in a personal relation. That it was so is fairly plain, for in my letters to Katherine I was emphatic on the reality of his affection for us. On December 24th I wrote to her:

> Last night Lawrence left London for Ripley. He is going to stay there for Christmas, and then he is going to the Beresfords' house in Cornwall. Though he hurts and blunders sometimes, I am sure that he really loves us – and that he is the only one. Therefore we must guard him. I don't think he will ever understand us completely, but he can feel enough to take us on trust.

For me to have written that in my condition of sick hypersensitiveness is certain proof that Lawrence's affection towards me was very marked. Yet I can understand that with his doctrine he reacted against it, and judged it as falsity to himself. I do not think it was; but then I have my own opinion concerning the nature of Lawrence's real self.

Anyhow, when Lawrence left Hampstead and distributed the furnishings of No. 2 Byron Villas, he left for Katherine (I told her) and me 'his Endymion rug' – a beautiful sky-blue Persian rug – 'his clock, his fender, his kitchen-table and chairs and a camp-bed'. The rest was trivial, but the Endymion rug stood for something, for Lawrence had bought it, extravagantly (with a present of ten pounds made to him) because he loved it. And, indeed, from his point of view Lawrence might fairly say, as he did, that 'we kept far less faith with him than he did with us at the centre of things'. But he was not an easy person for us to keep faith with. His repudiation of the personal was really baffling. He made new friends, whom we distrusted profoundly and at sight, and then rebuked me for 'sneering at them', because I said that I did mistrust them. 'It doesn't matter what they are personally', he said. To us, to whom nothing else mattered, such a remark was sheer lunacy; and to me it is next door to lunacy still. Unless I trust a man, as a person, I cannot trust him at all. It is as vain to-day, as it was twenty years ago, to tell me that it is loyalty to the impersonal cause that matters. No doubt it does; but that is abstract and unreal. For whose loyalty to the impersonal cause shall I trust but his whom I trust as a person? I am of the old mind still, but more convincedly. What was then merely an instinct with me, has become a conviction of experience, in these later days when I have an impersonal cause to serve.

But in those days, there was no impersonal cause for Katherine or me. No doubt Lawrence had to choose: between others who professed loyalty to his impersonal cause, and us who felt loyalty to himself. And the bitterness was that he would not choose. He tried his disciples, whose persons did not matter, and found them wanting, and yearned for us. He wanted us as persons, called for us as persons, and when we responded as persons, he repudiated us as persons.

That is the substance of this complex relation at this critical time, as I disentangle it now. For no matter what he might say concerning his greater faith to us 'at the centre of things', Katherine and I made a great sacrifice when we returned from the South of France to live with him in Cornwall in the following spring: it was not – and Lawrence knew it was not – a sacrifice to his cause (which we neither understood nor believed in) but a sacrifice to him. If he did not want it, he ought not to have asked for it. But once it had been made, he should have kept faith with us who made it, in the same order as that in which we made it. If that was not 'at the centre of things' as Lawrence conceived it, it was the centre of *our* universe. The pound of flesh he asked for and we gave him came from very near our hearts. No doubt our hearts were no 'solar plexuses', but just ordinary traditional hearts; but for all that they deserved better treatment than he dealt them then.

CHAPTER XXVI

VILLA PAULINE

My final decision to return to France to Katherine – trivial though it may seem – was a real victory over myself, or at least a victory over myself of the only kind that I have ever won: the victory which consists in the strange discovery, after a period of hesitation and agony, that one's self does not exist. It will emerge again, infallibly, from the shadowy limbo of not-being; but for the moment, it does not exist. Such a moment had overtaken me now. After days of sick apprehension, I discovered suddenly that I did not exist, but that Katherine did. Nothing that might happen to me mattered, for there was nobody for it to happen to.

'Your awful loneliness has shaken me; I have lost the old confidence', I wrote to Katherine on December 22nd, when I had received telegrams from her to say that her illness was over. This confidence I realized that I had possessed only when it was gone. It was an absolutely naive faith that our love, by its own nature, was immune from all assault. Certainly, it seems an incredible faith to hold; but there is no doubt that I held it, and perhaps many young people hold it in some form or another. Perhaps my only peculiarity was that I had held it undiminished for three years. Nothing disturbed it. My wise friends might look meaningly at me, and darkly hint that, if I did not mend my ways, I would 'lose Katherine'; but I knew better. Nor in the sense in which they meant it, did I ever believe that I might 'lose Katherine': in that sense my faith was not naive, and it endured undimmed from the day we came together until the day we were parted for ever. It was not essentially shaken by the knowledge that she would leave me, or that I was momentarily shut out from her heart by the barrier of a brother's death. That was a horrible experience, but I knew it would end, even though I could not wait patiently for it to end, but ate out my heart like a soul on the banks of Styx, 'staying for waftage'. But this unshaken faith was mixed with a faith that was naive: because I believed that I could not lose her in this order, I had believed that I could not lose her in any other. Suddenly, I realized that in the material world our love was not secure. Anything might happen. The world of existence had no respect for love. It was not that I believed she might die – nothing so definite or unthinkable entered my mind – but that I had learned that the bond between us was vulnerable. The nature of things was, if not hostile, totally indifferent to its continuance. The further we were apart in physical space, the more vulnerable was the bond between us.

The childishness of some of the beliefs revealed in my letters at this time is astonishing. I was genuinely dumbfounded by the realization that at a moment when I was thinking of Katherine with tender and absorbed affection, she was quite unconscious of it. I reckoned out the times at which she had uttered her agony of loneliness, and found that sometimes at that very moment I had been pouring out my heart to her; and I felt a panic terror at what seemed to me the positive malignity of things, and a kind of stupor at the incomprehensibility of a world in which the motion of one loving heart is imperceptible to another. That a day, which seemed a lifetime, of pure suffering should hang on the delay of a letter for twenty-four hours; that one should write gaily and confidently, secure in the warm presence of the other, while the other was in the depths of barrenness and despair; that if one were, not rich, but less desperately poor, a great part of this insane suffering might be mitigated, by the speed which money can buy – over these things I brooded for hours, until it seemed to me that I must have been possessed by madness to allow this space, with all its potentiality of torments and treacheries, to come between us.

Your letters – just one word or one sentence of them – stab me. When you wrote in your Friday-Saturday letter about the villa at 88 francs, and I read, 'But no, I won't speak of

384

these things – for it's useless and foolish – I'll remember that England and the printing-press won the day and left me on the field' – that has haunted me all the day. Why did I leave you? I keep on asking myself the question, and I find no answer. I can remember nothing of what urged me back. It must have been strong and overwhelming – but it is all gone. There is no printing-press – that vanished like smoke. There is no England. There is only you, whom I left. Why, how, did it all seem so simple and natural then, and now it is like a nightmare that never ends?

Is it all too late? Could you not even now get a villa, and I could come. I should not go away again. England is simply a foolish word without you. You are everything – everything. Will you not get a villa – surely you could find one; I could find the money to come, and even if I could earn nothing, surely I might live on a tiny bit of your money?

The last words are significant. I was now suggesting what had to me for three years been the impossible thing. What Lawrence had urged me to do in the summer of 1913, and I had rejected with an indignation which had nearly killed our nascent friendship, I was myself proposing to do – timidly indeed, but clearly. The little gentleman was leaving me. The letter goes on:

For an hour, I've stopped – just thinking. Shall I borrow the money and come to you now? Shall I wait in the hope that you will come back? Shall I wait a little while until you have found a villa and then come? For I should have nothing at all and could not afford to stop in the hotel.

These three chase one another through my brain incessantly till I am dizzy with them. I don't exist any longer – I am only a torment of longing to be with you. And then – if I come – I am terrified that I should be a burden.

Your Sunday letter has just come, while I was writing. Another stab. 'I have a presentiment that I shall never see

385

Albion's shores again'. Oh, if it's only a jest, it nearly tears my heart out.

Darling, will you promise me this? That you will try to get a villa for us both immediately – that, if you can, you will telegraph to me: 'Come immediately. Ill.' (Then they will *visa* my passport immediately. I have arranged it with the nice man who took me last time.) I will borrow £10 – Lorenzo has £100 – and come, just as I am. I will be there in three days from the moment when you wire. I can't live away from you. I don't desire even to be alive. It is one incessant hunger. I implore you to do this, if you can. We could live in a villa for £3 a week, easy, couldn't we, darling?

The crucial decision was taken, and it had not been a decision. I knew better than ever how impossible it was for me to keep myself abroad by my writing; but now my immense and obstinate reluctance to be dependent on Katherine had given way. But that was only the outward symptom of deeper resistances that had given way. That independence, on which I set such store and which I stubbornly regarded as a virtue, had collapsed, because it was the defence behind which I shielded myself from the knowledge of my dependence on Katherine. That I had always refused to admit. But suddenly, she had spoken as she had never spoken before, called for me as she had never called before, flung herself to the winds in acknowledging that she was dependent on me. And at that, my last defences dissolved away. I knew that I was dependent on her, and I was free to acknowledge it.

This mutual self-surrender, from which I, and perhaps both of us, had fought away so long, had taken us both by surprise. So that Katherine could write: 'It is strange. I feel that I only really know you since you went back to England. I feel as though a miracle had happened to you, and you are rich and bathed in light. While I sit here writing to you, time is not. I am one with our love for ever.' And, veritably, a miracle had happened to me; but it had happened first to her.

I have loved you before for three years (she wrote) with my heart and my mind, but it seems to me I have never loved you *avec mon âme*, as I do now. I love you with all our future life – our life together which seems only now to have taken root and to be alive and growing up in the sun. I do not love you – but Love possesses me utterly: love for you and for our life and for all our richness and joy. I have never felt anything like it before. In fact I did not comprehend the possibility of such a thing. I seem to have only played on the fringe of love, and lived a kind of reflected life that was not really my own, but that came from my past. Now all that is cast away. Oh, my soul, if you come now we shall realize something that it seems to me never has been – such warmth and such richness and such virtue there is in you and me. Is it too late? You are *really* coming?

This morning I went to the little church and prayed. I prayed for us three – for you and me and my brother. It was so gay and yet solemn there.

Come quickly, quickly. My heart will break. Love presses on my forehead like a crown – my head is heavy, heavy. I must not think of you.

This Katherine I had never known. I had had glimpses of her in the old days at Runcton, when the world's great snare had begun to entangle us; but the effort of living, the struggle to keep afloat, had been too hard. Always between us there had been, in each, something that did not yield, something that claimed its freedom, and refused to say 'TOUJOURS'. A Katherine who gave herself away utterly, and bowed beneath the weight of her love, and let drop in a sort of childlike anguish all her armour, made my heart swell to breaking. Where now, in this, was the Katherine who claimed and granted 'freedom'?

Before I write any more I must tell you something. I hope you don't kiss anybody at Garsington. After all I have said, it does sound absurd. But I minded you kissing even Anne

387

'seriously'. I minded you *really* kissing. For this reason. If I
wished to I could not. There is no question of will or reason;
but I have to be physically faithful to you, because my body
wouldn't admit anyone else – ever to kiss *really* you know.
That was why I wrote so stiffly about your going to Garsington for Christmas. Is this jealousy? I suppose it is. But you're
mine – you're mine, and then we have not been lovers for
so long. I feel I could not bear anyone else to touch even the
threshold of your lips.

Or, in this, the Katherine who rebelled against domesticity?

Even if you never came, I cannot but love you more for
the evening and the night and the early morning I have spent
thinking that you *are* coming. It was Sunday, so I could not
send you a telegram until to-day. I somehow – oh, how did
I? – got through last evening, but sitting in the salon among
small fantastic people and sewing and talking. For I knew I
would not sleep. What drowsy bliss slept in my breast! A
woman here told me how to buy our stores, and how to make
soup with 2 sous' worth of bones, and what day the woman
with the good apples was at the market and how to manage
une femme de ménage. I heard. I dared not look at her. I felt
my smiles chasing in my eyes. I saw the villa – perhaps a
cactus near the gate – you writing at a little table, me arranging some flowers and then sitting down to write, too. Both of
us gathering pine cones and driftwood and *bruyère* for our
fire. I thought of what I would have ready for you, soup and
perhaps fish, coffee, toast (because *charbon de bois*, which is
much cheaper than coal, makes lovely toast, I hear), a pot of
confitures, a vase of roses . . .

But in this, I have represented my surrender as more instant
than it really was. The old Adam – though that is a name too
robust by far for his analogue in me – died terribly hard; and
though his struggles are complex and tedious to be told, to pass

over them in silence at this point would be to weaken the one claim this record has to attention – namely, its effort to extenuate nothing.

The day after I had written the letter in which I resigned my independence, I received a letter from Katherine reassuring me. What she had written to Lawrence was a cry of despair, not her own, a betrayal of 'us'. She was better. All was well between us.

> I have just got the letter you wrote me on Thursday night . . . I want to speak to you *très sérieusement*. Your letter made you 'real' to me in the deepest sense of the word, I believe, almost for the first time. You say just those things which I have felt. I am *of* you as you write, just as you are *of* me. Now I will say *Toujours*, because now at last I know you. We are in a world apart and we shall always be in a world apart, in our own kingdom which is finer and rarer. Shut the gates of it for a moment, and let us stand there. Let us kiss each other, we three. Yes, Bogey, I shall love you *for always*.

'We three . . .' I wonder whether I grasped the significance of it at that moment. I doubt it. My reaction to Katherine's letters was always childishly simple. Was it happy, or was it sad? And I was happy or sad, accordingly. But, now that I have time to be wise, the meaning of her letter comes clean across the years. I was received into the company of her dead brother and herself.

The words of mine which called forth this response from Katherine were these:

> For you and I are not of the world, darling; we belong to our own kingdom . . . I cannot speak save to you, and to you I have no need of words.
>
> Oh, my dearest, I must not write any more like this; I do not believe it will make you any happier, but rather sadder, for something in real love *is* sad – that knowledge of apartness, of an enemy world in which we dare not stay too long for the peril of our souls. And that is the sadness which has

hold of me to-night. It is not sadness at all, but the final triumph of our love. Darling, it is *toujours*. If you would not say the word now that I have opened all my heart, I feel that I should die.

It was true enough; it was what I felt and meant. But the assurance that Katherine understood, and felt and meant the same was enough for me. In a sense what I have said before, that I was 'in love with love', was true of me still; it always would be. But subtly I made this an excuse for the inertia that came of my overwhelming fear. If all that mattered was the reality of the love that was between us, and one was sure of that once more, why should we not stay as we were? Why should I go south again? I had offered to go, in a fit of desperation. Now, in the letter which assured me there was no cause for despair, Katherine had written: 'At the end of your letter you ask me how long I am going to stay. I do not know at all. You'd better tell me what you think.' In the letter which had comforted her completely, there had been no talk of my returning; I had promised that only afterwards, in the desperation caused by her despair. I was going because I would rather go than lose her; positive desire to go I had none, far less than none; I shrank from it. Since all was now well, why go? And so I wrote:

What a heavenly letter you sent me . . . Do you think I am mad? In two minutes – all that load which has been pressing on me for days and days – is utterly lifted. I am back again in the old confidence. I wrote you all my secret heart, and you knew. Now I feel I can work, do anything, wait till you return . . . I want you back, terribly, of course; but even if you stay, I know you are mine and I am yours. I should be always preparing my heart for you. You see, I never knew how much I loved you before – I never realized all the things which stood between us, all of my own making. I never knew that my life from minute to minute utterly depends on you . . .

Forget all my latest letters – even that of yesterday in which I said, 'Find a villa'. It was mainly cowardice. I was frightened that you were loving me less while I was not with you. I could not bear it . . . If you want me, I will come *immediately*.

A subtle letter; subtle because so completely sincere. Not a word in it was not absolutely true. And, naturally, instinctively, I had used the new confidence between us to let it appear that I had no positive desire to go; I had used the very freedom of my declaration of total dependence upon her to retain my practical independence. Rather than lose her, I would surrender that; but short of that desperate extremity I wanted to keep it. On that level it holds water. There was nothing wrong. But mixed with my independence was a fear: I was afraid of breaking completely away from my small security. I wanted the security of love, and I wanted the security of myself; I wanted to be safe in both worlds.

Fortunately, it was not allowed me. Katherine had taken my desire to be with her at its face-value. She did not want to return to England, where she always felt herself a stranger – 'a little Colonial' – she wanted to be happy in the sunshine which she loved. Since I was ready to return, she was free to realize her dream of a little house for us both under a sky which smiled on her. Straightway, she had sent the telegram arranged between us, 'Come immediately. Ill.' Now my letter had dashed her hopes again. It was all very well for me to have said, 'If you want me, I will come *immediately*.' That was putting on her the onus of dragging me to her. In that sense she did not want me: her isolation and anguish were over. What she wanted was her vision of 'us', happy, careless, rich, living one life together; and she wanted me also to obey that vision. If it was enough for me to live with the 'idea' of the love between us – and such was I that it nearly was enough – something was lacking. Therefore she telegraphed again: 'Letters received, implore don't come, don't want, understand perfectly.'

Then at last I had no hesitation any more. I had learned my lesson, and I had her joyous letters of anticipation before me; I knew that what I had written had been the chill wind on the opening rose, and that her disappointment was not to be borne.

> I came back from Garsington to-day (I wrote from Hampstead). There this morning I had both your telegrams saying that I should come. When I arrived here, another came, imploring me not to. That one finished me. It seemed suddenly so childish – no, not childish, but criminal – to stay away from you a day longer. Whatever happens, I must be with you . . .

I was with her before the letter. We laughed over it together.

It was not surprising, since this was passing within us and between us, that Lawrence's response to her despairing letter to him gave her no sustenance. Quite naturally, he was trying to use her moment of disenchantment to enlist her on the side of his new impersonal relation. She now, he believed or wanted to believe, had shared his experience; she also had 'gone down into death and been extinguished', whereas I ran away from mine. It was true of me – how true, I have tried to convey; but not in the sense that Lawrence meant it. And the 'dying in the self' which Katherine had experienced was a dying into, not away from personal love; it had not brought her one step nearer to the condition in which 'oneness in spirit was all, and what we are personally is of second importance'. On the contrary, what we were personally mattered more acutely than ever. 'I heard from Lawrence to-day', she wrote. 'Shall I send you his letter? It left me cold. He wants us to join him, but you know we are not made to do that kind of thing ever. We are two, rich and happy apart.'

It was hard: this problem of the relation between the Lawrences and ourselves. 'There remain only you and Murry in our lives', he had written. And we, I think, would have said the same of the Lawrences. Yet there was an insuperable difference between us. Our conceptions, our experiences, our ideals of love simply denied each other. Each was, no doubt, merely partial. But the strange thing was that as the Lawrences excluded ours, so we excluded theirs. Lawrence's conscious attitude was based on a denial that we existed; ours on a denial that they existed. Unity in spirit between us was a dream. But, unfortunately, at this time Lawrence's need of us was greater than our need of him.

Katherine and I now entered on a period of simple happiness together, when every day was pure delight. The victory over our selves that had been won passed naturally into all our doings. I who was wont to explore myself with such sick and sensitive fingers, forgot myself entirely. There was Katherine, there was the book I was writing: both engrossed me. And there was no need to turn away from her to concentrate. We sat on each side of a tiny table, interrupting one another continually; and yet I seemed to think with more strength and precision than ever before in my life. I did not have to cling to my thoughts to hold them; I could let them go, in the certainty that they would return. It was not that writing came easy to me: it never did nor would; but all the desperation and strain had gone from the effort. I could work on confidently, knowing that at some point or other, I should have a glimpse, and the way lie plain before me. And on her side of the table Katherine was writing the first draft of *Prelude* – wherein, for the first time, her inimitable magic passed wholly into her work.

The Villa Pauline – it was to be a memory of beatitude between us for ever, of a time when we were 'in some perfectly blissful way, at peace'. The beatitude would have ended; it could not have lasted. We could not go on triumphing over a world-war, as we were triumphing then. And perhaps it was as well that it ended as it did, by our deliberate surrender of it. To have felt that it was being slowly drained away, would have been far more bitter. Even though, in the dark days in Cornwall, we grievously repented our return, and believed that, had we chosen, we might still have been the children of the sun, it could not have endured. Two months, four months, a year perhaps; but the moment would

393

have come when Bandol began to change from the city of sunlight to the city of despair to which Katherine returned two years later.

Life at the Villa Pauline was good, it was perfect: the best we were ever to know, and better two human beings never could know. But perhaps it was what it was because we sacrificed it; and that is the reason why I find no answer to the strange question I have put to myself many times in the past, and now find myself putting again: whether it is indeed in the nature of things that such a condition between a man and a woman cannot endure. That it could not have endured then and there is plain. The surge of the War was bound to break our island down. But take the war away! whispers my heart; set it in the years to come when, as I must needs believe, there will not be war any more, and the long travail of the world will be over, and men shall have learned to live in the reality of brotherhood. Will such beatitudes happen then and endure? Or will they fall beneath the sentence of Keats, who pondered these things? 'I can imagine such happiness carried to an extreme: but what will it end in – Death.'

That I do not know nor any man; but after twenty years, my heart is older and wiser, and it answers quietly: 'Take the War away? But think! Was it not perhaps the War that made you what you were, even then? Was it not the War that struck Katherine in her brother, and parted you? Was it not the War that made you conscious of the vast hostility of things to the love which was between you? Was it not the War which caused you to cling together so desperately and make your other kingdom a reality?'

I think it was, and I think it was good that we surrendered as we did, at the claim of friendship. Perhaps we deceived ourselves, and merely forestalled the end of which we had a premonition. In March came the news, or what little of it the French censor let through, of the great German attack on Verdun. We mused over the white spaces in *Le Radical*, and wondered which was real – that world or ours.

Meanwhile Lawrence had won back all our affection by his generosity: he seemed to take a simple and unfeigned delight in our happiness. 'I am very glad you are happy', he wrote. 'That is the right way to be happy – a nucleus of love between a man and a woman, and let the world look after itself. One should be in love, and be happy – no more. Except that if there are friends who will help the happiness on, *tant mieux*. Let us be happy together.' But there was the rub. This happiness together – was it possible? And did we really desire it? It seemed to us absolutely sufficient that we two should be happy alone. With all sincerity we wished that the Lawrences might enjoy the like. But what was the need that we should live together? Katherine was definitely opposed.

Yet the appeal of Lawrence could not be ignored. 'Let us make some plans for March – let us live somewhere together', he urged. 'You make the plans this time – for us. I am done.' We wanted to respond, and we would have responded immediately; but in the same breath he told us, 'Heseltine is here – I like him – you will like him', and we knew instantly that we shouldn't. We had some painful experiences, only a little while before, with some of Lawrence's new 'disciples'. If living together meant living in peace and amity with people whom we instinctively disliked, as we had good reason to fear it did, it was impossible. So we temporized, saying only that we might come back in March and live *near*.

But Lawrence wanted us to live together. He returned to the charge a month later. 'I have been thinking with much affection and some longing of you two lately. I feel you are my only real friends in the world. I have really been badly seedy this time . . . One feels the slithery edge of oblivion under one's feet . . . Shall we all live together?' And 'all' still included the stranger Heseltine. Katherine thought that utterly exorbitant; and I was piqued that the scheme of publishing our books for ourselves, which I had broached to Lawrence on my return to England, and in which Koteliansky alone was included, had been given over to Heseltine without a word to me. 'Heseltine also talks of a publishing scheme; he would combine with you.' So once more we were non-committal.

With Lawrence's answering letter, which showed he was hurt by our reluctance to bind ourselves, came the bewildering notes on Dostoevsky, of which I have already spoken. In our publishing venture, he said, we were to go the whole hog, and the whole hog seemed to consist in *The Rainbow*, only more so; and a foretaste of the 'more so' was these strange views on Dostoevsky. It was a forbidding prospect of collaboration. In the world of ideas we could not understand him, in the world of persons he could not understand us, or he would never have tried to thrust this stranger among us. Lawrence reassured us: 'Don't think his friendship hurts ours. It doesn't touch it.' But that was not the point. It was a difference of personal sensibilities. We would never have dreamed of imposing even one of our old friends upon Lawrence. And though we might admit some truth in his claim that 'he had waited for us two years now, and was far more constant to us than ever we were to him', the fact was that he hadn't waited. He couldn't wait; it was contrary to his nature. He had changed and grown, and grown along a certain way where it was for ever hard to follow him. Katherine and I were now the two people he had wanted and needed in Italy more than two years before. If he could have written to me now the letter he wrote in the autumn of 1913, I could have responded to it. What he was trying to tell me then I had learned.

But now we were required to be 'co-believers' in something to which personal love was secondary and subservient. At the same time that we could not understand what it was we were required to believe in, we had the feeling that Lawrence didn't quite believe in it either. We were conscious of some contradiction between his insistence on the death of the personal and his insistence that we should join him. The happy community of Rananim had been a daydream – we knew that as well as he – but there was something sombre and sinister and sacrificial about his new idea of community into which we could not enter. It was to be one with 'the black rocks and the torn sea' of the Cornish coast in winter, in which he was finding comfort for his soul, where 'all was forsaken, not linked up'. Just as that coast gave its stark endorsement to his sense of personal annihilation, so the sunny Mediterranean shore, warm with centuries of human civilization, was in harmony with our sense of personal fulfilment.

That was blissful and overflowing. Katherine went away for two days in March to meet her sister at Marseilles. 'Oh, Bogey', she wrote from the room where we had been so wretched. 'How *can* you be such a darling? I shall sit here and write all the afternoon. I feel so "settled". It is because of our love. I feel so rich and my heart is quiet. Do you know that feeling?' And again, 'Life isn't half long enough to love all the different things about you in. I shall die in the middle of a little laugh at some new funny thing that I adore you for. Now I must go out and stop writing love-letters. Perhaps I didn't quite know until I came away what these months have brought, or how they have changed everything'. That was the feeling: that our life at the Villa Pauline had changed everything. Two new persons had been born, to whom every detail of life and of each other was lovely and full of meaning. Childish it may have been; but it was real, and for me the outward world was richer in those days than it ever had been or would be again. A thousand vivid memories crowd upon me, and one seems dear above the rest: the pink almond petals stuck all over the window one morning when, after a stormy night, I came down to light the fire. The storm must have happened on the night when we set ourselves for the theme of our nightly verses, 'Camomile Tea'. My version is lost; but Katherine's remains.

> Outside the sky is light with stars;
> There's a hollow roaring from the sea,
> And, alas for the little almond-flowers,
> The wind is shaking the almond tree,

How little I thought, a year ago,
In that horrible cottage upon the Lee,
That he and I should be sitting so
And sipping a cup of camomile tea.

Light as feathers the witches fly,
The horn of the moon is plain to see;
By a fire-fly under a jonquil flower
A goblin toasts a bumble-bee.

We might be fifty, we might be five,
So snug, so compact, so wise are we!
Under the kitchen table-leg
My knee is pressing against his knee.

Our shutters are shut, the fire is low,
The tap is dripping peacefully;
The saucepan shadows on the wall
Are black and round and plain to see.

In the daytime we worked in the little salon which looked over the serried rows of Monsieur Allègre's kitchen-garden on to the sea; but in the chill of the evening we retired to the warmth of the kitchen where our small cooking-fire was sinking to embers. There the table was infinitesimal.

We lived with extreme frugality, for I don't suppose I earned £10 during the whole of the time. I was writing the book on Dostoevsky to pay off a debt, so that there was nothing to hope for from that. Dates and honey were our only extravagance. But since my clothes were in a bad way, I managed to buy a remarkable corduroy suit in Toulon for nineteen shillings. It was a beautiful dark brown, almost black, and in combination with an impressive pair of side-whiskers and a big felt hat, which Campbell had given me long ago, it earned for me the name in the town of 'l'Espagnol'. That corduroy suit still flourishes. I wore it for more than ten years; and then passed it on to my brother. I saw him wearing the coat only the other day and it looked good for another twenty years. But its initial stink was proportionately enduring.

A more immediate consequence of our frugality – for we must have been living on less than a pound a week together for food – was the ravenous hunger which would possess us at about eleven o'clock in the morning. We rose every morning at six, and had finished our marketing by eight. At half-past we would settle down to writing. Before eleven we would be conscious of our stomachs. Katherine would begin to groan, then slip into the kitchen for two slices of bread. That only seemed to make things worse. But it was a law that we must not begin to cook our lunch till midday. The extremities we endured during that hour were farcical. Katherine would murmur, 'Beefsteak *and* fried potatoes!' cast up her eyes in despair, and struggle on. The original manuscript of *Prelude* is interlarded with such evocations. 'I'm so hungry, simply empty', she wrote at one such moment, 'and seeing in my mind's eye just now a sirloin of beef, well-browned, with plenty of gravy *and* horse-radish sauce and baked potatoes, I nearly sobbed.' But one morning I was so engrossed in what I was writing that when she raised the joyful cry 'Midi sonné!' I realized with astonishment that I had had no hunger-pangs that morning. When lunch was ready – we were always too tense to talk much while it was preparing – I began to plume myself on my superior powers of concentration. Katherine listened and agreed, very seriously. 'You didn't even notice when I put the clock on a whole hour.'

Strangest of all to me, however, was the ease with which I made friends with the shopkeepers there. That was quite unprecedented in my life, though normal enough in other people's. The chemist on the quay, who began by being a little distant towards me, seemed to change his opinion after one day when, for the appropriate reason, I went to him for castor oil. I asked him for 'huile de castor'. He stared at me, and said in a loud voice:

'Qu'est-ce que vous dîtes là, Monsieur?'

'De l'huile de castor.'

'De l'huile de cas-TORR!' he echoed and amplified in slow, reverberant words. 'Je n'ai jamais entendu parler de cette huile-là. Je ne sais même pas si ça ex-*iste*.' And castor-oil seemed instantly to vanish from the pharmacopoeia – from the universe.

I was nonplussed. We looked at each other, and I caught the authentic meridional twinkle in his eye. Suddenly, in tones absolutely stentorian, he cried: 'C'est pour vous *purr-ger*?' It rang along the quayside; the idlers at the café put down *Le Radical*; the passers-by stopped dead; the two or three cronies in the shop laughed outright: and after a second of consternation, inevitable in one not prepared to have the fact of his constipation proclaimed by the town-crier, I laughed also.

'Et pourquoi ne m'avez-vous dit cela, d'abord? De l'huile de cas-TORR! C'est l'huile de *ric-in* dont vous avez besoin. Émile! Apportez-moi un flacon de l'huile de ricin pour Monsieur!'

On another day I was walking, preoccupied, on a path about a mile from the town. Suddenly, I was called to myself by a ringing 'Salut!' I saw in front of me a portly man with a wheelbarrow full of dung, and a capacious smile. 'Salut!' I murmured, as I walked on. But no! Down went the legs of his barrow, blocking my way. The fat man stared me full in the eyes, and while he hitched his patchwork trousers, delivered himself of this staggering question:

'Et qu'est-ce que vous pensez de la Ré-pub-lique?'

My astonishment was palpable. I could *feel* my eyebrows arch with amazement. Then I saw the laughter in his eyes.

'Evidém-maing, vous n'y pensez pas du tout. C'est pour rien, pour vous, la Ré-pub-lique. Vous êtes heureux. Salut!' And he lifted his wheelbarrow and passed on.

'Happy? I was happy *once*,' wrote Robert Louis Stevenson. 'That was in Hyères.' I could almost write the same, with the small and insignificant change of Hyères into Bandol, for the places are not far apart, and the people are the same. The War had not yet entered into their souls.

And Lawrence was writing: 'As far as I possibly can, I will stand outside this time, I will live my life, and, if possible, be happy though the whole world slides in horror down into the bottomless pit . . . As far as I can, I will save myself, for I believe that the highest virtue is to be happy, living in the greatest truth, not submitting to the falsehood of these personal times.' These pursy times, said Shakespeare; these personal times, said Lawrence. There was the difference. And we, whose happiness was at the zenith, and as personal a thing as it was possible to conceive, could not but wonder why our presence should be necessary.

Then suddenly, early in March, Lawrence discovered two cottages at Higher Tregerthen, as he truly said, 'like a little monastery'. In a twinkling he had taken the cottage on the road. 'Really you must have the other place. I keep looking at it. I call it Katherine's house, Katherine's tower'. It was impossible, even for Katherine, to resist his urgency; but she never concealed the misgiving in her heart. My resistance had vanished, and had it not been for the requirement that I should like Heseltine, I should have been without a qualm. For now that the prospect had been held before me, the nostalgia for England had vaguely re-awakened. Katherine never felt this. Her country was New Zealand, and more than ever was it her country at this moment, when she had overcome her old resentment against it and taken it, by imagination, to her heart anew. Still more ominous, she cherished something of an old dislike of Cornwall. In August, 1914, when we were walking from Truro to St. Just, she had seen some women pitilessly harrying a cat, and she had decided that Cornish women were cruel; they were the 'countrywomen' of her sardonic verses:

> And such eyes!
> Stupid, shifty, small and sly
> Peeping through a slit of sty.

It is good to think that her prejudice was later charmed away by the loving simplicity of old Mrs. Honey at Looe. But that was two years after. And above all, Katherine distrusted the very idea of a community.

CHAPTER XXVII

HIGHER TREGERTHEN

It was no wonder that I was commanded by Lawrence to tell Katherine '*not* to be so queasy'. But the prospect of parting from Bandol and the Villa Pauline made her wretched. When the little iron gate finally clashed behind us and we called at the Allègres' to leave the key and say 'Good-bye', she was in tears. On the journey down to Cornwall, she grew more and more depressed. The blue sky seemed to her steely, and the sea grey; the cry of the gulls bleak and forlorn. What was spring to the Lawrences was no spring to her; and it was an obvious effort to her to conceal her disenchantment. But in the room at the Tinners' Arms, where we were to stay while we made ready the Long House, she confessed: 'I shall *never* like this place.'

It was a bad beginning; and I was not the person to make a recovery. If I had had any confidence about the whole affair, I might have withstood her depression, for I vastly enjoyed 'messing about' with Lawrence. And at first there was plenty to be done, in painting and furnishing the Long House on the money we had. But things were cheap at Benny's sale-room in St. Ives, and with Lawrence at hand to restrain me from any flightiness and to suppress firmly any aesthetic misgivings I might have about Victorian furniture that was solid and cheap and useful, I did pretty well. And it was good fun to hitch on my rucksack while Lawrence hitched on his – more substantial altogether: an authentic German affair – and march with him over the hill and down into St. Ives. As a companion, Lawrence was a nonpareil. His off-hand, half-schoolmastery way of imparting his amazing range of country lore suited me perfectly; for I made no pretensions in that kind. But it wasn't what the man said, so much as the warm and irresistible intimacy with which he surrounded one, an atmosphere established as it were by a kindly gardener who had, very precisely, decided that you were to grow, and who, by that act, awakened in you the feeling that there was something in you which could grow.

That was good, for me at any rate; but it quickly passed. The solid ground beneath my feet was slipping away again. With Katherine miserable I was half a man, wretchedly aware that she was only pretending to enter into our common concerns. The sensation that she was merely acting her part was sickening, and I was now far more sensitive than I had been before to her essential absence. Six months before it had taken nothing less than her complete self-withdrawal, at her brother's death, to arouse me to the real situation between us; but now that I had known what it was to live as one being with her, I was instantly aware of its cessation. Whereas six months before I was aware only when the situation was extreme and desperate, and had fled to the security of England and Lawrence, now I instinctively withdrew along with her, conscious all the while that I was disappointing Lawrence's expectation. For though, no more than before, did I understand his idea of community, I did understand something of his need of friendship. I knew how glad he had been that we had come, and I knew that I was glad to be with him again. I did not want to withdraw from him; but still less could I withdraw from Katherine. Within three weeks of our entering into the Long House, she was writing to Koteliansky, to whom she always turned at such a moment:

> I have not written before because everything has been so 'unsettled' . . . I am very much alone here. It is not really a nice place. It is so full of huge stones, but now that I am writing I do not care, for the time. It is so very temporary. It may all be over next month; in fact, it will be. I don't belong to anybody here. In fact, I have no being, but I am making preparations for changing everything.

I don't suppose she showed me that letter; but I well remem-

ber the effect on me of the condition in which she wrote it, and
which I now knew so well: that condition of complete apartness,
when she would sit in her room, smoking cigarettes, meditating
one of her 'cynical' stories: probably that 'EXTRAORDINARILY good
story about Marseilles', of which she wrote to Beatrice Campbell
at this moment. She added, 'I've re-read my novel to-day,
too, and now I can't believe I wrote it'. That novel was the
first draft of *Prelude*, and now to Katherine it seemed to have
come from another being, as indeed it had. Now she disowned it.
The contradiction or alternation in her being, which she was so
clearly to acknowledge two years after, was manifest.

> I've two 'kick-offs' in the writing game (she wrote in
> February, 1918). One is joy, real joy, the thing that made me
> write when we were at Pauline, and that sort of writing I could
> only do in just that state of being, in some perfectly blissful
> way at peace . . . The other is my old original one, and, had
> I not known love, it would have been my all. Not hate or
> destruction (both are beneath contempt as real motives), but
> an extremely deep sense of hopelessness, of everything doomed
> to destruction, almost wilfully, stupidly, like the almond-tree
> and 'pas de nougat pour le noël'.

In a less acute form the sense of hopelessness had begun to
invade her now, and I who used to be insensitive to it even in
mid-career, now felt it from the beginning of the onset. When
the chairs I had bought at Benny's came up to Tregerthen, I
spent a morning in the sunshine painting them a dull, funereal
black. I did not do it deliberately, but just as Lawrence had
expressed his feeling of spring in painting his dresser royal blue,
and his walls pink, so I expressed my sense of winter. Lawrence
and Frieda, when they emerged from their cottage to view my
handiwork, were comically dismayed; but Katherine knew what
I had been about.

The old, sickening feeling of rootlessness began to take hold
of me again, and with it the old agony of self-consciousness.

405

Among my few papers of this period is a queer effusion which reflects my condition.

I am tired with the effort to suck life from the words of another man, to kindle with my own breath the dead embers of his thought. They will not live, they will not flame, to me they are dead.

Is it I who am dead, or they?
Is it I who ask that question and of whom do I make
    demand?
I of myself demand: 'Is it I who am dead, or they?'
    'Like a bit of cold pasty.'
Am I dead?
How shall I know that I live?
'As I live, and as my soul liveth,' said the Lord.
'As I die, and as my soul dieth,' say I.
No voice sounds;
No power holds my hand;
No conscience writhes for blasphemy;
I am dead.
    'How abominably this book has been cut!'
If I were dead,
I should be still,
My cords unfretted by the idle rasping bow
Of such vain, self-important questionings.
I should be laid quite still,
And the melancholy twist of my mouth would grow strong
    and severe.
Some one would say:
'Surely, he suffered.'
    But I am that some one who says:
'What a miserable dog!
'He did not even know whether he suffered,
'Whether he was alive or dead.'

But the wise men say:
Not to know
Is the deepest pain of all.
They are wise, and I
Do not know whether I am foolish or wise.
I, the wise-foolish, the living-dead,
Utter my word:
'Not to know
'Is not to be.
'Not to be
'Is not to feel.
'And how shall not to feel
 Be such intolerable pain?'
Am I in torment now?

I look at my half-inch of cigarette; I smoke it only because
not to smoke it would leave a little nudging emptiness. There was
another little nudging void, I fancy, and I wrote these lines to
fill it.
I wrote them deliberately.

'*Is this the jug you want?*'
I held her in my arms
And we were one, and I
A love.
Was it from her I drew a moment's breath taken with joy?
Caught from her a moment's fire?
Even though she was tired,
Weary,
Yet had she enough to give?
Or does a glow remain
Within the ashes
Of me
Who am dead?

Dead.
If I were dead, it would be terribly simple –
Simple and terrible.
But I am not.
I am dead to the me-ness of me.
In her I am, and then
Not-I.
That which I am not is now become essential me.
How surely I breathe,
The breath being mine no more!
How firmly I stand,
When I lean upon her, and she
Curls and lifts up her body like a bird to my arms!
Calmly, ineffable
Being, in a warm soft flood
Rises up from the secret springs,
Descends from I know not where,
And I, not-I
Am a conquest, a triumph, a voice in the night, an assurance
    of victory,
Of life over death.

Ah, my philosopher,
My mouse-haired, intolerant prophet,
What do you know? Shall your knowledge outweigh my
    ignorance? Shall you tell me how
I may love, that this certainty
Shall never lie dead, like an ugly root,
Forgotten?

There was the sickness. My certainty was real and present
only in the self-obliteration of the love between Katherine and me.
Let that be taken from me and I relapsed into a deathly self-
consciousness. I must turn where I knew my life was. If I turned
towards Lawrence, then Katherine's feeling of 'belonging to no
one' engulfed her completely, and I was outcast and had no

strength at all. And Lawrence would not see or acknowledge that this was so. His relation with Frieda left room, and perhaps need, for a relation with a man of something of the kind and quality of my relation with Katherine; and he wanted this relation with me. It was possible only if it left my relation with Katherine intact, and indeed were based on that relation: for I was I only in that relation; or at any rate, only in that relation was I a man who had anything to give to Lawrence. My relation with Katherine was not of the same order as his relation to Frieda. It is no question whether it was better or worse; it simply was different. When it was whole, I had no need of Lawrence. I could love him tenderly and affectionately, as I believe I did, but I did not depend on him. If ever I did depend on him, it was because the relation between Katherine and me was not whole.

So at this critical moment, I began to withdraw towards Katherine. And as he felt my withdrawal, Lawrence became more urgent to bind me to him. He talked of the blood-brotherhood between us, and hinted at the need of some inviolable sacrament between us – some pre-Christian blood-rite in keeping with the primeval rocks about us. Timidly, I withdrew only the more. And his exasperation increased. The clashes between him and Frieda became more frequent, and to me more desperate and frightening. One evening, when Katherine and I were sitting by our fire – in the long room where Lawrence had dreamed that the community would eat together – we heard a shriek. Suddenly, Frieda burst in at the door crying, 'He'll kill me!' Lawrence followed, white as a ghost, but in a frenzy of fury. Round and round the long table they went, Lawrence crying, 'I'll *kill* her, I'll *kill* her!' The chairs were scattered; I just managed to save the lamp. Katherine sat still in a corner, indifferent, inexpressibly weary. I was terrified. That he would have killed her, I made no doubt; and yet, for some strange reason, I had no impulse to intervene. Things had reached such an extremity that it was no use to intervene. Life was mad, let it rip! It was all beyond me, anyhow.

Quite suddenly, Lawrence collapsed into a chair by the fire. The frenzy had left him, bleached, blanched and inert. And there was a great silence, which no one dared to break. At last Frieda went back to the cottage. The three of us sat on, without stirring – each, in our different ways, utterly exhausted. Then Lawrence rose, pale and unsteady, and said 'Good night'. It was over.

I will not pretend that I now find that outburst as incomprehensible and frightening in itself as I did then. I have lived to learn that there is a truly fearful power of exasperation in a woman, and even to understand that the consequent explosion in a man of a frenzy which seems, and may actually be, murderous, is an elemental happening, really quite outside the scope of a moral judgment, or any judgment at all. Not that we passed any moral judgment on the Lawrences. The thing was too obviously outside the range of our experience: we were astonished and scared at the thing itself. But a tinge of superiority certainly did enter into our bewilderment the next day, when, after nervously approaching the Lawrences' cottage, apprehensive of we knew not what, we discovered them sitting side by side, to all appearance blissfully happy, while Lawrence trimmed a hat for Frieda. That was a relief, indeed, but it was a shocking relief. I was very far from understanding, as I now dimly do, that the murderous frenzy is, in the pre-mental realm to which these happenings belong, a kind of electrical discharge that establishes a completer contact than before. When Lawrence talked, as he afterwards did, of 'the sympathy of pure hatred', he was not talking nonsense, as I so long believed. But such 'sympathy' is pre-mental; and to ordinary experience 'pre-mental sympathy' is a contradiction in terms. Whether, as Lawrence came to hold, it is necessary that our mental consciousness should acknowledge these things, instead of trying to outlaw and ignore them, I do not know. That they do veritably exist is certain; it is equally certain that nothing of the kind existed between Katherine and myself. We were merely the astonished and uneasy witnesses of a phenomenon to which we had no clue.

That was only the worst of many outbreaks, and I did not see it originate. But those which I witnessed from start to finish almost always had their origin in some apparently trivial occurrence. Frieda would contradict one of Lawrence's more dogmatic pronouncements; there would be a few quick ripostes; the atmosphere would become electric, and Bang! the explosion came. Only one recurrent pattern do I remember: which was when Frieda would take it on herself to defend one of Lawrence's discarded prophets – Shelley, for example, or Nietzsche – against his sudden sentence. Frieda's remonstrance would sound sweetly reasonable. No sedate, circumspect and catholic professor of literature could have recalled Lawrence more gently to a sense of the *juste milieu*; but somehow one wasn't taken in. After one had recovered from the initial shock of surprise at Lawrence's vehemence – 'That's *false*! What do you know about Shelley? What do *you* care? If you *dare* to say another word about Shelley, I'll . . .' one felt that there was some right on his side, and that Frieda was not altogether ignorant that she would lash Lawrence into a frenzy by this bland pretence of sympathy with his past heroes, whom she, more than anybody, had taught him to discard.

During this time Lawrence began to write the novel *Women in Love*. The theme, or at least the germ of it, was the relation and the situation between the four of us. Yet I have to confess that, such was my unawareness, that even four years later when it was published, and I read it thoroughly and wrote a full and hostile review of it, I did not recognize this. I was really astonished when, one day, Frieda told me that I was Gerald Crich. Anyhow, that was a rough way of putting it; I was not Gerald Crich, but it probably is true that Lawrence found the germ of Gerald in me, as he found the germ of Gudrun in Katherine. Those two characters are, so to speak, our counterparts in the pre-mental realm of which we had no cognizance and in which Lawrence's imagination liked to dwell. It is scarcely to be wondered at that we did not recognize ourselves.

Nevertheless, just as a few of the incidents of Gudrun's life were taken without any sea-change from Katherine's, so were a few of the episodes between Rupert and Gerald taken from conversations between Lawrence and me.

You've got (says Rupert to Gerald) to take down the love-and-marriage ideal from its pedestal. We want something broader. I believe in the *additional* perfect relationship between man and man – additional to marriage.

That is more or less what Lawrence said to me, and no doubt the queer wrestling-match between the two is more or less what he meant by the 'blood-sacrament' between us at which he hinted. But I, being a little scared and more than a little naive, envisaged it rather as some sort of ceremony of black magic to be performed amid the great stones of the eerie Cornish moors. What I was certain of was that Lawrence had subtly changed, and was subtly changing while I was there. He was not at all the same man who had written to us at Bandol, rejoicing in our happiness, that 'one should be in love and happy – no more . . . Let us be happy together.' Granted that it was inordinately difficult under the circumstances for us to be happy together, it was plain that Lawrence was now to be satisfied with no such thing. What he really wanted of me he never put into words, and to this day I am doubtful whether he ever knew. But what he imagined he wanted is stated clearly enough in the novel. There Gerald puts away Rupert's offer of union between the two men, and chooses marriage with Gudrun instead. This marriage of Gerald and Gudrun comes to disaster because it is wholly 'under the dominion of Aphrodite the deadly', that is to say, even the physical bond between them is conscious and mental.

The other way (which Gerald refused) was to accept Rupert's offer of alliance, to enter into the bond of pure trust and love with the other man, and then subsequently with the woman. If he pledged himself with the man, he would later be able to pledge himself with the woman: not merely in legal marriage, but in absolute, mystical marriage.

I do not believe that this was ever more than an idea or a theory with Lawrence; but that he took it with intense seriousness at this time is manifest. At the very end of the book, when Gerald and Gudrun have met their consummation in their death, Rupert refuses to admit that what he wanted was 'false and impossible'. 'I don't believe that', are his final words.

There is not much doubt that this was how Lawrence conceived the situation between us; or that *Women in Love* gives the real clue to much that was at the time quite baffling to me. Lawrence believed, or tried to believe, that the relation between Katherine and me was false and deadly; and that the relation between Frieda and himself was real and life-giving: but that his relation with Frieda needed to be completed by a new relation between himself and me, which I evaded. I am not concerned to judge this conception of Lawrence's, which (I now think) contained elements both of truth and falsehood. But its curious structure is evident. The foundation of it all is the relation between Lawrence and Frieda. That is, as it were, the ultimate reality. That foundation secure, Lawrence needs or desires a further relation with me, in which Katherine is temporarily but totally ignored. By virtue of this 'mystical' relation with Lawrence, I participate in this pre-mental reality, the 'dark sources' of my being come alive. From this changed personality, I, in turn, enter a new relation with Katherine.

Whether such a theory could have been accepted deliberately by any man in my situation I cannot say. I was very, very far from being aware of what was going on in Lawrence. But I was quite conscious that the obscure struggle between us was a struggle between two conceptions, or two experiences of love between a man and a woman. I was being definitely required to accept the relation between Lawrence and Frieda as a sort of bed-rock on which life must be builded; and I have no doubt, we

413

were unconsciously but quite as stubbornly requiring that Lawrence and Frieda should accept our relation as the ideal. Inevitably, the evidence seemed to us to point our way.

We were fresh from the actual experience of a great and real happiness, achieved after a struggle. It was not at all the boy-and-girl beatitude of first love, which we had known, but something different, something which, even now, my human heart pronounces to have been a blessed and wonderful condition. Out of this we had been plunged, at Lawrence's summons, into a closer contact than ever before with the utterly different relation that held between him and Frieda. It was humanly impossible for us to accept that relation as the norm of marriage and the basis of the community that should grow between us. On the contrary I felt that his demand for a more intimate relation with me sprang from the fact that some element in his nature was left profoundly unsatisfied by his marriage. Since our experience was that, the closer the relation between Katherine and myself, the less need we had of any relation beyond, it was impossible for us not to believe that this new demand of Lawrence came from a deep inward estrangement between him and Frieda. That what we saw was evidence of such estrangement was, of all things to us in those days, most certain.

I am older now and see things differently. It was not, I believe, a struggle between truth and falsehood, as both sides saw it then: between their truth and our falsehood, as Lawrence saw it, between our truth and their falsehood, as we saw it It was a struggle between two half-truths. We represented something that Lawrence and Frieda had to acknowledge; they represented something that we had to acknowledge. And to neither of us was this acknowledgment really possible. What took the place of it, what might in a different order of existence have been the earnest that it could be achieved, was the very real bond of affection between us all. Quite simply, as four human beings, we were fond of one another. Towards the end of his life, Lawrence put it that 'we all had to pretend a little, and we couldn't keep it up.' That was true, but yet only partly true. Where we met, and we did really meet, was on a simple level, which, for all that, was not superficial. When we four 'messed about gaily' together, we were veritably at one, and there was no pretending. And when we meet in the fields of Elysium, we shall do it again.

But to bring us together on a deeper level required a super-human power; we should have needed to be born again and born different. It would, I think, have been possible only if the marriage-relations on either side had been of the same kind, or at any rate if my relation with Katherine had been of the same kind as Lawrence's with Frieda. Then I can imagine that Lawrence and I could have closed in 'a bond of pure trust and love with the other man'. But that may be mere imagination. Shaped as we had been by life, it was impossible. It was impossible, unthinkable that I should have entered on such a marriage as that of Lawrence and Frieda, before I had learned by bitter experience that the kind of love that I desired and which was once the breath of life to me, does verily end in death. And the real reason why Lawrence entered into such a relation was that he had some such bitter experience of the self-consuming nature of agonizing personal and 'spiritual' love – not with a woman in marriage, but with his mother. So that his knowledge was only half-knowledge, premonitory rather than experiential, and there remained in him the feeling that a different kind of marriage than his own might have been possible. Hence the undoubted fascination that Katherine and I had for him.

But the more I meditate on the situation between us then, the more evident is the impossibility of it all. Let those who will take sides between us: I cannot. I am conscious only that one of the deepest and most mysterious problems of life was in question then: that on my side I fought and suffered blindly, while Lawrence on his fought and suffered with more understanding. But that there could have been no solution, I am convinced. Whether there is, in the world of existence, a solution to the problem itself, I do not pretend to know. What I am convinced of is that it is no solution to the problem to declare, as Lawrence did, that we have gone all wrong, that we have to unlearn our desire for 'spiritual' and personal love, which (as he truly saw) is in the last resort Christian love – Christian love carried into the relation between a man and a woman, where Lawrence came to believe it had no place at all. That he persuaded himself, in this matter, against his deeper instinct, is apparent to my perception in the unbearably beautiful story of *The Man who Died*. There the great problem is revealed anew, and I think I detect in it the solution which is true to Lawrence's own heart, and of which he dreamed: the death and the rebirth of Christian tenderness – a condition in which the physical and the spiritual, the personal and the impersonal are one.

But, as things happened then in Higher Tregerthen, the tension between us became unbearable as I blindly fought away from him. There were peaceful and happy interludes, as when a Spanish coal-ship, the *Manu*, ran aground on the rocks below; when we bid for shilling bargains together at the cottage-sales; or we drove together over the moors to Penzance and went to Marazion and played with heaps of tiny white shells. But they were interludes of convalescence, mere intervals in a struggle which was wearing us down to the naked nerves. Marazion brought Katherine's determination to a head. The south side was kindly: we must move to it. And a few days later, giving as our reason that Katherine felt herself in a foreign country on the northern shore, we told Lawrence that we had made up our minds to look for a cottage on the south side. He heard it with an unmoved indifference which did not deceive us. Soon afterwards, he began to have fits of a kind of delirium at nights. We were hardly surprised. The background of life at Higher Tregerthen was too mysterious and inscrutable for us to be surprised at anything any more. But one night I heard him crying or moaning that I was 'an obscene bug that was sucking his life away', and my blood went cold. Again, I will not pretend that I cannot now find a meaning in his feeling; it was not simply, as I then felt, the raging

416

of some awful mania. But now as then, it horrifies me that Lawrence should have been in a condition in which his feeling sought such words.

I went on with my search for a cottage and at length found one at Mylor, on a creek of the Truro river, at £18 a year, and a landlord as pleasant as his name, Barnicoat. We lost no time in moving. Katherine went ahead by train, while I remained behind to see our things loaded on the cart. It would have been unlike Lawrence, even at such a moment, not to have lent a hand; and he did. But our hearts were sore. When the last rope was tied, I said good-bye and hoped they would come over to see us. Frieda, who took such incidents lightly, said they would; but Lawrence did not answer. I wheeled my bicycle to the road and pedalled off, with the feeling that I had said good-bye to him for ever.

CHAPTER XXVIII

CAUGHT IN THE MACHINE

OUR cottage at Mylor was a pleasant and peaceful place, with syringa and magnolia in the front garden and, behind it, a kitchen garden which ran in a sort of clumsy terrace down to the water's edge. An arm of the creek divided us from our next-door neighbour, whom Katherine christened Mr. Mustard. At last we possessed a clock – one of those pleasant oblong pendulum clocks made in America a hundred years ago, which hang on a nail on the wall. They were always going begging at the sales, and their works were so obvious that they were easy to put to rights. The drowsy ticking of this clock was the voice of that quiet and sunny cottage.

There was much sunshine that summer. We had a little maid called May, slow in the uptake, but a gentle and willing soul, who brought us every day while they lasted a rhubarb-leaf of raspberries from her own garden. May gave us a little black kitten, whom we christened 'Peter Wilkins, or the Flying Indian'; because Peter, when he found a great shaft of sunshine pouring down upon the garden path, was rapt into an ecstasy. He leapt madly up and down in it, as though chasing some invisible presences, till he was exhausted. And Katherine and I would stand in the cottage door watching him. He was an adorable kitten, with fierce tiny black eyes and an ineradicable suspicion that somewhere about my person, preferably between my coat and waistcoat, he would find the teat of which he had been too early bereft.

Katherine did not like the place so well as I, partly because there were neighbours who tried to interest her in parish-work and jumble-sales, partly because she could not help comparing it with Villa Pauline, but mainly because the unsettled feeling that had taken hold of her in Higher Tregerthen had her strongly in its grip. She went, as often as we could afford it, to London; and, for the first time, went to stay with Lady Ottoline Morrell at Garsington, which she enjoyed.

Early in July Lawrence wrote of her to Mrs. Carswell, 'I told you the Murrys had gone away to South Cornwall. Now she doesn't like that. I believe she is in London at present. She is very dissatisfied with him'. Possibly she was, but I would not have taken Lawrence's word for it. Dissatisfied with herself was quite as likely true. Certainly my most vivid memories of the cottage at Mylor are of my being alone in it. I read a great deal that summer.

At a sale in Falmouth we had bought two easy-chairs for ten shillings each, and a whole pile of French books for a shilling. To save money, I brought them home in a little dinghy which I had hired for five shillings a month. I dearly wanted a small sailing-boat with a centre-board – a life-long and ever-frustrated ambition of mine – and I was offered a beauty for £7, but with a sigh I refused it, and contented myself with this little sailing dinghy. But it served me well that day. I brought my chairs down from the hill to the quayside on my back and discovered what a perfect protection is an easy-chair on top of one's head. I could have walked down Bond Street as gaily as I did through Falmouth with such a helmet. And, indeed, I was extraordinarily happy rowing that cargo home. Perhaps there was some truth in Katherine's joke that I would have been at my best on a desert island – by myself.

Among these books was a charming little edition of Rousseau's *Confessions*, and one or two odd volumes of Sainte-Beuve's *Lundis*, as well as a fine assortment of Dumas the elder and George Sand. For the first time, for many months, perhaps years, I read again for the sheer pleasure of reading. Of Rousseau's *Confessions*, which I finished on July 28th, I recorded my opinion.

Jean-Jacques can hardly be called detestable, yet he is certainly not likeable. And it is hard to say why. For the things for which De Quincey detests him – throwing the

419

pebble at the tree to find out whether there was a God – I love him; I love his temperament when he was on his little island – 'J' aime à commencer un travail de dix ans et de l'abandonner en dix minutes' – and yet I really dislike him. Why, in the name of glory, tell me why?

Is it his femininity, his parade of his own sensibility? Seeing that it was displayed deliberately to achieve his literary purpose, it is hard if one must condemn him for it. And yet there is something in it which is at bottom revolting. He is totally without some hard aristocratic stuff which is necessary to the ideal composition. That is, it is not his sensibility as such that is at fault, but the colour and quality of it.

Maybe the demand for the 'hard aristocratic stuff' came from my reading of Nietzsche at this moment. It was now that I conceived a great admiration for the critical power of Nietzsche which, unlike my disapproval of Rousseau, has endured.

The memorable and true thing in Nietzsche's criticism is its incessant and fundamental humanism. It is the never-failing sympathy with the torments of the creative soul, and an almost unique understanding of them. He is therefore essentially self-guarded against the boorish insensitiveness of *soi-disant* disciples, Nietzscheans and *hoc genus omne*, for he has given us the touchstone to try his own achievements. His absolutes are as personal to him as they are to any great artist. Doubtless he knew it; he cannot not have known it. Therefore he is doubly great in that, having a conscious understanding of his own creative soul, he yet could so well wear the mask he knew was necessary, that at times, even many times, looking in the glass, he straightway forgot what manner of man he was.

I was now well established as a reviewer of French books for *The Times Literary Supplement*. The writing of my book on

Dostoevsky had loosened my muscles as a critic; I could think and write freely. My reviews were no longer task-work, but a genuine satisfaction to myself. So that I easily earned all that we needed at Mylor, and I could read and read. Rousseau, Nietzsche, Disraeli, Kinglake, De Quincey, Sainte-Beuve: there were few periods of my life when I devoured books more eagerly than I did now. I was conscious of the stirrings of a new power to connect what I read; at any rate it all began to fall into some kind of pattern, and I was coming to believe that my once doubtful hope of having an independent mind might prove to be not wholly unfounded.

I was now exactly twenty-seven. At last, after being rejected by many publishers, my novel, which I had finished a year before, had been accepted. With the proofs of that and those of my book on Dostoevsky before me at the same moment I had no doubt in which direction lay such literary ability as I possessed. My novel was quite obviously half-dead; my Dostoevsky book was not. It might be partial, but I could see that, so far as it went, it was good.

I had advanced a perceptible stage in knowledge of myself, and of others. My mind had cleared; the obscure unease of Tregerthen had lifted. For the time I no longer thought, as I had done there, of the War as a great black wave of Death which must sooner or later engulf all Life. It became what Lawrence would have called 'personal' once more. In quick succession came the news of the deaths of Porky Allen and Elliot Crooke; Goodyear came down to stay with me, on a few days' leave because he had accepted a commission. He was bored, he explained, with his job of meteorological observer in the R.E., simply bored. To take a commission was the only way to get into the line. He didn't believe he would come back. But what of that? Life was a boring business, anyhow. He had returned from India, where he might have stayed, because he had thought he was missing an experience by not enlisting; it had turned out to be just as boring as any other experience. The great thing in life, he thought, was to retain enough illusions to take things seriously; and somehow he had lost the capacity. Dostoevsky – he read the proofs of my book with approval – had illusions, 'so have you', he added. But when one had stood a few times in a queue in front of a red-light shop behind the lines, illusions disappeared, and one knew how thin a veneer was spread by civilization and the ideal over the primitive animal that was man.

He wanted to see Lawrence again: and we arranged to go to Tregerthen and stay the night, sleeping together on the floor room of 'Katherine's Tower'. Lawrence received us kindly, though I don't think he particularly wanted to see us. Nor did I want to see him; but Goodyear's desire was paramount, for I had it in my head that I should not see him again. Lawrence and Goodyear got on well enough together, and Lawrence was rather surprised to find that Goodyear's knowledge of birds and beasts and flowers was greater in its own way even than his own. But he was baffled and disturbed by Goodyear's combination of a fundamental indifference with a delighted interest in things. I see Lawrence squatting like a pitman, in his little kitchen garden with the rough rock wall, uncovering with delicate hands his beetroots from the pea-haulm that straggled over them. Goodyear watched him with a quizzical admiration. And I watched them both. Then my eyes turned down the hill to the great, still, shining sea below and beyond; and it was all sad and beautiful and beyond understanding.

Meanwhile I had been called up to Bodmin, classified as B2, and told I must hold myself in readiness for home-service. I asked what it was likely to be. The sergeant glanced at the chit where I had boldly described myself as an author, and guessed it would be some clerical work. I hated the idea of totting up figures in a depot, and began to wonder whether I might not be able to find something a little more interesting. But I didn't know how to begin. So I lapsed back into my reading, with no more than fitful moments of resentment at the idea that I was now at the beck and call of the authorities. But nothing happened.

Before Goodyear and I went over to see the Lawrences, they

had come to see us. Lawrence, in his white linen sun-hat and his rucksack, as we crossed on the ferry from Penrhyn, seemed to show something of an apostolic contempt for our soft south and us. 'They should have a soft valley with leaves, and a ring-dove cooing', he wrote to a friend concerning us. 'And this is a hillside of rocks and magpies and foxes.' Nevertheless Mylor managed to put up a show. We went for a picnic in the dinghy, and sailed softly enough in the sunshine to a pleasant beach some miles up the river. But when we had finished our lunch, the sky was grey and the wind beginning to get up. There was nothing for it but to row home. Like a slim St. Peter, Lawrence put his back into it; but he was no waterman. Worse still, he was no swimmer, neither was Frieda. Frieda began to be frightened. The dinghy had just as much as it could carry. With Lawrence pulling so erratically, it was a terrible job to keep our head to the wind, in what was rather more than a choppy sea. I was seriously alarmed. But by hugging the shore, though the course added miles to the distance, we had the comfort of feeling that there would be some chance of a rescue if we did overturn. However, after a long and tiring struggle we got into the sheltered water of Mylor Creek and could laugh at our escape. But we had been well scared.

Lawrence remembered this visit to us at Mylor as one in which I had shown my hostility to him. There was truth in the memory; for though I did not feel exactly hostile, I did feel entirely separate from him. I wanted to be left alone. One of my moods of self-sufficiency was upon me. But I certainly do not remember that my hostility to him was greater than his to me. The fact that I now accepted it that our ways were different seemed to annoy him; and that I wanted to remain personal friends with him to exasperate him. He had discovered that 'Murry and I are not associates'; in the sense that I was not prepared to enter into 'an eternal bond' with him, it was true. But I didn't see why we should not be friends. My persistence in this attitude made him furious; and he irritated me by showing contempt for what I offered. I was ordinary enough to be hurt when my overtures were treated as a peculiarly putrid sort of humbug. I knew they were not that, just as well as I knew that they were not what he wanted.

Then he jumped on my Dostoevsky book, which I had sent him. He didn't trouble to read it, but hastened to assure me that 'Dostoevsky, like the rest, can nicely stick his head between the feet of Christ and waggle his behind in the air'. Since there was a good deal of hero-worship of Dostoevsky in the book, he had me fairly on the raw by suggesting that posture of the man whom I admired, and have not ceased to admire, was contemptible. It is much easier to accept an insult to oneself than one's hero; for then one's whole being is involved in the contempt. And seeing that Lawrence's own expressed view of Dostoevsky was completely incomprehensible to me, I felt that he only wanted to insult me. I didn't mind so much as I would have done a year before. There was now something in me that could stand up to him; and since I had no desire to enter into a slanging match, I let the thing slide, and went on with my reading. Except for his sending me Crèvecœur in return for a George Sand, there was silence between us for a while.

I was hauled up to Bodmin Barracks again. I had always been treated decently before, but this time I was examined by a young cub of a doctor. When he asked me if I had ever had a long list of diseases, including pleurisy, and I replied that I had had an attack of pleurisy two years before, he said: 'I can't find a trace of it' in such an incredibly insulting voice that I nearly lost control. 'Nevertheless, I had pleurisy', I said in a tone that was meant to annoy him, and did: for he went red and called out to the sergeant who had roughly examined my eyes by the card. 'Examine this man's eyes again.' I couldn't help saying, 'Do you imagine I am *pretending* to be short-sighted?' By this time, I was raging inwardly: and wondering what on earth would happen if I had to endure being ordered about by such a man. My ticket was altered from B2 to B1, and I was called before the Colonel. Once more I was being treated as a human being.

'You're an educated man, aren't you?'

I supposed so.

'Well, we haven't any jobs here for educated men of your grade. Why don't you try for a suitable job? I wonder you're not in one already.'

I replied that I didn't know how.

'I don't myself, either,' he said frankly. 'But I tell you what. I'll write to the local M.P. about you.'

This was so astonishingly decent that I didn't know what to say.

'All I can tell you is that there's not much chance of your being called up before Christmas' – it was now October – 'and if you don't want to put in a spell of navvying, I would advise you to find something if you can.'

The idea of navvying didn't upset me – though no doubt the reality would have done – but the idea of being ordered about by someone like that doctor did. I realized that I was totally unused to it, and that I really did not know how I should react. And I had been under the impression that I had had a fairly hard life. My eyes were opened to quite new possibilities.

Anyhow, I was taking no chances if I could help it. But I knew nobody who could give me a hand; I could do nothing but wait. The M.P. sent me a letter to somebody at the War Office whom I was to interview about an interpretership. And off I went. It was a wasted fare. The young staff-officer who interviewed me said that I was too late, with the plain implication that it was my own fault for not having tried long before. I couldn't gainsay it. There was no doubt about it; I had kept out of the machine as long as I could; and only when I was really up against it, was I bestirring myself. My position was distinctly ignominious. Still, I forced my interviewer to admit that if his only prospect had been a labour battalion he would have tried to do something about it. But even then, I felt I was being disingenuous. I just hadn't the courage to tell him, in his red tabs and his high brown boots, what I really felt about it all. I don't suppose he would have been interested to hear.

But here it is – not indeed as I felt it then – but as I felt it six months later, after four months' hard work at the War Office, and recorded it. I do not think my feeling had changed much in the interval.

Now before I got to bed to wake up to-morrow to the corvée of the office (I wrote on Easter Day, 1917) I want to unburden my soul. I have been disturbed thinking that there is after all quite a chance that the War will swallow me up quick – disturbed, not frightened. Perhaps it will all come very quickly, and I shall not have time ever to record my thoughts. I think they are worth recording. Of course, I have written a good deal about it before. But now I have it clearly. Before, I was distraught by contradictory desires.

It is clear just because I have been more of the artist lately. My desires and my ideas have taken their right pattern, just as when the grains of sand fall into place when a bow is drawn across the edge of the glass on which they are spread.

As an artist – there is no doubt about it – I am non-social, perhaps anti-social. No doubt I recognize, definitely recognize and make it my duty to obey, a moral code that is not obviously aesthetic. (It probably is at the last wholly so.) But that resembles hardly at all the code of social and citizen duties. From the point of view of that code I do not exist; and it is unreal for me. I don't care about the England I may have to fight for. I don't hate it; I rather love it. But to die for it would be simply an irony. I don't recognize the obligation. That is not pretence: I simply do not feel it.

I would die if – the case is hardly conceivable – the battle were being waged against a tyranny which would deny me the right to do the work I can do. No other battles concern me. Their results do not interest me. If I am killed in this war – that is, for the purposes indicated in the Entente reply to America – I should be killed not merely in a quarrel with which I have no concern, but for a cause which is, I am convinced, unjust. That doesn't make the irony any greater. It is merely a fact worth recording.

Nor do I pretend that I don't have any patriotic feelings, or national pride. I have, and I don't crush them, for I don't see why I should. But, though they are real, they are utterly negligible as compared to the really profound feelings I have about the work to be done. That is my purpose; all outside must be subordinate to it. If it will subordinate itself, well. If like this war, and the services it may demand from me, it will not, then . . .

There was nothing particularly glorious in that; but it is clear enough. I was not going to meet the war a step nearer than I could help. But now that I was cornered and really had to choose between some such ineffably boring job as the Colonel had hinted at and the chance of doing something interesting, I bestirred myself indeed. I made the round of a half-dozen departments, and I was put upon as many waiting-lists. But the end of it all was that there was nothing to do but go home – and wait.

Meanwhile, Katherine was bemoaning the fact that she had not come to London with me. 'What is £2 10s. to us?' she said. But I, with my congenital money-fears, was incapable of this regal indifference. £2 10s. (which was the fare to London) was a lot. I felt I dared not go back without something, in case I could not afford to come to London again. Just at that moment I had an invitation to Garsington, which was a godsend, for it happened that J. M. Keynes and J. T. Sheppard were there, and both disposed to help, out of sheer kindness. Sheppard's suggestion that I should become a translator in the department where he was working seemed the more hopeful, for one of my meagre qualifications. I presented myself, and I was taken on. Not merely was I taken on, but I was to receive a salary of £5 a week: more than I had ever earned since the war began. To me, that was Eldorado.

What followed is really a blank in my memory, for several

months. I became a mere automaton. I worked desperately hard in a kind of mental stupor. Life, or what I regarded as life, had simply ceased. I passed into a quite mysterious state of unawareness, from which I did not emerge for fully six months, and by that time, by what process I know not, my salary was almost doubled. I had mysteriously become some one of importance in the department, and was more or less the editor of an impressive sheet called *The Daily Review of the Foreign Press*.

There were a great many able people in the department, and most of them were remarkably pleasant, too. In fact, I don't believe a nicer set of educated Englishmen could have been gathered together. Capacity and decency went hand in hand.

They formed a rare combination of ability and humanity, so that I was at first distinctly dubious of my own qualifications to be of the company. However, I came to feel that I could hold my own, at any rate in the particular job we were engaged on – which was to construct as accurate a picture as we could, using with discrimination the evidence of the foreign press, of the internal condition, political, economic and moral, of the enemy countries. It was interesting, even absorbing work, and I was quickly absorbed by it. Since I was unused to regular work in an office, I probably pushed myself too hard. At any rate it seemed to me that there was nothing left of me for any save a superficial contact with my colleagues. One day, as the result of one of the periodical 'combings-out' from which the department suffered, one of them went into khaki and into a training camp. A day or two afterwards I received a letter from him to the amazing effect that he did not mind leaving Watergate House, but he did mind leaving me; that my advent to the office had made life different for him. It was a letter full of a manly and tender affection, which I had done nothing to deserve. Again, I was bewildered. Here was the very thing I chiefly valued, yet, because I had attracted it unconsciously, I was rather distressed than delighted. There must be, I felt, something uncanny about me – a sort of shadow personality whom I could not see. Sometimes this shadow personality was wise, sometimes charming; or he may have been both together: but the deference or the affection he seemed to elicit were alike mysterious to me. The effect was out of all relation to the cause. There was an unknown quantity somewhere.

This was a new and alarming realization: so alarming that I did my utmost to suppress it. If I had admitted it fully into my consciousness, I felt, I should go mad, or be mad. I had a presentiment that I was not far from that condition. For this sudden plunge into a multitude of contacts with men whom for various reasons I admired and liked, had convinced me that I was a very queer fish. I was of their tribe, and I was not. I seemed to understand them all, quite simply, and yet to know that they could not understand me. When they talked to me and I to them, I had the queer sensation of not being really there. But where *I* was I did not know. Was *I*, as I felt, really present in my brief moments with Katherine, or was I the curious consciousness that began to be travailed with all manner of strange thoughts, which I could not impart to anybody at all? When, about this moment in the spring of 1917, Lawrence suddenly wrote to me, asking me what 'I had been thinking and doing apart from the office', and saying that he 'didn't know why I had been in his mind lately', I felt that I did know why I had been in his mind, but that I could not possibly explain either that, or my own thoughts. I was so near the verge of madness that I was afraid any attempt to express myself would carry me over. I don't believe I even answered Lawrence's letter.

CHAPTER XXIX

HUMAN OR INHUMAN?

INSTEAD, I buried myself in work. I wanted to depart altogether from life; and I found it the quickest way to work myself to a standstill. I had a prodigious faculty for work in those days; and the work came to me. Now, I really knew what I was writing about when I wrote my reviews of French books for *The Times Literary Supplement*: I had something to say, and I said it well. Again, I could see that a serious peace move was preparing in Austria, now that the new Emperor had succeeded, and I was desperately anxious that something should be done about it. For one of the more comprehensible thoughts by which I was haunted and oppressed was that, if a peace by understanding were to be achieved in 1917, Europe would be saved from cracking altogether. 'Europe' had suddenly become real and precious to me. It would be hard to explain what I meant by it – it was almost identical with Humanity. And now that I could not turn away from Europe, and my eyes were riveted on its agonies every day, I saw how precious and precarious it was.

Now, *all* my friends who had entered the War were dead. Goodyear had gone the way of all the rest. It was all one happening. In them, and those like them, Europe was murdering its own soul. If Europe could awake to what was happening, then the life, the soul, the consciousness would be saved, and those men would not have died in vain. But if Europe did not awake, and the thing went on to the bitter end – then, there was no hope, no hope any more. Victory or defeat, it was all one. Europe would be dead.

I came into contact, which I sought deliberately, with politicians who were 'interested' in peace: the present Prime Minister among them. And I was heart-sickened by them. The only one of those I met who cared for 'Europe' – in this transcendental sense – was a Conservative: Lord Henry Bentinck, in whom I learned to admire what an aristocrat might be. He cared for Europe because he represented it, because he was by instinct what I was coming to be by thought. Yet it was another member of his party, who joined in the talks I sometimes had with certain members of Parliament concerning the imminent Austrian peace-move, solely for the purpose of trapping me. I found myself reported by him to my supreme head at the War Office, Sir Michael MacDonogh. When I was called before him, I explained exactly what I had done, and I tried also to explain why. To my relief my action was reckoned perfectly legitimate, and the informer dismissed as an interfering busybody. Though the word was not mentioned I was given to understand that he was considered to have behaved like a cad.

At this time I met H. W. Massingham – quick, querulous, lovable – who came to share with J. A. Spender the pedestal on which my heroes of political journalism were set. Both these men, I felt, were inspired by a passion for an ideal. The passion was nearer to the surface in Massingham, in Spender calmer; but that may be because I knew them at different moments. Perhaps Massingham was a calmer man before the war had fretted his soul to feverishness. Anyhow, I did not admire him the less for that; and when he asked me to write on the European situation for *The Nation* I felt honoured as well as pleased. From this time onward I saw a great deal of him. Two or three times a week I went to talk with him in his little office, until all his familiar gestures were dear to me, and I had come to share something of H. M. Tomlinson's feeling about him: that 'The Chief' had to be guarded and defended and preserved. Always when I entered he would be on his feet, waiting impatiently, as though he half-believed that the magic word of salvation might be at hand. Then he would push his gold spectacles on to his forehead and flutter through the pages of the outspread newspapers till he had found what he wanted. 'What do you think of *that*?' And his

431

indignation would run floodgate. When it had subsided, he would appear to settle in a chair, and the talk would begin. But he was out of his chair in a second, fluttering again. 'Have you seen this? That *bloody* man . . .' Massingham's 'bloody' was the man himself. He used it very frequently, and it had the effect of an oath on the lips of a saint. There was something childlike in Massingham.

He soon had me working for him as hard as I could, and harder than I ought, for to keep up with his demands meant writing in the small hours of the morning. But one had the feeling that it was all for the cause. And H. M. Tomlinson was there to confirm one in the faith. He had been sacked from his job of war-correspondent for telling the human truth, and had come temporarily to rest as the assistant editor of *The Nation*. Who shall describe 'Tommy'? Quiet, weary, sad, with his unforgettable face, carved and weather-beaten like the figure-heads of the sailing-ships under whose bowsprits he walked and dreamed as a boy on the East India Dock, with his elbow propped on the mantelpiece, sucking at his pipe, staring down into the fire, shut off, it seemed, from all commonplace vibration by his deafness, brooding, brooding . . . A man struck by a deep and incurable wound, to whom the war had been, and ever would be, a heart-ache and an agony. The boys, the boys . . . He stared into the fire, and one's soul stared with him.

Insensibly, inevitably, every faculty of mine was now strained upon the war. I was not. The thing engulfed me. I brooded on it incessantly. And even though I was working harder than I have ever worked in my life, I had to seek some escape in writing poetry. Escape? Poetry was no escape for me. It was a kind of relief perhaps, in that it forced me to grapple with the thoughts that were wearing me down, and by the effort of mastering them induced in me a kind of intellectual ecstasy which may have served me as an opium-dream. All my veritable life was gathered into these moments of hallucination, if it was hallucination. Obstinately, instinctively, I was driven on by the conviction that

432

one must face the War completely, in imagination and consciousness, to the end; that one must behold it until something happened
to the sight, until one was blinded, or one saw. And there were
moments when I seemed to see. But the person who saw, at those
moments, was assuredly not myself. Long ago, *I* had disappeared:
'something' supervened upon the eclipse of my conscious self with
its intolerable hopes and fears, its ache of longing and its presentiment of disaster, and that 'something' understood, and against
its understanding I rebelled in vain.

What kind of human thing I was in those days, I have no
idea. That Katherine went to live apart from me seemed to
me only natural. In my own way, I also had passed beyond the
personal. Where my life was, love had ceased to have meaning.
She took a studio at 141a Church Street, Chelsea; and I went to
live in two ground-floor rooms at 47 Redcliffe Road. I went to
see her every day; but life with her was no part of the texture of
my life any more. It was only a strange interlude.

Katherine was refashioning what she had written at the Villa
Pauline into *Prelude*, and the beauty of it took my breath away, as
she read it to me. And that beauty was not alien to me; on the
contrary, I was more sensitive to it than I had ever been before.
Her work seemed to utter the very voice of the soul that was being
killed in the giant agony of the world. About this time I wrote in
my diary:

> To-night Katherine read me three 'Spring Pictures', which
> she wrote in France in the spring of 1915, when she was in
> the flat on the Quai aux Fleurs. They are such stuff as only
> she can do; they have in them the tremulous, uncertain,
> fearful poise of spring. The spring of the spirit made manifest
> in the spring of the senses. They will not buy of the stalls.
> No one will buy. Every one knows the most famous singers of
> the world in the upper room – they are as old as the new songs.
> She has written the mistrust of spring, when the soul does not
> know whether to hide in the old or give itself to the new, when

433

> it dares not yet believe
And less dares doubt . . .

when it fears the eternal recurrence, and hears a whisper that
the new is only a name for the old, the bud for the bark –
when it is poised on the threshold of re-birth, and is not.

It is very wonderful. Katherine, when she is Katherine,
writes like the South-West Wind. The world is moist, calm,
urgent under its touch. All colours have a new life. There is a
plenitude of re-birth; a passing of one life into another: a
creation that is, is divined. Thus she reveals the secret life,
not merely of minds (which I may sometimes do) – not
merely of men and women (which again even I *might* do) –
but of the whole vast world. And all in the thousand lines
of three 'Spring Pictures'.

In that beauty I longed to believe. But the more desperately
I desired to believe in it, the more certain I became that the only
beauty in which one could believe was a terribly impersonal
thing. It arose out of the very shipwreck of human hopes; the
destruction of loveliness was the birth-throe of this beauty. And
what faith in it I could achieve must be purchased at the price
of a fearful unfaith in the power of all that humanly I longed for,
all that was precious to my heart. Faith of some kind I must
have, and the only faith I could conquer was to be bought at a
price I could not pay. And concerning this fearful struggle within
myself, I could unburden myself to no one at all. To Katherine
I simply dared not breathe that I was losing all belief in love: that
my childish faith in its human duration had crumbled away, and
that the love which was gradually taking possession of me – for
to such as I was, and am, there can be no faith without love –
was a love which arose out of the certainty of destruction of
personal love.

To unburden myself I turned towards a new friend I had
found. I had heard through Dan Rider that someone was anxious
to meet me because of my book on Dostoevsky, and on Dan's

assurance that he was a man I should like, I made a free evening
and invited him to my rooms. It was J. W. N. Sullivan. He came
in a big black hat and a khaki great-coat, the relic of a Serbian
campaign in which he had been a Red Cross orderly. It was a
rainy night; and I saw him as a big sheep-dog shaking himself.
One could not but like him, and I liked him at sight; I was deeply
attracted by an essential naivety which I sensed in him, and which
had taken shape in my mental picture of him. I suppose we talked
about Dostoevsky; but indeed I do not remember: I was grateful
enough for his friendly presence. At the end of the evening he
told me that he was on his beam-ends, and wanted a job. I
thought that his scientific knowledge and his knowledge of
German would make him welcome to the department, and
promised to interview the colonel the next morning. It was
arranged that Sullivan should wait at a nearby café, and I
would pop out and tell him the result. Meanwhile I offered to
lend him some money, which he refused.

All went well, and he was taken on. Five pounds a week was
even more a god-send to him than it had been to me eight months
before, and I was delighted that I had been able to do my new
friend a good turn. In a little while it became a regular habit with
us to have our tea together – gritty cake and sugarless tea – in a
shabby café in Villiers Street; and afternoon after afternoon I
would try to make him understand the strange faith that was
forming itself in me. When this had been a mere intellectual
possibility, and I had discovered it in Dostoevsky and had tried
to expound it, Sullivan had understood. He was the only man
I had met who had understood my book. He seemed marked out
to be the one man who would 'understand along with me' now
that an intellectual possibility had become a nightmare reality.
And I longed to convince him; I had a childish hunger to be rid
of the burden of my own isolation. There were moments when I
felt that he did understand, and that he was sharing the intellectual ecstasy of understanding and the faith and love in which
alone I now lived, if I lived at all.

In this belief I, too, was naive; as yet I was very far from understanding the sombre and salutary truth that in order to understand another man's faith, one must needs have undergone essentially the same experience. But Sullivan's companionship was precious to me in those days. I knew that he felt a certain affection towards me, and that was enough to enable me to persuade myself that he did understand what I was trying to say. For by now my isolation was extreme. I had drifted completely apart from Lawrence. I was quite separated from Koteliansky and all my former acquaintances. And now that my simple faith in the enduring power of the love between Katherine and myself was gone, I knew not where to turn. I felt that I had not the strength to accept the reality of my own complete isolation. At the critical moment I wanted someone to go with me. If I tried, as I did try, to go alone, I passed inevitably into an ecstasy in which I could not live. So I turned to Sullivan. And, for a time, his companionship was my only comfort. What my companionship was to him, he himself has set on record.

I was, undoubtedly, exceptionally fortunate in the people I met at this time. Two of them, in particular, caused me to make a singular and profound discovery about myself. I realized that, as a person, I was quite extraordinary undeveloped and even chaotic. It was not that I found them in any specific direction more sensitive or more mentally active than myself. But whereas I was an unco-ordinated bundle of appetites and perceptions, they had achieved a sort of integration, a degree of self-awareness, that was quite strange to me . . .

One of these men, the more powerful of the two, was a professed mystic . . . The other was a younger man who had already acquired a literary reputation as a poet and critic. The first man obviously had a heart of gold; the second attracted and repelled me in about equal measure. On the whole, I thoroughly distrusted and disliked him, and yet he could, at times, touch me more intimately than any-body else. He professed a great affection for me, meaning, I think, that I amused him, that my attitude to him flattered him, and that he also found me somewhat pathetic. He immensely valued his sentimentality; it made him feel more alive; and in order to awaken it he would sometimes use the vivisector's art with great subtlety and complete ruthlessness.

His mind was, in some respects, not unlike Woods', and I have always been attracted by enigmatic profundities. But he was altogether more penetrating and discriminating than Woods. He had quite unusual and perfectly genuine insight which was often so singular and unexpected that one never felt quite safe in supposing that he was talking nonsense. He was perfectly aware of this insecurity in his hearer and it amused him to bully one into a pretended agreement with his most 'transcendental' remarks. We had wonderful conversations, especially on Dostoevsky, and the 'higher' consciousness. They would last for hours, and during them he would mount, as it were, from one transcendental height to another, the ascent culminating with some such remark as 'the inhuman is the highest form of the human', and in the ensuing silence he would gaze vaguely at a corner of the ceiling with a faint, wondering smile. The self-restraint and the unceasing agility necessary to support these conversations was terrible. But it was worth it. I am quite sure now that it was worth it. I had, I admit, to lie and pretend very extensively through these séances, but it would be wrong to suppose that the whole thing was humbug. On the contrary, I regard the efforts that resulted in these mental contortions as of very great value. I developed a sensitiveness, as it were, to states of consciousness quite outside my normal range. I became aware, in a con-fused way, that there were adventures of the spirit of which I had never dreamed. The impression made by these con-versations, which often affected me as revelations, was permanent. I have always found, since then, that the literature or music that most matters to me is that which reveals this superior consciousness . . .

There is more than one portrait of myself lurking in the pages of contemporary literature, and with one or two of them I may have to be concerned. All alike are hostile: which is significant. But this one differs from the various attempts made by Lawrence, and the distinctly pointed one by Aldous Huxley, in that it is a serious effort of a man who knew me intimately at this period of my life to define what seemed to him my enigmatic personality. It is an honest attempt at a truthful picture of me, as I appeared. The contradiction between it and the picture I am drawing of myself, is striking and salutary; but far more interesting, to me, is its own inward contradiction. The man who deliberately exercised his unusual powers of insight to arouse insecurity in his companion and bully him into agreement with his own most obscure statements is also the man who awakened him to a realization of a superior mode of consciousness which, since that time of initiation, has been for him, although he has never directly experienced it, the highest human possibility. Objectively, such a creature appears to me a monster. I am not conscious of possessing any unusual powers of insight; but such as I have forbid me to believe in the real existence of such a man. But others may find him more credible than I do; and they have full liberty to believe that he is, or was, myself.

But I can discover in the monster elements which I recognize to be an exaggeration of elements that I recognize as mine. I can even recognize, and readers of this narrative may also recognize, my 'characteristic' culminating remark as probably authentic words of my own. But the difference between what they meant to me and what they meant to my friend is great. I suspect that he had really forgotten what they once meant even to him, and that he has carried away only the words, and a vague memory of a moment of intellectual communion, which, because it was

438

strange to him, was memorable. All that remains is a memory of the words. 'That was the kind of remark,' my friend, grown wise, now says to himself, 'with which Murry used to excite me, deliberately, almost maliciously, to show his power over me. But what it meant, I have forgotten, if I ever knew. I even suspect it meant nothing at all'.

But what *did* it mean – this saying that 'the inhuman is the highest form of the human'? Perhaps this whole book will prove to be no more than an unconscious exposition of all that it meant – of the meaning that I knew, and the meaning which I had yet to learn. But at that moment it meant that the highest condition possible to man, as I dimly perceived it then, was to be able to accept the necessity, and discern the beauty, of the denial of his own deepest heart's desire. That I was, as I believed, on the brink of being able to do this was no achievement of my own. Indeed, I would a thousand times rather have lacked this knowledge, or been unvisited by this surmise for ever, than have had it proved upon my pulses. For I paid for this vision with my all. That I had not much, I know as well as anybody; but it was my life. Again, and yet again, I trembled and drew back; again and yet again I was driven on.

That there were moments when I appeared veritably inhuman, in the common sense, to my friend, I can well believe. Even then I wonder whether he has not read into his immediate experience of me some of his subsequent conclusions as to what I was. But I will not deny that the epithet 'inhuman' has been fastened on to me by others besides him. Maybe I am inhuman: I cannot tell. But I know I was suffering then. Though I could not speak my thoughts, or hint at them, to any person – neither to Katherine nor Sullivan – I could utter them in a kind of poetry. Whether it has merits as poetry I neither know nor care; for me it is simply an authentic record of what I then endured. Perhaps those who read, with this commentary, the lines called 'An Induction to an Unwritten Poem' will gain from them an inkling of what went to the making of them.

To such high themes I turn that higher none
  May haunt my soul with a presentiment
Of unsubstantial victory. There is One
  That will not suffer that this instrument
Should sound to less intention, though the strings
  May shatter at the strain, the heart be rent
By longing for that Beauty, whose dark wings
  Do fan the mind to a bewilderment
Of destiny, and dumbness, and forgotten things.

Therefore do thou, O Power, O Influence
  That turns me thus aside from old delights,
Robbing them of their subtlest quintessence
  By the strange poison of more perfect sights,
And premonitions of a mastery
  To which the slow-ascending step affrights
With knowledge of the impossibility
  Of any backward turning: – let thy spirits
Attend me now and whisper of supremacy.

Tell me that I may know thee, comfort me
  With dream-beholden stirrings of thy veil
That I may know thou livest; let me see
  Faint fragmentary lights which may prevail
Down-darting on to my mortality,
  Against the child within me who doth quail
At his cold-gazing brother's cruelty,
  And with imploring eyes and forehead pale
Weeps for the icy stillness of his destiny.

O comfort this my brother, lest he die;
  Send down on him thy blinding anodyne
He may not hear me when my lips deny
  The warm love that he gave to me, at thine

HUMAN OR INHUMAN?

Unswerving and inexorable demand;
　　And let my backward eyes behold no sign
That he hath felt the coldness of my hand,
　　His arms unlacing, that my neck entwine
And will not let me go to thy forgetful land.

The parable seems as simple to me now as it was natural then.
The child, my brother, was my heart that longed to love and to
be loved, and in this alone could find happiness and peace. That
I should have imagined the bond between my heart and my mind
one of mutual love is not strange to me, nor is the adjuration with
which in the final verses I (now become the Mind, and strained to
the uttermost by the new love which it glimpses and which it
knows is to be bought only by the death of the old) turn to the
child who was my brother, calling upon him to love me no more.

Love not the scapegoat of humanity;
　　Love me no longer: yea, love thou not aught;
And love not love, for this shall truly be
　　A sudden spear thrust through thy living thought,
A poison that will chill thy warmest blood,
　　To strange adventure in the desert brought
Or in the frozen wastes of the great flood,
　　Within the toils of lonely knowledge caught
Of that which lies beyond the evil and the good.

Then shalt thou leave thy brother, as I thee;
　　He shall thy child-heart be, as thou art mine;
And he shall bend his head as I now see
　　Thy bended head; and so his arms shall twine
About thy neck as thine press me forlorn.
　　Then shall thou shut thy staring orbs, as I
Shut mine; and as thine arms are torn,
　　With this same chill despairing ecstasy,
So shalt thou kill the child of thine own soul's love born.

Thou canst not love me now, for thou art dead
   And I who killed thee shall as surely die.
O mighty, bitter love that enterèd
   A soul so frail and loving-kind as I –
Passion of love and beauty, fire transcending
   The mortal substance of the clay it burns;
Light that revealeth purer light unending
   Till at the pinnacle of flame it turns
And pierces him who fed it to his own heart-rending –

   Thee will I sing, or in sad incantation
      Knowing no joy, but such necessity
As shall inform my speech with desolation
      Of highest human purpose, call to thee!
Visit me now, for I the latest-born
      Of all thy priests do stand in agony,
A weaker soul by greater longing torn
      Called, in despite of all humility,
To sadder ministration, keener woe to mourn.

Such was the *Induction*, or part of it. The poem itself was completely beyond my power to write. I attempted it, but it shaped itself incessantly into a parable of my own life; and then I knew that what I had written was not the opening, but the ending of a poem.

Nevertheless, I may have been the man to use his uncanny skill in soul-anatomy in ruthlessly dissecting his friend in order to have the pleasure of commiserating with the pain which he inflicted. It may have been so. But if it was so, then I must assuredly build up my knowledge of myself all over again, on quite different foundations. It is beyond my power to do so.

CHAPTER XXX

IMMORTAL SICKNESS

MY activity was intense during the autumn of 1917. With my
ordinary waking mind in the War Office and as a journalist I
was working to the limit of my power, and the only relief I could
take from it was in an intensity of speculation – using the word in
Keats' sense – far more consuming than ordinary work could ever
be. For a time this alternation appeared to suffice, and even to
be in itself restorative. But, quite suddenly, about the middle of
November, I passed, rather joyfully than otherwise, into a condition of sleeplessness. I lay with my eyes shut, for many nights,
in a sort of beatific wakefulness; my consciousness seemed to be
working itself free of its slavery to the body. As I felt that I
had no desire, so I felt that I had no need to sleep. It was
sufficient to lie contemplating the Truth to be renewed by the
Truth, which I was wont to call in my own mind, the Beauty of
Necessity.

I saw Katherine every evening. At her studio she would
prepare a dinner for me. For the rest of the day it was then simpler
to solve the problem of food by ignoring it. The business of
providing oneself with one's ration of butter and bacon, if one
lived alone and was working all day, was too burdensome to be
borne; and I suppose I neglected myself. Anyhow, I woke one
morning with the astonishing feeling that I – or my physical being
– did not want to go to the office, and that in fact it would have
difficulty in getting there. My wrists seemed to have turned to
damp string and my knees to water. So I sent a note to Katherine
to ask her to summon our generous and faithful doctor to see me.
He came, sounded me, pulled a long face, took me off in a taxi to
have me weighed, discovered that I was under eight stone instead

of my normal nine stone and a half – I am 5 ft. 8½ in., and have always been a light-weight – declared once again that I was in imminent danger of tuberculosis, and that I must go into the country.

It was my first, and probably it will be my last, experience of sick-leave on full pay: therefore my one authentic taste of the condition of a future society in which there is economic security for all. My verdict is that it is a blessed condition, and if my example goes for anything I can assure the stern moralists who live on unearned increment that it does not result in laziness. What it may, and I hope will, result in is that men will work quite hard at something different from their normal and regular occupation. I did: I wrote, in about four weeks, a little poetic drama called, to the distress of some people who rather liked it, *Cinnamon and Angelica*. The only people who really seemed to understand why all its characters had the names of condiments were Katherine and Walter de la Mare. H. W. Massingham, I remember, was positively angry with me, and seemed to feel that I had played an unfeeling practical joke on his tender sensibility: that I had deliberately roused his emotions only to laugh discreetly at them. That verdict interestingly implies very much the same judgment of my nature as Sullivan has expressed. And that consensus calls to my mind that five years after this H. M. Tomlinson came to stay a week-end with me in Ashdown Forest, where I was living alone after Katherine's death. When he left, he said to me that he had been dubious of coming, but now was glad. 'For,' said he, 'I always wondered whether you had a soul at all: now I know you have.' Probably, he has changed his mind since. People generally do.

Yes, I am afraid the evidence is more impressive than I was inclined to allow that I am not quite human: and the main question among my acquaintances has been whether it is a respectable big devil that inhabits me, or a little mean one. It does not matter: neither conclusion can comfort or discomfit me. But if the strange reaction of H. W. Massingham to *Cinnamon and Angelica* is any indication of what may hâve been meant by the charge that I arouse emotional response only to blow cold upon it, I can say that I gave my characters the names of spices, because I felt the exceeding smallness of all things human. It is not, as I understand the matter, cruel or cold to remember oneself, or to remind others that, though the desires and the sufferings of the human heart are infinite, there is an infinity beyond them compared to which they are as grains of mustard seed. Whether or not this is a comfortable knowledge, it seems tò me cowardly not to face it, and by that I mean really to face it, not as intellectual possibility, but as an experienced reality. I believe that it is our human duty to suffer that knowledge as immediately as we suffer a heartbreak, so that it is, for ever, as intimate a part of our being as the wounds to our emotional or physical bodies. That was the persuasion I attempted to convey in my little play; and I tried to convey it as I had experienced it, and was to experience it more fully. This sense of the infinite littleness of things human was, with me, no intellectual after-thought; I felt it simultaneously with the utmost pang of human desire and disappointment of which I was capable. They were inextricably mixed together, and the one exacerbated the other. My desire was only the more eager because it was blent with the anguish that it could not be, and the anguish the more bitter because the desire was extreme. Maybe it is more human to let each in turn have its sway: to indulge the heart's desire to its fullness, and when it sinks to quiescence to let the knowledge of the mind have its hour of mastery. If that is, indeed, the human way, then I must acknowledge that mine is the inhuman one. But I did not choose it; it chose me. Nor was I the first to be chosen by it. Keats at least had known all that I knew long before me, and when he was years younger than I. In him I recognized my malady, and recognized his recognition of it.

Thou art a dreaming thing,
A fever of thyself; think of the earth;
What bliss, even in hope, is there for thee?
What haven? every creature hath its home,
Every sole man hath days of joy and pain,
Whether his labours be sublime or low –
The pain alone, the joy alone, distinct:
Only the dreamer venoms all his days,
Bearing more woes than all his sins deserve.
Therefore, that happiness be somewhat shar'd,
Such things as thou art are admitted oft
Into like gardens thou did pass erewhile
And suffer'd in these temples: for that cause
Thou standest safe between this statue's knees.

There, bating the poetry, was I. And I remember the very moment at which I recognized myself.

It was in November, 1917, in the drawing-room at Garsington Manor, whither Lady Ottoline Morrell's generosity had invited me to recuperate. That autumn Sir Sidney Colvin's *Life of Keats* was published. It lay in my way at Garsington, and I read it. I had never read any life of Keats before; nor even a word of his letters. His poetry I admired, as one admires a lovely thing, which has never entered into one's soul. But the fragments from the letters in Colvin's *Life* stirred me deeply. I began to read the poetry with a new understanding – a very partial understanding, for there is no end to the process of understanding Keats, but a real one. The barriers were down. Though it might take me a lifetime to explore the world of human feeling and thought before me, the gate at least was open, and I had entered in. One evening, sitting in an armchair in the drawing-room, I re-read *The Fall of Hyperion*. Before that moment, it had seemed to me merely the lamentable failure of the effort of a sick and desperate mind to improve on the perfect *Hyperion*. But now it was the voice of very Truth, speaking from the tomb. When I came to the lines:

> Then saw I a wan face
> Not pin'd by human sorrows but bright-blanch'd
> By an immortal sickness which kills not . . .
> But for her eyes, I should have fled away.
> They held me back with a benignant light,
> Soft-mitigated by divinest lids
> Half-clos'd, and visionless entire they seem'd
> Of all external things – they saw me not
> But, in blank splendour, beamed like the mild moon
> Who comforts those she sees not, who knows not
> What eyes are upward cast . . .

When I read, for the first time really *read*, those words, they made my heart too small to hold its blood. As was Keats in his vision before Moneta, so was I before him.

> I ached to see what things the hollow brain
> Behind enwombed: what high tragedy
> In the dark secret chambers of his skull
> Was acting, that could give so dread a stress
> To his cold lips, and fill with such a light
> His planetary eyes, and touch his voice
> With such a sorrow.

In that vision of Moneta, I had no doubt, was the Truth – Truth palpable, irresistible, ultimate. What I had groped for and glimpsed, there was seen; that of which I was afraid, there was realized. A kind of chill crept over me, a foreboding sense that I had not paid the price of the knowledge that was there, and that it would have to be paid. The vanward cloud of evil days had spent their malice; that was true. Was I not at peace and resting now? But,

> the sullen rear
> Was with its stored thunder labouring up.

Yet, at the very instant that I was chilled with the premonition of disaster, I was thrilled with the ecstasy of discovery. This was for

447

me; this was mine: to this voice my ears were sensitive. I listened to the solemn words, which before had gone unheeded.

> Whether the dream now purposed to rehearse
> Be poet's or fanatic's will be known
> When this warm scribe, my hand, is in the grave.

More than a hundred years had passed, and always it had been a fanatic's dream. So it had seemed to me. But now the scales were lifted from my eyes. And why not? The only qualification I had was the only qualification that Keats demanded.

> Since every man whose soul is not a clod
> Hath visions and would speak, if he had lov'd
> And been well-nurtur'd in his mother-tongue.

To speak them, good nurture; but to understand them only this: 'If he had lov'd'. In my heart I knew that was my only claim. Whatever I knew, I knew because of that. And I was learning more.

Perhaps I had been a fortnight at Garsington when Katherine came down for the week-end to see me. It was a bitterly cold night, and when she got down from the high dog-cart she said she felt frozen. The next day she stayed in bed in a big attic-room, and I read to her part of my play. It was agreed that she had 'a bit of a chill', but neither of us took it seriously. I, at that time, was supposed to be the ill one, not she. We talked of our plans. We were not going to live apart from each other any longer. She would give up her studio, and rent two rooms next door to mine in Redcliffe Road. But she confessed that my play, which had for its background a kind of idealized Bandol, had aroused in her a great longing to leave England. She frowned decisively on the idea of a comfortable flat (which we could have afforded now); she said she positively liked Redcliffe Road, with its feeling of impermanency. It left us free to fly.

She returned to her studio in Chelsea. A day or two after she wrote that the chill had developed into a high fever, and that she had had to call in the doctor. It was a sharp attack of pleurisy. Since pleurisy was an old friend to both of us, the mere fact did not alarm me unduly; but there was something queer about her letters. She described it herself exactly in one of them. 'I am still feeling *prestissimo*. In fact I can't sleep for a nut. I lie in a kind of *furious bliss*!' And the fury of the bliss would suddenly change into a fury of irritation.

> That man has just been – the doctor – and thumped away. He says I must lie very low for a week. I have taken it beautifully in time and *all is well*. He is so fearfully nice *and* kind *and* has read Tolstoi. What a pearl to find in these oceans of sillies! I feel an atom bit dashed, I confess.
>
> *Knock*. Now I really *am* dashed. Two loathsome females have come to look over the studio. FROM MISS WRIGHT. [K.M.'s landlord.] Is that legal? I thought only 6 weeks beforehand. I'm jiggered! They made my floor filthy – said it was a quaint little place!! but not big enough for *real* furniture.
>
> Oh, Hell. Oh, how I loathe these English!
>
> Courage. Keep calm, Wig. It ain't so bad. But I feel a snip furious, I must allow.
>
> It's all right. I am angry, but not in the you-and-me country. There, all is radiant. If I shut my eyes, will the train carry me away? No. So keep them open and try to be sensible. But it was a push in the face, I must say.

In that letter was a quite unfamiliar note of exasperation which did alarm me. I had already journeyed to London to see Katherine, and she had seemed convalescent. Now I went again. She looked thin and bright-eyed in her little bed; but insisted that she was mending fast. The chief cause of her jumpiness, she said, was that kindly meant interruptions continually prevented her from work. She was engaged, when she had the chance, in putting the final touches to *Prelude*. I suggested that the English winter was really more than she could bear. Why should she not go to

449

the South of France? I was earning enough now to make it possible
for her to travel there in comfort, or what we thought of as
comfort. But she put the idea aside. She had actually signed the
agreement for the rooms in Redcliffe Road. Anyhow, her illness
wasn't serious. We knew all about pleurisy, didn't we?

I stayed the night near by and the grim sense of foreboding
that had been gathering in me fairly took possession of me. I
was engulfed in a black wave of unfaith. And such was the state
of mind which lay in wait for me that the sudden reversal of our
rôles – my illness as it were in a moment transferred to her – was
sinister with destiny. That possibility had never entered my mind;
but now that it was a reality, it seemed to be self-evident. That
was precisely how Necessity – the Beauty of Necessity – would
reveal itself in us!

I tried to keep this horrible foreboding in control. My duty,
as it was to be for years to come, was to be cheerful and confident –
to believe. I knew my duty well enough. But I was past believing.
Deep in my heart was the black stone of unbelief. And yet,
though that is true, it is less than half the truth. Obstinately, in
spite of all fear and all knowledge, there would rise up again in me
the ghost of a naive faith that, somehow, all would be well. It
slowly reasserted itself in me as Katherine persisted in regarding
as a heaven-sent deliverance the doctor's final order that she must
leave England. 'As I am going,' she wrote, when sending me her
passport to be renewed, 'I have a great longing to be ready, and I
feel to-day absolutely strong enough to travel. The spiritual fact
qu'on voyage vers le soleil is such a staff!' 'I feel now that I've only to
get into the sun,' she wrote again, 'and I'll simply burst into leaf
and flower again.' Because she believed that, I came to believe it,
too. She was so certain that I could not help feeling that, in some
mysterious and simple way, she knew.

For, in some ways, she had suddenly become a different
person. Her 'furious bliss' and her furious exasperation belonged to
another Katherine than I had known. 'Yet a funny feature about
this sort of illness is one's temper,' she wrote. 'I get so irritable,

so nervous that I want to *scream*, and if many people start talking, I just lose my puff and feel my blood getting *black*. Perhaps that is because one is a bit weak. I only tell it you to put in your symptom-book.' Possibly it was only a physical symptom, if that 'only' has any meaning. But it seemed to me that there was taking place a deeper change, hard to define. There is a glimpse of it in Katherine's description of herself in the last letter she wrote before she left England.

> These my present letters are really such *self-engrossed dull* affairs that I groan to think of them after they are gone. But you see I feel that life has changed so, and it has all happened so quickly. All my plans are altered. All my future is touched by this – all *our* future rather. It's like suddenly mounting a very fresh, very unfamiliar horse – a *queer, queer* feeling.

As the change appeared to me, it was a sort of rarefaction of her sensitiveness, and I was only too ready to believe that her certainty of a happy issue was due to a keener vision and a more immediate knowledge than I possessed.

But beyond and beneath this childish expectation of a minor and not unfamiliar miracle was a quite different condition: in which the sheer intensity of the love between us was the obscure warrant of its own everlastingness. This 'faith' – for this condition was not undeserving of the name – had nothing to tell me concerning the simple human question of what would happen. Somehow, mere 'happening' was indifferent and unessential to my mind in this condition, which was, perhaps, not unlike Shelley's when he believed that 'the pure spirit' was

> A portion of the Eternal, which must glow
> Through time and change, unquenchably the same.

But this condition was precarious; it was always on the brink of, and passing into, that ecstatic worship of the Beauty of Necessity of which I have spoken: nor was it ever totally distinct from it. Probably, I am trying, even now, to express the inexpressible.

But perhaps some tremor of an experience which is now faint in my memory is still distinguishable in this poem, called 'Surmise'.

> Whether this painèd longing that is mine
>   Is incident to true humanity,
>   Whose slumbering soul has slowly woke in me
> And stretched his quivering arms to some divine
> Immutable perfection that doth shine
>   Most certain and most manifest in thee,
>   Most potent with a sweet serenity
> That serves a final harmony for sign –
> God knows: or that remote unsleeping eye
>   Which smiles upon the pattern which our joys
> Weave on the warp of pain, and silently
>   Mirrors the unknown Beauty in the poise
> Of sad-sweet contemplation, whereof I
>   Through love of thee make surmise, and rejoice.

Perhaps it is a poor poem; but it has the power to recreate in me the strange condition in which I could, by no conscious or desperate effort, identify the extreme anguish of my human love with the extreme ecstasy of my divine love. Nor even to-day could I, nor would I, entirely disown the faith that fumbled for expression there.

CHAPTER XXXI

EINE ALTE GESCHICHTE

GAY and confident, Katherine left London for Bandol on Tuesday, January 8th, 1918. As the curving train left Waterloo Station, we waved to one another, a long time. So sure of the outcome was she that she made me promise to write to her only twice a week because I was so thronged with work. With some such sensible businesslike arrangement our partings always began.

I received a joyful letter from her in Paris. Everything had gone wonderfully, she wrote. France had wrought the usual miracle: all her indifference to the visible world, to life, had left her. She was 'unreasonably, deeply happy'. So all was well. And, as usual, the aura of her presence remained with me for several days, during which the fact that we were separated, and both alone again, was not real to me. Not until the Sunday following, when the pressure of my routine work was lifted, did her absence come home to me.

This evening I felt the desire not to be alone. I thought of all the people whom I might go and see. *All*. At most, three . . . It is curious that I have all the old temptations of Christianity. They have other colours and contexts; but essentially they are the same. There is an hour of loneliness, when one is weak, and the self one has conquered trembles and would not stand alone. 'Lead us not into temptation!' It is an evil thing to seek to escape our own loneliness. Of that I am certain. Perhaps we are not really worth much until we love our loneliness and consort with her for ever. Perhaps loneliness is not the terrible thing we believe it to be. Perhaps achievement begins at the point when we have changed it from a negative to a positive state, from a barren to a pregnant.

I overcame the temptation to escape my loneliness. From this time forward I strove to make my loneliness my friend. If others sought me out, well and good; but there should be no motion of mine towards them. I would have either love or loneliness. And now that silence had descended between me and Katherine since she had left Paris, I would be the lover of loneliness itself. At the end of the entry in the journal is the draft of a sonnet.

> O Loneliness, of my proud heart be queen!
>> Grant me a lover's privilege: to hold
>> Thee ever closer to my soul, be bold
> To lift the veil that hides thy form unseen,
> To trample down the terrors that have been
>> Thine own grim guardians, driving me to old
>> Back from the brink of new, and from the untold
> Back to the weary lie . . .
> Let drop thy veil, let lift my weight of fear,
>> And let me gaze in thy cold lucid eyes
>>> Till I shall see the Void become the All
> And, pressed to thy slow-heaving bosom, hear
>> Thy silence fill the world, and I am wise
>>> Yet without pride, and sad, yet without gall.

Into the peace thus glimpsed, or half-achieved, came the next day the shattering news from Katherine that her journey south had been one long agony, mocking all her confidence, and that she was seriously ill. It was a cry of anguish.

Tuesday, January 15. Yesterday, I had the first letter from Bandol, and to-day a second. She asks me to write to her every day: 'parceque je suis tellement malade'. Oh, why did she ever go so far away? It seems as though, because we are more in love than any other man or woman in the world, we must go through a perpetual torment of absence and illness – and, most awful of all, illness in absence. I do not believe that

454

anyone has ever had, more than we, the sense of the vastness and inhumanity of the world and of our own frailness and smallness.

Wednesday, January 16. As usual, it has taken a day for the sense of her loneliness and my fear to *penetrate me*. It is the old story of two years ago [i.e. of December, 1915], with this ironic difference that I am now finally caged. I cannot move hand or foot. Nor can I think about it. I merely feel that the ground has given way beneath my feet. No, it is something more subtle and awful than this. The ground has given way beneath my soul. And to me, I know not why, one of the most awful elements in my situation is that the ground has *not* given way beneath my body also. I worked harder at the office to-day (S—— and V—— being away) than I have ever done, and probably better, and certainly more swiftly; I am now drinking hot milk and eating biscuits. Talk of irony! The Mind that imagined this conjuncture of soul and body had a conception of Irony that would freeze the human mind alive if it could but grasp it. What about Ivan's dream? Just let the soul achieve its purpose; just let it flood out into an overwhelming emotion – and see the body! *Mens insana in corpore sano*: no, just *mens in corpore*, it's quite enough. The essence and the culmination of the Timeless Jest is there. And we don't see it! 'O'er-informed his tenement of clay': yes, but they don't see that the very juxtaposition of the two is so utterly grotesque, so indelibly insulting!

Yet the paradox, I suppose, is resolved, the insult washed out, the grotesque antinomy made harmony, at one moment: when we are passionate lovers. When we are not passionate lovers, we are the fools of Time. Nothing then but passionate love, yes, love that should be all passion, at every moment of its being, is the salvation of man from the derision of Eternity. *Amor intellectualis, amor corporealis, amor angelicus, amor animalis.*

No, *tout se paie*. The passionate lovers who burn out the

brand on humanity, have it most deeply burned in them. *Amor intellectualis Dei.* Yes, I can well imagine that, once you apprehended the nature of the God who had done this thing with his material, you would love him intellectually. What else, in God's name, would there be to do? Besides, it was, at least, an aesthetic triumph. After all, art in its wildest dreams and its wildest dreamer, Dostoevsky, has only begun to touch the furthest fringe of this 'utter beauty in utter grotesqueness' – which is no less than the secret of the world, the mystery of being, and the heart of God!

So my lucid and desperate mind struggled with the pain that now engulfed me. I was in such a condition that I could seriously wonder whether even the invincible springing of hope within myself was a symptom of callousness.

Thursday, January 17. How I clutch at straws! How I persuade myself that that which I want to be, is! Two letters from K—— and I am ready to believe that she is getting better. I wonder: Is it coldness in me? Inhumanity? Is it that by some instinct I refuse to face a truth which hurts me, as I refuse to face life itself? Or do I grow petrified and turn to insentient, immovable stone? Or is there just some fibre of feeling lacking in me? Or is it faith, a profound conviction that our love is eternal as the stars?

I do not put these questions to myself mechanically, or idly as a *jeu de mots*, or by some irrepressible casuistry, or out of a mere desire to write (though for some reason I have to write it well); but because each one in turn seems to have as much truth in it as the others. At one moment I caught myself thinking what would happen if she were to die, and I am horrified at my own callousness. What is a lover made of? Is it, after all, ordinary clay that claims the right to speak in undefended moments? Or is it that love contains within itself something inhuman – so superhuman a belief in its own duration that it becomes hard and cruel to all thoughts of mortality? Does it trample underfoot all fears, however just and tender? Or is it so full of fears that it will not think on them? Or is it . . . I could go on asking these questions of my inscrutable soul, I think, for ever, or until I made myself sick with the many cigarettes I smoked.

I was seeking to impose an impossible discipline upon myself. I was trying to apply the same intolerable 'honesty' to my human love as I did to my concern for Europe and for Peace. I was asking myself: Had I the *right* to hope and believe? Was it not conniving, for the sake of happiness, at a self-deception which, by my creed, was ignoble? Truly, now, the dreamer had venomed *all* his days. There was not, and perhaps there never could be again, any possibility of returning to that condition wherein the joy was joy, and the pain, pain. If the joy of confidence returned to me, I shrank away from being possessed by it as from an ignominious and cowardly connivance at my own deception. I was forgetting, and only the coward forgets. And yet, at the same moment, quite clear before my mind was the absolute necessity of turning a brave and smiling face to Katherine. Under such conflicting tensions, it seemed that something was bound to crack.

Whether it did crack or not, I do not know; but I know that I felt that my existence was impossible. Yet I existed. Yet existence was impossible: impossible. I had to think and feel and act on two levels, from two beings, simultaneously. The simplest acts became nightmarish in their perplexity. Thus, for example, if I had not agreed, or if I had even hesitated in agreeing, that it was enough that we should write to each other twice a week, I should have shown Katherine that I did not share her confidence. Whether I did share it or not, I did not know. And when, before the appointed time, the desire seized me to write to her, I felt 'ashamed of my own incontinence' (as I put it in my journal) and feebly excused myself by saying it was merely a part of a letter, sent in advance because I might not have time to write fully when the appointed day came. But when her anguished, lonely letters reached me I straightway fell to accusing myself of unimaginative stupidity.

Why am I such an unimaginative fool? I should have known – I did know – I should have *realized*, how different France had become in the exhaustion of these last two years of war. I should have *realized* (in spite of her telegrams from Havre and Paris) that the journey would be awful. I should have *realized* that even if France had been at peace and *riante*, she would be lonely when she arrived. It has happened before: I had only to remember.

So I accused myself bitterly; but the accusation was preposterous. For the necessary condition of Katherine's former confidence had been that I should not allow myself to *realize* those things. She had set her heart on the sun and I dared not deny her. What I could have accused myself of – if I had been capable of it in those days – was weakness in not having firmly taken control and commanded her to stay in England. Instead of that, through the eagerness of my desire that she should be happy, and still more through some renascent spark of faith in our 'star', I had allowed myself to dream her dream; and now, in consequence, I was caught in a position where my own instinct for right action with regard to her was undermined. I blamed myself for things that were not blameable; I made impossible demands upon myself.

I am glad (I wrote in my journal) that I had decided to write every day before she asked me: no, more than *glad*. It was evidence – and I needed it – in my own eyes that I was not utterly worthless, nor utterly unworthy of her. I acted all through on impulse. Not till I *felt* she was absent did the desire to call to her come upon me. But that is not enough; love demands more than that one should act on impulse. A lover is not a true lover unless he thinks, calculates and imagines what the other will need and desire. And he must do this so often that it becomes almost an instinct, too. It is not sufficient for him to say: I am by nature this. He has no right to claim that allowance should be made, or indulgence given. He has to be more than himself.

That was an exacting creed; evidence of how literally true it was that I had 'made love all my religion'. Of course, I failed to live up to it, precisely as the sincere Christian must fail to live up to his creed. But I was in a worse case even than the Christian, for I was binding myself to supply all that another human being 'needed and desired'. And what, above all things else, she needed and desired was to be strengthened in the faith that her dream of happy love would come true. To satisfy that need and desire I had to become either credulous or omnipotent: to be as a child, or to be as God.

I sought in both directions, according to my nature. It was no accident that at this moment I turned towards Spinoza, and copied into my journal on January 20th words which, as the years have passed, have become more and more indisputable to me.

> Most who have written on the emotions, the manner of human life, seem to have dealt not with natural things which follow the general laws of Nature, but with things which lie outside the sphere of Nature; they seem to have conceived man in Nature as a kingdom within a kingdom. For they believe that man disturbs rather than follows the course of Nature, and that he has absolute power in his actions, and is not determined in them by anything other than himself.

Yet, at the very moment that I was saturating myself with this bitter and sustaining truth, I was also committing myself to an extreme assertion of the independent sovereignty of the human emotions. While I bowed to the truth of Spinoza, I clung desperately – for Katherine's sake rather than my own – to the faith that love like ours, by its very extremity, must prevail. And, alas, I was not made like Katherine; I could not surrender myself

459

wholly to the emotion as it came. I could not pass from total confidence to total despair and back again. Behind my confidence was a despair; and likewise, behind my despair, a confidence. But the confidence behind my despair was not a confidence in any future happiness: on the contrary, it was a confidence in a power that wrought beauty out of human disaster. My veiled goddess dwelt with beauty, indeed; but with 'Beauty that must die'.

Since that was no faith on which to draw to comfort Katherine, I turned avidly to the comfort of a dream. In the previous summer we had imagined between us what our life should be after the war. We had built in our dream a farmhouse-cottage, where we would live together as we had lived at the Villa Pauline, the only difference being that we would have many children. There we would set up a printing-press, and print our own writings bit by bit – my brother Richard helping us – and live frugally yet bounteously on the proceeds. We would be as far as might be self-supporting, and we would ignore the world which was actively or unconsciously hostile to what we stood for. This little house, where the life of love was to be lived, as we, by experience, knew it could be lived, in a condition of 'being in some perfectly blissful way at peace', we called The Heron Farm, in memory of Katherine's brother Leslie, whose second name was Heron. The Heron Farm was the concrete symbol of that happiness in love which we knew was not altogether a dream; and it was our secret. To this I turned. Did I believe in it? God knows. It depends on what is meant by belief; but if ever a man tried to believe in something I tried to believe in The Heron.

As the strain of separation became more intense, we found ourselves frequently expressing the same thought at the same moment, quite unknown to one another. Thus, a letter would come from Katherine pointing me to a sonnet by Wordsworth which, reckoning backward, I found that I had been reading on the very day her letter was written; or she would be telling me to read a poem by Wyatt, on the same afternoon that I was buying, on nothing but vague impulse, a copy of his poems. It was for

K. M., photographed by Walter Bennington, 1917

this reason chiefly that we began at this moment systematically to preserve each other's letters; we conceived the idea that one day we would prepare a record of these strange correspondences between us. After one such correspondence, when I received from her a post-card of 'Les Charmettes' at the moment I was pondering upon J.-J. Rousseau, I wrote to her:

It's no use talking about these identities of ours. I have not the slightest doubt (seriously) that we are manifestations of the same being. One might be a coincidence, two might be; but ever since the Heron began, we have gone on and on. Don't think I'm mystical if I explain it like this. The night *when we discovered the Heron together*, we became one being. The quality of that evening I shall always remember; and with these correspondences it recurs to me again and again. I feel certain that what I say is true. We became one being and this one being expressed itself that night in the Heron. Therefore, the Heron is more than the symbol of our love, it is the creation of our one being. From that night on we have been fused in soul, so that our correspondences now seem to me the most natural and inevitable thing in the world. Now, I am perfectly aware that if I were to say this to anybody else but you, they would think me raving. But to me it is simple truth in exactly the same way as $2+2=4$. Everything now conspires to tell me that I am right . . .

Sometimes now I begin to think tremulously *high* thoughts, thoughts which make me dizzy. Suddenly, I seem to know the secret of the universe. And this at least I know, beyond all doubt, that I know the way to the secret, and that my life will be spent in trying to make the pathway clear. I know this, too, that you and I are *geniuses*. I didn't know it before the real meaning of the Heron began to dawn on me as it has lately done. You saw that into your work and mine a new strong wind of *power* had come. I didn't know *why* it had come – why we two, at the moment when we seemed more frail

than all the other creatures of the earth, should become
suddenly *strong-winged in the spirit*. Now, I begin to see. What
I said about the Heron just now is part of the explanation.
But that is outward merely; behind that I feel there is a
bigger explanation still. You and I are manifestations of the
same being; yes, but *that same being is also a manifestation*. I feel
I am on the way to discovering of what.

That way, no doubt, lay madness; but it was necessary for
me to go that way. I had somehow to twist the sense of destiny
and doom that was upon me into an assurance of comfort. For
the wail of anguish that came to me from Katherine was more
than I could bear. And when she wrote to say that she was better,
I was haunted by the undertone. 'It is quite true', she wrote on
January 20th, 'I have been *bloody ill*. But these last two days I
feel a good deal better, and quite a different child. Chiefly because I know I am not going to get worse and that we shall be
together again. I really did, at one or two times, think I would
"peg out" here, without ever having had a Heron or a Heronette,
and that simply horrified me.' The traces of her terror remained.
Within a week she was longing to return; but she could not come.
Not only was she totally unfit to travel; but the condition on which
the authorities had allowed her to leave England was that she
must not return for three months. Though she affected to make
light of this, and to be certain that she would be able to return as
soon as she could stand the journey, her underlying fear was
palpable. She might be too ill, or she might not be allowed to
come. 'I mean to come back next month, March', she wrote on
February 1st. 'By that time I shall be as well as I ever shall be
during this war – and – and – oh, I *must* come. I can't stick it out
for longer.' That was how she put it when she was calm. But
almost at the same moment, she was writing:

Darling, I do in a way live here. I see a great deal, am
very solitary and quiet: lead the life I tell you of, never speaking to anybody except *bon jour* and *bon soir* – and yet in a way

it is all absolutely unreal: it is all a dream. My mind seems
to do nothing but build and build and try and try that bridge
that brings me home. I get into *panics* that I shall not be
allowed home; the offensive will stop it; France will run out
of coal. No, you would laugh at my fears. But life as it is at
present *is* too terrifying to be endured alone . . . Even one
day without a letter is sufficient to start me off like this.

Laugh at her fears! My fears for her were even greater than
her own; for my hopelessness was deeper – or I thought it was.
But when, early in February, she began to write a story, and wrote
to explain that she was fully launched in her second writing-mood
– 'an extremely deep sense of hopelessness, of everything doomed
to disaster' – I knew that her truth was speaking. She was now
beyond trying to cheer me up. And I, in reply, said that her letter
'somehow told me more nearly what you felt and how you were
than any you have written me.' Now, for the first time, Katherine
was beaten down and engulfed by the War.

Except for the first few warm days here, when I really did
seem to forget it, it's never been out of my mind – and everything is poisoned by it. It's *here in me* the whole time, eating
me away, and I am simply terrified by it. It's at the root of my
homesickness and anxiety and panic. I think it took being
alone here and unable to work to make me fully *accept* it.
But now I don't think that even you would beat me.

But more instantly convincing even than that was the actual
story which she sent me. *Je ne parle pas français* is, I believe, a
great short story, with its quality stamped upon it for all time.
But there is also a moving personal symbolism in it which only I
could understand. The fate of the Mouse, caught in the toils of
the world's evil, abandoned by her lover, is Katherine's fate. She
sent it to me in two halves. Of the first part I was able to write
objectively.

463

Your MS. came this morning. It's not only first-rate; it's overwhelming. The description – no, not description, creation – of that café is extraordinary. The whole thing is extraordinary. I don't know what you are going to do at all. But I'm absolutely fascinated.

I'll try to tell you what I feel. In the first place my sensation is like that which I had when I read Dostoevsky's *Letters from the Underworld*. That is, it's utterly unlike any sensation I have ever yet had from any writing of yours, or any writing at all except Dostoevsky's.

Secondly, though it's like D—— in that unearthly way he has of putting you in a place and stopping the world – everything stands still, becomes timeless – and though you have (the Lord knows how) kept this up all through, so that the first page and the last seem to be simultaneous, happening in the same icy moment – and this is the final, large impression the whole chapter leaves . . . It's all of such a different kind from any of your other work – different, I mean, in scope and skeleton and structure. The exquisite exactness – the this and nothing else – of your vision is there just as before. How can I put it? This is the only writing of yours I know that seems to be *dangerous*. Do you understand what I mean by the adjective? It's *dangerous* to stop the world for a timeless moment.

To put it another way. Here you seem to have begun to drag *the depths of your consciousness*. Before, you did something quite different, and I am certain that you will again. But somehow it has happened that on this one occasion you were driven to make an utterly new approach, to express something different. I mean it like this. Ordinarily what you express and satisfy is your desire to write, because you are a born writer, and a writer born with a true vision of the world. Now you express and satisfy some other desire, perhaps because for a moment you doubt or have not got the other vision. The world is shut out. You are looking into yourself.

I did not realize, because the story was not complete, all the personal symbolism of *Je ne parle pas*; but I did realize, better than she herself, what a deep and icy despair underlay it. I was made aware of Katherine's secret thought, as she could never have told it directly; aware of the knowledge that lay hidden deep in her physical being. This she kept in subjection only by the intensity of her love, the ardency of her heart's desire. Out of that heart's desire she could write, with complete conviction, when she sent me the second part of the story:

> Again this fusion of our minds. You talk of love-poetry. All I write or ever, ever will write, will be the fruit of our love – love prose. This time, for instance, as I went on and *on*, I fed on our love. Nightingales, if you like, brought me heavenly manna. Could I have done it without you? No, a million times. I don't want to exaggerate the importance of this story or to harp on it; but it's a tribute to Love you understand, and the very best I can do just now.

Katherine meant this, and indeed it was only in part a self-deception, or a necessary illusion. It was true in the sense that only Love could feel and utter the agony of Love's disaster. But the deeper truth she herself had expressed when she first began to write the story, when she had said that, for her, there were two conditions of creativeness – the blissful peace of love, and the despair of hopelessness, and her story was born of the latter. True, the despair also was what it was 'because she had known love'. But it was in that tragic sense alone that her story was a love-story, born of love and sustained by it.

The second part which she sent me with this strange commentary, struck me dumb and numb, with pain. It hurt too much. 'Pas de nougat pour le noël', was bad enough; but when it was the blossom of the life and love between us that was stricken, I winced. For the Mouse *is* Katherine, the secret Katherine, the Katherine whom I alone knew, and the world never can. Mysteriously, unconsciously, she had spoken a doom. It had to be spoken; and it was not she who spoke it. It came from deeper than herself. But it was a knell in my heart.

I was not surprised that immediately she had emerged from the ecstasy of writing it, 'going on and *on*' through utter physical exhaustion – 'God, *how* tired I am! How I'd love to curl up against you and *sleep*!' – she was overwhelmed with the longing to get home again. While the story was writing she had been surrendered to a condition which her waking mind would flee. 'I am still in a state of work', she had written from the depth of it, 'dead quiet and spinning away. I feel rather that I ought to stick it till April'. She was then the impersonal Katherine, far removed, sunk into the silent centre of her own apartness, a prophetess of destiny, a Sibyl. But when the dead quiet lifted, she would be afraid like a child waked by an evil dream. Straightway she turned in panic towards home, arranging the telegram that I must send her, in order that she could persuade the authorities to let her go. And straightway, with the same motion of her being, she called upon me to believe in a future of happiness.

YOU ARE NOT TO THINK FOR ONE SECOND THAT THERE WILL BE THE SAME OLD WORLD AFTER THE WAR (she wrote on February 17th). All you have to think of is that it cannot NOT come true. It's so utterly simple. We shall live on honeydew and milk of Paradise; we shall be happy and free immediately. There's not a moment to lose. Ah, my soul, if you doubt *this*; if you feel for one moment that the big stone could fall on your head, then Love is not what I think it is . . . Bogey, what can I say? It makes me so unhappy when you doubt it. I want to wring my hands and run up and down. We know each other and our wants and ways are plain to us . . . Don't you want to be my mate and live with me in a tiny cottage and eat out of egg-cups? How *can* you torture me by thinking anything else is possible?

I did my best. But it was easier for her to forget her story than it was for me. It had come from that 'other' Katherine who

466

now was not. It had come from her unconsciousness, but it was imprinted on my consciousness. I remembered; I mistrusted her confidence, mistrusted it the more, the more confident it was. And her confidence had reached a fantastic height. Her friend, L.M., hearing the news of her illness, had insisted on going out to her. She had sent Katherine a telegram to say that she was coming, which Katherine in her paradoxical exaltation regarded as a sinister mystery. It must be, she argued, that something terrible had happened to *me* and that L.M. was coming to break the news. Letter after letter came to me, written between the receipt of the telegram and L.M.'s arrival, palpitating with anxiety for *me*. Anxiety for *me* was now eating her away! I felt that we were caught in the toils of a bitter madness – we had eaten 'the insane root that makes the reason prisoner'.

I ceased even to feel; I became numb, more or less as I described it in a later letter to Katherine:

Flat, stale and unprofitable, giddy with the immense and endless spinning of the world. How shall I say it? Neither despairing, nor depressed, but *grey*. That's my danger now. It's so hard to go on, so easy to be carried on. I can go on only by forgetting for a little while; I am carried on when I neither remember nor forget. The world just rushes, I don't know why or whither – to salvation, I try to believe when I can try; to ruin, I feel at other moments. I am like a man doing dumb-bell exercises incredible thousands of times. He doesn't doubt, he doesn't believe. He is just part of IT, doing dumb-bell exercises: perhaps IT is the soul of the universe. I don't know. I wish I could explain. It's as though I put out tendrils feverishly into something beyond, true, steady, outside this spinning world; but the world spins on and the tendrils are torn away – snap, snap, snap – and the place they are torn from goes numb. But I go on still. But never a tendril clings.

In such a condition I waited for the evil which I knew would come. Sure enough, it came.

467

I want to tell you some things which are a bit awful (she wrote on February 19th), so hold me hard. I've not been so well these last few days . . . Look here! I can't leave this place till April – it's no earthly go. I can't and mustn't. Can't risk a draught or a chill and mustn't walk. I've got a bit of a temperature, and I'm not so fat as I was when I came, and, Bogey, this is NOT serious, does NOT keep me in bed, but I have been spitting a bit of blood . . . Before the doctor came, I was so frightened. Now I'm confiding – it's not serious. But when I saw the bright arterial blood, I nearly had a fit . . . In April there can't be the same chance of a snow-storm or a wind that might make 'pas de nougat pour le noël' for us both. I think it must be. And then, please God, we'll be married.

That bright arterial blood – how well I knew it! How clearly I had foreseen it, ever since I had made the story of Keats part of my life! And how well I also knew the frightened heart that hid behind those brave words!

Ah, well; but Keats – that was a hundred years ago, and things have changed since then. Pulmonary tuberculosis was now curable – quite curable. Well, may be. But that girl, already devoured by anxiety to return, and fear that she never would return, was eating herself away. The tubercle might be the physical sign, but something deeper was gnawing at her. This sentence that she must not move till April would tighten the strings till they would snap. And it was all bound to be – as it was, and not otherwise. It was an old, old story, told ages ago.

> Es ist eine alte Geschichte
> Doch bleibt es immer neu.

The story of the Princess and the lover: how they were parted, and how she pined. Who does not know it? How romantic it is and lovely, and how long ago! How sweet and far! For in the modern world these things happen no more. Perhaps they do not

– I cannot tell. Perhaps we were indeed a terribly old-fashioned pair. 'I was thinking in bed this morning,' she wrote the day before the bright blood came, 'I can't think how we should have got on if we were not to be married in April. I felt it will make things go easy, all sorts of things, and the feeling will be quite different. Apart from thousands of other things, I know I shall take the most childish delight in speaking of you as my husband after you really are'. No, this Princess, for all her courage and her genius, was not modern; she felt and suffered in the old unfashionable ways.

> I feel much better to-day (she wrote the day after she had told of the bright blood) and the hæmorrhage is – hardly at all. Can't work much or think very sensibly, but I am ever so much better than I was. The worst of all this is *this*. I have such a longing for you. I feel once *you* had me, I should get well. Once we ate together, the food would go to the right spot. If I was in bed with you I'd sleep – and this is a sort of *deep, deep* conviction. I cannot help it. I *pine* when I am away from you just like the ladies do in old songs, and all my efforts seem to be in vain. However, I am making very great ones to be a strong girl for April. The absence from you eats at my heart.

In the silence of my room at night words like these became for me a physical sensation. I would *hear* the absence eating at her heart, the destruction eating at her body; and a lucid agony of despair would take hold of me. It was the time when the air-raids on London were at height, and I found some kind of relief in walking through the empty streets in the superstitious hope that a merciful bomb would drop near me. That we were marked down by destiny was plain to my sick and apprehensive soul, and I was weary of waiting for the issue.

Of the strange adventures of my soul during those days I had perforce to be silent in my letters to Katherine. My duty and my desire were to build up her confidence; and that I could only do, or try to do, by indulging my own childish faith. I sought to build up a dream-world, by letting my fancy play about the Heron, by dwelling on our 'correspondences', by weaving them both together.

On Sunday (I wrote on February 26th – a week after her hæmorrhage), when I was chewing the last straw and unable to work, I began Wordsworth's *Excursion*. I read 100 pages of it that night, and it did me good, I can tell you. It's all so honest, so desperately honest; and so *pure*. There isn't any other word for it. I began to feel calm: my jangling nerves began, if not to sing, at least to croon. When I have finished it (When will that be, say the bells of old Bailey?) I shall just turn it upside down and begin again. Like you I can read nothing but poetry, and no poetry but English poetry (if indeed there *is* any other) now. Of course, when you said that in a letter the other day, it was another pure case of our identical soul. I mean that just as a matter-of-fact truth. It doesn't even surprise me now, except in the way that any profound delight has in it an element of surprise. I want somehow to have a complete collection of English poetry gathered together before the end of the war.

You'd laugh at me for the way my thoughts are always turning to the details of preparation for this great voyage of ours on a tiny ship to a desert island. Every book I buy is bought with a kind of feeling that when the war is over we shan't be able to buy any books – not so much because we shan't have the money – I can't tell and don't vastly care about that – but because we shall somewhere, somehow have *weighed anchor*. All the stores will be aboard, all the books, all the saucepans, all the corduroy suits: we shall make all fast, shut the shutters, and look at each other, take a deep breath, and smile (you know *how* we'll smile), and then will begin such a voyage that no one will ever hear of us again. 'Oh, those two,' they'll say, 'they disappeared. They were very unpractical and ungrateful. No one ever hears of them' . . . Oh, all sorts of childish perfectly certain things fly through my mind.

What the Heron was is beyond my power to describe. It was the secret gathering-place of all that was true and pure and beautiful and human: of all that denied the war. As the war came nearer with its menace of death to our love, so the Heron became more lovely, and more near, and more inaccessible; and so we clung to it more desperately.

And now the menace of death began to come very near indeed. Early in March Katherine made up her mind that she must attempt to return to England. It was all very well for the doctor to assure her that she must wait till April to gain the strength to travel. She knew that she would get no more strength by waiting. The pang of absence went on eating her away; and also the pang of fear. There were rumours of a great German offensive. If that were to begin before she was on the way she might never return at all. All communication would be cut off, and she would die. So she determined to make the attempt. I sent her the telegram she had arranged, summoning her home, and she sent it to the Consulate in Marseilles. The Consul smiled at it. That was the kind of telegram which all the people who had come out to the Riviera 'for fun' were presenting to him. He could do nothing. She must get permission from the Military Permit Office in Paris, which might take ten days or a fortnight. She was plunged in despair. 'The idea that the war can do this' (she wrote) 'in addition to all that it has done to us, *strikes* me, and lays me low for the moment. I'll get up again. I'm only speaking "spiritually", but at present after I had packed and taken my tickets, I should cry if I wrote any more. I feel I can't bear this absence a great deal longer – and yet – they *will* torture me.'

She had sent L.M. to the Consul at Marseilles, for she herself was in a raging fever. Now she determined to go to see him herself. Her only chance of being allowed to board the Paris train, she felt, was to put before the authorities medical evidence which they could not ignore. But how was she to do that? For the doctor, shady and disreputable though he was, had professional conscience enough to insist that any attempt to travel in her condition was mere madness: and, this time because he was shady and disreputable, he would have no glimmering of the truth of her conviction that if she was not allowed to travel, she would die. Somehow she would contrive it. But she only half-believed it. 'I think I shall leave in the middle of next week', she wrote on March 15th. 'But though I write that, I don't feel it. Somehow a curious *numbness* is beginning in me about this journey – or a sort of feeling that it is all going to take place in the pitch-dark, with no thought of place or time.'

'Don't wait – don't wait so ardently,' she wrote the next day. 'They won't let me through yet, and while I know you wait like that my lamentable state in this prison is like to kill me. I could *break through* – and yet I can't.' In truth, we were like to kill each other now. Her words sometimes seemed to scald me. 'Every drop of blood that I have is *sick* for home,' she wrote; and straightway every drop of my blood went sick. She lived (she wrote) 'in that mingled fever, dread, and dismayed impatience that one must feel in a tumbril'; and long afterwards I was told that one of my colleagues at the office, glancing into my room, saw my queer pale face and said to another that 'I looked as though I were waiting to be taken off to execution.' I wrote to her about the Heron. 'I look, I see, I feel,' she answered, 'and then I say THE WAR, and it seems to disappear, to be taken off like a film, and I am sitting in the dark.'

Next I heard that she was in Marseilles. Here is the story as she told it me in a letter, written from a Marseilles café.

Last night after I wrote to you I felt desperate and sent L.M. after Doctor Poached Eyes, even though it was rather late. He was at dinner – fatal time! but promised to turn up. Whereupon I set to – threw L.M. out of my room – dressed in my old frock and a black swanny(?) round my neck, *made* up, drew chairs to the fire, and waited for this little toad. If you could have come in, you would have been horribly shocked, I think. I have not felt so cynical for years. I knew my man and determined to get him by the only weapon I could, and that *he* could understand. He came more than three parts drunk – and I sat down and played the old game with him – listened – looked – smoked his cigarettes – and asked finally for a chit that would satisfy the Consul. He gave me the chit but whether it will, I'll not know till to-morrow. It could not be more urgent in its way. I dictated it *and* had to spell it *and* lean over him while he wrote *and* hear him say – what dirty dogs do say. I am sure he is here because he has killed some poor girl with a dirty buttonhook. He is a maniac on *venereal* diseases and *passion*. Ah, the filthy little brute! There I sat and smiled and let him talk. I was determined to get him for my purpose in any way that didn't involve letting him touch me. He could say what he liked: I laughed and spelled and was so sweet and soft and so *obliged*.

Oh dear, oh dear! I feel so strange. An old, dead, sad, wretched self blows about, whirls about in my foolish brain – and I sit here in this café, drinking and looking at the mirrors and smoking and thinking how utterly corrupt life is – how hideous human beings are – how loathsome it was to catch this toad as I did – with *such* a weapon. I keep hearing him say, very thick, 'any trouble is a pleasure for a lovely woman', and seeing my soft smile . . .

I am very sick, Bogey. Marseilles is so hot and loud. They scream the newspapers and all the shops seem full of caged birds – parrots and canaries – shrieking, too. And the hags sell nuts and oranges – and I run up and down *on fire*. Anything – anything to get home. It all spins like a feverish dream. I am not unhappy or happy. I am just as it were in the thick of a bombardment, writing to you, here, from a front-line trench. I do remember that the fruit trees on the way were all in flower and there were such big daisies in the grass and a little baby smiled at me in the train . . . But this is all a dream, you see. I want to come home – to come home.

The prophetic vision of *Je ne parle pas* was now being realized in her actual life. The 'cry against corruption' was no longer her imaginative description of her motive and mood in writing such a story; the cry was real and physical, wrung from her heart and lips. 'I have lived through lives and lives since I last wrote to you in calm,' she wrote a little later from Marseilles, when she had produced her certificate to the Consul, and he had reluctantly given her permission to take the train as far as Paris. And I seemed to have lived through lives and lives with her.

She had been warned that she would not be allowed to go on from Paris until the Military Permit Office spoke the word; but she believed that she would be able to persuade them in person where they would disregard a letter; and, still more, she was hungry for the sense of being so many hundred miles nearer home. But all in vain. When at last she did arrive in Paris, on March 21st, she was told that she had no right to have come, and that she must wait for formal permission. It might take a week, it might take ten days, they told her. And just at this moment the regulations against strangers in Paris had been stiffened, and she was compelled to go every day to the police. To the police, to the Permit Office, to Cook's, where she hoped to find a message from me – such was her daily round in the extreme fever of phthisis.

My head is quite empty (she wrote when her hopes had been dashed in Paris) after the journey and getting about and the disappointment and the fatigue of this looking for rooms. Also the fact that I have not heard from you for days is *dreadful, dreadful* . . . Please wire, just a word, dearest. Oh God, it *is* a blow. Ten days more. This journey – it never, never ends. I seem to have been trying to get back to you from that moment we stopped waving.

The posts and telegraphs in France were now completely dis-
organized. Her letters reached me with some regularity; but my
letters and telegrams to her seemed to disappear entirely. Heart-
rending appeal after appeal came to me to break the silence. I
was impotent. Then came the final blow. The long-range bombardment of Paris began, and the cross-Channel boat service for
civilian traffic was completely cut off. Then for a while the silence
was complete.

It would be foolish to quote our letters any more. There they
lie, in order as they were written, before me now. They would
mean nothing to anyone who cannot imagine what they were.
But here is one of mine.

My own precious darling,

Somehow I survive from one day into another. But after
yesterday's news [that she would not be allowed to leave
Paris], to hear that they are shelling Paris with big guns – I
am just a blind thing made of impatience and fears. It is as
though our life consisted in saying, 'No, this is the worst
thing that can happen', and these words being always the
signal for something worse. I spend all my time trying to be
confident; but to-day I haven't made much of a success of it,
I'm afraid.

Therefore, I can say nothing. I would say – if it were not
so foolish – that I am frightened of saying how much I love
you, for fear that would bring disaster. This kind of love is
not an easy thing to tell, anyhow. I breathe with your breath;
I am not here, I am there where you are. When you are
calm, I am; when you are frightened, I am also. Every
moment just shows how *literally* true it was when I said that
I should not take a deep breath until I have you in my arms
again.

I can't, I never shall, understand how the world goes on
while these things happen. I can't imagine that there has
ever been anything like the derision and the mockery of these

gorgeous days. There's something so awful about their beauty that it terrifies me utterly.

Monday morning.

I have just got your letter from Paris saying you are looking for rooms. My darling, don't be anxious about *me*: it's too preposterous. I am perfectly well: no chimney-pots have fallen on my head: no motor buses have run over me. That I worry and worry about you just now – well, that can't be helped and nothing will change that.

I promise I'll make a valiant effort to keep heart; do you try to do the same. But oh, my darling.

Boge.

I had arranged to take a week's leave from the office when Katherine arrived. I had taken it for granted, when I had received her telegram that she was leaving Marseilles, that she would be in London in one, or at most two days. It never entered my head that she would take the fatal risk of going to Paris without the assurance that she would be allowed to travel on from there. When the news came that she was detained, I postponed my week's leave for a week. Nothing more was possible. Other people's leave depended on mine. But she was kept in Paris for twenty days. My leave came and went while she was there. I have not had many holidays in my life. But that was assuredly the strangest one I have ever spent. The irony of it was truly superb. The silence that had descended between us was still as death itself. Nevertheless, I wrote every day.

I spent the second day of my *holiday* (I wrote) wandering about London. I wandered up and down Tottenham Court Road and felt that all I saw was a dream in a fever. The sun was shining, though when I went out in the morning there was a fog. I looked in shop after shop and prayed for the Heron. I can't remember a single thing. The whole of London seems to be made of dirty cardboard. Someone has merely to touch it in the right place and it will all fall flat to the ground. I felt terribly hungry for real things – trees, and a solid oak floor, and copper pans thick as shell-cases. All the strong, solid things are being devoured by the war, and only the shams are left. And among all these shams one pines away, and my blood seems to get thin. Together, we were strong enough to battle through. Without you, I have absolutely nothing to fall back upon. I can almost believe that my imagination is only a queer unreal fever; it is so far divorced from the earth where its roots should be, like one of those freak flowers that grow when they plant the seed in the darkness, and it makes its painful way ever so far to a tiny speck of light, where it breaks into a too fragile blossom. I want to be a stout rose or an apple; I don't want to be anything orchidaceous. In other words, being parted from you, I used literature as a drug, and now, at the crisis, I feel that I've taken too many tabloids. A sense of emptiness hangs over me.

Nevertheless, in a state of still desperation, I went from place to place, trying to enlist the aid of the few people I knew who might have influence to secure that, when civilian communication between Paris and London was reopened, Katherine should be allowed to return. Rather grudgingly, a friend in the Foreign Office wrote to a colleague of his in the Embassy in Paris, and I received the assurance that Katherine had permission to travel on the first boat whenever traffic was resumed. My Foreign Office friend was genuinely fond both of Katherine and me. The cause of his unwillingness was that he held that it was best for her to go straight to a sanatorium in Switzerland. And he argued this with me. I stared at him uncomprehending. He meant well; I could feel his kindness. As I felt it and looked at him, a cold grey fear invaded me. I realized, as never before, that we were absolutely alone. In the last resort, no communication was possible between me and my friends. I had no friends, and never would have any.

477

On Thursday, April 11th, exactly three weeks after she had arrived in Paris, Katherine arrived in London. She was hardly recognizable. I have a little photograph of her, taken for passport purposes towards the end of her time in Paris. It is the portrait of a girl in prison, with alert and fearful eyes fixed on those who have entered her cell, seeking to read their thoughts, wondering what *they* have in mind to do to her, now.

On May 2nd the decree nisi in her husband's divorce suit against her was made absolute – six years after the original petition had been filed. On May 3rd we were married in the South Kensington registry office. J. D. Fergusson and Dorothy Brett were the witnesses.

CHAPTER XXXII

QUEER THOUGHTS

OUR marriage, which was to have meant so much, and did mean much, was a painful thing. It was so different from anything which, in the six thwarted and impatient years since Katherine and I first came together, I had dreamed our marriage would be. In spite of all my efforts of will, a wave of bitterness and dismay welled up and soured my heart. As ever, my unconsciousness has been at work for many years to make me forget, until I had forgotten and I remembered only that, like Juliet, 'I had no joy in this compact'.

But I have been compelled to remember. Among my letters to Katherine is one written about three weeks after our marriage, when we were separated again. It is a reply to one of hers in which she confessed her own disappointment. She wrote:

> Our marriage. You cannot imagine what that was to have meant to me. It's fantastic, I suppose. It was to have shone apart from all else in my life. And really it was only part of the nightmare after all. You never once held me in your arms and called me your wife. In fact, the whole affair was like my silly birthday. I had to keep on making you remember it.

It was true enough: our marriage was only part of the nightmare. But it was not in my power, as Katherine made believe, to take it out of the nightmare world and make it real. When she looked upon me, she saw me more or less as I had always been: when I looked upon her, it was hard to discover the Katherine whom I had known. The nightmare was in the reality itself. And I tried, as far as I dared, to tell her what I had felt.

479

I don't need to defend myself to you. The only thing I want to say is that perhaps you didn't quite know how *afraid* I was: how my soul was struck dumb with terror at your illness. I seemed neither to be able to speak nor to breathe, I could never say what I wanted to say to you, things that I cannot *say*. When we were married, my longing to hold you in my arms was terrible; but more terrible was the thought which held me back. 'No, I mustn't: I shall hurt her.' At that moment the knowledge of your illness blinded me like a flash of lightning – tore right through my heart. And from this there came another thing. I felt that I couldn't tell you all my love, because if I did, if I once let out the flower that was bursting in my heart, I could not have let you go, and you couldn't have gone. I felt that we were being killed by the devouring passion of our love: I chose to hold it back – it cost me more pain than I have ever known, or ever will know again. I was held up only by the one thought which never left my mind for an instant: She must rest, or she will die. One night I lay awake by your side for hours and listened to your breathing.

Our marriage meant, was to mean and has meant, as much to me as it did to you. Of that I am sure, even though you may smile a little and slowly shake your head. But my happiness withered in my heart. I shall never forget how it withered when I looked at you as you came into the restaurant. Perhaps I should have fought the devil of despair, but I am only – what I am.

One will never forget, and one does forget. The possibility of life lies in forgetting, not in remembering. For who, consciously remembering the agonies and disasters of the past, would dare to hope and be brave again? Consciousness would make cowards of us all. The only memory which belongs to life is the unconscious memory, the memory that forgets, whose incessant task it is to change consciousness into instinct, and to remind us that only when we have forgotten have we remembered indeed. It tells us, what some of us are loth to learn, that there is a great cynicism and a great comfort in the simple fact that we endure the unendurable. We suffer, but Life goes on in us. Our sensitiveness is not Life's sensitiveness. She accepts from our consciousness only what she needs for her purposes; and to know the truth we must return to her.

For nearly six weeks after her escape from Paris, Katherine lived in my two ground-floor rooms at 47 Redcliffe Road. They were gloomy and sunless, quite unsuited for one in her condition, and my one preoccupation was to get her away from them. She, on the other hand, was not only quite content to stay, but was almost suspicious of my eagerness to find a different place for her. I was 'trying to get rid of her'.

Once again, I was a divided man. What Katherine demanded was that I should ignore her illness altogether. It was impossible. I lay at night beside her, so sensitized to her, that her cough seemed to jar on my own spine. When I looked at her, a gaunt and bright-eyed shadow of what she had been only four months before, I felt sick with anguish. I struggled in queues to get her some decent food, and her attitude towards it was as though my insistence were somehow faintly indecent. Why did I not forget the disease which was not her? I had moments of a truly fearful exasperation, when I felt that I was caught in a trap. To have my anxiety for her interpreted as a desire to be rid of her was too much.

At last we agreed that I should look for a house in Hampstead, and I found a tall grey brick one, outwardly unprepossessing, but immediately overlooking the Heath. Because of its greyness and its size we christened it the Elephant. Having decided that we would take it if we could come to terms with the landlord, it was agreed between us that Katherine should go into Cornwall until the house was ready. Her friend Anne Estelle Rice was at Looe, and reported well of the place.

On May 17th, therefore, Katherine left London for Looe. I saw her into the train. We were both sad. It seemed devilish that, a bare six weeks after we had found each other in the dark forest, we should lose each other again. And immediately the familiar pattern returned. For a moment she was happy: the hotel was just what she wanted, the old Cornishwoman who tended her a dream of motherliness, Looe was what the South of France should have been. Straightway, when I received her telegram to say that it was all 'absolutely ideal', I was happy. But in a couple of days, she was ill and in despair. Probably, the effort of the journey had been too great a tax upon her strength. After two enthusiastic letters, she wrote, 'This place is very good for *just now*', and I knew that the old hopelessness and homelessness were upon her again. I knew also that my cheerful letters would reach her just at the moment when they were completely discordant.

My first letter after we had said good-bye had been sad; but when I heard that she was comfortable and happy, properly fed and well looked after, my spirits bounded up. As always at such a moment, I fell in love with the world again. As I put it to Katherine, 'I suddenly passed into a state of grace', and I described to her how, having promised to visit my generous and devoted Aunt, I bought a great bunch of roses to take with me, and how while buying them, I made the flower-woman laugh. Of the roses themselves I wrote:

I was staggered at them. I have never seen anything so rightly, sweetly passionate as the red ones. They were so utterly simple, and yet you could not understand their secret. I knew what it was – just *married love*. I shall think about them and you a lot while you are away.

No sooner had I written that than I received a panic-stricken telegram imploring me to write to her; yet I had already sent her four letters. Then, the next day, after telling me that all my letters were arriving perfectly now, she wrote this:

An idea . . .
Are you really only happy when I am not there? Can you conceive yourself buying crimson roses and smiling at the

flower-woman if I were within 50 miles? Isn't it true that, now, even though you are a prisoner, your time is your own? Even if you are 'lonely', you are not being 'driven distracted'. Do you remember when you put your handkerchief to your lips and turned away from me? And then you asked me if I still believed in the Heron? Isn't it true that if I were flourishing, you would flourish ever so much more easily and abundantly without the strain of my actual presence? We could write each other letters, and send each other work, and you would quite forget that I was 29 and brown. People would ask: 'Is she fair or dark?' And you would answer in a kind of daze, 'Oh, I think her hair's yellow'.

Well, well – it's not quite such a perfect scheme. For I should have to hack off my parent stem *such* a branch – oh, such a branch – that spreads over you and delights to shade you, and to see you in dappled light, and to refresh you, and to carry you a (quite unremarked) sweet perfume.

But it is NOT the same for you. You are always pale, exhausted, in a kind of anguish of set fatigue when I am by. Now I feel in your letters, this is lifting and you are breathing again. 'She's away and she is famously "all right". Now I can get on.'

That struck me then, and strikes me now, as a pretty cruel letter. Anyway, I winced under it, and I replied:

I've been rather depressed to-day. I started it by weeping over your letter. I send you what I wrote then: but it's not as bad as that now. It's really quite all right. But it gave me a fearful shock.

You see, it's true that I was happy when you went away. I was so confident that the sun and the food and Anne and the 'absolutely ideal' place would make you well. I wanted you to go, because I could see that London was knocking you up absolutely. Just because I care for nothing in the world but you, because the only thing I have to look forward to in life is living at your side – I wanted you to go away. I feel so sure that if I were ill, you would be the same; I felt so certain that you understood, that your letter this morning bowled me out.

But as I say, I'm better now. I know you can't have meant it *like that*, and that I have just been silly. I can't bear the thought that you should think my love so imperfect. It's the only thing I am jealous about, because I have fought a hard fight to make it perfect until it has become all there is of me. When I see you sick and ailing, I die; when I think that you are getting well, I straighten my stalk and begin to blossom like a flower.

And then you ask: 'Can you conceive of yourself buying crimson roses and smiling at the flower-woman if I were within 50 miles?' I feel I can't answer. More than that, I feel that I *ought* not to answer. But love casteth away pride – besides it's my love that's pierced and not my pride – so I reply.

If you were well and at my side and we were to buy roses together, I might not smile at the woman, I might be solemn even. But she would smile at us. We should leave such warmth in her heart that she would never, never forget.

Do you think that when I am away from you I *am* happy. Do you think I live at all? I go right apart from the world. I exist. But to think that you are getting well, that brings me happiness – compared to the utter grinding despair of watching you *not* eat, watching you *not* rest; it is heavenly. I'm not happy, though. I can never be happy apart from you. And just because I want to be with you, to live *our* life, I want you to get strong. I would wait years – yes, years – apart, if I knew that that was the only way we could make sure of having *our* life one day.

When I asked you if you still believed in the Heron – I meant only this one thing, that if you believed in it, then you would eat, then you would rest, no matter what it cost you.

I said it at a moment when I was mad, watching you. I'm not a cow, or a were-wolf, after all. I'm your lover. Everything rests on your wonderful body and lovely soul. I grow desperate seeing you pine; hearing that you are growing well, I lift up my head. 'You are always pale, exhausted, in a kind of anguish of set fatigue when I am by. Now I feel in your letters this is lifting, and you are breathing again.' It's absolutely true. But that you should have misunderstood!

I ought not to have written this, I know. But I have to tell the truth about what I feel, don't I? And you'll know where I'm all wrong and you'll set it all right again. But please don't doubt my love – it hurts too much.

Indeed, Katherine's letters at this moment drove me into a kind of delirium. I felt that it was literally true that we were killing one another. We had somehow entered into a nightmare world where love became poisonous and fatal. When she wrote to me to explain and told me that my reply to her letter had 'really nearly killed her' by its imputation that she doubted my love, when she assured me that I was 'all life to her. God, haven't my letters said just that. Hasn't all my suffering and misery been just because of that – because of my terrible – exhausting – utterly INTENSE love?' – I knew that she was speaking the truth, but it did not help. This love, which devoured her so, demanded for its fulfilment that she should never leave me, nor I her. It meant, in the world of cold reality, that I should stand by and simply watch her die. She could persuade herself, and truly believe, that she was 'only well when we are together: all else is a mockery of health'; but I knew it was only illusion. The ecstasy of love, which she required, was not health, but only a hectic hastening to death. Yet if I stood my ground against her fatal desire, she tore me to pieces by her suffering and her despair.

Far worse to endure than her momentary cruelties, which in a fashion I understood, was the icy cold despair which seized upon her, when she seemed to give way completely to the old profound hopelessness. Then the last thread of connection between herself and the world frayed and snapped. She felt 'utterly homeless, just uprooted', an atom of flotsam 'tossed about on any old strange tide'. She woke in the dark she dreaded and heard the wail of the sea, and 'her little watch raced round and round, and the watch was like a symbol of imbecile existence'. This was the bottomless pit, into which she fell, apart and alone. In such a moment she would, with a single gesture, scatter all my laborious plans for bringing us together again. She did not want a home, she wanted only to wander from place to place till the end came. What had she to do with houses and lands? She was by nature homeless and vagrant. Just as I was struggling to conclude some sort of bargain with the exorbitant landlord, 'Don't let's have the monster (she wrote). I hate the idea. *I don't want it at all.* Don't let's ever have a house in London. I am sure the whole idea is wrong. It is idiotic, I think, for us to be together when I am in the least ill. Waste of energy. I realize that.' And then she would announce her intention of leaving the hotel, because it was too expensive or too respectable, and in the same breath refuse to take any money from me.

In a day or two the mood would pass, but not before all my hopes and plans were in ruins. Then would come the explanation, which explained nothing. 'Oh God, I *do* get black . . . I simply go dark.'

God knows, my 'blackness' does not come from anything in your letters. Truthfully, I think it comes from my health; it's part of my illness – just that. I feel 'ill' and I feel a longing, longing for you: for our home, our life, and for a little baby. A very dark, obscure, frightening thing seems to rise up in my soul and *threaten* these desires . . . that is all. I know this will recur and when it is there I cannot put it away or even say: This is *temporary*, because of so and so. No, again I am enveloped and powerless to withstand it. So please try and understand it when it comes. It's a queer affair – rather horrible . . .

But what could 'to understand it' mean for me? Which was the real Katherine? Katherine in this icy aloofness of ultimate and impenetrable despair, or Katherine in the ecstasy of confidence, proclaiming her belief in a joyous future, as she did in the same letter that called upon me to 'understand' her blackness. Without a break, it ran on:

My whole soul waits for the time when you and I shall be withdrawn from everybody – when we shall go into our own undiscovered, darling country and dwell therein. That is the whole meaning and desire of life for me. I want nothing but you – and by you – I mean our home, our child, our trees and fruit, our flowers – our books – all our works, for they are all contained in you, and when I embrace you, all this treasure is in my arms. Oh God – that is so profoundly true. As I write, my happiness brims up. Do you feel it? You are everything, everything – and you are mine and I am yours.

Yet every effort of mine to bring this dream a little nearer to reality seemed to lead straightway to a recrudescence of the despair which repudiated it as a dream. One 'black' letter, which she did not send, but which I found sealed but unposted among her papers of this time, shows clearly the grim toil in which we were caught.

In the middle of last night I decided I couldn't stand – not another day – not another hour. But I have decided that so often. In France *and* in Looe. 'So *that* proves', as they would say, 'it was a false alarm.' It doesn't. Each time I have decided that, I have died again. Talk about a pussy's nine lives; I must have 900. Nearly every night at 11 o'clock I begin wishing it were 11 a.m. I walk up and down – look at the bed – look at the writing-table – look in the glass and am frightened of that girl with the burning eyes – think 'will my candle last until it's light?' – and then sit for a long time *staring* at the carpet – *so* long that it's only a fluke that one ever looks up again. And, oh God! this terrifying idea that one must *die*, and may be *going* to die . . . the Clovelly Mansions, South of France, 'writing a few last words' business . . . This will sound like exaggeration, but it isn't. If you knew with what feelings I watch the last gleam of light fade! . . . If I could just stroll into your room – even if you were asleep – and BE with you a moment – 'all would be well'. But I really have suffered such AGONIES from loneliness and illness combined that I'll never be quite whole again. I don't think I'll ever believe that they won't recur – that some grinning Fate won't suggest that I go away by myself to get well of something! Of course, externally and during the day one smiles and chats and says one has had a pretty rotten time, perhaps – but God! God!

I have discovered the ONLY TREATMENT for consumption. It is NOT to cut the *malade* off from life: neither in a sanatorium nor in a land with milk rivers, butter mountains and cream valleys. One is just as bad as the other. Johnny Keats' anchovy has more nourishment than both put together. DON'T YOU AGREE?

Do please give me every bit of your attention just to hear this. I MUST NOT BE LEFT ALONE. It's not a case of L.M. or a trained nurse. It's different.

But that really IS a cry for help. So do remember.

This letter is not to make you sad. I expect my to-morrow's will appear to deny it absolutely. But it will not really. This *does* stand for all time and I *must* let you know.

Why, then, did she not send it? It was, in itself, no more bitter than others which she did not withhold. But it came nearer to the naked truth. Johnny Keats' anchovy may have contained more nourishment than the things to which I tried, in vain, to persuade her; but it did not prevent Johnny Keats from galloping to death. And if the one true remedy for her disease was that the sick one

488

should not be cut off from life, did that not really mean that the only remedy for her consumption was to be cured of it? For she was cut off from life by the disease itself. To imagine that this could be otherwise, was only to imagine that she was whole. And that was a delusion, and she knew it. She knew that her black mood was elemental, the immediate outcome of her disease, but no sooner did she admit that to her consciousness than she put it away again, and persuaded herself that it was due to her separation and isolation. Let those be changed, and the blackness would not return. But they could not be changed; in truth, they were elemental. She could not escape them, as she imagined, by being near me. She never could be near me in the simple, elemental sense that she really desired. My anxiety alone would set a barrier between us; my consciousness that she was a creature now to be tended and cared for deliberately, and her inevitable knowledge that this was present to my mind, made an end for ever of the instinctive carelessness of natural living for which she pined.

And so, by an inexorable necessity, the moment would come when in her feverish search for this impossible condition – 'not to be cut off from life' – she, of her own motion would desire to go away and leave me. Thus, she dreamed, she would escape the isolation of which she was now conscious again. Again, for a little while, in new surroundings, the consciousness of isolation would leave her, but only to return with redoubled force. The old cry would go up to Heaven, and to me, with all its old terrible potency of tearing me to pieces, that although I had promised never to leave her alone, I had abandoned her again.

I did not understand the pattern then, as I understand it now; I seemed to myself to be engaged in a blind and weary struggle with an evil destiny. Whatever shelter I tried to build for us both came tumbling down. I felt that she was expecting some surpassing miracle to happen. Our marriage was to have been the miracle; it was not. Then the capture of the Elephant, as we called the final taking of the grey Hampstead house (which we entered on July 29th) would be the miracle; it was not. Then the end of the War – Peace – would be the miracle; it was not. And what was not the miracle, was nothing.

In October, shortly before the Armistice, a colleague of mine at the War Office kindly suggested that a friend of hers, a famous specialist in tuberculosis, should examine Katherine. I persuaded Katherine to agree. He came. I liked him at sight, for I saw he would be honest with me. Honesty was what I wanted; but now that I knew I was going to get it, I was afraid. He came down from Katherine's room. 'There's one chance for her – and only one. If she goes into a *strict* sanatorium immediately. Switzerland is not an atom more good to her than England is. Climate means nothing. Discipline everything. If she will go somewhere for a year and submit to discipline, then she has about an even chance. If not, she has two or three years to live – four at the outside.' So that was that. I thanked him, showed him out, and went up to Katherine.

'He says I must go into a sanatorium', she said. 'I can't. A sanatorium would *kill* me.' Then she darted a quick, fearful glance at me. 'Do *you* want me to go?'

'No,' I said dully. 'What's the good?'

'You do believe it would kill me?'

'Yes, I do,' I said.

'You do believe I shall get well?'

'Yes,' I said.

There was no escape. We were trapped. And I was caught in a web of strange and subtle falsity. Did I really believe that a sanatorium would kill her? I did not know. What I did know was that, if she went into one, her cries of anguish would tear me to pieces. Did I really believe that she would get well? I did not know. What I did know was that I must say so, again and again – for ever.

I knew what was required of me: that I should give her faith. I had a faith; but it was not of the kind she needed. She, for all her brilliance and her genius, required the simple faith of a peasant-woman in the Virgin – faith in the miracle. Not only had I no such faith, but I should have fought against it, if ever the impulse towards it had come to me, as against a temptation to treachery.

The Armistice came. Peace, and there was no peace. In Katherine's little bedroom at the top of the grey house, with its window looking south over all London, we could hear the noise of the celebrations, and I wished that I were dead. Night after night I went to bed, with the simple longing that I might never wake up again. What I had avoided, that I now desired. The wheel had turned full circle.

As I lay listening to Katherine coughing in the next room, thoughts, unfamiliar and beautiful thoughts, formed themselves in my brain. I had glimpses of the pattern, and it unfolded itself before me somehow thus.

My faith in love was shattered now, beyond all repair. If I dreamed of a happiness to come, I knew it was only a dream, which I indulged to keep heart in Katherine. For myself now, to believe in the dream was the subtlest agony of all.

But out of these ruins and this pain, and beyond them, a new faith was being born. It was, and it had to be, a faith which had no consolation for my heart, for it was being born of the bitter knowledge that there was no consolation to be had. But why should there be? What right had I to consolation? What right to happiness? My friends had perished. The fact that I had not perished with them – did that entitle me to happiness? The very thought was ignoble – obscene.

Since I had been spared, it must somehow be that I had been spared, as it were, for a purpose; and this purpose was to experience, in full consciousness, the *meaning* of their disaster. Disaster, it was – unmitigated disaster. Always the figure of Elliot Crooke rose before me: partly, no doubt, because of that last evening together, of which I have written, but there was an intrinsic cause besides – something in the man himself which made him symbolical of the hidden meaning of the War. For

491

others, Elliot Crooke will be only a name among a thousand forgotten names; but for me he embodied a type which was the fine
flower of European 'civilization'. The Christian religion speaks
of 'the beauty of holiness' – a wonderful phrase, indeed, but the
phrase for such as Elliot Crooke I seek in vain. But if to be a man
means to be just, to be brave, to be tender, to be generous, to seek
the truth in singleness of soul, to have understanding and imagination and sympathy, to be delicate and strong, to be independent
and modest, to have the gift of laughter yet to be grave and
gracious, to bear in one's heart without presumption a sense of
responsibility for all mankind – if this it is, as I believe it is, to be a
man, then the phrase I seek for such as Elliot Crooke is at least
echoed in the words: 'the beauty of manliness'.

That – all that there was of this rare essence in a whole
generation – had been sacrificed, wantonly sacrificed. For I
believed that all that for which they fought could have been
won, if they had been remembered. But they, and the ideals for
which they gave up their lives, ideals which were incarnate in
them, were forgotten. And what was remembered? Not they,
but profits and possessions and revenge – everything which they
despised, that was remembered. And everything they fought for –
generosity and justice and peace – that was forgotten. The death
of my friends had been sheer waste. I had now no doubt of that.
Yet there could be a meaning in their extinction and my survival,
if I became their consciousness. By that alone could I be justified;
by that alone would my continued existence be something better
than ignominy. And that, it seemed, was happening to me. It
was not a function which I could deliberately choose, a duty which
I could elect to fulfil. No such overweening thought entered into
my mind. This was a meaning of which one could only be the
passive and unconscious vehicle. One woke to discover that one
was being used.

This I seemed to be discovering now. How many times of
late had I desired, simply and hungrily, that their fate should be
mine! I, who at the first had so jealously saved my personality

492

from the vortex, had come all unaware to the point where it seemed the only happiness thus to have lost it. If 1914 had been all over again, I would have found some way to be swallowed up in it.

No, I would not. What I would not do then, for my own sake, now I could not do, for another's. Now my duty was to annihilate myself, to be completely annihilated. Now, not my physical life was required of me, but my living soul. Henceforward, my life would be one long lie – of Love. To have no faith, and pretend one; to have no hope and pretend it; to watch day by day the circle round Katherine growing narrower and to feign not to see it; to learn every day anew the utter impotence of Love – this was to be my life.

Somehow, this was right, this was just, with a rightness and a justice my imagination dimly groped at, and slowly unravelled. I was now completely isolated. Now, between Katherine and me, a subtle and impassable barrier had descended. To speak my thoughts to anyone but her was unthinkable; it was more unthinkable to speak them to her. Now my heroes failed me: none of them that I could find, had endured this strange thing that was happening to me. Not one of them whispered a word of encouragement that I knew. How could this be? Surely, someone had been along this road before. There was nobody. Why, why did my heroes fail me now?

I grappled with the tangle again. Why was it that the War had passed me by? In the last resort, because I had, as I had told Katherine in a letter, 'a very timid, girlish, love-seeking sort of soul'. If I had had the positive will to enter it, doubtless I could have done; but I had shrunk from a mode of contact not my own. My rootless being had put out its tendrils towards a devouring personal love. That was my only mode of contact, my only way of life. I could not bear that it should be taken from me. And now it was being taken from me. Now one by one, those fibres of my being had been torn out of me. Now, at last, the War had sought me out. In my own mode it had come to me. That annihilation of the personal which I had evaded on alien ground, because I *could* not commit it through any deliberate act of mine, had overtaken me in my own world now, in the only world my heart acknowledged to be veritably mine.

It was well. Somewhere at the heart of things there was an eternal Justice, a mighty and ever-living Beauty of Necessity. I could trace out threads of the pattern, and I could dimly discern why there were no heroes to guide me. Life was never twice the same. Never before had there been a War which to refuse to enter left a doubt in the heart of the sequestered man; never before had there been a war which laid siege to all men's souls as this had done; never before had there been a war against which every conscious man *had* to pit some value, some faith of his own. All unknowing I had pitted mine against it. To the increasing tension of the War I had opposed an ever-increasing tension of personal love. As the war had threatened it the closer, so had I more totally surrendered myself to it, until it had become all my life.

Yes, though I could not fathom it wholly, I knew that the intensity of the love that was killing Katherine, and now had made my life a living death, was born of the War. I had used Love to deny the War, lived in and by Love to blot it out. But it could not be denied, it could not be blotted out. The War was the reality, the rest was dreams. And the reality, which was the War, would go on and on and on. Armistices and Peace and Treaties, these meant nothing – they were mere illusions. For the reality was not this war; that was only the shadow and outward form of the substance, which when it ceased to take this form would take another.

What that Reality was, I could not discern. My vision seemed to blur. I knew that I could follow only threads of the pattern that had taken my life for its material; and that I must be content. But there were moments when I also knew, or believed that I knew, something stranger: that this Reality, which had been the War, and was now the War no longer, would work itself out to consciousness in me. My life was now totally involved in this

494

secret process, that there was no longer any room for an 'I'. There were no choices to be made any more, the margin of 'freedom' which the conscious personality demands for its existence had been taken away from me. It was not deliberate in me that my life with Katherine had become one complete pretence: there was no possibility of its being otherwise. I was merely reacting like an animal to a situation. Truth, lies – these were meaningless conventions. There was only one Truth that mattered, the simple knowing of the human condition for what it really was – a tissue of futile dreams veiling a strange and simple and beautiful and terrible Reality.

And the most stubborn and enduring of these dreams was the 'I'. It was the 'I' which hid the Truth from us. One could not destroy it, for the will to destroy it was also 'I'. It could only *be* destroyed. There came a moment of clarity when it was revealed that the 'I' had been destroyed. Such a moment came to me now. 'I' was the mere consciousness of a process that had taken place, unknown to me, and would go on. I had done nothing either to force or evade the issue. What meaning there was in me struggled to self-awareness through my own passivity. And that was, in itself, the Justice and the Beauty. At the moment that I knew, I knew it was not I who knew. 'I' had never known, never could and never would know. There was a mighty comfort there.

For this 'I', who was thus rejected and surpassed, and become the dead husk of a seed of knowledge, was not simply the petty, anxious ego that had been so anxious for assurance of its own validity – the ego whom I myself despised; the 'I' who was now rejected was the self who had despised the ego, my own precious essence, the 'I' whom I had loved purely, the 'I' whom my unquiet and petty ego had so long betrayed. He also had fallen like a dead and empty husk. For the 'I' whom I loved was the I who loved – at first fitful, wavering, timid, a little flame which shone for a moment and disappeared like a ship's light in a storm at sea; then slowly grew stronger, came nearer and nearer, until it was my very life, all the all of me. He also was gone. He had no part in the knowledge that was not mine, but had come to birth in me.

The devastation of myself was vast and unbelievable; and I could not believe it. My life was now divided into these moments of solitary vision, when faith had vanished into sight and I was exalted and revivified by an awareness of an inscrutable process that was silently and inexorably at work in me to an unknown end; and the life of my waking dream, in which I was a lover, a husband, a man among men. Between the two worlds there was now an abyss. In the world of vision I was at home, because I was not; in the world of act and suffering, of love and friendship, I was, and was in anguish or in insentience.

INDEX

. (There are no entries in this index under the names of the author or of Katherine Mansfield)

INDEX

Father, 17, 101 *sq.*
Fergusson, J. D., 191, 478
Fall of Hyperion, The, 446
Forgetting and remembering, 480
Fort, Paul, 129
Fox, H. F., 88 *sq.*, 110, 189
Fox-hunting, Defence of, 107
Freedom, negative and positive, 357
Freud, D. H. Lawrence and, 287
Fulham Road, rooms off, 281 *sq.*

G——, THE HYPNOTIST, 70 *sq.*
G——, the artist, 145, 244 *sq.*
Garsington, 307, 427
Gaudier-Brzeska, Henri and Sophie, 221 *sq.*, 245, 283
—— and Lawrence, compared, 223
George, W. L., 183 *sq.*
Georgian Poetry, 238
German Pension, In a, 184
Gertler, Mark, 321
Gibson, W. W., 236
Gipsy the mare, 98
Gittins, Mr., 30
Gods, the three, 28
Gonorrhœa, 183
Goodyear, Frederick, 86, 376, 421, 430
—— —— and Katherine Mansfield, 199
Grandmother, 33-4
Grecians, at Christ's Hospital, 50-1
Gyp, 23

HÆMORRHAGE, K. M.'s, 468
Hardy, Thomas, 223, 263
Harmony, 370
Harris, Frank, 174 *sq.*
Hastings, 33
Hazlitt, Mr., 42
Health in the Home, 14
Hearth and Home, 178
Hedgehogs, 35-6
Heidelberg, 171, 293
Heron Farm, The, 460 *sq.*, 470
Heseltine, Philip, 352, 395
Higher Tregerthen, 401 *sq.*
Homer, 57, 63
Homosexuality, schoolboy, 74
Hope, Lord Charles, 123
Hopetoun House, 125
Horses and Immorality, 102
Huile de castor, 400

Induction to an Unwritten Poem, An, 439
Inertia, the value of, 338-9
Intellectual Mysticism, the author's, 267-8, 311

'JACK', THE ICE-CREAM, 25
Jackson, Holbrook, 191
Jealousy, 374, 379
Je ne parle pas français, 463 *sq.*
Jersey, 33
Jesus Christ, 29, 363
Johnson, Dr., 13, 62

KEATS, 63, 112, 247, 328, 443, 446-8, 468
Keynes, J. M., 427
Kingsmith, Hugh, 175, 177, 181, 296
Koteliansky, S. S., 304, 321-2, 341-4, 376, 404

L.M., 346, 467, 471
Lamb Medal, The, 61
Larrouy, Maurice ('René Milan'), 120 *sq.*
—— —— and Gaudier, compared, 223
Lawrence, D. H., Review of Georgian Poetry, 239
First meeting of J.M.M. with, 261
Advice to J.M.M., 279
's first Dress Suit, 291
and Dostoevsky, 314, 369
at Greatham, 331 *sq.*
and Revolution, 333 *sq.*
and Florida, 353, 380
and Blood-brotherhood, 409
at Mylor, 324
and Gaudier compared, 223 *et passim*
—— Frieda, 261, 291-2, 294, 351 *et passim*
Lee, the Rev. Richard, 44
Lefebvre, M. (concierge), death of, 277
Letters, unpublished, of K. M., 277, 342, 345, 374-5, 378, 387, 397, 465-6, 468-9, 471-3, 479, 482-3, 487-8
Life of Katherine Mansfield, The, correction of, 189
Lil, 213 *sq.*
Little Governess, The, 343
Loneliness, 453-4, 488
Looe, 481 *sq.*
Love, the anguish of, 160

498

INDEX

499

INDEX